This Book Comes With Lots of FREE Online Resources

Nolo's award-winning website contains thousands of articles on everyday legal and business issues, plus a plain-English law dictionary, all written by Nolo experts and available for free.

You'll also find more useful **books, software, online apps, downloadable forms,** plus a **lawyer directory.**

GET DISCOUNTS ON NOLO PRODUCTS. Get discounts on hundreds of books, forms, and software.

READ BLOGS. Get the latest info from Nolo authors' blogs.

LISTEN TO PODCASTS. Listen to authors discuss timely issues on topics that interest you.

WATCH VIDEOS. Get a quick introduction to a legal topic with our short videos.

www.nolo.com

10th Edition

Nolo's Encyclopedia of Everyday Law

Answers to Your Most Frequently Asked Legal Questions

Shae Irving, J.D. & the editors of Nolo

TENTH EDITION	JANUARY 2017
Editor	MARCIA STEWART
Cover design	SUSAN PUTNEY
Book design	TERRI HEARSH
Proofreader	ROBERT WELLS
Index	SONGBIRD INDEXING SERVICE
Printer	BANG PRINTING

Names: Irving, Shae, editor. | Nolo (Firm)
Title: Nolo's Encyclopedia of everyday law : answers to your most frequently asked legal questions / Shae Irving, J.D. & the editors of Nolo.
Other titles: Encyclopedia of everyday law
Description: 10th ed. | Berkeley, CA : Nolo, 2017. | Includes index.
Identifiers: LCCN 2016026441 (print) | LCCN 2016026493 (ebook) | ISBN 9781413323436 (pbk.) | ISBN 9781413323443 (ebook)
Subjects: LCSH: Law--United States--Popular works. | Law--United States--Miscellanea.
Classification: LCC KF387 .N65 2017 (print) | LCC KF387 (ebook) | DDC 349.73--dc23
LC record available at https://lccn.loc.gov/2016026441

This book covers only United States law, unless it specifically states otherwise.

Please note

We believe accurate, plain-English legal information should help you solve many of your own legal problems. But this text is not a substitute for personalized advice from a knowledgeable lawyer. If you want the help of a trained professional—and we'll always point out situations in which we think that's a good idea—consult an attorney licensed to practice in your state.

Dedication

For Edward F. Dolan

Acknowledgments

Thanks to Jake Warner for inspiring and supporting this project. And thanks to all the Nolo editors and hardworking production folks who keep the book on track.

We're also grateful to every Nolo author whose fine work has shaped these pages. We want to give special thanks to:

Paul Bergman and **Sara Berman,** authors of *Represent Yourself in Court* and *The Criminal Law Handbook*

David W. Brown, author of *Beat Your Ticket* and *The California Landlord's Law Book*

Denis Clifford, author of many Nolo titles, including *Quick & Legal Will Book*, *Make Your Own Living Trust*, and *Plan Your Estate* and coauthor of *A Legal Guide for Lesbian & Gay Couples*

Frederick W. Daily, author of *Stand Up to the IRS* and *Tax Savvy for Small Business*

Emily Doskow, author of many Nolo books, including *Nolo's Essential Guide to Divorce*, *Nolo's Essential Guide to Child Custody & Support*, *A Legal Guide for Lesbian & Gay Couples*, *The Legal Answer Book for Families*, *The Sharing Solution*, and *Neighbor Law*

Stephen R. Elias, author of numerous Nolo books, including *The New Bankruptcy*, *How to File for Chapter 7 Bankruptcy*, *Chapter 13 Bankruptcy*, and *Legal Research: How to Find & Understand the Law*

Lisa Guerin, author of many Nolo books, including *The Manager's Legal Handbook*, *Create Your Own Employee Handbook*, *Dealing With Problem Employees*, *The Essential Guide to Federal Employment Laws*, *The Essential Guide to Workplace Investigations*, *The Essential Guide to Family and Medical Leave*, and *Smart Policies for Workplace Technologies*

Mimi Lyster Zemmelman, author of *Building a Parenting Agreement That Works: Child Custody Agreements Step by Step*

Anthony Mancuso, author of *Incorporate Your Business*, *How to Form a Nonprofit Corporation* (national and California editions), *Form Your Own Limited Liability Company*, *The Corporate Records Handbook*, and *LLC or Corporation?*

Joseph Matthews, author of *How to Win Your Personal Injury Claim*, *Long-Term Care: How to Plan & Pay for It*, and *Social Security, Medicare & Government Pensions*

Peri Pakroo, author of *The Small Business Start-Up Kit* (national and California editions), *The Women's Small Business Start-Up Kit*, and *Starting & Building a Nonprofit*

Mary Randolph, author of several Nolo books, including *The Executor's Guide: Settling a Loved One's Estate or Trust*, *8 Ways to Avoid Probate*, and *Every Dog's Legal Guide: A Must-Have Book for Your Owner*

Fred S. Steingold, author of *Legal Guide for Starting & Running a Small Business* and *The Employer's Legal Handbook*

Richard Stim, author of many Nolo books, including *Music Law: How to Run Your Band's Business; Patent, Copyright & Trademark: An Intellectual Property Desk Reference;* and *Profit From Your Idea*

Ralph (Jake) Warner Ralph, a cofounder of Nolo, is a lawyer who became fed up with the legal system and dedicated his professional life to making law more accessible and affordable to all Americans. He is the author of many Nolo books, including *Every Landlord's Legal Guide*, *Everybody's Guide to Small Claims Court*, *Form a Partnership*, and *Get a Life: You Don't Need a Million to Retire Well.*

Contributors

Sachi Barreiro Sachi is a legal editor at Nolo, specializing in employment law and workers' compensation law. After graduating from the University of San Francisco School of Law, Sachi practiced law for several years in San Francisco. She has litigated a variety of employment matters and advised businesses on their obligations to their employees. Sachi is coauthor of *The Manager's Legal Handbook* and *The Essential Guide to Federal Employment Laws.*

Ilona Bray Ilona's legal background includes solo practice as well as experience in the nonprofit and corporate worlds. She has written or coauthored over a dozen Nolo titles, including *Effective Fundraising for Nonprofits, Becoming a U.S. Citizen, Nolo's Essential Guide to Buying Your First Home, Selling Your House,* and *First-Time Landlord.* Ilona is a graduate of Bryn Mawr College and the University of Washington Law School.

Stephen Fishman Stephen has dedicated his career as an attorney and author to writing useful, authoritative, and recognized guides on business, taxation, and intellectual property matters for small businesses, entrepreneurs, independent contractors, and freelancers. He is the author of many Nolo books, including *Every Landlord's Tax Deduction Guide, Deduct It! Lower Your Small Business Taxes, Working for Yourself: Law and Taxes for Independent Contractors, Freelancers & Consultants,* and *Consultant and Independent Contractor Agreements.*

Diana Fitzpatrick Diana worked at the San Francisco City Attorney's office before joining Nolo. She also worked at a law firm in New York for several years before moving to the Bay Area. Diana is a graduate of New York University School of Law and Barnard College.

David Goguen David is a legal editor at Nolo, focusing on claimants' rights in personal injury cases. He is a member of the California State Bar with over 15 years of experience in litigation and legal publishing. David is a graduate of the University of San Francisco School of Law.

Lina Guillen Lina joined Nolo as a legal editor in 2012. Specializing in family law, Lina writes and edits articles on a variety of topics including custody, visitation, support, and the financial aspects of divorce. She is the coauthor of *Neighbor Law: Fences, Trees, Boundaries & Noise* and *Divorce & Money: How to Make the Best Financial Decisions During Divorce.* Before arriving at Nolo, Lina practiced family law and civil litigation at several law firms in the San Francisco Bay Area. Lina received her J.D. from the University of California, Hastings College of the Law and is an active member of the California State Bar.

Shae Irving Shae graduated from Berkeley Law (Boalt Hall School of Law) at the University of California at Berkeley in 1993 and began editing and writing for Nolo soon after. She has written extensively on durable powers of attorney, health care directives, and other estate planning issues.

Bethany K. Laurence Beth is a longtime Nolo editor and author. She holds a law degree from University of California, Hastings College of the Law, a B.A. degree from Boston University (Phi Beta Kappa, magna cum laude), and is a member of the California State Bar. Beth is editor of *Nolo's Guide to Social Security Disability and Social Security, Medicare & Government Pensions,* and the popular website *Disability Secrets.* She has also coauthored several Nolo books, including *Business Buyout Agreements: Plan Now for All Types of Business Transactions.*

John McCurley John is a legal editor at Nolo, focusing on DUI and driving law. He has a degree in engineering physics from U.C. San Diego and completed law school at the University of San Francisco School of Law. Before joining Nolo, John practiced criminal defense and juvenile dependency law, primarily doing writs and appeals. John maintains a small private practice in San Diego, California.

Cara O'Neill Prior to joining Nolo, Cara served as an Administrative Law Judge; taught undergraduate and graduate courses in the areas of employment law, business law, and criminal law; and served as house counsel for a large insurance company. She earned her law degree in 1994 from the University of the Pacific, McGeorge School of Law, where she graduated Order of the Barristers, an honor society recognizing excellence in courtroom advocacy. Cara maintains a bankruptcy practice in Rosesville, California.

Janet Portman Janet received undergraduate and graduate degrees from Stanford University and a law degree from the University of Santa Clara. She was a public defender before coming to Nolo. Janet is the author of *Every Landlord's Guide to Finding Great Tenants*, and the coauthor of many Nolo titles, including *Every Landlord's Legal Guide, Every Tenant's Legal Guide, Renters' Rights*, and *Negotiate the Best Lease for Your Business.*

Micah Schwartzbach Micah joined Nolo's editorial staff in 2013. Beforehand he practiced criminal defense law, specializing in research and writing. He writes and edits content across a range of practice areas. Micah earned his B.A. from the

University of California, Davis, where he graduated with highest honors, and his J.D. from the University of California, Hastings College of the Law, where he graduated cum laude.

Betsy Simmons Hannibal Betsy is a Nolo editor specializing in estate planning books and software. She graduated with The Honors Lawyering Program from Golden Gate University School of Law where she was research editor of the law review. Prior to joining Nolo, she trained at two private law firms as well as the San Francisco Superior Court and the Federal District Court of Northern California.

Marcia Stewart Marcia is a long-time Nolo editor and author of several books, including *Every Landlord's Legal Guide, Every Tenant's Legal Guide, Renters' Rights, Leases & Rental Agreements, Nolo's Essential Guide to Buying Your First Home,* and *First-Time Landlord.*

Stephen Stine As a research specialist and editor at Nolo, Stephen conducts legal research and writes and edits content for Nolo's books and websites. Previously, Stephen worked at the American Bar Association's Legal Technology Resource Center, where he assisted attorneys with technology, performed research, and wrote and edited articles, blog posts, and the annual ABA Legal Technology Survey Report. Stephen earned an undergraduate degree in Psychology from the University of California, Berkeley, and J.D. and Master of Science in Information degrees from the University of Michigan.

Table of Contents

About Nolo's Encyclopedia of Everyday Law

Whether we like it or not, the law touches our personal lives in many ways each day. We may not think much about the laws that affect us as we carry out simple tasks such as driving a car, making a phone call, or shopping at the farmer's market. But every now and again, we're sure to need an answer to a common legal question that arises in the course of daily life:

What can I do about my noisy neighbor?

What are my rights if I'm fired from my job?

Do I really need to make a will?

What should I do if I can't pay the child support I owe?

And so on.

This book provides answers to frequently asked questions about hundreds of subjects you might encounter in your personal life—topics that range from buying a house to getting a divorce, from paying your debts to starting and running a small business. Obviously, we can't answer every question on a particular subject, but we've answered many common ones to get you started.

Throughout each chapter, you'll find resources for additional information, including websites that will help you learn more about a specific area of the law, find the answer to your legal question, connect you with a government or community agency, or lead you to the form you need to accomplish a specific legal task. And if you need to go further, and read the text of a specific law or court case, the appendix in this book explains how to do basic legal research online or at the library.

Think of this book as a desk reference —a little encyclopedia that explains what the law really means in a language you can understand. But remember that the law changes constantly, as legislatures pass new statutes and courts hand down their rulings. We will publish new, revised editions of this book periodically, but it will never be perfectly current. It's always your responsibility to be sure a law is up to date before you rely on it. Check for legal updates on our website at www.nolo.com for the most current legal information affecting Nolo books and software.

CHAPTER

1

Houses

Home is heaven for beginners.

—Charles H. Parkhurst

Buying or selling a house is both exciting and demanding. To do either successfully, you need to understand how houses are priced, financed, and inspected; how to find and work with a real estate agent; how to protect your interests when negotiating a contract; and how legal transfer of ownership takes place. This chapter covers many of the basics for buyers, sellers, and owners.

Buying a House

Before you fall in love with a house, it's essential to determine how much you can afford to pay and what your financing options are. You'll also need to choose a good real estate agent or broker, decide whether to buy an old house, new house, or condo, and finally, even if you think you've found your dream home, understand house inspections, and insure your new home against unforeseen problems.

How do I determine how much house I can afford?

Don't rely on abstract formulas. Instead, take a close look at how much of your monthly income you can realistically set aside after you stop paying rent. Then, when considering a particular house, total up the estimated monthly loan payments (including principal and interest) plus one-twelfth of your yearly bill for property and homeowners' insurance and other house-related costs like utilities and maintenance. Now compare that to your monthly income.

Lenders expect you to make all monthly housing payments with 28% to 38% of your gross monthly income (before taxes). The exact percentage depends on the amount of your down payment, the interest rate on the type of mortgage you want, your credit score, the level of your long-term debts, and other factors.

It's best to run the numbers yourself before you talk to a bank or lender. Various online mortgage calculators, such as those at www.nolo.com/legal-calculators, will help you get a realistic picture of your budget.

Next, ask a lender or loan broker for a preapproval letter saying that you will (subject to later review) be approved for a loan of a specified amount based on your income and credit history.

Having lender preapproval makes you more financially attractive to sellers than simple loan "prequalification" (which involves less scrutiny by the lender). It's crucial in competitive markets or where sellers are wary of accepting any offer that might not close successfully.

How important is my credit history in getting loan approval?

Your credit history plays a vital role in determining the type and amount of loan lenders offer you. Expect your prospective lenders to request your credit score from the credit bureaus. This score is a statistical summary of the information in your credit report, such as:

- your history of paying bills on time
- the level of your outstanding debts
- how long you've had credit
- your credit limit, and
- the types of credit you have.

The higher your credit score, the easier it will be to get a loan. If your score is low, a lender may either reject your loan application altogether or insist on a very large down payment or high interest rate to lower the lender's risk.

To avoid problems, always check your credit report and clean up your file if necessary—before, not after, you apply for a mortgage. For information on how to order and clean up your credit report, see Chapter 9.

How can I find the best home loan or mortgage?

Banks, credit unions, savings and loans, insurance companies, mortgage bankers, and others make home loans. Lenders and terms change frequently as new companies appear, old ones merge, and market conditions fluctuate. To get the best deal, compare loans and fees from at least a half-dozen lenders. This information is widely available online.

Mortgage rate websites come in two basic flavors: those that don't offer loans (called "no-loan" sites) and those that do. No-loan sites are a great place to examine mortgage programs, and crunch numbers.

Many mortgage websites also offer direct access to loans from one or more lenders. However, many customers report dissatisfaction with online mortgage services and prefer to complete their transaction with a "live" lender or broker. See the end of this chapter for addresses of some mortgage websites.

To avoid all the legwork involved in shopping for mortgages on your own, you can also work with a loan broker, who specializes in matching house buyers with an appropriate mortgage lender. (Check the broker's qualifications carefully—not all are licensed.) Loan brokers usually collect their fee from the lender, not from you.

What are alternative options for home loans?

You may also be eligible for a government-guaranteed loan, offered by:

- the Federal Housing Administration (FHA), an agency of the Department of Housing and Urban Development (HUD) (see www.hud.gov)
- the U.S. Department of Veterans Affairs (see www.benefits.va.gov/homeloans), or
- a state or local housing agency.

Government loans usually have low down-payment requirements and sometimes offer better-than-market interest rates as well.

Also, ask banks and other private lenders about any "first-time buyer programs" that offer low down-payment plans and flexible qualifying guidelines to low- and moderate-income buyers with good credit.

Finally, don't forget private sources of mortgage money—parents, other relatives, friends, or even the seller of the house you want to buy. Borrowing money privately is usually the most cost-efficient method of all.

What's the difference between a fixed and an adjustable rate mortgage?

With a fixed rate mortgage, the interest rate and the amount you pay each month remain the same over the entire mortgage term, traditionally 15 or 30 years.

With an adjustable rate mortgage (ARM), your interest rate will fluctuate in step with the interest rates in the economy. Initial ARM interest rates are usually offered at a discounted ("teaser") rate, which is lower than those for fixed rate mortgages. Over time, however, initial discounts are filtered out. To avoid constant and drastic changes, ARMs typically regulate (cap) how much and how often the interest rate and/or payments can change in a year and over the life of the loan.

How do I decide between a fixed and an adjustable rate mortgage?

Because interest rates and mortgage options change often, your choice of a fixed or an adjustable rate mortgage should depend on their respective interest rates, how much you can afford in the short term, your view of the future (generally, high inflation will drive ARM rates up and vice versa), and how willing you are to take a risk.

Risk-averse people usually choose the certainty of a fixed rate mortgage, even if an ARM might be cheaper in the long run. However, some people can't afford the relatively higher interest rates at which fixed rate mortgages usually begin.

Keep in mind that if you take out a loan now, and several years from now interest rates have dropped but your home has retained its value, refinancing may be an option. But if the only way you can afford your home over the long term given your expected income is to count on a refinance, don't take the risk—many others have done so and lost.

What's the best way to find and work with a real estate agent or broker?

Get recommendations from people who have bought or sold a house in the past few years and whose judgment you trust. Don't work with an agent you meet at an open house or see advertised unless and until you call references and thoroughly check the person out. (In fact, it's best to line up an agent before visiting open houses, because if you visit an open house unaccompanied and wish to make an offer, some listing agents have been known to claim that they found you first, and are therefore owed the full commission.)

The agent or broker you choose should be in the full-time business of selling real estate and should have the following five traits: integrity, business sophistication, experience with the type of services you need, knowledge of the area where you want to live, and sensitivity to your tastes and needs.

All states regulate and license real estate agents and brokers. You may have different options as to the type of legal relationship you have with an agent or broker. Typically, the seller pays the commission of his or her listing agent, who splits it with the real estate salesperson who helps the buyer locate the seller's house. The total commission is a percentage (usually 5%–6%) of the sales price of the house (so 2.5%–3% per agent). What this means is that your agent or broker has a built-in conflict of interest: Unless you've agreed to pay the agent separately, there's no payday until you buy a home, and the more you pay for a house, the bigger the agent's cut.

To offset this conflict, you need to become knowledgeable about the house-buying process, your ideal affordable house and neighborhood, your financing needs and options, your legal rights, and how to evaluate comparable prices.

What's the best way to get information on homes for sale and details about the neighborhood?

Most people begin their search online, scanning listings to see which homes are worth a visit, how much they cost, and what amenities they offer. Virtual tours often include floor plans and room-by-room photographs.

Once you see a house you like, you can email the address or identification number to your agent, the listing agent, or the owner (if it's a listing by a FSBO—for sale by owner) to obtain additional information or to set up an appointment to see the home.

The list of websites at the end of this chapter includes some of the major national real estate listing sites. Your state or regional realty association or multiple listing service (MLS) should also have a website listing homes for sale. Major real estate companies, including ERA, RE/MAX, Coldwell Banker, Prudential, and others offer home listings on their websites.

Many online editions of newspapers offer a homes-for-sale section where you can browse listings.

Advice on relocation decisions and details about your new community are also readily available online. For valuable information about cities, communities, and neighborhoods, including schools, housing costs, demographics, crime rates, services, and jobs, see the websites listed at the end of this chapter.

The Internet is, however, no substitute for your own legwork. Ask your friends and colleagues, walk and drive around neighborhoods, talk to local residents, read local newspapers, visit the local library and planning department, and do whatever it takes to help you get a better sense of a neighborhood or city.

I want to buy a newly built house. Is there anything special I need to know?

The most important factor in buying a newly built house is not what you buy (that is, the particular model and customized finishes), but rather from whom you buy. New is not always better, especially if the house is slapped together in a hurry—or months late. And as the first person to live in the house, you could be in for unpleasant surprises, such as water pipes that aren't connected to the sewer or light switches that don't work.

Shop for an excellent builder—one who builds quality houses, delivers on time, has adequate cash reserves to finish the job (your home plus any promised community amenities such as a clubhouse or pool), and stands behind the work. To check out a particular builder, talk to existing owners in the development you're considering, or ask an experienced contractor to look at other houses the developer is building.

Keep tabs on the builder as work on the home you've contracted for is done, by scheduling regular home inspections. (You'll need to negotiate for these in your purchase contract.)

Many developers of new housing will help you arrange financing; some will also pay a portion of your monthly mortgage or subsidize your interest payments for a short period of time (called a "buydown" of the mortgage). As with any loan, be sure you comparison shop before arranging financing through a builder.

Also, be sure to negotiate the prices of any add-ons and upgrades, such as a spa or higher-quality appliances. These can add substantially to the cost of a new home.

What should I know before buying a home in a development run by a homeowners' association?

When you buy a home in a subdivision or planned unit development, chances are good that you also automatically become a member of an exclusive club—the homeowners' association or "HOA." Its members (including a volunteer board of directors) are the people who own homes in the same development. The HOA will probably exercise a lot of control over how you use and alter your property. You'll not only have to pay regular dues (often several hundred dollars per month), but count on your fellow members to also pay their dues in order to maintain the common areas and deal with any issues that come up, such as major repairs or sudden damage that's not covered by your insurance.

Deeds to houses in new developments almost always include restrictions—from the size of your dog to the colors you can paint your house to the type of front yard landscaping you can do to where and what types of vehicles you can park in your driveway. Usually, these restrictions, called covenants, conditions, and restrictions (CC&Rs), put decision-making rights in the hands of the HOA. Before buying, study the CC&Rs carefully to see if they're compatible with your lifestyle.

If buying a resale home, check into the HOA's finances, looking for issues like unpaid dues, debts, or pending lawsuits. If you don't understand something, ask for more information and seek legal advice if necessary.

It's not easy to get out from under overly restrictive CC&Rs after you move in. You'll likely have to submit an application (with fee) for a variance, get your neighbors' permission, and possibly go through a formal hearing. And if you want to make a structural change, such as building a fence or adding a room, you'll probably need formal permission from the association in addition to complying with city zoning rules.

How can I make sure that the house I'm buying is in good shape?

In most states, you have the advantage of a law that requires sellers to disclose considerable information about the condition of the house, on a standard, written form. (See "Selling Your House," below.) Regardless of whether the seller provides disclosures, however, you should have the property inspected for defects or malfunctions in the building's structure and components. Such inspections are traditionally done after your offer has been accepted but before the deal closes.

Start by conducting your own inspection. To help you learn what to look for, see *Nolo's Essential Guide to Buying Your First Home*, by Ilona Bray, Alayna Schroeder, and Marcia Stewart. Ideally, you should take a close look at a house on your own before you make a formal written offer to buy it so that you can save yourself the trouble should you find serious problems. (Believe it or not, people have bought houses on the Internet sight unseen. Don't do that!)

If a house passes your inspection, hire a general contractor to check all major house systems from top to bottom, including the roof, plumbing, electrical and heating systems, and drainage. This will take two or three hours and cost you anywhere from $200 to $500 depending on the location, size, age, and type of home. Accompany the inspector during the examination so that you can learn more about the maintenance and preservation of the house and get answers to questions, including which problems are important and which are relatively minor. The inspector should prepare a written report.

Depending on the property, you may want to arrange specialized inspections for pest damage (your mortgage lender may require a pest inspection), hazards from floods, earthquakes, and other natural disasters, and environmental health hazards such as asbestos, mold, and lead.

If the house is in good shape, you can proceed, knowing that you're getting what you paid for. If an inspector discovers problems—such as an antiquated plumbing system or a major termite infestation—you can negotiate for the seller to pay for necessary repairs or lower the purchase price. Finally, you can back out of the deal if an inspection turns up problems, assuming your purchase contract is properly written to allow you to do so.

When making an offer to buy a house, how do I avoid locking myself into a deal that might not work out?

Real estate contracts almost always contain contingencies—events that must happen within a certain amount of time (such as 15 days) in order to finalize the deal. For example, you may want to make your offer contingent on your ability to qualify for financing, the house passing certain physical inspections, it being appraised for the amount you're paying for it, or even your ability to sell your existing house first.

Be aware, however, that the more contingencies you want, the less likely the seller is to accept your offer or sign the purchase agreement. See "Selling Your House," below, for more on real estate offers.

When should I start looking for homeowners' insurance?

A house may be the biggest investment you make in your life, so you'll want to fully insure it against damage (by fire, wind, vandalism, earthquakes, floods, and mold, for example). A comprehensive homeowners' insurance policy should cover the replacement value of your house and other structures, and partial replacement of valuable items of personal property like art and computers. But beware: So-called "replacement cost coverage" for your house pays you only a preset amount if your house is destroyed, so you'll want to make sure that's enough to cover your actual rebuilding costs. You'll want some liability coverage as well, in case visitors to your property slip and fall or are otherwise injured.

Start shopping for homeowners' insurance soon after your purchase agreement has been signed. Don't put this off until escrow is about to close—finding a good policy at a reasonable price can be hard.

The problem is particularly acute in states such as California and Texas, where expensive mold claims have pushed the industry into a state of panic. Homebuyers who have filed past claims for water damage (a precursor to mold) or who are buying a house with a history of mold problems may find themselves unable to get any insurance at all. Homebuyers with a history of making frequent claims on their insurance policies have similar problems. Some homebuyers now add a contingency to their purchase contract stating that the deal can be cancelled if they can't find adequate insurance.

Strategies for Buying an Affordable House

To find a good house at a comparatively reasonable price, you may need to make some sensible compromises as to size and amenities, be patient, and employ one of the following strategies:

1. Buy a fixer-upper cheap (preferably one that needs mostly cosmetic fixes).
2. Buy a small house (with remodeling potential) and add on later.
3. Buy a house at an estate or probate sale.
4. Buy a house subject to foreclosure (when a homeowner defaults on the mortgage).
5. Buy a shared-equity house, pooling resources with someone other than a spouse or partner.
6. Rent out a room or two in the house.
7. Buy a duplex, triplex, or house with an in-law unit, to get rental income.
8. Lease a house you can't afford to buy now, with an option to buy later.
9. Buy a house at a short sale (where the seller's mortgage is higher than the home can be sold for, and the lender agrees to accept a lower amount from a willing buyer).
10. Buy a house at an auction.

Shop carefully—and if you're in a state with a troubled insurance industry, buy a policy with a high deductible. This will lower your premium cost and prevent you from racking up a history of claims that could endanger your ability to renew your policy or get future insurance.

RESOURCE

For more information about buying a home, see these Nolo books:

- *Nolo's Essential Guide to Buying Your First Home,* by Ilona Bray, Alayna Schroeder, and Marcia Stewart. Provides all the information you need to select the best house, mortgage, agent, inspections, and much more.
- *How to Buy a House in California,* by Ralph Warner, Ira Serkes, and George Devine. Explains the details of the California house-buying process.

Selling Your House

If you're selling a home, you need to time the sale properly, price the home accurately, and understand the laws (such as disclosure requirements) that cover house transactions. These questions and answers will get you started.

I don't need to sell in a hurry. When are the best and worst times to put a house on the market?

Ideally, you should put your house on the market when there's a large pool of buyers—causing prices to go up. This may occur in the following situations:

- Your area is considered especially attractive—for example, because of the schools, low crime rate, employment opportunities, weather, or proximity to a major city.
- Mortgage interest rates are low.
- The economic climate of your region is healthy, and people feel confident about the future.
- There's a jump in house-buying activity, as often occurs in spring or due to a time-sensitive tax credit.

Of course, if you have to sell immediately—because of financial reasons, a divorce, a job move, or an imperative health concern—and you don't have any of the advantages listed above, you may have to settle for a lower price, or help the buyer with financing, in order to make a quick sale.

I want to save on the real estate commission. Can I sell my house myself without a real estate broker or agent?

Usually, yes. This is called a FSBO (pronounced "fizzbo")—for sale by owner. You must, however, look into the legal rules that govern real estate transfers in your state, such as who must sign the papers, who can conduct the actual transaction, and what to do if and when disputes or other problems arise. You also need to be aware of any state-mandated disclosures

Preparing Your House for Sale

Making your house and garden look as attractive as possible may put several thousand dollars in your pocket. At a minimum, sweep the sidewalk; mow and fertilize the lawn; put pots of blooming flowers by the front door; clean the windows; and fix chipped or flaking paint.

Clean and tidy up all rooms and remove clutter, personal items (including photos), and some furniture, to make them look bigger.

Be sure the house smells good—hide the kitty litter box and bake some cookies.

Check for loose steps, slick areas, or unsafe fixtures, and deal with everything that might cause injury to a prospective buyer. Take care of minor maintenance issues that might make buyers think you've taken poor care of the house, such as a cracked window, overgrown front yard, leaking faucet, or loose doorknob.

You can improve the look of your house without spending much money—a new shower curtain and towels might really spruce up your bathroom, and freshly cut flowers or bowls of fruit will improve every room. Or you can spend several thousand dollars to have a professional "stage" your house with rented furniture and accessories, a technique some real estate agents swear by for increasing buyer excitement and yeilding greater returns.

as to the physical condition of your house. (See the discussion below.)

If you want to go it alone, be sure you have the time, energy, and ability to handle all the details—from setting a realistic price to negotiating offers to closing the deal. Also, be aware that FSBOs are usually more feasible in hot or sellers' markets, where there's more competition for homes, or when you're not in a hurry to sell.

And you may not be able to save the whole 5%–6%. For example, a buyer who is represented by an agent may approach you and agree to complete the transaction only if you pay the commission for the buyer's agent. (Traditionally, that's one-half of the total 5%–6%.)

ONLINE HELP

For more advice on FSBOs, including the involvement of attorneys and other professionals in the house transaction, contact your state department of real estate. Also, check online at www.owners.com.

Is there some middle ground where I can use a broker on a more limited (and less expensive) basis?

Yes. You might consider doing most of the work yourself—such as showing the house—and hiring a real estate broker for such crucial tasks as:

- setting the price of your house
- advertising your home in the local multiple listing service (MLS) of homes for sale in the area, an online database managed by local boards of realtors, and
- handling some of the more complicated paperwork when the sale closes.

If you work with a broker in a limited way, you may be able to negotiate a reduction of the typical 5%–6% commission, or you may be able to find a real estate agent who charges by the hour for specified services.

How much should I ask for my house?

No matter how much you love your house, or how much work you've put into it, you must objectively determine how much your property will fetch on the market—called "appraising" a house's value. The most important appraisal factors are recent sales prices of similar properties in the neighborhood (called "comps").

Real estate agents have access to sales data for the area and can give you a good estimate of what your house should sell for. Many agents will offer this service free, hoping that you will list your house with them. You can also hire a professional real estate appraiser to give you a documented opinion as to your house's value. A number of companies also offer detailed comparable sales prices online, though the information isn't always as recent as you might need. (See the list of recommended websites at the end of this chapter.) Public record offices, such as the county clerk or recorder's office, may also have information on recent house sales.

The asking prices of houses still on the market can also provide guidance (adjusting for the fact that asking prices can vary greatly from the ultimate selling price). For example, the asking price might be 10% or more above the usual sales price in slow markets, in order to allow buyers room to negotiate downward, or up to 25% below the selling price in hot markets, to generate interest and encourage multiple offers. To find out asking prices, go to open houses and check newspaper real estate classified ads and online listings of homes for sale.

I checked my home's supposed value on an online site, and it looks to be way low. Who's right, me or them?

Online sites such as Zillow will give you an estimate of your home's value based on information drawn from public records about the house and past sales of (theoretically) comparable properties. Don't be surprised if your estimate (or in Zillow-talk, your "Zestimate") looks to be way off the mark, or even if estimates from different sites are tens of thousands of dollars different from each other. As many experts have commented, generating a number via a computer algorithm is no substitute for having a live human not only check the accuracy of the basic data, but adjust for all the factors the computer can't see.

But there's a good reason to check your online estimates: Buyers will be looking at them! If the estimates are far lower than your list price, the buyers may underbid. If the estimates are far higher, that's better—but cases have been reported of buyers who shied away from such houses, worried that the seller knew of some deep dark reason that the place wasn't worth what the online estimates said. Be proactive about your online estimates, particularly if they're low. You can go onto the sites and enter data about your own house, which will both give the public a better sense of the place and might actually raise your estimates.

Do I need to take the first offer that comes in?

You're under no obligation to accept the first or any other offer (except in a few states where you must accept a full price offer that has no contingencies). In fact, offers, even very attractive ones, are rarely accepted as written. More typically, you will negotiate to accept some, maybe even most, of the offer terms, while also proposing certain changes, for example:

- price—you want more money
- financing—you want a larger down payment
- occupancy—you need more time to move out
- buyer's sale of current house—you don't want to wait for this to occur, or
- inspections—you want the buyer to schedule them more quickly.

A contract is formed when either you or the buyer accept all of the terms of the other's offer or counteroffer in writing within the time allowed.

What are my obligations to disclose problems about my house, such as a basement that floods in heavy rains?

In most states, it is illegal to fraudulently conceal material defects in your property, such as your troublesome basement. And states are increasingly requiring sellers to take a proactive role by making written disclosures on the condition of the property.

California, for example, has stringent disclosure requirements. California sellers must give buyers a Transfer Disclosure Statement listing such material defects as a leaky roof, faulty plumbing, deaths that occurred within the last three years on the property, and even the presence of neighborhood nuisances, such as a dog that barks every night.

In addition, California sellers must disclose potential hazards from floods, earthquakes, fires, environmental hazards (such as mold, asbestos, and lead) and other problems. The form for this is called a Natural Hazard Disclosure Statement. California sellers must also tell buyers about a state database maintained by law enforcement authorities on the location of registered sex offenders.

Generally, you are responsible for disclosing only information within your personal knowledge. However, many sellers hire a general contractor to inspect the

Sellers of Older Homes Must Disclose Lead-Based Paint and Hazards

If you are selling a house built before 1978, you must comply with the federal Residential Lead-Based Paint Hazard Reduction Act of 1992 (42 U.S. Code § 4852d), also known as Title X (Ten). You must:

- disclose all known lead-based paint and hazards in the house
- give buyers a pamphlet prepared by the U.S. Environmental Protection Agency (EPA) called *Protect Your Family From Lead in Your Home*
- include certain warning language in the contract, as well as signed statements from all parties verifying that all disclosures (including giving the pamphlet) were made
- keep signed acknowledgments for three years as proof of compliance, and
- give buyers a ten-day opportunity to test the house for lead.

If you fail to comply with Title X, the buyer can sue you for triple the amount of damages suffered—for example, three times the cost of repainting a house previously painted with lead-based paint.

For more information, contact the National Lead Information Center, 800-424-LEAD (phone) or www.epa.gov/lead.

property. The inspection report will help you determine which items need repair or replacement and prepare any required disclosures. The report is also useful in pricing your house and negotiating with prospective buyers.

Full disclosure of any property defects will also help protect you from legal problems from a buyer who seeks to rescind the sale or sues you for damages suffered because you carelessly or intentionally withheld important information about your property.

Check with your real estate broker or attorney, or your state department of real estate, for disclosures required in your state and any special forms you must use. Also, be aware that real estate brokers are increasingly insisting that sellers complete disclosure forms, regardless of whether it's legally required.

What are home warranties, and should I buy one for the buyer?

Home warranties are service contracts that cover major housing appliances and systems—electrical wiring, built-in refrigerators or dishwashers, heating, plumbing, and the like—for one year from the date the house is sold. (But note they don't cover basic structural components like the roof, windows, or foundation.) Most warranties cost $300 to $500 and are renewable. If something goes wrong with any of the covered systems after the sale closes, the repairs are paid for (minus a modest service fee)—and the new buyer saves money. Many sellers find that adding a home warranty to the deal makes their house more attractive and easier to sell.

Before buying a home warranty, be sure you don't duplicate coverage. You don't need a warranty for the heating system, for example, if your furnace is just six months old and still covered by the manufacturer's three-year warranty.

Your real estate agent or broker can provide more information on home warranties.

What is the "house closing"?

The house closing is the final transfer of ownership from the seller to the buyer. It occurs after both you and the buyer have met all the terms of the contract and the deed is recorded. (See "Deeds," below). Closing also refers to the time when the transfer will occur, such as "The closing on my house will happen on January 27 at 10:00 a.m."

Do I need an attorney for the house closing?

This depends on state law and local custom. In some states, attorneys are not typically involved in residential property sales, and an escrow or title company handles the entire closing process. In many other states, particularly in the eastern part of the country, attorneys have a more active role in all parts of the house transaction; they handle all the details of offer contracts and house closings. Check with your state department of real estate or your real estate broker for advice and local rules.

I'm selling my house and buying another. What are some of the most important tax considerations?

If you sell your home, you may exclude up to $250,000 of your profit (capital gain) from tax. For married couples filing jointly, the exclusion is $500,000. (Unmarried co-owners may also divide the profit and each take a $250,000 exclusion.)

To claim the whole exclusion, you must have owned and lived in your residence an aggregate of at least two of five years before the sale. You can claim the exclusion once every two years.

Even if you haven't lived in your home a total of two years out of the last five, you are still eligible for a partial exclusion of capital gains if you sold because of a change in employment or health, or due to unforeseen circumstances. You get a portion of the exclusion, based on how long you lived in the house. To calculate it, take the number of months you lived there before the sale and divide it by 24.

For example, if you're an unmarried taxpayer who's lived in your home for 12 months, and you sell it for health reasons at a $100,000 profit, the entire amount would be excluded from capital gains. Because you lived in the house for half of the two-year period, you could claim half the exclusion, or up to $125,000. (12/24 × $250,000 = $125,000.)

For more information on current tax laws involving real estate transactions, see Publication 523, *Selling Your Home*, available from the IRS at 800-829-1040 or at www.irs.gov.

RESOURCE

For more about selling a home, see *Selling Your House: Nolo's Essential Guide,* by Ilona Bray (Nolo). This book offers practical strategies on pricing, staging, marketing, and negotiating the sale of your home.

Deeds

Castles in the air are the only property you can own without the intervention of lawyers. Unfortunately, there are no title deeds to them.

—J. Feidor Rees

Remember playing Monopoly as a kid, where amassing deeds to property—those little color-coded cards—was all-important? Real-life deeds aren't nearly so colorful, but they're still very, very important.

What is a deed?

A deed is the document that transfers ownership of real estate. It contains the names of the old and new owners and a legal description of the property, and is signed by the person transferring the property.

Do I need a deed to transfer property?

Almost always. You can't transfer real estate without having something in writing.

I'm confused by all the different kinds of deeds—quitclaim deed, grant deed, warranty deed. Does it matter which kind of deed I use?

Probably not. Usually, what's most important is the substance of the deed: the description of the property being transferred and the names of the old and new owners. Here's a brief rundown of the most common types of deeds:

A **quitclaim deed** transfers whatever ownership interest you have in the property. It makes no guarantees about the extent of your interest. Quitclaim deeds are commonly used by divorcing couples; one spouse signs over all rights in the couple's real estate to the other. This can be especially useful if it isn't clear how much of an interest, if any, one spouse has in property that's held in the other's name.

A **grant deed** transfers your ownership and implies certain promises—that the title hasn't already been transferred to someone else or been encumbered, except as set out in the deed.

A **warranty deed** transfers your ownership and explicitly promises the buyer that you have good title to the property. It may make other promises as well, to address particular problems with the transaction.

Does a deed have to be notarized?

Yes. The person who signs the deed (the person who is transferring the property) should take the deed to a notary public, who will sign and stamp it. The notarization means that a notary public has verified that the signature on the deed is genuine. The signature must be notarized before the deed will be accepted for recording. And in some states, deeds must also be witnessed, just like wills.

After a deed is signed and notarized, do I have to put it on file anywhere?

Yes. You will need to "record" (file) the deed in the land records office in the county where the property is located. This office goes by different names in different states; it's usually called the county recorder's office, land registry office, or register of deeds. In most counties, you'll find it in the courthouse.

Recording a deed is simple. Just take the signed, original deed to the land records office. The clerk will take the deed, stamp it with the date and some numbers, make a copy, and give the original back to you. The numbers are usually book and page numbers, which show where the deed will be found in the county's filing system. There will be a small fee, probably about $5 to $10 a page, for recording. If you're buying or selling a house, the escrow company will normally take care of this for you.

What's a trust deed?

A trust deed (also called a deed of trust) isn't like the other types of deeds; it's not used to transfer property. It's really just a version of a mortgage, commonly used in some states.

A trust deed transfers title to land to a "trustee," usually a trust or title company, which holds the land as security for a loan. When the loan is paid off, title is transferred to the borrower. The trustee has no powers unless the borrower defaults on the loan; then the trustee can sell the property and pay the lender back from the proceeds, without first going to court.

What's a transfer-on-death deed?

A transfer-on-death (TOD) deed (called a beneficiary deed or transfer-on-death instrument in some states) lets you name a beneficiary to inherit real estate at your death, without the need for probate court proceedings. A TOD deed looks a lot like any other real estate deed but contains a statement, making it clear that the deed does not take effect until the current owner's death.

After you've signed the deed, you must record it with the local county land records office before your death. Otherwise, it won't be valid. You can revoke the TOD deed at any time.

These deeds are allowed only in certain states:

Alaska
Arizona
Arkansas
California
Colorado
District of Columbia
Hawaii
Illinois
Indiana
Kansas
Minnesota
Missouri
Montana
Nebraska
Nevada
New Mexico
North Dakota
Ohio
Oklahoma
Oregon
South Dakota
Texas
Virginia
Washington
West Virginia
Wisconsin
Wyoming

ONLINE HELP

The following sites are excellent resources for buying or selling a home:

- **www.nolo.com** Information on a wide variety of legal topics, including real estate matters of interest to home buyers, sellers, and owners. Use several real estate calculators at www.nolo.com/legal-calculators.
- **www.homefair.com** Lots of information and calculators that will help you move and make relocation decisions. Good local information on home prices, schools, crime, salaries, and other factors.
- **www.bestplaces.net** Run by Bert Sperling, the guru of "Best of" lists, this site ranks everything from the best towns for affordable housing to the worst for getting a good night's sleep.

- **www.msn.com** (Click "Money" and then "Real Estate") A roundup of recent news, plus help with all aspects of buying or selling a home.
- **www.trulia.com** Award-winning site containing home listings, comparable values, mortgage rates, and more.
- **www.ashi.org** The American Society of Home Inspectors offers information on buying a home in good shape, including referrals to local home inspectors.
- **www.fanniemae.com** Fannie Mae, which provides financing for mortgage lenders, offers a useful "Helping Homeowners & Communities" section with information on credit, qualifying for a mortgage, and more.
- **www.hsh.com** Detailed information on mortgage loans available from lenders across the United States.
- **www.realtor.com** The National Association of Realtors website offers a list of U.S. homes for sale that's updated every 15 minutes and provides links to real estate broker websites and a host of related services.
- **www.owners.com** Find homes sold without a broker, also known as FSBOs (for sale by owner), and useful information if you're considering selling your home without a real estate agent.
- **www.sandygadow.com** Sandy Gadow, author of *The Complete Guide to Your Real Estate Closing*, offers FAQs and articles on this key part of the purchase process.
- **www.homegain.com** An agent-finding service, with home value estimates, calculators for a wide variety of tasks, survey results, and other resources.
- **www.zillow.com** Home and mortgage listings, articles and advice, and estimates of specific homes' values.

CHAPTER

2

Neighbors

People have discovered that they can fool the devil, but they can't fool the neighbors.

—Edgar Watson Howe

Years ago, problems between neighbors were resolved informally, perhaps with the help of a third person respected by both sides. These days, neighbors—who may not know each other well, if at all—are quicker to call the police or head for court. Usually, of course, lawsuits only cost everyone money and exacerbate bad feelings, which makes it even harder for neighbors to coexist peacefully. But knowing the legal ground rules is important; it can help you figure out who's right, who's wrong, and what your options are—without having to call in a judge.

Boundaries

Most of us don't know, or care, exactly where our property boundaries are located. But if you or your neighbor want to fence the property, build a structure, or cut down a tree close to the line, you need to know where the boundary actually runs.

How can I find the exact boundaries of my property?

You can hire a licensed land surveyor to survey the property and place official markers on the boundary lines. A simple survey usually costs about $500; if no survey has been done for a long time, or if the maps are unreliable and conflicting, be prepared to spend $1,000 or more.

My neighbor and I don't want to pay a surveyor. Can't we just make an agreement about where we want the boundary to be?

You and the neighbor can decide where you want the line to be, and then sign deeds that describe the boundary. If you have a mortgage on the property, consult an attorney for help in drawing up the deeds. You may need to get the permission of the mortgage holder before you give your neighbor even a tiny piece of the land.

Once you have signed a deed, you should record (file) it at the county land records office, usually called the county recorder's office, land registry office, or something similar. Deeds are discussed in more detail in Chapter 1.

What can I do if a neighbor starts using my property?

If a neighbor starts to build or otherwise encroach on what you think is your property, do something immediately. If the encroachment is minor—for instance, a small fence in the wrong place—you may think you shouldn't worry. But you're wrong. When you try to sell your house, a title company might refuse to issue insurance because the neighbor is on your land.

Also, if you don't act promptly, you could lose part of your property. A person who uses another's land for a long enough time can gain a legal right to continue to do so and, in some circumstances, gain ownership of the property.

Talk to your neighbor right away. Most likely, a mistake has been made because of a conflicting description in the neighbor's deed or just an erroneous assumption about the boundary line. Try to get your neighbor to agree to share the cost of a survey. If your neighbor is hostile and insists on proceeding without the survey, state that you will sue if necessary. Then send a firm letter—or have a lawyer send one. If the building doesn't stop, waste no time in having a lawyer get a judge's order to temporarily stop the neighbor until you can bring a civil lawsuit for trespass before the judge. (Usually, mediation, discussed in Chapter 16, is a good way to resolve neighbor issues, but time is of the essence in this situation, so you need to call a lawyer right away if you can't agree.)

A Little Common Sense

If you are having no trouble with your property and your neighbors, yet you feel inclined to rush out and determine your exact boundaries just to know where they are, please ask yourself a question. Have you been satisfied with the amount of space that you occupy? If the answer is yes, then consider the time, money, and hostility that might be involved if you pursue the subject.

If a problem exists on your border, keep the lines of communication open with the neighbor, if possible. Learn the law and try to work out an agreement. Boundary lines simply don't matter that much to us most of the time; relationships with our neighbors matter a great deal.

Fences

Local fence ordinances are usually strict and detailed. Most regulate height and location, and some control the types of material that can be used and even the fence's appearance. Residents of planned unit developments and subdivisions are often subject to even pickier rules. On top of all this, many cities require you to obtain a building permit before you begin construction.

Fence regulations apply to any structure used as an enclosure or a partition. Usually, they also include hedges and trees.

How high can I build a fence on my property?

In residential areas, local rules commonly restrict artificial (constructed) backyard fences to a height of six feet. In front yards, the limit is often four feet.

Height restrictions may also apply to natural fences—fences of bushes or trees—if they meet the ordinance's general definition of fences. Trees that are planted in a row and grow together to form a barrier are usually considered a fence. When natural fences are specifically mentioned in the laws, the height restrictions commonly range from five to eight feet.

If, however, you have a good reason (for example, you need to screen your house from a noisy or unsightly neighboring use, such as a gas station), you can ask the city for a onetime exception to the fence law, called a variance. Talk to the neighbors before you make your request, to explain your problem and get them on your side.

My neighbor is building a fence that violates the local fence law, but nothing's happening. How can I enforce the law?

Cities are not in the business of sending around fence-inspection teams, and as long as no one complains, a nonconforming fence may stand forever.

Tell the neighbor about the law as soon as possible. If the fence is still being built, your neighbor may be able to modify it at a low cost. If the neighbor suggests that you mind your own business, alert the city. All it takes in most circumstances is a phone call to the planning or zoning department or the city attorney's office. If the neighbor refuses to conform, the city can issue a citation, impose a fine, and even sue.

My neighbor's fence is hideous. Can I do anything about it?

As long as a fence doesn't pose a threat of harm to neighbors or those passing by, it probably doesn't violate any law just because it's ugly. Occasionally, however, a town or subdivision allows only certain types of new fences—such as board fences—in an attempt to create a harmonious architectural look. Some towns also prohibit certain materials—for example, electrically charged or barbed wire fences.

Even without such a specific law, if a fence is so poorly constructed that it is an eyesore or a danger, it may be prohibited by another law, such as a blighted property ordinance. And if the fence was erected just for meanness—it's high, ugly, and has no reasonable use to the owner—it may be considered a "spite fence," which means you can sue the neighbor to get it torn down.

The fence on the line between my land and my neighbor's is in bad shape. Can I fix it or tear it down?

Unless the property owners agree otherwise, fences on a boundary line belong to both owners as long as both are using the fence. Both owners are responsible for keeping the fence in good repair, and neither may remove it without the other's permission.

A few states impose harsh penalties on neighbors who refuse to chip in for maintenance after a reasonable request from the other owner. Connecticut, for example, allows one neighbor to go ahead and repair the fence, then sue the other owner for double the cost.

Of course, it's rare that a landowner needs to resort to a lawsuit. Your first step should be to talk to the neighbor about how to tackle the problem. Your neighbor will probably be delighted that you're taking the initiative to fix the fence. When you and your neighbor agree on how to deal with the fence and how much you'll each contribute to the labor and material costs, put your agreement in writing. You don't have to make a complicated contract. Just note the specifics of your agreement and sign your names.

Trees

Woodman, spare that tree!
Touch not a single bough!
In youth it sheltered me,
And I'll protect it now.

—George Pope Morris

We human beings exhibit some complicated, often conflicting, emotions about trees. This is especially true when it comes to the trees in our own yards. We take ownership of our trees and their protection very seriously in this country, and this is reflected in the law.

Can I trim the branches of the neighbor's tree that hang over my yard?

You have the legal right to trim tree branches up to the property line. But you may not go onto the neighbor's property or destroy the tree itself.

Most of a big oak tree hangs over my yard, but the trunk is on the neighbor's property. Who owns the tree?

Your neighbor. It is accepted law in all states that a tree whose trunk stands wholly on the land of one person belongs to that person.

If the trunk stands partly on the land of two or more people, it is called a boundary tree, and in most cases it belongs to all the property owners. All the owners are responsible for caring for the tree, and one co-owner may not remove a healthy boundary tree without the other owners' permission.

My neighbor dug up his yard, and in the process killed a tree that's just on my side of the property line. Am I entitled to compensation for the tree?

Yes. The basic rule is that someone who cuts down, removes, or hurts a tree without permission owes the tree's owner money to compensate for the harm done. You can sue to enforce that right—but you probably won't have to, once you tell your neighbor what the law is.

Deliberately Harming a Tree

In almost every state, a person who intentionally injures someone else's tree is liable to the owner for two or three times the amount of actual monetary loss. These penalties protect tree owners by providing harsh deterrents to would-be loggers.

My neighbor's tree looks like it's going to fall on my house any day now. What should I do?

You can trim back branches to your property line, but that may not solve the problem if you're worried about the whole tree coming down.

City governments often step in to take care of dangerous trees or make the owner do so. Some cities have ordinances that prohibit maintaining any dangerous condition—including a hazardous tree—on private property. To enforce such an ordinance, the city can demand that the owner remove the tree or pay a fine. Some cities will even remove such a tree for the owner. To check on your city's laws and policies, call the city attorney's office. Search for your city or town's municipal codes online. American Legal Publishing Corporation maintains an online library of many local codes at www.amlegal.com/code-library.

You might also get help from a utility company, if the tree threatens its equipment. For example, a phone company will trim a tree that hangs menacingly over its lines.

If you don't get help from these sources, and the neighbor refuses to take action, you can sue. The legal theory is that the dangerous tree is a "nuisance" because it is unreasonable for the owner to keep it in its current state, and it interferes with your use and enjoyment of your property. You can ask the court to order the owner to prune or remove the tree. You'll have to sue in regular court (not small claims court) and prove that the tree really does pose a danger to you.

Views

The privilege of sitting in one's home and gazing at the scenery is a highly prized commodity. And it can be a very expensive one. Some potential buyers commit their life savings to properties, assuming that a stunning view is permanent. However, that isn't always the case.

If a neighbor's addition or growing tree blocks my view, what rights do I have?

Unfortunately, you have no right to light, air, or view unless it has been granted in writing by a law or subdivision rule. The exception to this general rule is that someone may not deliberately and maliciously block another's view with a structure that has no reasonable use to the owner.

This rule encourages building and expansion, but the consequences can be harsh. If a view becomes blocked, the law will help only if:

- a local law protects views
- the obstruction violates private subdivision rules, or
- the obstruction violates some other specific law.

How can a view ordinance help?

A few cities that overlook the ocean or other desirable vistas have adopted view ordinances. These laws protect property owners from having their view (usually, the view that they had when they bought the property) obstructed by growing trees. The laws don't cover buildings or other structures that block views.

The ordinances allow someone who has lost a view to sue the tree owner for a court order requiring the tree owner to restore the view. A neighbor who wants to sue must first approach the tree owner and request that the tree be cut back. The complaining person usually bears the cost of trimming or topping, unless the tree was planted after the law became effective or the owner refuses to cooperate.

Some view ordinances contain extensive limitations that take away much of their power. Some examples:

- Certain species of trees may be exempt, especially if they grew naturally.
- A neighbor may be allowed to complain only if the tree is within a certain distance from the neighbor's property.
- Trees on city property may be exempt.

I live in a subdivision with a homeowners' association. Will that help me in a view dispute?

Often, residents of subdivisions and planned unit developments are subject to a detailed set of rules called covenants, conditions, and restrictions (CC&Rs). They regulate most matters that could concern a neighbor, including views. For example, a rule may state that trees can't obstruct the view from another lot, or may simply limit tree height to 15 feet.

How to Approach a View Problem

Before you approach the owner of a tree that has grown to block your view, answer these questions:

- Does the tree affect the view of other neighbors? If it does, get them to approach the tree owner with you. You could all pitch in to cover trimming costs.
- Which part of the tree is causing view problems for you—one limb, the top, or one side?
- What is the least destructive action that could be taken to restore your view? Maybe the owner will agree to a limited and careful pruning.
- How much will the trimming cost? Be ready to pay for it. Remember that every day you wait and grumble is a day for the trees to grow and for the job to become more expensive. The loss of your personal enjoyment is probably worth more than the trimming cost, not to mention the devaluation of your property (which can be thousands of dollars).

If someone violates the restrictions, the homeowners' association may apply pressure (for example, by taking away swimming pool or clubhouse privileges) or even sue. A lawsuit is costly and time-consuming, however, and the association may not want to sue unless there have been serious violations of the rules.

If the association won't help, you can take the neighbor to court yourself, but be prepared for a lengthy and expensive ordeal.

I want to buy a house with a great view. Is there anything I can do to make sure I won't ever lose the view—and much of my investment?

First, ask the property owner or the city planning and zoning office whether the property is protected by a view ordinance. Then check with the real estate agent to see whether neighbors are subject to restrictions that would protect your view. Also, if the property is in a planned unit development, find out whether a homeowners' association actively enforces the restrictions.

Check local zoning laws for any property that might affect you. Could the neighbor down the hill add a second-story addition?

Finally, look very closely from the property to see which trees might later obstruct your view. Then go introduce yourself to their owners and explain your concerns. A neighbor who also has a view will probably understand your concern. If someone is unfriendly and uncooperative, you stand warned.

Cities Without View Ordinances

If your city (like most) doesn't have a view ordinance, you might find help from other local laws. Here are some laws that may help restore your view:

Fence height limits. If a fence is blocking your view, it may violate a local law. Commonly, local laws limit artificial (constructed) fences in backyards to six feet high and in front yards to three or four feet. Height restrictions may also apply to natural fences, such as hedges.

Tree laws. Certain species of trees may be prohibited—for example, trees that cause allergies or tend to harm other plants. Laws may also forbid trees that are too close to a street (especially an intersection), to power lines, or even to an airport.

Zoning laws. Local zoning regulations control the size, location, and uses of buildings. In a single-family area, buildings are usually limited to heights of 30 or 35 feet. Zoning laws also usually require a certain setback (the distance between a structure and the boundary lines). They also limit how much of a lot can be occupied by a structure. For instance, many suburban cities limit a dwelling to 40% to 60% of the property.

Noise

Nothing so needs reforming as other people's habits.

—Mark Twain

If you are a reasonable person and your neighbor is driving you wiggy with noise, the neighbor is probably violating a noise law.

Do I have any legal recourse against a noisy neighbor?

You bet. The most effective weapon you have to maintain your peace and quiet is your local noise ordinance. Almost every community prohibits excessive, unnecessary, and unreasonable noise, and police enforce these laws.

Most laws designate certain "quiet hours" —for example, from 10 p.m. to 7 a.m. on weekdays, and until 8 or 9 a.m. on weekends. So running a power mower may be perfectly acceptable at 10 a.m. on Saturday, but not at 7 a.m. Many towns also have decibel level noise limits. When a neighbor complains, they measure the noise with electronic equipment. To find out what your town's noise ordinance says, you can run a search online, or ask at the public library or the city attorney's office.

Once you've figured out that your neighbor is in fact violating a noise ordinance, try approaching the neighbor in a friendly way and letting the neighbor know the noise is disturbing you. It's always possible that you'll get an apology and the noise will stop. If the noise continues, the next step would be to ask the neighbor to attend a mediation session and try to work it out. (To learn about mediation, see Chapter 16.) If all else fails and your neighbor keeps disturbing you, you can also sue and ask the court to award you money damages or to order the neighbor to stop the noise ("abate the nuisance," in legal terms). For money damages alone, you can use small claims court (also covered in Chapter 16). For a court order telling somebody to stop doing something, you'll have to sue in regular court.

Of course, what you really want is for the nuisance to stop. But getting a small claims court to order your neighbor to pay you money can be amazingly effective. And suing in small claims court is easy and inexpensive, partly because you don't need a lawyer.

Noise that is excessive and deliberate may also violate state criminal laws against disturbing the peace or disorderly conduct. This means that, in very extreme circumstances, the police can arrest your neighbor. Usually, these offenses are punishable by fines or short jail sentences.

The neighbor in the apartment next to mine is very noisy. Isn't the landlord supposed to keep tenants quiet?

In addition to the other remedies all neighbors have, you have another arrow in your quiver: You can lean on the landlord to quiet the neighbor. Standard rental and lease agreements contain a clause entitled "Quiet Enjoyment." This clause gives tenants the right to occupy their apartments in peace, and also imposes upon them the responsibility not to disturb their neighbors. It's the landlord's job to enforce both sides of this bargain.

If the neighbor's stereo is keeping you up every night, the tenants are probably violating the rental agreement, and could be evicted. Especially if several neighbors complain, the landlord will probably order the tenant to comply with the lease or face eviction. For more information about tenant rights and responsibilities, see Chapter 3.

Tips for Handling a Noise Problem

- Know the law and stay within it.
- Be reasonably tolerant of your neighbors.
- Communicate with your neighbors—both the one causing the problem and the others affected by it.
- Try mediation before taking more aggressive steps.
- Assert your rights.
- Ask the police for help when it is appropriate.
- Use the courts when necessary.

My neighbor's dog barks all the time, and it's driving me crazy. What can I do?

Usually, problems with barking dogs can be resolved without resorting to police or courts. If you do eventually wind up in court, however, a judge will be more sympathetic if you made at least some effort to work things out first. Here are the steps to take when you're losing patience (or sleep) over a neighbor's noisy dog:

1. **Ask your neighbor to keep the dog quiet.** Sometimes owners are blissfully unaware that there's a problem. If the dog yaps for hours every day—but only when it's left alone—the owner may not know that the barking is driving you crazy.

   If you can establish some rapport with the neighbor, try to agree on specific actions to alleviate the problem: for example, that your neighbor will take the dog to obedience school, get the dog a citronella collar to prevent barking, or consult with an animal behavior specialist, or that the dog will be kept inside after 10 p.m. After you agree on a plan, set a date to talk again in a couple of weeks.
2. **Try mediation.** Mediators, both professionals and volunteers, are trained to listen to both sides, identify problems, keep everyone focused on the real issues, and suggest compromises. A mediator won't make a decision for you but will help you and your neighbor agree on a resolution.

Many cities have community mediation groups that train volunteers to mediate disputes in their own neighborhoods. You can ask for a referral from:

- the small claims court clerk's office
- the police
- the local district attorney's office—the consumer complaint division, if there is one
- radio or television stations that offer help with consumer problems, or
- a state or local bar association.

For more information on mediation, see Chapter 16.

3. **Look up the law.** In some places, barking dogs are covered by a specific state or local ordinance. If there's no law aimed specifically at dogs, a general nuisance or noise ordinance makes the owner responsible. Local law may forbid loud noise after 10 p.m., for example, or prohibit any "unreasonable" noise. And someone who allows a dog to bark after numerous warnings from police may be arrested for disturbing the peace.

   To find out what the law is where you live, call the local animal control agency or city attorney. Or go to a law library and check the state statutes and city or county ordinances yourself. Look in the index under "noise," "dogs," "animals," or "nuisance." For more information on how to do this, see the "Legal Research" appendix. You can run a search online, since most cities maintain online libraries of their municipal codes and ordinances; www.amlegal.com/code-library (mentioned in the "Fences" section above) is also a good resource.
4. **Ask animal control authorities to enforce local noise laws.** Be persistent. Some cities have special programs to handle dog complaints.
5. **Call the police if you think a criminal law is being violated.** Generally, police aren't too interested in barking dog problems. And summoning a police cruiser to a neighbor's house obviously will not improve your already-strained relations. But if nothing else works, and the relationship with your neighbor is shot anyway, give the police a try.

My neighbor just started giving piano lessons at her home—very loud lessons, starting at 7 a.m. on the weekends. What can I do about this?

The first thing you should do is figure out whether your neighbor is breaking any laws. Check your local zoning law to find out whether your neighborhood is zoned for residential use only—if so, your neighbor is in violation. Next, find out whether your neighborhood imposes "quiet hours," during which neighbors can't make excessive noise. Typically, quiet is enforced until at least 8 a.m. on weekends.

Once you know your rights, talk to the other folks on your block (and perhaps those who live behind your noisy neighbor). Are others also bothered by the noise? If so, approach the piano teacher as a group. Explain the problem and present some possible solutions. For example, perhaps your neighbor can soundproof her practice room and agree to hold her first lesson of the day at 9 a.m.

If your neighbor is breaking the law, make that clear—but also emphasize that you have not yet spoken to the police or any other local authority, and that you'd like to work the problem out informally. Don't let yourself get pushed around, however—if your neighbor refuses to be reasonable, explain that you know your legal rights and are prepared to enforce them. And remember, even if your neighbor isn't violating a particular zoning or noise regulation, she may be creating a nuisance.

If your neighbor agrees to your proposed solution, great. If not, you might try to solve the problem through neighborhood mediation. (For information about mediation, see Chapter 16.) If all efforts at compromise fail, you can either complain to local authorities (such as the zoning board, if your neighbor is violating the zoning laws, or the police if your neighbor is breaking a noise ordinance) or take your neighbor to court.

RESOURCE

For more about dealing with neighbors, see these Nolo books:

- *Neighbor Law: Fences, Trees, Boundaries & Noise,* by Lina Guillen and Emily Doskow. Explains laws that affect neighbors and shows how to resolve common disputes without lawsuits.
- *Every Dog's Legal Guide,* by Mary Randolph. A guide to the laws that affect dog owners and their neighbors.

ONLINE HELP

The following sites are good resources for dealing with neighbors:

- **www.nolo.com** Information about a wide variety of legal topics, including neighbor law disputes, from trees and noise to secondhand smoke and easements.
- **www.statelocalgov.net** Comprehensive index of websites for states, counties, cities, and towns. Check here first for the local laws that are so important in neighbor disputes.
- **www.amlegal.com** American Legal Publishing Corporation maintains a free online library of local municipal codes.

CHAPTER

3

Landlords and Tenants

Property has its duties as well as its rights.

—Thomas Drummond

Fifty years ago, custom, not law, controlled how most landlords and tenants interacted with each other. This is no longer true. Today, whether you focus on leases and rental agreements; habitability; discrimination; the amount, use and return of security deposits; how and when a landlord may enter a rental unit; or a dozen other issues, both landlord and tenant must understand their legal rights and responsibilities.

Here's an overview of the key legal issues affecting both landlords and tenants. Because landlord–tenant laws vary significantly depending on where you live, you'll need to check your state and local laws for specifics. The Nolo resources listed at the end of this chapter provide the detailed legal information landlords and tenants need, including state statutes on security deposits, late rent fees, repairs, and evictions.

Leases and Rental Agreements

It's important to carefully read—and fully understand—the terms of your lease or rental agreement. This piece of paper is the contract that describes many important aspects of the landlord–tenant relationship.

Why is it important to sign a lease or rental agreement?

The lease or rental agreement is the key document of the tenancy. A thorough lease or rental agreement will cover important issues such as:

- the length of the tenancy
- the amount of rent and deposits the tenant must pay
- the number of people who can live on the rental property
- who pays for utilities
- whether the tenant may have pets
- the landlord's access to the rental property
- grounds for termination, and
- who pays attorneys' fees if there is a lawsuit over the meaning or implementation of the agreement.

Leases and rental agreements should always be in writing, even though oral agreements are enforceable for up to one year in most states. Though oral agreements can be easy and informal, they often lead to disputes. If a tenant and landlord later disagree about key issues, such as whether the tenant can add a roommate, the result is all too likely to be a court argument over who said what to whom, when, and in what context.

What's the difference between a rental agreement and a lease?

The biggest difference is the length of occupancy. A rental agreement provides for a tenancy of a short period (often 30 days). The tenancy automatically renews at the end of this period unless the tenant or landlord ends it by giving written notice, typically 30 days. For these month-to-month rentals, the landlord can change the terms of the agreement with proper written notice, subject to any rent control laws. This notice is usually 30 days, but it can be shorter in some states if the rent is paid weekly or biweekly or if the landlord and tenant agree to a shorter notice period. In some states, the notice period is longer.

A lease, on the other hand, gives a tenant the right to occupy a rental unit for a set term—most often for six months or a year, but sometimes longer—as long as the tenant pays the rent and complies with other lease provisions. Unlike a rental agreement, when a lease expires it does not usually automatically renew itself. A tenant who stays on with the landlord's consent usually becomes a month-to-month tenant (with the same terms and conditions that were present in the lease).

In addition, with a fixed-term lease, the landlord cannot raise the rent or change other terms of the tenancy during the lease, unless the changes are specifically provided for in the lease or the tenant agrees.

What happens if a tenant breaks a lease?

As a general rule, a tenant may not legally move out during the lease period unless the landlord consents or has significantly violated its terms—for example, by failing to make necessary repairs or failing to comply with an important law concerning health or safety. Several states have laws that allow tenants to break a lease because of domestic violence or because health problems or a job relocation require a permanent move. A tenant who begins active military service for more than a month at a time, may break a lease after giving 30 days' notice.

A tenant who breaks a lease without a legally recognized cause will be responsible for the remainder of the rent due under the lease term. In most states, however, a landlord has a legal duty to use reasonable efforts to try to find a new tenant—no matter what the tenant's reason for leaving—rather than charge the tenant for the total remaining rent due under the lease. Once the next tenant starts paying rent, the old tenant's responsibility for the rent will stop.

When can a landlord legally break a lease and end a tenancy?

A landlord may legally break a lease if a tenant significantly violates its terms or the law—for example, by paying the rent late, keeping a dog in violation of a no-pets clause in the lease, substantially damaging the property, or participating in illegal activities on or near the premises, such as selling drugs.

To end the tenancy for these reasons, the landlord sends the tenant a notice stating that the tenancy has been terminated. State laws are very detailed as to how a landlord must write and deliver (serve) a termination notice. The termination notice may state that the tenancy is over and advise the tenant to vacate the premises or face an eviction lawsuit. Or, the notice may give the tenant a few days to remedy the problem—for example, pay the rent or find a new home for the dog—and thus avoid termination of the tenancy. If a tenant doesn't comply with the termination notice, the landlord can file a lawsuit to evict the tenant.

See "Tenancy Terminations and Evictions," below, for more on the subject

Tenant (and Rental) Selection

Choosing tenants is the most important decision any landlord makes. To do it well, landlords need a reliable system that helps weed out tenants who will pay their rent late, damage the rental unit, or cause legal or practical problems later.

And for tenants, finding a place to live is an extremely important decision, also requiring a systematic approach—in this case, identifying and checking out potential rentals and getting chosen by the landlord.

What's the best way for landlords to screen tenants?

Savvy landlords should ask all prospective tenants to fill out a written rental application that asks for the following information:

- employment, income, and credit history
- identification, such as a Social Security number or Individual Taxpayer Identification Number (ITIN)
- details on past evictions and bankruptcies, and
- references.

Before choosing tenants, landlords should check with previous landlords and other references; verify income, employment, and bank account information; and obtain a credit report. The credit report is especially important because it will indicate whether an applicant has a history of paying rent or bills late, has gone through bankruptcy, or has a heavy debt load compared to income.

How can a landlord avoid discrimination lawsuits when choosing a tenant?

Fair housing laws specify clearly illegal reasons to refuse to rent to a tenant. (For details, see "Housing Discrimination," below.) Landlords are legally free to choose among prospective tenants as long as their decisions comply with these laws and are based on legitimate business criteria. For example, a landlord is entitled to reject someone with a poor credit history, insufficient income to pay the rent, or past behavior—such as damaging rental property—that makes the person a bad risk. A reasonable occupancy policy limiting the number of people per rental unit—one that is clearly tied to health and safety—can also be a legal basis for refusing tenants.

What's the best way for a tenant to find a good apartment or rental house?

Finding a good place to rent, at a reasonable price, is often difficult, especially in tight rental markets, such as Oakland or New York City. Here are some specific steps tenants can take to land a rental that meets their needs:

- firmly establish your rental priorities, such as maximum rent, number of bedrooms, location, budget, or pet policy
- use a variety of resources (depending on the market, these may include Craigslist, your social media contacts, newspaper ads, real estate brokers and property management companies) to tap into available rentals
- get a copy of your credit report (free from annualcreditreport.com) and clean up any problems or errors before you fill out a rental application
- pull together names and contact information for references, such as your current landlord or boss and other information you'll need for the rental application
- understand your legal rights and responsibilities under both state and local law before signing a lease, including limits on roommates and subletting, use of security deposit, grounds for termination, and anything else that's important to you (such as restrictions on home businesses or guests), and
- check out the landlord, rental property, and neighborhood before signing a lease (other tenants are a great source of information).

Housing Discrimination

Not so long ago, a landlord could refuse to rent to an applicant, or could evict a tenant, for almost any reason. If a landlord didn't like your race or religion, or the fact that you had children, you might find yourself out on the street. But times have changed. To protect everyone's right to be treated fairly and to help people find adequate housing, Congress and state legislatures passed laws prohibiting discrimination, most notably the federal Fair Housing Acts.

What types of housing discrimination are illegal?

The federal Fair Housing Act, Fair Housing Amendments Act, and Civil Rights Act prohibit landlords from choosing or rejecting tenants (or treating tenants differently) on the basis of a group characteristic such as:

- race
- religion
- ethnic background or national origin
- sex
- familial status (including age)
- the fact that the prospective tenant has children (except in certain designated senior housing)
- mental or physical disability, or
- color.

In addition, some state and local laws prohibit discrimination based on a person's marital status, sexual orientation, or gender identity; or because an applicant or tenant receives financial assistance from the government. And some cities and counties have added other criteria, such as one's personal appearance or occupation.

On the other hand, landlords are allowed to select tenants using criteria that are based on valid business reasons, such as requiring a minimum income or positive references from previous landlords, as long as these standards are applied equally to all tenants.

How does a tenant file a discrimination complaint?

A tenant who thinks that a landlord has broken a federal fair housing law should contact the U.S. Department of Housing and Urban Development (HUD), the agency that enforces the Fair Housing Act. To find the nearest office, check the "Housing Discrimination" section (under "Topic Areas") of the HUD website at www.hud.gov. You can file a complaint online or through a regional HUD office (you'll find a complaint form and phone numbers of the local offices on the HUD website, under "State Info"). Or you can call HUD's Fair Housing Hotline at 800-669-9777. HUD will provide a complaint form, which tenants can fill out online, and will decide whether to pursue the claim. A tenant must file a complaint within one year of the alleged discriminatory act. If HUD decides that the complaint may have merit, it will appoint a mediator to negotiate with the landlord and tenant and reach a settlement (called a "conciliation"). If a settlement can't be reached, the fair housing agency will hold an administrative hearing to determine whether discrimination has occurred.

If the discrimination is a violation of a state fair housing law, the tenant may file a complaint with the state agency in charge of enforcing the law. (In California, for example, the Department of Fair Employment and Housing enforces the state's fair housing laws.) The HUD website (www.hud.gov) includes links to state and local fair housing agencies in the "State Info" section.

Examples of Housing Discrimination

The Fair Housing Act and Fair Housing Amendments Act prohibit landlords from taking any of the following actions based on race, religion, or any other protected category:

- advertising or making any statement that indicates a preference based on group characteristic, such as color or race
- falsely saying that a rental unit is no longer available
- setting more restrictive standards, such as higher income requirements, for certain tenants
- refusing to rent to members of certain groups
- failing to accommodate the needs of tenants with a disability, such as refusing to allow a guide dog or other service animal
- setting different terms for some tenants, such as adopting an inconsistent policy of responding to late rent payments, or
- terminating a tenancy for a discriminatory or retaliatory reason.

Instead of filing a complaint with HUD or a state agency, tenants may file lawsuits directly in federal or state court. If a state or federal court or housing agency finds that discrimination has taken place, a tenant may be awarded damages, including any higher rent the tenant had to pay as a result of being turned down, and damages for humiliation and emotional distress.

Rent and Security Deposits

Landlords may charge whatever the market will bear for rent, except in areas covered by rent control. Many states do, however, have rules as to when and how tenants must pay the rent and how landlords may increase it.

Security deposits are more strictly regulated by state law. Most states dictate how much money a landlord can require, and when and how the deposit must be returned.

What laws cover rent due dates, late rent, and rent increases?

By custom, leases and rental agreements usually require the tenant to pay rent monthly, in advance. Often rent is due on the first day of the month. However, it is legal for a landlord to require rent to be paid at different intervals or on a different day of the month.

Unless state law or the lease or rental agreement specifies otherwise, there is no legally recognized grace period—in other words, if a tenant hasn't paid the rent on time, the landlord can usually terminate the tenancy. In some states, a landlord may do so the day after rent is due; in others, the landlord must give the tenant a set number of days to come up with the rent before sending a termination notice.

Some landlords charge fees for late payment of rent or for bounced checks; these fees are usually legal if they are within state guidelines or, when the state has not legislated on the issue, they are reasonable.

How Rent Control Works

Communities in only four states—California, Maryland, New Jersey, and New York—and the District of Columbia have laws that limit the amount of rent landlords may charge. Rent control ordinances also limit the circumstances in which rent may be increased. Many rent control laws require landlords to have a legal or just cause (that is, a good reason) to terminate a tenancy—for example, if the tenant doesn't pay rent or if the landlord wants to move a family member into the rental unit. Landlords and tenants in New York City, Newark, San Francisco, and other cities with rent control should get a current copy of the ordinance and any regulations interpreting it. Check local government listings for the address and phone number of the local rent control board, or go online to your city's website (all cities with rent control ordinances post them online).

For month-to-month rentals, the landlord can raise the rent (subject to any rent control laws) with proper written notice, typically 30 days. With a fixed-term lease, the landlord may not raise the rent during the lease, unless the increase is specifically called for in the lease or the tenant agrees.

Landlords may not legally raise rent as retaliation (for example, in response to a tenant's withholding rent for a habitability problem) or in a discriminatory manner.

How much security deposit can a landlord charge?

All states allow landlords to collect a security deposit when the tenant moves in. Landlords use the deposit to cover unpaid rent and damages or cleaning beyond ordinary wear and tear. Half the states limit the amount landlords can charge, usually to not more than a month or two's worth of rent.

Many states require landlords to put deposits in a separate account. Some states (and a few cities) require landlords to pay tenants interest on deposits.

What are the rules for returning security deposits?

The rules vary from state to state, but landlords usually have a set amount of time in which to return deposits, usually 14 to 30 days after the tenant moves out.

Landlords may deduct from a tenant's security deposit as long as they do it correctly and for an allowable reason. Most states require landlords to provide a written, itemized accounting of deductions for unpaid rent and for repairs for damage that was beyond normal wear and tear, together with payment for any deposit balance.

A tenant may sue a landlord who fails to return the deposit in the time and manner required; or who violates other provisions of security deposit laws (such as interest requirements). Tenants often bring these lawsuits in small claims court (the subject of Chapter 16). If the landlord has intentionally and flagrantly violated the ordinance, in some states a tenant may recover the entire deposit—sometimes even two or three times this amount—plus attorneys' fees and other damages.

Tenants' Privacy Rights

In most states, landlords have a legal responsibility to keep fairly close tabs on the condition of the property. Tenants however, have the right to be left alone. To balance landlords' responsibilities with tenants' rights to privacy in their homes, laws in many states set rules about when and how landlords may legally enter rented premises.

Under what circumstances may a landlord enter rental property?

Typically, a landlord has the right to legally enter rented premises in cases of emergency, in order to make needed repairs, or to show the property to prospective tenants or purchasers.

Several states allow landlords the right of entry during a tenant's extended absence (often defined as seven days or more), to maintain the property as necessary, and to inspect for damage and needed repairs. In most cases, a landlord may not enter just to check up on the tenant or the rental property.

Must landlords provide notice of entry?

States that specify entry requirements typically require landlords to provide advance notice (usually 24 hours) before entering a rental unit. Without advance notice, a landlord or manager may enter rented premises while a tenant is living there only in an emergency, such as a fire or serious water leak, or when the tenant gives permission.

Is it legal for a landlord to answer questions about a tenant's credit?

Creditors, banks, and prospective landlords may ask a landlord to provide credit or other information about a current or former tenant. A landlord who sticks to the facts that are relevant to the tenant's creditworthiness (such as whether the tenant paid rent on time) may respond to these inquiries without fear of legal liability. To be extra careful, some landlords insist that tenants sign a release giving the landlord permission to respond to such requests. Landlords must be very careful to give accurate information that they can document if challenged.

What options are available if a landlord violates a tenant's privacy rights?

A tenant's first step should be to communicate privacy concerns to the landlord or manager (a written request is best). In some cases, a formal letter, setting forth the tenant's legal rights and options (such as a lawsuit for unlawful entry or breaking the lease or moving out) may be appropriate.

Roommates, Sublets, and Airbnb

Leases and rental agreements typically limit who and how many people may live in a rental unit and restrict subletting.

What's the best way to choose roommates?

The greatest place in the world won't make up for a bad roommate. Before you move in with roommates (even your closest friends), it's a good idea to make sure you're compatible on issues such as neatness, cleaning standards, and household chores; privacy needs, amount of entertaining, and overnight guests; noise; food sharing; bill paying; smoking, and anything else that's important to you. Many people report that making a written roommate agreement goes a long way toward avoiding problems living together.

And if things don't work out, keep in mind that, as a general rule, one roommate can't terminate another's tenancy by filing an eviction action. Only landlords can evict tenants.

What are a tenant's rights as to who lives or stays in a rental unit?

A landlord my restrict the number of occupants in a rental unit, as long as there is a legitimate health, safety, or business reason for doing so, such as the size and number of bedrooms, or the limitations of the plumbing system. Occupancy limits are not legal if they are based on the age or sex of the occupant, and landlords cannot use overcrowding as an excuse for refusing to rent to tenants with children.

Savvy landlords will also require that all people living in a rental unit (including both members of a married couple) are full-fledged tenants who have been screened and approved and signed the lease. Most landlords will insist that a new roommate become a cotenant, sharing the same rights and responsibilities for the rent and other terms of the lease or rental agreement.

If you live or own rental property in New York, be sure to check out New York's Roommate Law, which gives tenants the right to bring in certain additional roommates without obtaining the landlord's prior approval, subject only to applicable local laws on overcrowding.

Can a landlord restrict tenants from having overnight guests or subletting the rental?

Leases and rental agreements typically prohibit sublets (such as having a person stay in the rental and pay rent while a tenant is gone for an extended period of time), without the prior written consent of the landlord. Some leases even require a landlord's written consent for guest stays over a set limit, such as up to ten days in any six-month period.

And, increasingly, landlords are specifically prohibiting tenants from opening their rentals to paying guests through Airbnb or similar services. Many cities also restrict or prohibit short-term rental housing, even if the landlord does allow it. Airbnb's website (www.airbnb.com) has a summary of the legal requirements of many cities, with links for more information (check "Responsible Hosting" under the "Hosting" section).

Repairs and Maintenance

In 1863, an English judge wrote that "Fraud apart, there is no law against letting [leasing] a tumble-down house." But in 21st-century America, it's no longer legal to be a slumlord. Landlords must repair and maintain their rental property or face financial losses and legal problems from tenants—who may withhold rent and pursue other legal remedies —and from government agencies that enforce housing codes.

What are the landlord's repair and maintenance responsibilities?

Under state and local laws, rental property owners must offer and maintain housing that satisfies basic habitability requirements, such as adequate weatherproofing; available heat, water, and electricity; and clean, sanitary, and structurally safe premises. Local building or housing codes typically set specific standards, such as the minimum amounts of light, ventilation, and electrical wiring. Many cities require the installation of smoke detectors in residential units and specify security measures involving locks and keys.

To find out more about state laws on repair and maintenance responsibilities, check your state's landlord-tenant statutes. Your local building or housing authority and health or fire department can provide information on local housing codes and penalties for violations.

What are a tenant's rights if the landlord refuses to maintain the property?

A landlord who doesn't meet legal responsibilities leaves a tenant with several options, depending on the state. These options include:

- paying less rent
- withholding the entire rent until the problem is fixed
- making necessary repairs or hiring someone to make them and deducting the cost from the next month's rent
- calling the local building inspector, who can usually order the landlord to make repairs, or
- moving out, even in the middle of a lease.

A tenant who has lived under substandard conditions can also sue the landlord for a partial refund of rent paid during that time. In some circumstances, the tenant can sue for the discomfort, annoyance, and emotional distress caused by the substandard conditions.

Tenants should check state and local laws and understand available remedies and required procedures before taking any action, especially before using "repair and deduct" or withholding rent.

What must tenants do to keep the rental property in good shape?

All tenants have the responsibility to keep their own living quarters clean and sanitary, and to carefully use common areas and facilities, such as lobbies, garages, and pools. A tenant who damages the premises—for example, by breaking a window or scratching hardwood floors—is responsible for the damage (typically the landlord will deduct the cost of damage repair from the tenant's security deposit). Leases typically forbid tenants from making any repairs or alterations to the premises (such as painting the rental unit or rekeying the locks) without the landlord's permission.

A landlord can usually delegate repair and maintenance tasks to the tenant in exchange for a reduction in rent. If the tenant fails to do the job well, however, the landlord is not excused from his responsibility to maintain habitability.

Is a landlord liable if a tenant or visitor is injured on the rental property?

A landlord may be liable to the tenant (or others) for injuries that resulted from:

- the landlord's negligence or unreasonably careless conduct
- the landlord's violation of a health or safety law
- the landlord's failure to make certain repairs
- the landlord's failure to keep the premises habitable, or
- the landlord's reckless or intentional acts.

A tenant can file a personal injury lawsuit for medical bills, lost earnings, pain and other physical suffering, permanent physical disability, disfigurement, and emotional distress. A tenant can also sue for property damage that results from faulty maintenance or unsafe conditions.

RESOURCE

For more about personal injury lawsuits, *How to Win Your Personal Injury Claim,* by Joseph L. Matthews (Nolo), provides step-by-step details on how to understand what a claim is worth, prepare a claim for compensation, negotiate a fair settlement, and manage a case without a lawyer.

How can property owners minimize financial losses and legal problems related to repairs and maintenance?

Landlords who offer and maintain housing in excellent condition can avoid many problems. Here's how:

- Clearly set out responsibilities for repair and maintenance in the lease or rental agreement.

- Use a written checklist to inspect the premises and fix any problems before new tenants move in.
- Encourage tenants to immediately report plumbing, heating, weatherproofing, or other defects or safety or security problems—whether in the tenant's unit or in common areas such as hallways and parking garages.
- Keep a written log of all tenant complaints and repair requests, with details as to how and when problems were addressed.
- Handle urgent repairs as soon as possible. Take care of major inconveniences, such as a plumbing or heating problem, within 24 hours. For minor problems, respond in 48 hours. Always keep tenants informed as to when and how the repairs will be made and the reasons for any delays.
- Twice a year, give tenants a checklist on which to report potential safety hazards or maintenance problems that might have been overlooked. Use the same checklist to inspect all rental units once a year.

Landlord Liability for Criminal Acts and Activities

Can a law-abiding landlord end up financially responsible for the criminal acts of a total stranger? Yes—especially if the crime occurred on rental property where an assault or other crime occurred in the recent past. Rental property owners are being sued with increasing frequency by tenants injured by criminals.

What are the landlord's responsibilities for tenant safety and security?

Property owners are responsible for keeping their premises reasonably safe for tenants and guests. Landlords in most states now have at least some degree of legal responsibility to protect their tenants from would-be assailants and thieves and from the criminal acts of fellow tenants. Landlords must also protect the neighborhood from their tenants' illegal activities, such as drug dealing. These legal duties stem from building codes, ordinances, statutes, and, most frequently, court decisions.

How can a landlord limit responsibility for crime committed by strangers on the rental property?

Effective preventive measures are the best ways to avoid being held liable for others' criminal acts and activities. The following steps will not only limit the likelihood of crime but also reduce the risk that the property owner will be found responsible if a criminal assault or robbery does occur. A landlord should:

- Meet or exceed all state and local security laws that apply to the rental property, such as requirements for deadbolt locks on doors, good lighting, and window locks.

- Safeguard keys (for example, don't label keys with the rental unit numbers, and rekey a rental unit every time a new tenant moves in or loses a key).
- Realistically assess the crime situation in and around the rental property and neighborhood and implement security that provides reasonable protection for the tenants—both in individual rental units and in common areas such as parking garages and elevators. Local police departments, the landlord's insurance company, and private security professionals can all provide useful advice on security measures. Often, the most effective measures are the easiest and cheapest, like properly trimming trees and bushes and installing adequate lights. If additional security requires a rent hike, the landlord should discuss the situation with the tenants. Many tenants will pay more for a safer place to live.
- Educate tenants about crime problems in the neighborhood and describe the security measures provided by the landlord—including their limitations.
- Maintain the rental property and conduct regular inspections to spot and fix any security problems, such as broken locks or burned out exterior floodlights. Asking tenants for their suggestions as part of an ongoing repair and maintenance system is also a good idea.
- Handle tenant complaints about dangerous situations, suspicious activities, or broken locks and security items immediately. Failing to do this may saddle a landlord with a higher level of legal liability should a tenant be injured by a criminal act after the landlord learned of a complaint.

The Costs of Crime

The money a landlord spends today on effective crime-prevention measures will pale in comparison to the costs that may result from crime on the premises. Settlements paid by landlords' insurance companies for horrific crimes such as rape and assault are likely to be hundreds of thousands of dollars; jury awards are even larger.

What kinds of legal trouble do landlords face from tenants who deal drugs on the property?

Drug-dealing tenants can cause landlords all kinds of practical and legal problems:

- It will be difficult to find and keep good tenants, and the value of the rental property will plummet.
- Anyone who is injured or annoyed by drug dealers—be it other tenants or people in the neighborhood—may sue the landlord for violating nuisance laws and building codes.

- Local, state, or federal authorities may levy stiff fines against the landlord for allowing the illegal activity to continue.
- Law enforcement authorities may initiate eviction proceedings on their own against drug-dealing tenants. They can also seek criminal penalties against the landlord for knowingly allowing drug dealing on the rental property.
- In extreme cases, the presence of drug dealers may result in government confiscation of the rental property.

Protecting Tenants From the Manager

Rental property owners should be particularly careful when hiring a property manager—the person who interacts with all tenants and has access to master keys. Landlords should scrupulously check a manager's background to the fullest extent allowed by law to avoid hiring a manager with a criminal conviction that would render the person unsuitable for the job. In addition, landlords should closely supervise the manager's job performance. A tenant who gets hurt or has property stolen or damaged by a manager could sue the property owner for failing to screen or supervise the manager properly. If tenants complain about illegal acts by a manager, landlords should pay attention. Property owners should also make sure their insurance covers illegal acts of their employees.

How can a property owner avoid legal problems from tenants who deal drugs or otherwise break the law?

Landlords can take several practical steps to avoid trouble from tenants and limit their legal exposure:

- Screen tenants carefully and choose tenants who are likely to be law-abiding and peaceful citizens. Weed out violent or dangerous individuals to the extent allowable under privacy and antidiscrimination laws, which may limit questions about a tenant's past criminal activity, drug use, or mental illness.
- Don't accept a cash deposit or rental payments.
- Do not tolerate tenants' disruptive behavior. Include an explicit provision in the lease or rental agreement prohibiting drug dealing and other illegal activity by tenants or guests, and promptly evict tenants who violate the clause.
- Be aware of suspicious activity, such as heavy traffic in and out of the rental premises.
- Respond to tenant and neighbor complaints about drug dealing on the rental property. Get advice from police immediately upon learning of a problem.
- Consult with security experts to do everything reasonable to discover and prevent illegal activity on the rental property.

Landlord Liability for Lead Poisoning

Landlords are increasingly likely to be held liable for tenant health problems resulting from exposure to lead and other environmental toxins, even if the landlord didn't cause—or even know about—the danger.

What are a landlord's legal responsibilities regarding lead in rental property?

Because of the health problems caused by lead poisoning, the federal Residential Lead-Based Paint Hazard Reduction Act was enacted in 1992. This law is commonly known as Title X (Ten). Environmental Protection Agency (EPA) regulations implementing Title X apply to rental property built before 1978.

Under Title X, before signing or renewing a lease or rental agreement, a landlord must give every tenant the EPA pamphlet, *Protect Your Family From Lead in Your Home,* or a state-approved version of this pamphlet. At the start of the tenancy, both the landlord and tenant must sign an EPA-approved disclosure form to prove that the landlord told the tenants about any known lead-based paint hazards on the premises. Property owners must keep this disclosure form as part of their records for three years after the tenancy begins.

A landlord who fails to comply with EPA regulations faces penalties of more than $10,000 for each violation. And a landlord who is found liable for tenant injuries from lead may have to pay three times what the tenant suffered in damages.

Are there any special rules for renovations?

Landlords who are renovating property that contains lead paint must alert tenants to the planned work. The EPA Lead Renovation, Repair and Painting (RRP) rule requires landlords to hire only EPA-Certified contractors. If the landlord or the landlord's employee will do the work, then the landlord and the worker must be certified. Landlords must take reasonable steps to ensure that the contractor is following lead-safe practices. If an occupied rental unit is being worked on, landlords or their contractors must also give tenants a copy of the EPA booklet, "The Lead-Safe Certified Guide to Renovate Right." If common areas will be affected, the landlord or contractor must distribute the pamphlet to every unit.

RESOURCE

More information about lead hazard resources. You can get information on the evaluation and control of lead-based paint and other hazards, and copies of the *Protect Your Family From Lead in Your Home* and *Renovate Right* pamphlets, by calling the National Lead Information Center at 800-424-LEAD, or checking the Lead section of the EPA website at www.epa.gov/lead. In addition, state housing departments have information on state laws and regulations governing the evaluation and control of lead hazards.

Are there any rental properties exempt from Title X regulations?

These properties are not covered by Title X:

- housing for which a construction permit was obtained, or on which construction was started, after January 1, 1978
- housing certified as lead-free by a state-accredited lead inspector
- lofts, efficiencies, and studio apartments
- short-term vacation rentals of 100 days or less
- a single room rented in a residential dwelling
- housing designed for persons with disabilities, unless any child under the age of six lives there or is expected to live there, and
- retirement communities (housing designed for seniors, where one or more tenants is at least 62 years old), unless children under the age of six are present or expected to live there.

State law may still apply, even if the property is not subject to federal rules.

Landlord Liability for Exposure to Asbestos, Mold, and Bedbugs

In addition to lead, property owners may be liable for tenant health problems caused by exposure to other environmental hazards such as asbestos and mold, and to bedbugs.

What government agency regulates asbestos?

Regulations concerning asbestos are issued by the Occupational Safety and Health Administration (OSHA). They set strict standards for the testing, maintenance, and disclosure of asbestos in buildings constructed before 1981. For information, check the Asbestos section of the "A–Z Index" of OSHA's website at www.osha.gov.

What are landlord responsibilities for mold in rental properties?

Mold is an environmental hazard fueling lawsuits against rental property owners. Across the country, tenants have won multimillion-dollar cases against landlords for claims of significant health problems—such as rashes, chronic fatigue, nausea, cognitive losses, hemorrhaging, and asthma—allegedly caused by exposure to "toxic molds" in their building.

No federal law sets permissible exposure limits or building tolerance standards for mold in residential buildings. Only a few states have taken steps toward establishing permissible mold standards. California, Indiana, Maryland, New Jersey, Texas, and Virginia are among the few that have passed laws aimed at developing guidelines and regulations for mold in indoor air. A few cities, including New York City and San Francisco, have enacted ordinances related to mold.

For information on the detection, removal, and prevention of mold, see www.epa.gov/mold.

What are tenant rights when it comes to bedbugs?

Bedbugs have increasingly become a problem in residential multifamily housing. Because an infestation is often difficult to trace to a particular unit, it's hard to know for sure who bears financial responsibility for the problem. But one thing is clear: Regardless of who should be stuck with the bill, the landlord has the responsibility to treat the infested areas. Tenants must cooperate with extermination and cleaning plans, which may involve moving out for a time. The law is not settled on who must pay relocation costs, though increasingly, landlords are assuming that burden.

The Bedbugs section of the EPA website (www.epa.gov/bedbugs) has extensive information about bedbugs, including relevant regulations. For the definitive guide to the eradication and prevention of bedbugs, see www.techletter.com, a website maintained by a pest management consulting firm. You can read dozens of articles on the site or order the comprehensive *Bed Bug Handbook: The Complete Guide to Bed Bugs and Their Control.*

Insurance

Both tenants and landlords need insurance to protect their property and bank accounts. Without adequate insurance, landlords risk losing hundreds of thousands of dollars of property to fire or other hazards. While tenants may not have as much at stake financially, they also need insurance—especially tenants with expensive personal belongings. Tenant losses from fire or theft are not covered by the landlord's insurance policy.

How can insurance help protect a rental property business?

A well-designed property insurance policy can protect rental property from losses caused by many perils, including fire, storms, burglary, and vandalism. (Earthquake and flood insurance are typically separate and, in some areas, coverage for mold claims may not even be available.) A comprehensive general liability policy will include liability insurance, covering injuries or losses suffered by others as the result of the landlord's negligence.

Equally important, liability insurance covers the cost (including lawyers' bills) of defending personal injury lawsuits.

Here are some tips on choosing insurance:

- Purchase enough coverage to protect the value of the property and assets.
- Be sure the policy covers not only physical injury but also libel, slander, discrimination, unlawful and retaliatory eviction, and invasion of privacy suffered by tenants and guests.

- Carry liability insurance on all vehicles used for business purposes, including the manager's car or truck.
- Make sure your policy is "occurrence based," not "claims based." Here's the difference: A claims-based policy must be in effect on the date you make the claim—even if it was in place when the incident leading to the claim occurred. Under an occurrence-based arrangement, you can make the claim after the policy has ended, as long as the claim arose while the policy was in effect—which is obviously to your advantage.
- Check out pet restrictions as to breeds of dog, or weight and number of pets allowed.
- Insist on a highly rated carrier (the most recognized rater is the A.M. Best Company, which rates a company based on criteria such as financial stability).

What does renters' insurance cover?

The average renters' policy covers tenants against losses to their belongings that occur as a result of fire and theft, up to the amount stated on the face of the policy, such as $25,000 or $50,000.

Most renter policies include deductible amounts of $250 or $500. This means that if a tenant's apartment is burglarized, the insurance company will pay only for the amount of the loss over and above the deductible amount.

In addition to fire and theft, most renters' policies include personal liability coverage ($100,000 is a typical amount) for injuries or damage caused by the tenant—for example, when a tenant's garden hose floods and ruins the neighbor's cactus garden, or a tenant's guest is injured on the rental property due to the tenant's negligence.

Renters' insurance is a package of several types of insurance designed to cover tenants for more than one risk. Each insurance company's package will be slightly different—types of coverage offered, exclusions, the dollar amounts specified, and the deductibles will vary. Tenants who live in a flood- or earthquake-prone area will need to pay extra for coverage. Policies covering flood and earthquake damage can be hard to find; tenants should shop around until they find the type of coverage that they need.

RESOURCE

More information on insurance. Whether you're a landlord or a tenant, you'll find lots of useful information on the website of United Policyholders (www.uphelp.org), a highly regarded consumer advocacy group. Another useful resource is the Insurance Information Institute (www.iii.org).

Resolving Disputes

Legal disputes—actual and potential—come in all shapes and sizes for landlords and tenants. Whether it's a disagreement over a rent increase, responsibility for repairs, noise, or return of a security deposit, rarely should lawyers and litigation be the first choice for resolving a landlord-tenant dispute.

How can landlords and tenants avoid disputes?

Both landlords and tenants should follow these tips to avoid legal problems:

- Know your rights and responsibilities under federal, state, and local law.
- Make sure the terms of your lease or rental agreement are clear.
- Put it in writing. To help avoid legal problems in the first place, and minimize those that can't be avoided, landlords should document important facts of their relationship with tenants (in addition to the lease or rental agreement), by using a written move-in letter, for example. Tenants should do the same. The key is to establish a good paper trail from move in to move out.
- Keep communication open. If there's a problem—for example, a disagreement about the landlord's right to enter a tenant's apartment—first try to resolve the issue by talking it over, without running to a lawyer. In some situations, it may be appropriate to give a tenant a written warning notice to correct a problem or stop a disruptive activity (such as a loud party), particularly if the tenant has not created other problems; in other situations, a formal termination notice may be more appropriate.
- Keep copies of any emails and correspondence, and make notes of conversations about any problems. For example, a tenant should ask for repairs in writing and keep a copy of the letter. The landlord should keep a copy of the repair request and note when and how the problem was repaired.

What if you've talked about the problem and still don't agree. What should you do next?

If you can't work out an agreement on your own but want to continue the rental relationship, consider mediation by a neutral third party. Unlike a judge, the mediator has no power to impose a decision but will simply work with you both to help find a mutually acceptable solution to the dispute. Mediation is often available at little or no cost from a publicly funded program.

RESOURCE

For information about local mediation programs, call your mayor's or city manager's office and ask for the staff member who handles "landlord–tenant mediation matters" or "housing disputes." That person should refer you to the public office, business, or community group that handles landlord–tenant mediations.

You can learn more about mediation in Chapter 16 of this book.

If mediation doesn't work, is there a last step before going to a lawyer?

If you decide not to mediate your dispute, or mediation fails, it's time to pursue other legal remedies. If the disagreement involves money, such as return of the security deposit, you can take the case to small claims court. A few states use different names for this type of court (such as "justice court"), but the purpose is the same for all: to provide a speedy, inexpensive resolution of disputes that involve relatively small amounts of money.

Keep in mind that your remedy in small claims court may be limited to an award of money damages. The maximum amount you can sue for varies from $2,500 to $25,000, depending on your state.

You can find more information about small claims court in Chapter 16; that chapter also provides advice about finding and working with a lawyer.

Tenancy Terminations and Evictions

Despite a landlord's best efforts, some disputes are unavoidable, or unsolvable—for example, if a tenant stops paying rent. In that case, evicting the tenant may be the landlord's only option.

A tenant who wants to end a tenancy early may also have options. See the section on "Leases and Rental Agreements," above, for advice for tenants who want to break a lease and move out early.

What are the basic steps in evicting a tenant?

Eviction itself (that is physically removing the tenant and the tenant's possessions from the rental property) generally can't be done until the landlord has gone to court and proved that the tenant did something wrong that justifies ending the tenancy. States set out very detailed requirements for landlords who want to end a tenancy. Each state has its own procedures as to how termination notices and eviction papers must be written and delivered.

Different types of notices are often required for different types of situations (such as late rent versus a tenant's illegal activity on the premises), and landlords must follow state rules and procedures exactly or experience delays in evicting a tenant (or even losing the lawsuit).

Are there any eviction shortcuts?

Landlords who attempt to bypass state eviction rules, by taking direct and immediate action to get a tenant out, may face a tenant lawsuit for wrongful eviction.

Landlord efforts at "self-help" evictions, such as changing the locks, threatening or intimidating the tenant, or shutting off the utilities, are illegal and may (depending on the situation) result in a tenant lawsuit for trespass, assault, battery, or intentional infliction of emotional distress.

A landlord who properly brings and conducts an eviction lawsuit for a valid reason is not guaranteed winning if the tenant mounts a legitimate defense—for example, that the landlord's action is motivated by a retaliatory reason, such as the tenant filing a complaint about uninhabitable housing.

RESOURCE

For detailed information about landlord–tenant law from the landlord's point of view, see these Nolo books:

- *Every Landlord's Legal Guide,* by Marcia Stewart, Ralph Warner, and Janet Portman. Extensive state-specific legal and practical information on leases, tenant screening, rent, security deposits, privacy, repairs, property managers, discrimination, roommates, liability, tenancy termination, and much more. Includes more than 30 legal forms and agreements.
- *Every Landlord's Tax Deduction Guide,* by Stephen Fishman. Explains the many tax write-offs available to landlords and provides advice on maximizing deductions, claiming credit and losses, filling out necessary tax forms, and much more.
- *Every Landlord's Guide to Finding Great Tenants,* by Janet Portman. Provides a system (including over 40 detailed forms) for finding, choosing—and legally rejecting—tenants.
- *First-Time Landlord,* by Janet Portman, Ilona Bray, and Marcia Stewart. Explains how to rent out a single-family home, including how to evaluate costs and profits, qualify for tax deductions, and comply with legal obligations, such as repairs.
- *Every Landlord's Guide to Managing Property,* by Michael Boyer. Provides practical and legal compliance advice for small-time landlords who manage property and tenants on the side (while holding down a day job). Includes do-it-yourself advice on handling day-to-day issues, such as nitty-gritty maintenance and conflicts with tenants regarding late rent, pets, and unauthorized occupants.
- *Mold and Your Rental Property: A Landlord's Prevention and Liability Guide,* by Ron Leshnower. An overview of landlord legal responsibilities for mold problems, mold prevention and identification techniques, insurance coverage, and more.
- California landlords and property managers should consult *The California Landlord's Law Book: Rights & Responsibilities,* by David Brown, Janet Portman, and Nils Rosenquest, and *The California Landlord's Law Book: Evictions,* by David Brown and Nils Rosenquest, for detailed legal advice and forms for the Golden State.

Nolo books from the tenant's point of view:

- *Every Tenant's Legal Guide,* by Janet Portman and Marcia Stewart. Gives tenants in all 50 states the legal and practical information they need to deal with their landlords and protect their rights when things go wrong. Covers all important issues of renting, including signing a lease, getting a landlord to make needed repairs, fighting illegal discrimination, protecting privacy rights, dealing with roommates, getting the security deposit back fairly, moving out, and much more.
- *Renters' Rights,* by Janet Portman and Marcia Stewart. A concise, highly accessible guide for tenants in every state, loaded with tips and strategies.
- California tenants should check out *California Tenants' Rights,* by Janet Portman and Scott Weaver. Detailed legal advice and forms for the Golden State, including rent control rules and eviction defense.

Nolo book for both landlords and tenants:

- *Everybody's Guide to Small Claims Court,* by Ralph Warner (National and California Editions). Explains how to evaluate your case, prepare for court, and convince a judge you're right. Also tells you what remedies (money only, or enforcement of the lease) are available in your state.

Nolo book for tenants renting commercial property:

- *Negotiate the Best Lease for Your Business,* by Janet Portman and Fred S. Steingold. Gives commercial tenants the information they need to understand and negotiate a commercial lease, plus tips on finding suitable space, choosing and working with brokers and lawyers, and bargaining effectively for the best terms and conditions.

ONLINE HELP

The following sites are good resources for landlords and tenants:

- **www.nolo.com** Information about a wide variety of legal topics, including state-specific charts on security deposits, small claims court, rent rules, landlord access to rental property, evictions, and other landlord–tenant laws (in two separate sections: "Landlords" and "Tenants"). Downloadable state-specific leases and other useful forms are also available for sale on the Nolo site. In addition to the landlord-tenant sections of Nolo.com, other sections of the site provide relevant articles, including the Accidents & Injuries, Small Claims Court & Lawsuits, Real Estate, and Taxes sections.
- **www.statelocalgov.net** Links to local and state resources, including many cities that have posted their ordinances (and often their rent control laws) online.
- **websites of relevant associations for landlords** (such as the National Apartment Association, www.naahqa) **and tenants** (such as New York City's TenantNet, www.tenant.net).

CHAPTER

4

Workplace Rights

I like work; it fascinates me. I can sit and look at it for hours.

—Jerome K. Jerome

If you're like most workers, you have experienced occasional job-related problems or have questions about whether you are being treated fairly—and legally—on the job. Here are some common problems:

- You were not hired for a job and you suspect it was because of your race, national origin, age, sex, sexual orientation, religion, or disability.
- Your employer promoted a less-qualified person to fill a position you were promised.
- You are regularly required to work overtime but are not given extra pay, or you are paid for your overtime hours at your regular pay rate (rather than time-and-a-half).
- You need to take a leave of absence from your job to care for a sick parent or child, but you are concerned that this will jeopardize your job or your eligibility for a promotion.
- You have been called to serve on a jury and wonder whether your employer must pay you for this time.
- You want to know whether your employer can read your emails or monitor your telephone conversations.
- You have been laid off and you want to know whether you're entitled to unemployment compensation or severance pay, and when you will get your final paycheck.

Federal laws provide a number of basic guarantees for most workers, such as the right to work free from discrimination, to take leave for certain reasons, and to be paid minimum wage and overtime. Many states give workers additional rights, including the right to receive a higher minimum wage than the federal rate or to take time off to attend a child's school conference or serve on a jury. And some local governments provide even more protections. Your employer must follow whichever law—federal, state, or local—that provides you the most protection.

For related questions from the employer's perspective, such as running background checks when hiring employees, see Chapter 5.

Fair Pay and Time Off

I do not like work even when someone else does it.

—Mark Twain

These days, most of us spend at least half of our waking hours working. Ideally, this time will be spent on jobs that are fulfilling. But whether or not we enjoy our work, all of us want to be paid fairly and on time, and to be able to take time off to tend to important obligations and emergencies. Fortunately, both state and federal laws protect these rights.

Which laws cover pay and work hours?

The Fair Labor Standards Act (FLSA), is the major federal law that covers wages and hours of work. (29 U.S.C. §§ 201–219.) It regulates how much workers must be paid, how many hours they can be required to work, and the special rules that apply to younger workers. The law includes provisions on:

- the minimum wage
- hours worked
- overtime, and
- child labor.

The FLSA applies to most employers, including the federal government, state and local governments, schools, and virtually all private employers.

In addition, your state probably has a wage and hour law that covers the same basic topics. Many state laws give workers more rights than the FLSA, so it's always a good idea to become familiar with what your state requires. And a few cities and counties also impose rules on local employers, including setting a higher minimum wage.

What is the minimum wage?

The current federal minimum wage is $7.25 per hour. Additionally, states have their own minimum wage laws that require a higher rate of pay. For example, the state of Washington's current minimum wage is $9.47 per hour. Employers must pay whichever minimum wage rate is higher. To find out the minimum wages in the 50 states and the District of Columbia, Puerto Rico, and Guam, go to www.nolo.com/legal-encyclopedia/fair-pay, and select your state from the list. You can also contact your state labor department for information; you'll find contact information on the U.S. Department of Labor website (www.dol.gov/whd/contacts/state_of.htm).

In addition, some cities and counties have enacted so-called "living wage" ordinances, which require certain employers to pay a higher minimum wage. Many of these laws cover only employers that have contracts with, or receive subsidies from, the state or county. However, some apply more broadly to private employers in the area. In San Francisco, for example, any employee who works at least two hours per week in the city is entitled to a minimum wage of $13 per hour as of July 1, 2016. To find out whether your area has a living wage ordinance, contact your local government offices.

How can I figure out whether I am entitled to overtime pay?

First, check to see whether your employer is covered by the FLSA or your state's wage and hour law. Because the coverage of these laws is so broad, you can be pretty sure that your employer must comply with them.

The next step is to figure out whether you are considered an "exempt" employee under these laws: If you are exempt, then you are not entitled to overtime.

The FLSA has exemptions for certain types of workers, including:

- outside salespeople
- independent contractors
- certain computer specialists, including computer system analysts, programmers, and software engineers, as long as they are paid at least $27.63 per hour or at least $455 per week
- employees of seasonal amusement or recreational businesses
- farmworkers
- transportation workers
- newspeople
- employees of motion picture theaters, and
- commissioned employees of retail or service businesses, if their regular rate of pay is more than one and a half times the minimum wage and more than half their pay comes from commissions.

The largest categories of exempt workers that employers are most likely to try to shoehorn their workers into are executive, administrative, and professional workers. To fall under one of these exemptions, you must receive at least $455 per week on a salary basis—meaning that you are paid the same amount each week, regardless of the quality or quantity of your work. (The minimum weekly salary will increase from $455 to $913 on December 1, 2016.) You must also have certain qualifications and/or perform certain duties, such as routinely exercising discretion, supervising other employees, making high-level decisions, having an advanced degree, or working in a creative field. However, some employers—in an effort to avoid paying overtime—claim that their employees fall into one of these categories even though the employees actually perform fairly routine tasks. For example, a fast-food restaurant might classify many of its employees as exempt assistant managers (and schedule them to work lots of unpaid overtime) but assign them the same basic tasks as the rest of its workforce. Employers can face significant penalties—and costly lawsuits—for misclassifying employees in this manner. Some states have their own exemption rules. So even if an employee is exempt under the FLSA, he or she might not be exempt from overtime state law.

If you are not exempt, then you are entitled to overtime if you work more than 40 hours in a week or, in a few states, more than eight hours in a day. To learn more about your state's overtime requirements and exemption rules, contact your state department of labor.

Does my employer have to pay me overtime if I work more than eight hours in a day?

Under the FLSA, your employer does not have to pay you overtime if you work more than eight hours in any given day. As long as you work 40 hours or less in a week, you aren't entitled to overtime.

In this area, however, it's definitely worth checking to see if your state has an overtime law. Some states, such as California, require employers to pay overtime to employees who work more than eight hours in a day.

Can my employer require me to take time off instead of paying me time-and-a-half for overtime hours?

Most workers are familiar with compensatory or comp time: the practice of offering employees time off from work in lieu of overtime pay.

However, compensatory time is generally illegal under federal law, except for state and federal government employees. Some states allow private employers to give employees comp time instead of cash. However, these are complex, often conflicting laws. Check with your state's labor department for special laws on comp time in your area.

Employers and employees routinely violate the rules governing the use of compensatory time in place of overtime wages. However, such violations are risky. Employees can find themselves unable to collect money they are owed if a company goes out of business or they are fired before they can use their comp time. And employers can end up owing large amounts of overtime pay to employees if a labor department pursues compensatory time violations.

If you would prefer to have time off rather than overtime pay, you can ask your employer to rearrange your work hours to accomplish this without violating the law. This is done by giving you an hour and a half of time off for each overtime hour you worked during the same pay period. For example, suppose you worked 50 hours in the first week of a pay period. Because you worked ten overtime hours, you would get 15 hours of time off in the second week of the pay period. That way, you get time off and your paycheck remains the same.

Can my boss force me to work overtime?

Under the federal FLSA, your employer can require you to work overtime and can even fire you if you refuse to do so.

The FLSA does not limit the number of hours in a day or days in a week that an employer can schedule an employee to work. It only requires employers to pay nonexempt employees overtime (one and a half times the worker's regular rate of pay) for any hours over 40 that the employee works in a week.

However, your state law may provide additional rights, such as the daily overtime standard explained above. Contact your state labor department to learn more.

My boss says that because I earn tips on the job, he can pay me less than the minimum wage. Is this true?

It depends on how generous your customers are. Generally, employers must pay all employees at least the minimum wage. If an employee routinely receives at least $30 per month in tips, however, federal law allows employers to credit a portion of those tips against the minimum wage requirement. Employers can pay you as little as $2.13 an hour, as long as you earn enough in tips to bring your hourly pay up to at least the federal minimum wage of $7.25 per hour.

> EXAMPLE: Alphonse is a waiter and earns more than $10 per hour in tips. Denis, the restaurant's owner, is required to pay Alphonse at least $2.13 per hour on top of his tips. If business slows and Alphonse's tips dip to, say, $1 an hour, Denis must pay him at least $6.25 per hour, so that Alphonse makes at least the $7.25 minimum wage when taking his tips into account.

Some states set a lower tip credit than federal law. And some states don't allow employers to pay tipped employees less than the minimum wage, no matter how much the employees earn in tips. If you work in one of those states, your employer may not take a tip credit and must pay you at least the minimum wage for each hour worked. Contact your state labor department for information on your state's law.

I am required to be reachable by phone 24 hours a day, seven days a week for my job. I am occasionally called on my days off. Am I entitled to be paid anything for on-call time?

When your employer requires you to be on call but does not require you to stay on the company's premises, the following two rules generally apply:

- On-call time that you control and use for your own enjoyment or benefit is not counted as payable time.
- On-call time over which you have little or no control and which you cannot use for your own enjoyment or benefit is payable time.

Disputes usually boil down to the meaning of control and use of time. If you receive only the occasional call, and you are otherwise free to spend your time any way you want, your employer does not need to pay you for the on-call time. However, if your employer insists that you be available to return to work on short notice and puts constraints on your behavior—you cannot consume alcohol, or you must stay within a certain radius of work, for example—you may be entitled to compensation for your on-call time.

Similarly, if you receive five or six calls on every day off, and if each of those calls requires you to come into the office or be in a specific place, then a court will certainly see that your time isn't your own and will require that your employer compensate you.

And—as always—be sure to check with your state labor department to see whether your state has different rules.

How can I tell if I'm really an intern or just an employee who isn't getting paid?

Internships are a time-honored method of gaining valuable experience in a new field. But some employers are willing to call just about anyone an "intern" to get free labor. Calling a job an "internship" doesn't relieve an employer of the obligation to pay for your time. An employer that wants to pay less than the minimum wage (or nothing at all) to an intern must meet a strict six-part test, intended to ensure that the position really is a learning experience:

- The internship must be similar to training that would be provided in an educational environment. An internship that centers on academic experience is more likely to meet this requirement, as is one that trains the intern for multiple employment settings rather than just to do the work of the employer.
- The internship must be for the benefit of the intern. The more the business depends on the work of the intern, and the more time the intern spends on routine, regular work of the business, the more likely the intern will be considered an employee who is entitled to minimum wage and overtime.
- The intern must not displace regular employees and must work under close supervision of existing staff. A company that is using interns rather than regular employees (either because it has let employees go or put off hiring) is likely to be seen as an employer that must follow wage and hour obligations. Similarly, if an intern receives the same supervision as regular employees, that argues against a true internship experience.
- The employer gets no immediate advantage from the intern's work and may, on occasion, find its operations impeded by the internship. Having to provide an intern with extra training, special learning opportunities, and additional supervision and guidance, for example, cost the employer in time and resources.
- The intern is not necessarily entitled to a job once the internship ends. An internship that is actually a trial period, the successful completion of which will lead to a job, will be considered regular employment that should be paid.
- Both the employer and the intern understand that the intern is not entitled to wages for time spent in the internship. If the intern thought the position would be paid, that argues in favor of employment status.

What laws ensure my right to take vacations?

Here's a surprising legal truth that most workers would rather not learn: No federal or state law requires employers to pay you for vacation or holidays. This means that if you receive a paid vacation, it's because of custom, not law.

And just as vacation benefits are discretionary with each employer, so are the rules about how and when they accrue. For example, it is perfectly legal for an employer to require a certain length of employment—six months or a year, for example—before an employee is entitled to take any vacation time. It is also legal for employers to prorate vacations for part-time employees, or to deny them the benefit completely. Employers are also free to set limits on how much paid time off employees may earn before it must be taken.

However, some states prohibit "use it or lose it" vacation policies, which take away accrued vacation hours if employees don't use their time off by a certain deadline (often, the end of the year). To find out whether your state has such a rule, contact your state labor department.

Even in states with this kind of rule, it is still legal for employers to set a vacation cap, which prohibits you from accumulating more hours once you have a certain number of hours in the bank.

If I lose or leave my job, when will I receive my final paycheck?

State law, not federal law, determines when employees must receive their final paychecks, so the answer to this question depends on where you live. Laws relating to final paychecks usually distinguish between employees who quit and those who are fired; the latter are often entitled to receive their paycheck a bit sooner. For example, a fired employee might be entitled to receive all accrued wages and vacation pay immediately, but an employee who quits has to wait 72 hours to be paid, or even until the next regularly scheduled payday. To find out what your state's law requires, contact your state labor department.

Independent Contractors Are Exempt

The Fair Labor Standards Act covers only employees, not independent contractors, who are considered independent business-people. The FLSA was passed to clamp down on employers who cheated workers of their fair wages. As a result, employee status is broadly interpreted so that as many workers as possible are protected by the law. In recent cases on this issue, courts have leaned toward classifying workers as employees rather than independent contractors.

Among other things, a worker is more likely to be considered an independent contractor under the FLSA when:

- the worker is retained for a definite period of time or on a project basis
- the worker is not performing work that is an integral part of the employer's business
- the worker has an opportunity to make a profit or suffer a loss
- the worker has invested in facilities and equipment
- the worker competes in the open market and is not economically dependent on one business, and
- the worker has control over how and when the work is performed.

Am I entitled to take time off from work if I get sick?

No federal law requires an employer to offer *paid* time off for illness. (A handful of states and cities require employers to offer at least a few days of paid sick leave per year.) However, the Family and Medical Leave Act (FMLA), a federal law passed in 1993, gives workers some rights to *unpaid* leave for their own serious health conditions, among other things. Under the FMLA, you may be eligible for up to 12 weeks of unpaid leave during a 12-month period. Your employer can count your accrued paid benefits—vacation, sick leave, and personal leave days—toward the 12 weeks of leave allowed under the law. But many employers give employees the option of deciding whether to include paid leave time as part of their 12 weeks of sick leave.

The FMLA applies to all private and public employers with 50 or more employees. To be covered under the law, you must:

- be employed within a 75-mile radius of 50 or more employees of the same company
- work for the employer for a year or more, and
- work at least 1,250 hours (about 24 hours a week) during the year preceding the leave.

There are a number of loopholes in the FMLA. For example, schoolteachers and instructors who work for educational agencies and private elementary or secondary schools may have restrictions on their FMLA leave. If you and your spouse both work for the same employer, your total leave allotment may be restricted when taking leave to bond with a new child. And if you are among the highest-paid 10% of your company's employees, you may not be entitled to be reinstated to your job as normally required.

A number of states have passed their own versions of family leave laws, and most of them give workers more liberal leave rights. A number of laws, for example, apply to smaller workplaces and extend to workers who have been on the job only a short time. Check with your state's department of labor for more information.

Can I take time off if a member of my family gets sick?

Possibly. The FMLA—or your state's version of it—also allows you to take leave to care for a spouse, parent, or child with a serious health condition. And your state may allow you to use at least some of your paid sick leave (if your employer provides it) to care for a sick family member. A few states even allow paid time off for this purpose (whether through a state insurance fund or a requirement on employers). Contact your state's department of labor to find out whether your state has this kind of leave law.

My employer refused to grant me the time off for sick leave guaranteed by the FMLA. What can I do?

The FMLA is enforced by the U.S. Department of Labor. If you have specific questions about the law, including how to file a claim against your employer for failing to comply, contact your local Department of Labor office. You can find a list of local offices at the Department of Labor's website at www.dol.gov.

You generally must file a claim or lawsuit under the FMLA within two years of an employer's violation. If the violation was willful (intentional), you'll have up to three years.

Does my employer have to pay me for time I spend on jury duty?

No federal law requires employers to pay employees for jury duty. Most states prohibit employers from penalizing an employee who is called for jury duty or actually serves on a jury. However, only a few states require private employers to pay their workers for this time. And some of these states place limits on the amount an employer must pay (for example, by allowing the employer to pay only for a certain number of days off or to subtract any amounts the employee receives in jury fees from the court from his or her regular wages). To find out about any protections offered in your state, contact your state labor department.

The rules are different for exempt employees. One of the requirements for classifying employees as exempt under the FLSA is that they are paid the same amount each week, regardless of a variation in work hours. For that reason, employers generally cannot dock an exempt employee's paycheck for jury service, except to offset jury fees that the employee receives from the court.

Can I take time off work to vote?

This is another state law issue. Many states require employers to give employees some time off to cast their ballots—and prohibit employers from disciplining employees who take time off for this purpose—but a number of restrictions apply. For example, some states give an employee the right to take time off only if the employee doesn't have enough time to vote outside of work hours. Some states require employers to pay workers for this time; others do not. And a few states allow employers to require workers to give advance notice or provide proof that they actually voted to take advantage of these legal protections. For information on your state's rules, contact your state labor department.

If I am called to serve in the military, does my employer have to hold my job open for me until I return?

Federal and state laws provide strong protections for workers who must leave their jobs for military service. Under the Uniformed Services Employment and Reemployment Rights Act of 1994 (USERRA), employers may not discriminate against employees who are called to serve in the armed forces, National Guard, or Reserve. (38 U.S.C. §§ 4301 and following.)

USERRA also entitles an employee who takes time off to serve in the armed forces to job reinstatement, if the employee meets these conditions:

- the employee must have given notice, before taking leave, that the leave was for military service
- the employee must have spent no more than five years on leave for military service (with some exceptions)
- the employee must have been released from military service under honorable conditions, and
- the employee must report back to work or apply for reinstatement within specified time limits (these limits vary depending on the length of the employee's leave).

Workers must be returned to the positions they would have held had they been continuously employed throughout their leave, as long as they are otherwise qualified for the job. This means that you are entitled to more than simple reinstatement to your old position; you also have the right to receive any promotions, increased pay, or additional job responsibilities you would have received had you never taken leave. If you are not qualified for the job, your employer must try to get you qualified. You are also entitled to the benefits and seniority you would have earned had you been continuously employed. For purposes of your employer's benefits plans and leave policies, the time you spent on leave must be counted as time worked.

Returning members of the military receive one additional benefit: You cannot be fired without cause for up to one year after you are reinstated (the exact length of this protection depends on the length of your military service), regardless of your employer's policies or practices.

To find out more about USERRA, check out the website of the Department of Labor, at www.dol.gov/vets/programs/USERRA. For lots of free information on the law, see the website of the National Committee for Employer Support of the Guard and Reserve, at www.esgr.mil.

In addition to these federal protections, almost every state has a law prohibiting discrimination against those in the state's militia or national guard. Some of these laws provide the same protections available under USERRA. Most state laws also require employers to grant leave to employees for certain types of military service. Some states require leave only for those employees called to active duty; other states require leave for those called for training as well. Employees who take military leave are not generally entitled to pay, although many private employers choose to pay at least a portion of the employee's salary for time spent on leave. To find out about your state's law, contact your state department of labor.

My daughter has been called to active duty abroad; can I take time off work to help her and her kids prepare for her departure?

As long as you and your employer are covered by the FMLA, the answer is yes. The FMLA was amended in 2008 to add a couple of new reasons for taking leave. One of them, called "qualifying exigency" leave, allows employees to take FMLA leave when a child, spouse, or parent is deployed to a foreign country for active military duty. Employees in this situation may take leave to:

- handle issues arising from a military member's short-notice deployment (up to seven days' advance notice)
- attend military programs, ceremonies, and family support and assistance programs
- provide assistance to a military member's parent who is incapable of self-care
- arrange child care and school activities
- help make financial and legal arrangements, including wills, powers of attorney, and bank account transfers
- attend counseling for oneself, the member, or the military member's child
- spend time with the military member who is on temporary rest and recuperation (R&R) leave, or
- attend postdeployment ceremonies, briefings, and events, including homecoming activities, and to address issues arising from the death of a military member on active duty.

In addition, an employee may use qualifying exigency leave for other activities, if the employer agrees.

The employee is entitled to use the regular 12 weeks of FMLA leave for qualifying exigency leave. For certain categories of leave, however, the employee's time off is limited. For example, employees may only take up to five days off to spend with a military member on temporary R&R leave (if the military member takes more R&R leave later, the employee can take another five days off then).

Can I take time off work to attend school conferences with my child's teacher?

Although the federal leave laws do not require employers to provide time off for their employees to attend a child's school events, some state laws do. These laws vary in their particulars, including which employees are eligible for leave, which employers have to provide leave, and how much time an employee may take off during the course of a year. To find out whether your state has a leave law that applies to school activities, check with your state's department of labor.

RESOURCE

For more information about wages, hours, and time off, call your local U.S. Labor Department, Wage and Hour Division office, listed in the federal government section of your telephone directory, or available at www.dol.gov. You can also get contact information by calling the toll-free number of the U.S. Department of Labor Wage and Hour Division at 866-487-9243.

The Department of Labor's website (www.dol.gov) offers many helpful materials, including the full text of the FLSA and its regulations; fact sheets on federal wage, hour, and leave laws; information on state wage and hour laws; and links to other resources.

You can find detailed information on wage and hour laws, including each state's laws, at Nolo's Fair Pay page, www.nolo.com/legal-encyclopedia/fair-pay.

Workplace Health and Safety

Several laws establish basic safety standards aimed at reducing the number of illnesses, injuries, and deaths in workplaces. Because most workplace safety laws rely on employee complaints as a primary enforcement tool, most laws also prevent employers from retaliating against employees who report unsafe conditions to proper authorities.

Do I have any legal rights if I feel that my workplace is unsafe or unhealthy?

Federal and state laws protect you from an unsafe workplace. The Occupational Safety and Health Act of 1970 (OSHA) is the main federal law covering threats to workplace safety. (29 U.S.C. §§ 651 and following.) OSHA requires employers to provide a workplace that is free of dangers that could physically harm employees.

In addition to the basic right to a safe workplace, OSHA gives you the following rights:

- You can get training from your employer on the health and safety standards that your employer must follow.
- You can get training from your employer on any dangerous chemicals you are exposed to and on ways you can protect yourself from harm.
- You can get training from your employer on any other health and safety hazards (such as construction hazards or blood-borne pathogens) that might exist in your workplace.
- You can request information from your employer about OSHA standards, worker injuries and illnesses, job hazards, and workers' rights.
- You can ask your employer to cure any hazards or OSHA violations.
- You can file a complaint about unsafe working conditions with OSHA.
- You can request that OSHA inspect your workplace.
- You can find out the results of an OSHA inspection.

What to Do After an Injury

Workplace hazards often become obvious only after they cause an injury. For example, an unguarded machine part that spins at high speed may not seem dangerous until someone's clothing or hair gets caught in it. But even after a worker has been injured, employers sometimes fail—or even refuse—to eliminate the danger.

If you have been injured at work by a hazard that should be eliminated before it injures someone else, take the following steps as quickly as possible after obtaining the proper medical treatment:

- Immediately file a claim for workers' compensation benefits so that your medical bills will be paid and you will be compensated for your lost wages and injury. In some states, the amount you receive for a workers' comp claim will be larger if a violation of a state workplace safety law contributed to your injury. (For more information, see "Workers' Compensation," below.)
- Tell your employer that a continuing hazard or dangerous condition exists. As with most workplace safety issues, the odds of getting meaningful results will be greater if other employees join in your complaint.
- If your employer does not eliminate the hazard promptly, file a complaint with OSHA and any state or local agency that you think may be able to help. You can obtain a list of state health and safety agencies on the OSHA website at www.osha.gov/dcsp/osp/index.html.

- You can file a complaint with OSHA if your employer retaliates against you for asserting your rights under the law.
- You can request the federal government to research possible workplace hazards.

Most states also have their own OSHA laws, most of which offer protections similar to the federal law.

How do I assert my rights to a safe workplace?

If you feel that your workplace is unsafe, your first action should be to make your supervisor aware of the danger. If your employer doesn't take prompt action, follow up in writing. Then, if you are still unsuccessful in getting your company to correct the safety hazard, you can file a complaint at the nearest OSHA office.

Look under the U.S. Labor Department in the federal government section of your local telephone directory. You can also file a complaint online at www.osha.gov/workers/file_complaint.html.

If you feel that a workplace hazard poses an imminent danger (a danger that could immediately cause death or serious physical harm), you should immediately call the agency's hotline at 800-321-OSHA (6742).

Can I refuse to do work that puts me in danger?

OSHA gives you a very limited right to refuse to do a job if you have a reasonable, good faith belief that you will be exposed to imminent danger. As you might imagine, not every unsafe condition qualifies as an imminent danger. A workplace danger is imminent if:

- you face a threat of death or serious physical injury, and
- the threat is immediate (that is, you believe that death or serious injury could occur within a short time period, before OSHA could take steps to remedy the situation).

If you are facing an imminent danger, you should ask your employer to correct the problem or to assign you other work, tell your employer that you won't perform the work until the problem is resolved, and remain at the workplace unless and until asked to leave by your employer. You should also immediately call OSHA's hotline at 800-321-OSHA.

Does OSHA protect against the harmful effects of tobacco smoke in the workplace?

OSHA rules apply to tobacco smoke only in rare and extreme circumstances, such as when contaminants created by a manufacturing process combine with tobacco smoke to create a dangerous workplace air supply that fails OSHA standards. Workplace air-quality standards and measurement techniques are so technical that typically only OSHA agents or consultants who specialize in environmental testing are able to determine when the air quality falls below allowable limits.

If OSHA won't protect me from secondhand tobacco smoke at work, is there anything I can do to limit or avoid exposure?

If you are bothered by coworkers' smoking, there are a number of steps you can take.

Check local and state laws. Most states and many cities prohibit or place significant restrictions on smoking in the workplace. Most of them also set out specific procedures for making complaints. Your state's labor department should have up-to-date information about these laws. If you can't find local laws that prohibit smoking in workplaces, check with a national nonsmokers' rights group, such as Americans for Nonsmokers' Rights, www.no-smoke.org.

Ask your employer for an accommodation. If you have a disability caused by or aggravated by smoke, you may be entitled to a reasonable accommodation. For example, your employer may have to install additional ventilation systems, restrict smoking to outdoor areas or special rooms, or segregate smokers and nonsmokers. See "Discrimination," below, for more information on disabilities and reasonable accommodation.

RESOURCE

For more about workplace health and safety, the Occupational Safety and Health Administration publishes pamphlets about workplace safety laws. Visit www.osha.gov for more information.

You can also read a summary of OSHA in *The Essential Guide to Federal Employment Laws,* by Lisa Guerin and Sachi Barreiro (Nolo).

Workers' Compensation

If you are injured on the job—or suffer a work-related illness or disease that prevents you from working—you may be eligible to receive benefits from your state workers' compensation program. Among other things, worker's compensation will cover your medical bills and pay you for your time off work and any permanent injury you suffer. If you are eligible for workers' compensation benefits, however, you typically cannot sue your employer for the injury in court.

Who pays workers' compensation benefits?

In most states, employers are required to purchase an insurance policy from a workers' compensation insurance company. In some states, larger employers that are clearly solvent are allowed to self-insure or act as their own insurance companies, while small companies (with fewer than three or four employees, for example) are not required to carry workers' compensation insurance at all. When a worker is injured, the employee's claim is filed with the insurance company—or self-insuring employer—which pays medical and disability benefits according to a state-approved formula.

Are all on-the-job injuries covered by workers' compensation?

The workers' compensation system is designed to provide benefits to injured workers, even if an injury is caused by the employer's or employee's carelessness. But there are some limits. Usually, injuries caused by an employee's intoxication or use of illegal drugs are not covered by workers' compensation. Coverage may also be denied for:

- self-inflicted injuries (including those suffered by a person who starts a fight)
- injuries suffered while a worker was committing a serious crime
- injuries suffered while an employee was not performing work-related tasks, and

- injuries suffered when an employee's conduct violated company policy.

If your employer's conduct is especially egregious (for example, your employer did something intentional or reckless that harmed you), you may be allowed to bypass the workers' compensation system and sue your employer in court. Although you won't be assured of the outcome (because you'll need to prove that your employer is at fault for your injury), you could win much larger amounts of money than you could collect through workers' compensation.

Does workers' compensation cover only injuries, or does it also cover long-term problems and illnesses?

Your injury does not need to be caused by an accident—such as a fall from a ladder—to be covered. Many workers, for example, receive compensation for repetitive stress injuries (such as carpal tunnel syndrome and back problems) that are caused by overuse or misuse over a long period of time. You can also be compensated for some illnesses and diseases that are the gradual result of work conditions or toxins, such as heart conditions, lung disease, cancer, and stress-related digestive problems.

Do I have to be injured at my workplace to be covered by workers' compensation?

No. As long as your injury is job-related, it's covered. For example, you'll be covered if you are injured while traveling on business, running a work-related errand, or even attending a required, business-related social function.

Are You Covered by Workers' Compensation?

Most workers are eligible for workers' compensation coverage, but every state excludes some workers. Exclusions often include:

- business owners
- independent contractors
- casual workers
- domestic employees in private homes
- farmworkers
- maritime workers, and
- railroad employees.

Check the workers' compensation law of your state to see whether these exclusions affect you.

Federal government employees are also excluded from state workers' compensation coverage, but they receive workers' compensation benefits under a separate federal law.

In addition, some states don't require smaller employers—those with fewer than three to five employees, depending on the state's rules—to carry workers' compensation insurance. If you work for one of these employers, you may be excluded from the state program.

How do I claim workers' compensation benefits?

First, promptly report the work-related injury or sickness to your employer. Most states require you to do this within two to 30 days following an injury. If an injury occurs over time (for example, a breathing problem or carpal tunnel syndrome), you must report your condition soon after you discover it and realize that it is caused by your work.

Next, get the medical treatment you need. In an emergency, you can go to the nearest hospital or emergency room. However, for nonemergency care, you must follow your state's rules on which doctors you can see for a work injury. See "Can I be treated by my own doctor?" below.

In many states, you will also need to file an official workers' compensation claim with the insurance company before you can receive benefits. Your employer should provide you with the necessary forms. You can also contact your state's workers' compensation agency.

Finally, make sure you save copies of all correspondence with your employer, its insurance carrier, and your doctor concerning your workers' compensation claim. You might need this paperwork if you run into problems later.

What kind of benefits will I receive?

The workers' compensation system provides wage replacement, medical expenses, and sometimes vocational rehabilitation benefits, such as job training, education, or job placement assistance, if you are unable to return to your former position. The benefits paid through workers' compensation, however, are relatively modest.

If you are temporarily unable to work, you'll usually receive two-thirds of your average weekly wage up to a maximum set by state law. But because these payments are tax-free, if you received decent wages prior to your injury, you'll fare reasonably well in most states. You will be eligible for these wage-loss replacement benefits as soon as you've lost a few days of work because of an injury or illness that is covered by workers' compensation.

If you become permanently unable to do the work you were doing prior to the injury, or unable to work at all, you may be eligible to receive permanent disability benefits. The amount of the payment will depend on the nature and extent of your injuries. If you anticipate a permanent work disability, contact your state workers' compensation agency as soon as possible; these benefits are rather complex and may take a while to process.

Can I be treated by my own doctor?

Some states allow the worker to choose the doctor, while other states allow the employer (or its insurance company) to choose. Other states have more complicated rules. For example, in some states, the worker can select the doctor, but it must be from a list approved by the employer.

The doctor's report will have a big impact on the benefits you receive. While it's crucial that you tell the doctor the truth about your injury and your medical history (your benefits may be denied based on fraud if you don't), be sure to clearly identify all possible job-related medical problems and sources of pain. This is no time to downplay or gloss over your injuries.

Keep in mind that a doctor selected by or paid for by your employer's insurance company is not your friend. The desire to get future business may motivate a doctor to minimize the seriousness of your injury or return you to work before you are ready, in order to please the insurance company.

Social Security Benefits for the Permanently Disabled

If you're permanently unable to return to work, you may qualify for Social Security disability benefits. Social Security will, over the long run, provide more benefits than workers' compensation. But be forewarned: These benefits are hard to get. They are reserved for seriously injured workers. To qualify, your injury or illness:

- must prevent you from doing any substantial gainful work, and
- must be expected to last at least 12 months or to result in death.

If you think you may meet the above requirements, contact your local Social Security office. For more information about Social Security benefits, see Chapter 13.

If I am initially treated by an insurance company doctor, do I have a right to see my own doctor at some point?

State workers' compensation systems establish technical and often tricky rules in this area. Often, you have the right to switch doctors at least once if you are not satisfied with the care you are receiving, although there is sometimes a waiting period before you can get a second doctor. Also, if your injury is serious, you usually have the right to a second opinion. And in some states, after you are treated by an insurance company's doctor for a certain period (90 days is typical), you may have the automatic right to transfer your treatment to your own doctor or health plan.

To understand your rights, contact your state worker's compensation office (sometimes called the industrial relations office); find yours on the U.S. Department of Labor website (www.dol.gov/owcp/dfec/regs/compliance/wc.htm). You can also get a copy of your state's rules—or, if necessary, research your state workers' compensation laws and regulations. The appendix explains how to do your own legal research.

Will I be covered if I suffer an injury to a part of my body that had been injured previously?

If the previous injury was also work-related, workers' compensation should provide full coverage. If it wasn't, you may receive lower-level benefits.

If your earlier injury occurred at a former job, it's generally up to your current employer's insurance company and your former employer's insurance company to sort out who's responsible for paying your benefits. Sometimes, they will split the costs between them. If your previous injury was not work-related, but it was aggravated due to your work activities, you may still be able to collect benefits. However, you will receive benefits only for the worsening of the condition caused by work.

How do I find a good workers' compensation lawyer and how much will it cost?

You usually don't need a lawyer unless you suffer a permanent disability or all or part of your workers' compensation claim is denied. If you find yourself in one of these situations, you'll probably want to do some research to learn your rights and duties. For example, many claims are denied based on a doctor's report claiming that you are not injured. If you dispute the report, you may have a right to obtain a second opinion from another doctor at the insurance company's expense.

If your claim is denied, consider hiring an experienced workers' compensation lawyer to help you navigate the appeals process. The best way to find a good lawyer is often through word of mouth. Talk to other injured workers or check with a local union or other workers' organization.

In most states, fees for legal representation in workers' compensation cases are limited to between 10% and 20% of any eventual award. Because these fees are relatively modest, workers' compensation lawyers customarily take on many clients and, as a result, do not have time to provide much individual attention. Most of your contacts with your attorney's office will be with paralegals and other support personnel. This is not a bad thing in itself, if the office is well run by support staff. Be sure that the office is able to stay on top of paperwork and filing deadlines, and that a knowledgeable person is available to answer your questions clearly and promptly.

If I receive workers' compensation, can I also sue my employer in court?

Generally, no. The workers' compensation system was established as part of a legal trade-off. In exchange for giving up the right to sue an employer in court, you get workers' compensation benefits—generally fairly quickly and without legal wrangling—no matter who was at fault. Before the workers' compensation system was in place, if you went to court, you stood to recover a large amount of money, but only if you could prove the injury was caused by your employer. And it could take years before you saw any money.

Today, workers' compensation is generally your only remedy against your employer for a work-related injury. However, there are a few exceptions to this rule. For example, in many states, you can sue your employer if it failed to secure workers' compensation insurance or if your injury was caused by your employer's intentional or reckless actions.

You can also sue any third party that might be responsible for your injuries, such as the driver of the car that hit you or the manufacturer of the machinery that injured you.

What if my employer tells me not to file a workers' compensation claim or threatens to fire me if I do?

In nearly all states, it is a violation of workers' compensation laws to retaliate against an employee for filing a workers' compensation claim. If this happens, immediately report it to your local workers' compensation office.

RESOURCE

For more information about workers' compensation, see *California Workers' Comp: How to Take Charge When You're Injured on the Job,* by Christopher Ball (Nolo), which includes all of the forms and instructions you need to file a workers' compensation claim in California. The book is also useful for people who live elsewhere, as it provides a good overview of how the system works in general.

ONLINE HELP

You can find more information on workers' compensation topics at Nolo's Workers' Compensation page, www.nolo.com/legal-encyclopedia/workers-compensation.

What to Do When the Insurance Company Won't Pay

Some workers' compensation carriers take an aggressive stance and deny legitimate claims for compensation. When this happens, it's often because the insurer claims you haven't been injured or, if you have, that it's not serious enough to qualify you for benefits. In some cases, this is done after a private investigator hired by the insurance company follows you and takes photographs of you engaging in fairly strenuous physical activity, such as lifting a box or mowing the lawn, despite claiming a disabling injury.

If your legitimate benefits are denied, you should immediately file an appeal with your state workers' compensation agency or workers' compensation appeals board. You may also want to hire an attorney to help you pursue your claim.

Discrimination

Sometimes, I feel discriminated against, but it does not make me angry. It merely astonishes me. How can any deny themselves the pleasure of my company? It's beyond me.

—Zora Neale Hurston

Since 1964, when the landmark federal Civil Rights Act was enacting prohibiting certain types of workplace discrimination, most employees have been protected from being fired or disciplined because of their race, color, national origin, sex, or religion. And more recent federal laws protect against discrimination based on age, disability, citizenship status, and genetic information. Despite these laws and similar laws in many states, however, workplace discrimination is still with us.

What is discrimination?

Legally, discrimination is treating someone differently because of a protected characteristic: a trait that the law has determined should not be the basis for employment decisions. Protected characteristics under federal law include race, color, national origin, religion, sex, disability, age (40 and older), and genetic information. Many states and local governments have enacted antidiscrimination laws that protect additional characteristics, such as marital status, sexual orientation, and gender identity.

What laws protect employees from discrimination?

The major federal law that prohibits discrimination is Title VII of the Civil Rights Act of 1964. (42 U.S.C. § 2000e.) This law protects employees from discrimination based on race, national origin, color, sex, and religion. Other federal antidiscrimination laws include the Age Discrimination in Employment Act (ADEA), which prohibits age discrimination against employees who are at least 40 years old (29 U.S.C. §§ 621-634); the Americans with Disabilities Act (ADA), which prohibits disability discrimination (42 U.S.C. §§ 12101 and following); the Equal Pay Act, which requires employers to pay men and women equally for doing the same work (29 U.S.C. § 206(d)); the Immigration Reform and Control Act (IRCA), which prohibits employers from discriminating against employees based on their citizenship status (8 U.S.C. § 1324 (a) and (b)); and the Genetic Information Nondiscrimination Act (GINA), which prohibits employers from gathering genetic information about employees and using that information as the basis for job decisions (42 U.S.C. § 200 and following).

In addition to these federal laws, all states prohibit some forms of discrimination in employment. Many of these laws mimic the federal protections, but some also protect against discrimination based on other characteristics, such as sexual orientation, gender identity, marital status, height or weight, and AIDS or HIV status. And some cities and counties also prohibit additional types of discrimination.

Are all employees protected from discrimination?

Some employees who work for smaller employers may not be protected from discrimination. For example, Title VII, GINA, and the ADA apply only to employers with at least 15 employees. The ADEA applies only to employers with at least 20 employees. The IRCA applies to employers with four or more employees.

Even if you are not covered by these federal laws, however, you may be protected by state or local antidiscrimination laws, which often apply to smaller employers. Contact your state's fair employment practices agency to find out more about your state's law. For information about local laws, contact your local government agency that deals with discrimination issues.

What should I do if I think I'm being discriminated against?

Your first step is to let your employer know that you believe you are a victim of discrimination. If your employer has a complaint procedure, make sure you follow it. If there's no formal complaint procedure, ask the human resources department or a manager how to complain. Filing a complaint will not only give your employer an opportunity to fix the problem, it will also protect your right to collect damages from your employer if it fails to act.

If complaining within the company isn't effective, you can file a discrimination charge at a government agency. The Equal Employment Opportunity Commission (EEOC) is the federal agency that handles discrimination complaints. To get information about how to file a charge—and to find an EEOC office near you—go to the agency's website at www.eeoc.gov. Many states also have an agency that deals with employment discrimination (sometimes called "fair employment practices," or FEP, agencies). You must file your charge within a certain amount of time, which might be as short as 180 days after the incident you believe was discriminatory. Therefore, it is important to act as soon as you realize that you might be the victim of discrimination; if you don't, you might lose your rights.

You must file a charge with an administrative agency before you can sue your employer for discrimination. The agency may investigate your complaint, propose that you and your employer try to settle or mediate the complaint, dismiss your complaint, or bring a lawsuit on your behalf in court.

In many cases, the agency will simply authorize you to file a lawsuit on your own by giving you a "right to sue" letter. If you decide to go this route, you should talk to an experienced employment lawyer first. (For information on finding the right lawyer, see Chapter 16.)

My boss seems to promote only white employees to work with customers, while African American and Latino employees hold mostly stockroom jobs with little customer contact. Is this legal?

If your employer is making these decisions based on race, this is illegal employment discrimination. Segregating employees based on race or preferring employees of one race for certain positions is discriminatory. Some employers try to justify this type of practice by claiming that their customers are "more comfortable" with employees of a particular race, or by making staffing decisions based on the race of their customers (for example, by hiring only Asian Americans to work in stores in Asian American neighborhoods). However, this kind of logic won't stand up in court. The EEOC has stated that these are not valid reasons for distinguishing among employees.

Can a company ask my race on its employment application?

Because an employer can't make hiring decisions based on race, it should not ask for this information on an employment application. If an employer has a legitimate need to keep track of the race of applicants and employees—for purposes of complying with a sanctioned affirmative action plan, for example—it should keep these statistics separately. Some employers accomplish this by asking applicants to state their race on a separate sheet of paper, which does not contain their name or other identifying information.

What is reverse discrimination?

In the context of race discrimination, "reverse discrimination" is a term sometimes used to describe discrimination against white employees or applicants. Because race discrimination laws traditionally were enacted to prevent discrimination against groups that were historically mistreated or denied opportunities, some employers believe that white employees are not protected by these laws. This belief is incorrect, however. Any time an employer makes a decision based on race, it commits illegal discrimination. So, for example, it is discriminatory for the owner of a Chinese restaurant or an African clothing boutique to refuse to hire white applicants based solely on their race.

Can my employer refuse to promote me to a customer service position because I speak with an accent?

There are two competing interests at work in this situation. On the one hand, diction and accent are closely associated with a person's nationality, so making employment decisions based on accent could constitute national origin discrimination. On the other hand, employers have a legitimate interest in making sure that their employees can communicate effectively with customers.

The law resolves the issue this way: An employer can make job decisions based on accent if the accent materially interferes with the employee's ability to do the job. If the job truly requires strong English communication skills (as many customer service positions do), the employer may refuse to hire or promote an employee with an accent that substantially impairs the employee's ability to communicate and be understood. On the other hand, if the employee has a perceptible foreign accent but can communicate clearly in English, the employer may not legally make decisions based on the employee's accent.

Can my employer impose a dress code that prohibits me from wearing traditional ethnic clothing?

An employer can require employees to follow a dress code, but the rules cannot single out particular types of ethnic dress. For example, a dress code that explicitly prohibited saris, turbans, or garments made of Kente cloth would be discriminatory. And your employer must make exceptions to the dress code to reasonably accommodate your religious beliefs (for example by allowing you to wear a religious headscarf to work).

Can my employer require me to speak only English at work?

Courts will take a very close look at English-only rules to determine whether they are discriminatory. Because the language we speak is closely connected to our nationality, English-only rules may very well discriminate on the basis of national origin.

Gather Your Evidence

If you believe you are being discriminated against, you should take some steps to make sure you will be able to prove your claims. Here are a few tips:

- **Take notes.** Start writing down every incident or statement that is offensive or just seems fishy. For example, you might make a log of every racist comment your supervisor makes, or note discriminatory statements made by company officials in speeches or presentations. And keep track of key employment decisions that you suspect could be discriminatory. Make sure to date your entries and to be very specific.
- **Collect documents.** Keep copies of any documents that seem to indicate discrimination. For example, print out copies of emails that contain religious slurs or jokes about older workers. Also keep copies of any discriminatory notes or items posted on company bulletin boards. You might also want to take pictures of discriminatory graffiti or cartoons on the walls. But make sure you don't take or copy any documents you are not entitled to have: If you steal or copy confidential company documents, you may lose your right to sue for money damages (and lose your job).
- **Talk to other employees.** If you have been discriminated against or harassed based on a protected characteristic, you might not be alone. Talk to your coworkers to find out whether they have faced similar problems or have seen or heard of any discriminatory behavior toward other employees.

Generally, employers have to show that there is a business necessity for the policy (in other words that the policy is necessary for the employer to operate safely and efficiently). For example, if an employer can show that safety requires all workers to speak a common language, or that an English-only rule is necessary to serve customers who speak only English, that would qualify as a business necessity.

Even if an employer has a good reason for requiring employees to speak English, however, it cannot adopt a policy that is too broad. For example, requiring employees to speak English to customers might pass muster; prohibiting employees from speaking any other language even while on breaks and making personal phone calls probably will not.

Can an employer refuse to hire me because of my religion—or lack thereof?

No. Title VII of the Civil Rights Act of 1964 prohibits employers from treating an employee less favorably because of the employee's religion or because the employee is not religious. For example, an employer commits illegal discrimination if it refuses to hire Jews, refuses to allow Sikhs to work with customers, or promotes only those who share the owner's religious beliefs.

However, in limited situations, employers are actually required to take an employee's religion into account. The law requires employers to accommodate an employee's religious beliefs and practices, if they can do so reasonably and without undue hardship. Examples of reasonable accommodations might include allowing an employee to wear traditional religious garb or allowing an employee to take time off during the workday to pray.

My boss requires all of us to attend a weekly meeting, where he says prayers and reads from the Bible. Is this legal?

No. An employer cannot require an employee to participate in religious observances or activities as a condition of employment. This prohibition extends to mandatory workplace programs that use yoga, meditation, biofeedback, or similar practices, if the program conflicts with an employee's religious beliefs.

I belong to a small religious group that isn't well-known; am I still protected from discrimination?

Yes. You don't have to belong to a mainstream or traditional religion to be protected. In fact, you don't even have to be a member of any recognized or organized religion. The EEOC defines religious beliefs as moral or ethical beliefs about right and wrong that are held sincerely, with the strength of traditional religious beliefs. Even if you can't point to an established religious group that holds the same beliefs, you are still protected. On the other hand, beliefs that are merely economic, social, or political are not protected.

Can my employer force me to work on my Sabbath day?

Employers are required to make reasonable accommodations for their employees' religious beliefs or practices unless doing so would create an undue hardship on the employer's business operations. For example, if your employer can arrange a voluntary job swap, shift change, flexible schedule, or job transfer that would allow you to take the day off, that might be a reasonable accommodation.

However, if the employer cannot give you the day off without incurring costs beyond ordinary administrative expenses, infringing on the rights of other employees, or diminishing workplace efficiency, it is not required to accommodate your request.

Can I proselytize in the workplace?

This is a complicated issue. Because employers are not allowed to make employment decisions based on religion, they may not single out employees of a particular religion for different treatment. In the context of workplace proselytizing, this means that an employer cannot clamp down on expressions of religious belief if the employer allows other kinds of personal expression at work.

On the other hand, an employer is obligated to prevent religious harassment, and proselytizing can cross this line if other workers find your religious discussions offensive based on their own religious beliefs (or the fact that they are not religious). For this reason, many employers prohibit employees from engaging in any type of personal expression that disrupts the workplace, from religious testifying to political discussions to displaying artwork that some might find offensive.

My boss rarely promotes women to positions requiring overnight travel—he says they won't want to spend time away from their families. Is this legal?

No. Title VII of the Civil Rights Act of 1964 prohibits sex discrimination, which includes discrimination based on stereotypes about men and women. So, for instance, an employer refuse to promote women to sales positions based on a belief that women are less aggressive than men, nor can an employer promote only women to management positions based on a belief that women are more nurturing and better at fostering teamwork than men. In your situation, your employer seems to be making a number of assumptions about female employees' feelings about their jobs and families, which is illegal.

My employer pays software salespeople—who tend to be men—more than employees who train customers on how to use the software, who tend to be women. Is this legal?

It depends on how similar the two jobs are. Under the Equal Pay Act, employers must pay men and women the same for doing substantially equal work in the same establishment. In deciding whether work is substantially equal, courts will look at the skill, effort, responsibility, and working conditions each job requires. Only jobs that are quite similar will qualify as substantially equal. And even for substantially equal jobs, differences in pay are allowed if they are based on merit, seniority, quantity or quality of work, or any other factor that isn't related to sex.

At first glance, it seems that salespeople have different job responsibilities (selling) than trainers (teaching) and that different skills are required for each job. However, some employers are in the habit of calling similar jobs by different titles. For example, male employees who handle appointments, telephone calls, correspondence, and other office work for more senior employees might be called "administrative assistants," while women who perform the same work might be called "secretaries." It doesn't matter what the jobs are called: If they are substantially equal, men and women must receive equal pay for doing them.

Also consider whether your employer has a practice of favoring men over women when hiring for sales jobs. If that's the case, your employer might be violating Title VII's prohibition against sex discrimination.

Can my employer require me to take time off during my pregnancy?

Not if you are able to work. In days gone by, employers routinely required women to stop working when they reached a certain stage of pregnancy or when they started to "show." Today, however, antidiscrimination laws prohibit these practices. An employer may not require a woman to take time off during her pregnancy or prohibit her from returning to work for a set period of time after she gives birth, as long as she is able to do the job.

Are all workers protected from age discrimination?

No. The federal Age Discrimination in Employment Act (ADEA)—which applies to workplaces with 20 or more employees —protects workers who are 40 or older from age discrimination. The ADEA does not, however, protect workers under the age of 40. The ADEA applies to federal employees, private sector employees, and labor union employees. It also protects state employees from discrimination, although they cannot file a lawsuit against the state to vindicate their rights.

There are several other exceptions to the broad protection of the ADEA, including:

- Executives or people "in high policy-making positions" can be forced to retire at age 65 if they would receive annual retirement pension benefits worth $44,000 or more.
- There are special exceptions for police and fire personnel, tenured university faculty, and certain federal employees working in law enforcement and air traffic control.

Most states have laws against age discrimination in employment, which often provide greater protection than the federal law. For example, some state laws protect workers under 40, and some apply to employers with fewer than 20 employees. And some allow state employees to sue the state directly for age discrimination.

To find out more about the laws of your own state, contact your state fair employment practices department; if you can't easily find it through an online search, check your state's home page, such as www.ca.gov or www.texas.gov.

I've noticed a pattern where I work: Older workers tend to be laid off just before their pension rights lock in or vest. Is that legal?

Using ploys like this one to cheat workers out of their promised pensions is a technique some employers use to save money. But it's not legal. The federal Older Workers Benefit Protection Act forbids:

- using an employee's age as the basis for discrimination in benefits, and
- targeting older workers for their staff-cutting programs.

Out From Under the Golden Parachute

A growing number of employers ask older workers to sign waivers (also called releases or agreements not to sue). In return for signing the waiver, the employer offers the employee an incentive to leave the job voluntarily, such as a significant amount of severance pay. The Older Workers Benefit Protection Act places a number of restrictions on such waivers:

- The waiver must be written in language that can be clearly understood.
- The waiver may not cover any rights or claims that arise after you sign it, and it must specify that you are agreeing to waive your rights under the ADEA.
- Your employer must offer you something of value (such as severance pay)—over and above what is already owed to you—in exchange for your signature on the waiver.
- Your employer must advise you, in writing, that you have the right to consult an attorney before you sign the waiver.
- If the offer is being made to a group or class of employees, your employer must inform you in writing how the class of employees is defined; the job titles and ages of all the individuals to whom the offer is being made; the ages of all the employees in the same job classification or unit of the company to whom the offer is not being made; and any time limits or eligibility rules for participating in the offer.
- Your employer must give you at least 21 days to consider the waiver (or 45 days, if the offer is made to a group of employees). You also have the right to revoke the agreement for up to seven days after you sign it.

Can my employer force me to take early retirement?

No, your employer cannot require you to retire because of your age. An early-retirement plan is legal only if it gives you a choice between two options: keeping things as they are or choosing to retire under a plan that leaves you better off than you previously were. This choice must be a genuine one; you must be free to reject the offer.

What laws protect workers with disabilities from workplace discrimination?

The Americans with Disabilities Act (ADA) prohibits employment discrimination on the basis of workers' disabilities. Generally, the ADA prohibits employers from:

- discriminating on the basis of physical or mental disability
- asking job applicants questions about their past or current medical conditions
- requiring job applicants to take medical exams before they have received a conditional offer of employment, and
- refusing to provide reasonable accommodations to qualified employees with disabilities.

The ADA covers companies with 15 or more employees. Its coverage broadly extends to private employers, employment agencies, and labor organizations. A precursor of the ADA, the Vocational Rehabilitation Act prohibits discrimination against disabled workers in state and federal government.

In addition, many state laws protect against discrimination based on physical or mental disability. To find out about your state's antidiscrimination laws, contact your state fair employment practices agency.

Whom does the ADA protect?

The ADA's protections extend to workers with disabilities, defined as those who:

- have a physical or mental impairment that substantially limits a major life activity or major bodily function
- have a record or history of such impairment, or
- are regarded as having such an impairment.

An impairment includes physical disorders, as well as mental and psychological disorders.

The ADA protects job applicants and employees who, although disabled as defined above, are still qualified for a particular job. In other words, they must be able to perform the essential functions of a job with or without a reasonable accommodation, such as wheelchair access, a voice-activated computer, or a customized workspace. Whether a worker with a disability is qualified for a given job depends on whether the person has the appropriate skill, experience, training, or education for the position.

If I have a disability, how do I get my employer to provide an accommodation?

The first step is simple, but often overlooked: Ask. The ADA places the burden on you to tell your employer that you have a disability and need an accommodation.

When you ask for an accommodation, you do not need to use formal legal language or even do it in writing (though it's always a good idea to document your request). Tell your employer that you have a disability and explain why you need an accommodation.

Once you request the accommodation, your employer should engage in an informal process of determining whether and how it can accommodate you. As part of this process, your employer is allowed to ask you for documentation, or proof, of your disability. It is important that you comply with this request to the best of your ability; if you don't, you may lose your right to an accommodation.

If an accommodation is not "reasonable" (see below), your employer does not have to provide it. Nor does your employer have to provide you with the accommodation that you want, as long as it provides another one that is effective. If you don't accept a particular accommodation, be prepared to defend your choice on the grounds that the accommodation isn't effective. If a court decides that the offered accommodation was reasonable, you may no longer be qualified for the job, and your employer can terminate you.

How can I tell whether the accommodation my employer offers is reasonable?

The ADA points to several specific accommodations that are likely to be deemed reasonable. Some of them are changes to the physical setup of the workplace, and some of them are changes to how or when work is done. They include:

- making existing facilities usable by disabled employees (for example, by modifying the height of desks and equipment, installing computer screen magnifiers, or installing telecommunications devices for the hearing impaired)
- restructuring jobs (for example, allowing a ten-hour/four-day workweek so that a worker can receive weekly medical treatments)
- modifying exams and training materials (for example, allowing more time for taking an exam or allowing it to be taken orally instead of in writing)
- providing a reasonable amount of unpaid leave for medical treatment
- hiring readers or interpreters to assist an employee, and
- providing temporary workplace specialists to assist in training.

These are just a few possible accommodations. The possibilities are limited only by an employee's and employer's imaginations, and the facts on the ground that might make a particular accommodation unduly burdensome for the employer.

When can an employer legally refuse to provide a particular accommodation?

The ADA does not require employers to make accommodations that would cause an undue hardship, defined as "an action requiring significant difficulty or expense." The Equal Employment Opportunity Commission (EEOC), the federal agency responsible for enforcing the ADA, has set out some of the factors that will determine whether a particular accommodation presents an undue hardship on a particular employer:

- the nature and cost of the accommodation
- the financial resources of the employer (a large employer may be expected to foot a larger bill than a mom-and-pop business)
- the nature of the business (including size, composition, and structure of the workforce), and
- the impact providing the accommodation will have on the employer's operations.

It is not easy for employers to prove that an accommodation is an undue hardship, as financial difficulty alone is usually not sufficient. Courts will look at other sources of money, including tax credits and deductions available for making some accommodations, as well as the disabled employee's willingness to pay for all or part of the costs.

Accommodations Don't Need to Cost a Bundle

According to ergonomic and job accommodation experts, the cost of accommodating a particular worker's disability is often surprisingly low:

- 31% of accommodations cost nothing
- 50% cost less than $50
- 69% cost less than $500, and
- 88% cost less than $1,000.

The Job Accommodation Network (JAN), which provides information about how to accommodate people with disabilities, gives the following examples of inexpensive accommodations:

- Glare on a computer screen, which caused an employee with an eye disorder to get eye fatigue, was solved with a $39 antiglare screen.
- A medical technician who was hearing impaired couldn't hear the buzz of a timer, which was necessary for laboratory tests. The problem was solved with an indicator light that cost $26.95.

To contact JAN, call 800-526-7234 or visit its website at www.askjan.org.

Can my employer require genetic testing?

In a word, no. The Genetic Information Nondiscrimination Act (GINA) prohibits employers from acquiring genetic information from their employees, except under very limited circumstances (for example, as part of a program to monitor the biological effects of toxic substances in the workplace). Before GINA was passed in 2008, some employers performed genetic testing for certain traits, sometimes on the sly (for example, as part of a medical "fitness for duty" exam, without telling the employee what the company was really testing for).

Even in the exceptional circumstances when employers may acquire genetic information about employees, they may not use that information as the basis for employment decisions.

Although I don't have breast cancer, I decided to have a double mastectomy after both my sisters were diagnosed with cancer and I tested positive for the BRCA-2 gene. When I returned from surgery, I was fired. Is this legal?

If you were fired because of your genetic discovery, that's illegal discrimination. GINA prohibits employers from making decisions on the basis of genetic information, including the fact that you carry certain genes or traits. Even if your employer found out about the situation legitimately (for example, because you were open about it), it cannot use that information against you.

Can I be fired because I'm gay?

Federal law does not explicitly protect private employees from discrimination based on sexual orientation. In recent years, though, the EEOC has taken the position that sexual orientation discrimination qualifies as illegal sex discrimination under Title VII, because it is based on stereotypes about how members of each gender should behave. A few courts have agreed in limited circumstances, but the issue is far from settled.

About half of the states and the District of Columbia explicitly prohibit private employers from making employment decisions based on sexual orientation. More than a hundred local governments also prohibit this type of discrimination. To find out more, go to the website of Lambda Legal at www.lambdalegal.org/in-your-state, for information on state and local laws prohibiting sexual orientation discrimination.

Can I be fired for being transgender?

Federal law does not explicitly protect employees from discrimination on the basis of gender identity. However, similar to its position on sexual orientation, the EEOC has declared that gender identity discrimination qualifies as illegal sex discrimination under Title VII. In 2014, the EEOC filed its first lawsuits against employers for discriminating against transgender employees. However, it remains to be seen whether the courts will uphold the EEOC's interpretation.

Nearly 20 states have clearly outlawed discrimination based on gender identity, however. Several cities have passed similar laws. To find out whether your area has such a law, check out the website of the American Civil Liberties Union, at www.aclu.org, and select "Know Your Rights."

Can my employer refuse to promote me to a position in which I would be supervised by my spouse?

It depends on your state's laws. Relatively few states prohibit marital status discrimination in the first place, so most employers are free to make employment decisions based on the fact that you are married, single, or divorced. Even if your state prohibits discrimination on the basis of marital status, employers may still be allowed to prohibit spouses from reporting to one another, in the interests of promoting efficiency and preventing favoritism (or the appearance of it).

To find out whether your state has a law prohibiting marital status discrimination (and if so, what the law requires), contact your state fair employment practices agency.

Harassment

Sexual harassment on the job took a dramatic leap into public awareness in 1991, when Professor Anita Hill made known her charges against Judge Clarence Thomas after his nomination to the U.S. Supreme Court. Many other incidents have erupted since then, from the Tailhook incident in the ranks of the U.S. Navy to Paula Jones's harassment claims against former President Clinton.

Although sexual harassment tends to get the most media coverage, other types of workplace harassment are also illegal, including harassment based on race, disability, and religion.

What is harassment?

Legally speaking, harassment is unwelcome conduct that is severe or pervasive enough to create an intimidating, hostile, or offensive work environment or results in an adverse employment action (such as being fired). Like discrimination, harassment is illegal only if it is based on a person's protected characteristic. Under federal law, protected characteristics include race, color, national origin, sex, religion, age (40 and older), disability, and citizenship status.

Harassment can take many forms, from racial or religious slurs to X-rated graffiti to cruel practical jokes played on employees with disabilities.

What is sexual harassment?

In legal terms, sexual harassment is any unwelcome sexual advance or conduct on the job that is severe or pervasive enough to create an intimidating, hostile, or offensive working environment or that results in an adverse employment action.

Sexually harassing behavior ranges from repeated X-rated or belittling jokes to a workplace full of offensive pornography to suggestive touching.

While a hostile work environment can arise from one serious incident (such as sexual assault), it is usually the cumulative effect of a number of smaller incidents occurring over time. The offensive conduct does not need to be of a sexual nature; for example, sexist comments about women can qualify as sexual harassment.

What laws prohibit workplace harassment?

The same federal laws that protect employees from discrimination also prohibit harassment. This means that you are protected from harassment only if your employer is subject to the federal antidiscrimination laws discussed in "Discrimination," above. For example, if you work for an employer with fewer than 20 employees, your employer does not have to comply with the federal laws that prohibit discrimination and harassment based on your age.

Many state laws also prohibit harassment. In some states, the same laws that prohibit discrimination also prohibit harassment. In other states, separate laws or provisions prohibit harassment, and these laws may apply to different employers. For example, California prohibits harassment by all employers regardless of size, while only those employers with at least five employees are prohibited from discriminating.

My coworkers like to tease me about my accent and nationality. When does this kind of joking around cross the line into harassment?

There's no clear point at which teasing becomes illegal harassment. Courts and the Equal Employment Opportunity Commission (EEOC), the federal agency that enforces federal laws prohibiting harassment, have said that one or two isolated jokes don't constitute harassment. On the other hand, repeated and offensive jokes—such as using racial slurs or belittling you because of your nationality—probably do. The test is whether the harassing conduct unreasonably interferes with your work performance or creates an intimidating, hostile, or offensive work environment. The more your coworkers tease you—and the more offensive their jokes are—the more likely you are facing illegal harassment.

I'm being harassed at work. What is the first thing I should do?

Consider telling the harasser to stop. This works surprisingly often, when the harasser doesn't realize how damaging the behavior is. For example, a coworker who doesn't understand that his jokes about your religion or his comments about your appearance are offensive might be embarrassed to learn that his behavior is upsetting you and be willing to change his ways.

If you are not comfortable confronting the harasser(s), go directly to your supervisor, human resources department, or other manager and make a complaint. The benefit of complaining directly to the harasser(s) is that doing so lets the harasser know that the behavior is unwelcome. Conduct is harassing only if it is not welcome to the person on the receiving end. This can be a disputed issue, particularly in sexual harassment cases—for example, if you have participated in sexual banter in the workplace or have a prior dating relationship with the harasser, the harasser may later argue (to your employer or in court) that he or she didn't know you were offended. Telling the harasser directly that you are upset is a surefire way to be clear about this.

However, if the conduct is severely disturbing or offensive, you may sensibly believe that the harasser must know that you are upset by it. For example, if you have been threatened with racial violence or sexual assault, there is no need to sit down with your persecutor and explain why you are upset.

Also, document what's going on by keeping a diary or journal noting important facts like what occurred, the full names of any witnesses, and the dates that the events took place. Your case will be stronger if you can prove that the harassment continued after you confronted the harasser or made a complaint.

What should I do if the harasser keeps it up or I'm too intimidated to tell the harasser to stop?

Complain, complain, complain. Start by finding out whether your company has a complaint procedure in place (check your employee handbook or ask a manager). If so, use that process to make a formal complaint. If your company doesn't have a complaint policy or procedure, talk to your supervisor, someone in your company's human resources department, or another manager. When you make your complaint, be thorough and honest. Don't leave anything out or exaggerate any details. If the person taking your complaint asks you to sign or fill out a written complaint, make sure everything in the document is accurate—and that nothing important has been omitted—before you sign.

You might be afraid to complain about harassment, perhaps because the harasser is your supervisor or has made threats against you. The laws that prohibit harassment also prohibit your employer from retaliating against you for complaining about harassment. Although this might be cold comfort if you fear for your job or your safety, the fact is that your legal rights might be limited if you fail to complain. An employer that can successfully argue that it didn't know about the harassment often has a defense to a harassment lawsuit. The best way to nip this argument in the bud is to complain to someone in authority, using the company's designated procedures.

What legal steps can I take to end harassment?

If complaining to the harasser and/or company officials doesn't stop the harassment, your next step is to file a charge of harassment at the federal EEOC or your state's fair employment practices agency. These agencies enforce federal and state laws prohibiting harassment; they are empowered to take complaints, investigate, try to settle or mediate the problem, and even sue on the employee's behalf, if they think the case warrants their involvement.

If you are considering suing your employer, you absolutely must take this step first. In most circumstances, courts will not allow your harassment lawsuit to go forward unless you have first filed with one of these agencies. And the deadlines for filing can be short; you might have only 180 days after the harassing incidents to file a charge.

These agencies don't often sue an employer on an employee's behalf. Usually, the agency will issue you a document referred to as a "right to sue" letter. This document allows you to take your case to court. If you decide to file a lawsuit, you will almost certainly want to hire an attorney to represent you.

RESOURCE

For more information about your right to be free of discrimination and harassment, check out the website of the EEOC, at www.eeoc.gov. It has many helpful materials on discrimination and harassment, as well as information on how to file a charge of discrimination or harassment. The EEOC website also has contact information for state fair employment practices agencies.

Nolo's website includes useful information on each state's discrimination laws at www.nolo.com/legal-encyclopedia/workplace-rights. Nolo's book, *Your Rights in the Workplace,* by Barbara Kate Repa, also includes a detailed discussion of discrimination and harassment.

9to5 is a national nonprofit membership organization for working women. It provides counseling, information, and referrals for problems on the job, including family leave, pregnancy disability, termination, compensation, and sexual harassment. 9to5 also offers a newsletter and publications. There are local chapters throughout the country. For more information, visit www.9to5.org.

Workplace Privacy

The common law secures to each individual the right of determining, ordinarily, to what extent his thoughts, sentiments, and emotions shall be communicated to others.

—Samuel Warren & Louis Brandeis

Technology has made it possible—sometimes even easy—to pry into people's lives, habits, and communications. Testing, background checks, social media, monitoring software, and surveillance equipment all make it possible for employers to find out more about you than you ever dreamed possible. As a result, many employees are understandably concerned about protecting their privacy.

At the same time, employers sometimes have good reasons to take a close look at what their employees are doing. If one employee is harassing another through the company's email or telephone system, for example, the employer has a legal obligation to look into it, which might require monitoring employee communications. And employers have a legitimate interest in hiring workers who are truly qualified for the position and have the experience, educational background, and skills they claim on their applications.

Can a prospective employer run a background check on me?

Yes, within limits. A prospective employer doesn't have the right to dig into all of your personal affairs, and generally shouldn't be investigating things that have no bearing on your ability to do the job. However, a prospective employer certainly has the right to verify the information on your résumé or job application by, for example, checking to make sure that you hold the degrees, licenses, and certifications you claim to have, and by calling former employers to confirm that you really did work for them.

In some cases, a prospective employer might want to take things a step further. For example, if you are applying for a delivery job, the employer will probably want to check your driving record. If you are applying for a position working with vulnerable clients—young children or the elderly, for example—the employer may want to make sure that you don't have a criminal record.

There are some limits on the information a prospective employer can gather. For example, federal law makes academic records confidential, so an employer might not be able to get your transcripts unless you consent or provide them. And, to get any but the most basic information about your military service, your employer must have your consent.

Special rules apply when an employer hires a third party, such as a private investigator or background check firm, to look into your background. In this situation, the federal Fair Credit Reporting Act (FCRA) requires that the employer follow certain procedures—such as getting your written consent and notifying you if it decides not to hire you based on the results of the background check. The same rules apply if the employer orders your credit report, although some states limit an employer's ability to collect this information.

Can a prospective employer ask whether I have a criminal record—and do I have to answer?

State laws determine whether a prospective employer can ask about prior arrests and convictions. Some states prohibit employers from asking about (or considering in their hiring decisions) arrests that did not lead to conviction, criminal records that have been sealed or expunged, convictions that are well in the past (for example, those that are more than ten years old), or juvenile convictions. Other states allow employers to consider an applicant's criminal record only for certain positions (most commonly, child care workers, private detectives, nurses, and other jobs requiring a license) or only if the conviction has some relationship to the job. And, a growing number of states and cities have passed "ban the box" laws, which prohibit an employer from asking about criminal history on a job application or before a certain point in the hiring process (for example, before an interview or a conditional offer of employment). To find out more about your state's rules, go to www.nolo.com/legal-encyclopedia/background-checks-testing.

Can my employer require me to take a drug test?

It depends on the laws of your state. Although most states allow employers to require job applicants to submit to drug testing, some states limit an employer's right to test current employees. For example, some states allow employers to test only employees who work in certain safety sensitive positions, employees who have been in workplace accidents, or employees whom the employer reasonably suspects of illegal drug use. To find out whether your state has a drug-testing law, go to www.nolo.com/legal-encyclopedia/background-checks-testing.

Can I refuse to take a lie detector test?

In most cases, yes. The federal Employee Polygraph Protection Act prohibits all private employers from requiring their workers to submit to lie detector tests—and from firing or otherwise disciplining employees who refuse to take a test. (29 U.S.C. §§ 2001 and following.) Certain employers—those that are authorized by the federal Drug Enforcement Administration (DEA) to manufacture, distribute, or dispense certain controlled substances and those that provide security services—have a very limited right to require employees to submit to polygraph testing, in a few situations.

The only exception that applies generally to all employers has to do with workplace investigations. An employer may ask an employee to take a polygraph (and may fire the employee for refusing to do so) if all of the following are true:

- the employer is investigating theft or loss of property

- the employee had access to the property
- the employer has a reasonable suspicion that the employee was involved, and
- the employer provides detailed information to the employee, before the test, about these facts.

Unless you are facing this situation, you may legally refuse to take a lie detector test, and your employer may not take action against you based on your refusal.

Can my employer read my email?

In most situations, yes. Employers generally have the right to read employee email messages sent and received on the employer's system, especially if they have a valid business purpose for doing so and have warned employees in advance that their emails are not private. As a result, the best course of action for employees is to follow your employer's email policy carefully, and never send an email on company equipment that you wouldn't want your boss to read.

My employer monitors our phone calls; is this legal?

Probably, as long as your employer has notified you of its monitoring. Under federal law, employers generally have the right to monitor employee conversations with clients or customers for quality control. Some states prohibit secret monitoring, though, and employers in those states must inform the parties to the call—by announcement or by signal (such as a beeping noise)—that someone is listening in.

Under federal law, once an employer realizes that a particular call is personal, it must immediately stop monitoring. However, if your employer has told you that particular phones are for business use only, it is probably within its rights to monitor all calls on those phones.

Can my employer monitor my Internet surfing?

Yes. Technology exists that allows employers to track the sites employees visit and how much time they spend there. Although employers should inform their employees about any Internet rules and monitoring systems they use, employers generally have the right to monitor what employees do on the company's computer system.

Given this state of affairs—and the possibility that your employer might be monitoring without your knowledge—it's best to limit Internet activities on the job to work-related sites, and save the surfing, shopping, tweets, and Facebook updates for another time.

Can my employer require all candidates for promotion to provide their Facebook passwords, so the company can make sure our online posts are consistent with the image it wants to promote?

It depends on how your state legislature and courts have defined employee privacy.

When some employers' practice of requiring employees or applicants to provide their social media passwords first surfaced, a number of states passed laws making it illegal. In these states, an employer who requires or requests that applicants or employees hand over their Facebook or other social media passwords is violating the law.

Congress has considered this issue as well, but has not yet passed a law outlawing these requirements. So, if your state hasn't explicitly prohibited employers from forcing employees to hand over their passwords, to their private accounts, it would be up to a court to decide whether this violates employee privacy.

In deciding workplace privacy issues, courts generally weigh the employer's need for the information against the employee's reasonable expectations of privacy. In this situation, there would be plenty of weight on the employee's side of the scale. The purpose of passwords and privacy settings, after all, is to restrict access to only those people with whom the employee chooses to share. This also diminishes the employer's need to see the information: If the employer is truly worried about its public image, there would seem to be no reason for it to look beyond the information that is publicly available, which it can do without passwords. But only time will tell how this issue plays out in court.

RESOURCE

Want more information on privacy issues? Check out Nolo's free information on workplace privacy at www.nolo.com/legal-encyclopedia/workplace-privacy. You can also find great information on a variety of privacy topics, including employee privacy, at the website of the Privacy Rights Clearinghouse, www.privacyrights.org.

Losing Your Job

It is easier for a man to be thought fit for an employment that he has not, than for one he stands already possessed of.

—François, Duc de la Rochefoucauld

The fear of being laid off or fired looms large for many workers. Employers have traditionally had a free hand to hire and fire, but a number of recent laws and legal rulings restrict these rights. If you do lose your job—or decide to leave it—you have certain legal rights on your way out the door.

For what reasons can I be fired?

Unless you have an employment contract with your employer, your employment is at will, which means that your employer can fire you for any reason that isn't illegal. Examples of illegal reasons for firing include firing a worker because of race, religion, or another protected characteristic (see "Discrimination," above); firing someone for filing a health and safety complaint or a charge of sexual harassment; or firing a worker for exercising a legal right, such as taking family and medical leave or taking leave to serve in the military. Even if you are employed at will, you can't be fired for reasons like these.

If you are employed at will, your employer can fire you for reasons that are job-related (incompetence, excessive absences, violating certain laws or company rules) or whimsical (your voice is abrasive, you tell corny jokes, you love Broadway musicals).

If you have an employment contract, for a certain length of time, the terms of your contract will determine the reasons for which you can be fired. Sometimes, contracts list specific reasons for which the employee can be fired (common examples include criminal acts, serious misconduct, or the employer's bankruptcy). Other contracts leave the issue open. In such a situation, the law usually says that you can only be fired for a legitimate, business-related reason (sometimes called "good cause"). Be aware, though, that some employers have employees sign "at-will contracts," which merely reinforce the fact that you are an at-will employee who can be fired for any legal reason.

How do I know whether I have an employment contract?

When most people think about contracts, they think of a formal written document. And many contracts do take that form. There are other kinds of contracts, however. You and your employer can make an oral agreement that is never put in writing, which has the same legal effect as a written contract (assuming you can prove the conversation took place).

Many states also recognize implied contracts, which are inferred from the comments and actions of you and your employer. For example, if your employee handbook says that employees will be fired only for good cause, or only after receiving every step in a progressive discipline policy, your employer might have limited its right to fire at will.

What are illegal reasons for firing?

Employers do not have the right to fire you in violation of federal or state antidiscrimination laws. (See "Discrimination," above, for more information.)

Separate state and federal laws protect workers from being fired for taking advantage of laws intended to protect them from unsafe working conditions. State and federal laws also protect whistleblowers (those who report an employer's illegal activity). In addition, many states protect workers from being fired for exercising a legal right or for refusing to comply with an illegal request by their employer (for example, to falsify tax records or rip off customers).

What can I do to protect any legal rights I might have before leaving my job?

Even if you decide not to challenge the legality of your firing, you will be in a much better position to enforce all of your workplace rights if you carefully document what happened. For example, if you apply for unemployment benefits and your former employer challenges your application, you will typically need to prove that you were dismissed for reasons other than misconduct.

There are a number of ways to document what happened. The easiest is to keep an employment diary where you record and date significant work-related events such as performance reviews, commendations or reprimands, salary increases or decreases, and even informal comments your supervisor makes to you about your work. Note the date, time, and location for each event, which members of management were involved, and whether or not witnesses were present.

Whenever possible, back up your log with materials issued by your employer, such as copies of the employee handbook, memos, brochures, employee orientation videos, and any written evaluations, commendations, or criticisms of your work. However, don't take or copy any documents that your employer considers confidential; this will come back to haunt you if you decide to file a lawsuit.

If a problem develops, ask to see your personnel file. If possible, make a copy of all reports and reviews in it. (Some states require employers to allow employees to copy at least some of the documents in their files; others don't.) Also make a list of every single document the file contains. That way, if your employer adds anything later, you will have proof that it was created after the fact.

Am I entitled to severance pay if I am fired or laid off?

It depends on your employer's policies and practices. In general, no law requires employers to provide severance pay. (Although a few states require a small amount of severance in mass layoff or plant closing situations.) Nevertheless, some employers give laid-off workers one or two months' salary as a sign of good will and to ease the employee's transition. And some employers are more generous to long-term employees, basing severance on a formula such as one or two weeks' pay for every year the employee has worked for the company.

Your employer may, however, be legally obligated to give you severance pay if you were promised it, as evidenced by:

- a written employment contract stating that you would receive severance
- a promise of severance pay in an employee handbook

- a long history of the company paying severance to other employees in your position, or
- an oral promise to pay you severance (although you may have trouble proving the promise was ever made).

What rights do I have if I get laid off?

In addition to any right to severance pay you may have (see above), you may have the right to advance notice of a layoff. The federal Worker Adjustment and Retraining Notification Act (WARN Act) requires employers with at least 100 full-time employees to give 60 days' written notice to workers who will lose their jobs in a plant closing or mass layoff. (29 U.S.C. §§ 2101 and following.) A plant closing is where an employer shuts down an employment site, causing 50 or more full-time employees to lose their jobs. A mass layoff is where an employer lays off 500 or more employees, or where the employer lays off 50 to 499 employees who make up at least one-third of the employer's workforce. There are a lot of exceptions to the WARN Act as well; as a result, lots of employees aren't subject to its protections.

The WARN Act only requires employers to give notice, not to pay severance. However, if an employer violates the law, a court can order it to pay back wages for every day that it failed to give notice, up to 60 days of pay. Some states have similar laws, and a few of them require employers to pay laid-off workers a small amount of money. Contact your state labor department to find out whether your state has a plant-closing law (find your state labor department at the U.S. Department of Labor website, www.dol.gov).

Do I have the right to continued health insurance coverage after I get fired?

Under the Consolidated Omnibus Budget Reconciliation Act (COBRA), employers with 20 or more employees must offer departing workers the option to continue coverage under the company's group health insurance plan for a specific period, usually 18 months. (29 U.S.C. §§ 1161 and following.) Family coverage is also included. In some circumstances, such as the death of the employee, the employee's surviving dependents can continue coverage for up to 36 months.

COBRA benefits are available only at the employee's expense: Employees have to pay the full premium to continue coverage, even if their employer picked up all or part of the tab while they were employed.

Your employer (or the administrator of your employer's insurance plan) is required to give you COBRA paperwork, allowing you to choose to continue your coverage, shortly after your employment ends. If you don't receive this paperwork, contact your former employer and ask for it.

Am I entitled to unemployment benefits if I get fired?

Fired employees can claim unemployment benefits if they were terminated because of financial cutbacks or because they were not a good fit for the job for which they were hired. They can also usually receive benefits if the employer had a good reason to fire but the infractions were relatively minor, unintentional, or isolated.

In most states, however, an employee who is fired for "misconduct" will not be able to receive unemployment benefits or will be disqualified for a period of time. Although you may think that any action that leads to termination would constitute misconduct, the unemployment laws don't look at it that way.

Common actions that result in firing but do not constitute misconduct are poor performance because of lack of skills, good faith errors in judgment, off-duty conduct that does not have an impact on the employer's interests, and poor relations with coworkers.

What qualifies as misconduct? Each state has its own definition of the term. Generally speaking, though, an employee who willfully does something that substantially injures the employer's business interests is engaged in misconduct. Revealing trade secrets or sexually harassing coworkers is misconduct; simple inefficiency or an unpleasant personality is not. Other common types of misconduct include extreme insubordination, chronic tardiness, numerous unexcused absences, intoxication on the job, and dishonesty.

ONLINE HELP

The following sites are good resources to obtain information on workers' rights:

- **www.nolo.com** Nolo offers information about a wide variety of legal topics, including workplace rights, from getting hired to losing your job.
- **www.eeoc.gov** The U.S. Equal Employment Opportunity Commission is the federal agency responsible for enforcing federal antidiscrimination laws, including Title VII, the Equal Pay Act, the Age Discrimination in Employment Act, the Genetic Information Nondiscrimination Act, and the Americans with Disabilities Act. The EEOC's website provides plenty of information about these laws. Among other things, it includes information on your workplace rights, the text of the fair employment laws, instructions on how to file a charge against your employer, and links to state fair employment practices agency websites.
- **www.dol.gov** The U.S. Department of Labor enforces many of the laws that govern your relationship with your employer, including wage and hour laws, health and safety laws, leave laws, and benefits laws. This website offers information about your rights, instructions on how to file a complaint, and links to state labor department websites.

- **www.osha.gov** The federal Occupational Safety and Health Administration interprets and enforces workplace safety laws. Its website offers information on the requirements of OSHA, provides detailed guidelines on a number of workplace safety topics, and explains how to file a complaint about unsafe working conditions.
- **www.law.cornell.edu** The Legal Information Institute at Cornell Law School provides information about discrimination in the workplace, including relevant codes and regulations.
- **www.privacyrights.org** The Privacy Rights Clearinghouse provides fact sheets, links, and other resources on privacy issues, including workplace privacy rights.

CHAPTER

5

Small Businesses

Business is never so healthy as when, like a chicken, it must do a certain amount of scratching for what it gets.

—**Henry Ford**

For all sorts of personal and economic reasons, more Americans are starting and running their own businesses today than ever before. With accessible technology, today's savvy small-time operator can often accomplish tasks that just a few decades ago could be tackled only by large corporations.

To be successful, however, requires understanding and staying on top of legal rules and regulations that affect almost every small business relationship in today's world, including organizing the business, dealing with co-owners, hiring and supervising employees, and relating to customers and suppliers. Fortunately, by using affordable, good-quality legal resources and getting additional help from a knowledgeable small business lawyer, you can master the laws you need to know to keep your business healthy.

Before You Start a Small Business

Your imagination is your preview of life's coming attractions.

—**Albert Einstein**

No matter what type of business you want to start, there are some practical and legal issues you'll face right away, such as choosing a name and location for your business, deciding whether or not to hire employees, writing a business plan, choosing a legal structure (sole proprietorship, partnership, corporation, or limited liability company), establishing a system for reporting and paying taxes, and adopting policies for dealing with your customers. This section addresses many of these concerns.

I'm thinking of starting my own business. What should I do first?

Be sure you are genuinely interested in what the business does. If you aren't, you are unlikely to succeed in the long run—no matter how lucrative your work turns out to be. Yes, going into business with a firm plan to make a good living is important, but so too is choosing a business that fits your life goals in an authentic way. Here are a few things you might want to consider before you take the leap:

- Do you know how to accomplish the principal tasks of the business? (Don't open a transmission repair shop if you hate cars, or a restaurant if you can't cook.)
- If the business involves working with others, do you have the necessary interpersonal skills? If not, look into the many opportunities to begin a business that doesn't rely on those skills.

- Do you understand basic business tasks, such as how to keep the books and prepare a profit and loss forecast and cash flow analysis? If not, learn before—not after—you begin.
- Does the business fit your personality?
- If you are a people person, make sure the business will provide you with enough opportunity to interact with others. If you prefer less social interaction, then a business that requires a lot of time at the computer might be a better fit for you.

What should I keep in mind when choosing a name for my business?

First, assume that you will have competitors and that you will want to market your products or services under the name you choose. (This will make your name a trademark.) For marketing purposes, the best names are those that customers will easily remember and associate with your business. Also, if the name is memorable, it will be easier to stop others from using it in the future.

Most memorable business names are made up words, like Google and Skype, or are somehow fanciful or surprising, like Three Twins Ice Cream and Penguin Books. And some notable names are cleverly suggestive, such as The Body Shop (a store that sells personal hygiene products).

Names that tend to be forgotten by consumers are common names (names of people), geographic terms, and names that literally describe some aspect of a product or service. For instance, Steve's Web Designs may be very pleasing to Steve as a name, but it's not likely to help Steve's customers remember his company when faced with competitors such as Sam's Web Designs and Sheri's Web Designs. Similarly, a name like Central Word Processing Services is not particularly memorable.

Of course, over time even a common name can become memorable through widespread use and advertising, as with Whole Foods. And unusual names of people can sometimes be very memorable indeed, as with Ben & Jerry's Ice Cream.

Choosing a Domain Name

If your business will have a website, part of choosing your business name will be deciding on a domain name. Using all or part of your business name in your domain name will make your website easier for potential customers to find. But many domain names are already taken, so check on what's available before you settle on a business name. After you pick an appropriate domain name, you'll need to register. See Chapter 8 for more detail.

How do I find out whether I'm legally permitted to use the business name I've chosen?

Your first step depends on whether you plan to form either a corporation or a limited liability company (LLC). If you are going to form one of these two types of entities, you will need to check with your secretary of state's office (or your state's equivalent corporate filing office) to see whether your proposed name is the same as or confusingly similar to an existing corporate or LLC name in your state. Most secretary of state office websites maintain a name database you can search online to see if your proposed name (or something very similar to it) is already in use. If it is, you'll have to choose a different name.

If you don't plan to incorporate or form an LLC, check with your county clerk to see whether your proposed name is already on the list maintained for fictitious or assumed business names in your county. In the states where assumed business name registrations are statewide, check with your secretary of state's office. The county clerk should be able to tell you whether you'll need to check the name at the state level. If you find that your chosen name or a very similar name is listed on a fictitious or assumed name register, you shouldn't use it.

If my proposed business name isn't listed on a county or state register, am I free to use it however I like?

Not necessarily. Even if you are permitted to use your chosen name as a corporate, LLC, or assumed business name in your state or county, you might not be able to use the name as a trademark or service mark. To understand the distinction, consider the potential functions of a business name:

- A business name may be a trade name that describes the business for purposes of bank accounts, invoices, taxes, and the public.
- A business name may be a trademark or service mark used to identify and distinguish products or services sold by the business (for example, Ford Motor Co. sells Ford automobiles, and McDonald's Corporation offers McDonald's fast food services).

While your corporate or assumed business name registration may legally clear the name for the first purpose, it doesn't speak to the second. For example, if your business is organized as a limited liability company or corporation, you may get the green light from your secretary of state to use Ikea's Toxics as your business name (if no other corporation or LLC in your state is using it or something confusingly similar). But if you try to use that name out in the marketplace, you're asking for a claim of trademark violation from Ikea's general counsel's office.

To find out whether you can use your proposed name as a trademark or service mark, you will need to do what's known as a trademark search. (See Chapter 8 for information.)

I've found out that the name I want to use is available. What do I need to do to reserve it for my business?

If you are forming a corporation or an LLC, every state has a procedure—operated by the secretary of state's office—under which a proposed name can be reserved for a certain period of time, usually for a fee. You can usually extend the reservation period for an additional fee. (For more information about corporations and LLCs, see "Legal Structures for Small Businesses," below.)

If you are not forming a corporation or an LLC, then you may need to file a fictitious or assumed business name statement with the agency that handles these registrations in your state (usually the county clerk, but sometimes the secretary of state). Generally speaking, you need to file a fictitious business name statement only if your business name does not include the legal names of all the owners.

If you plan to use your business name as a trademark or servicemark and your service or product will be marketed in more than one state (or across territorial or international borders), you can file an application with the U.S. Patent and Trademark Office to reserve the name for your use. (See Chapter 8 for information.)

What should I keep in mind when choosing a location for my business?

Commercial real estate brokers are fond of saying that the three most important factors in establishing a business are location, location, and location. While true for some types of businesses—such as a retail sandwich shop that depends on lunchtime walk-in trade—locating in a popular, high-cost area is a mistake for many businesses. For example, if you design computer software, repair tile, import jewelry from Indonesia, or do any one of ten thousand other things that don't rely on foot traffic, your best bet is to search out convenient, low-cost, utilitarian surroundings. And even if yours is a business that many people will visit, consider the possibility that a low-cost, offbeat location may make more sense than a high-cost, trendy one.

What about zoning and other rules that restrict where a business may locate?

Never sign a lease without being absolutely sure you will be permitted to operate your business at that location. If the rental space is in a shopping center or other retail complex, this involves first checking carefully with management, because many have contractual restrictions (for example, no more than two pizza restaurants in the Mayfair Mall). If your business will not be located in a shopping center, you'll need to be sure that you meet applicable zoning rules, which typically divide cities into residential, commercial, industrial, and mixed use areas.

You'll also need to find out whether any other legal restrictions will affect your operations. For example, some cities limit the number of certain types of business—such as fast food restaurants or coffee bars—in certain areas, and others require that a business provide off-street parking, close early on weeknights, limit advertising signs, or meet other rules as a condition of getting a permit. Fortunately, many cities have business development offices that help small business owners understand and cope with these kinds of restrictions.

Selling Goods and Services on Consignment

In a consignment agreement, the owner of goods (the consignor) puts the goods in the hands of another person or business—usually a retailer (the consignee)—who then attempts to sell them. If the goods are sold, the consignee receives a fee, which is usually a percentage of the purchase price, and the rest of the money is sent to the consignor. For example, a sculptor (the consignor) might place a work for sale at an art gallery (the consignee) with the understanding that if the artwork sells, the gallery keeps 50% of the sale price. Or a homeowner might leave old furniture with a resale shop that will keep one-third of the proceeds if the item sells. Typically, the consignor remains the owner of the goods until the consignee sells them.

As part of any consignment of valuable items, the consignor (owner) wants to be protected if the goods are lost or stolen while in the consignee's possession. The key here is to make sure that the consignee has an insurance policy that will cover any loss. When extremely valuable items are being consigned, it's often appropriate for the consignor to be named as a coinsured who can receive a share of the insurance proceeds if a loss occurs.

If you're a consignee, check your insurance coverage. Before you accept the risk of loss or theft, make sure your business insurance policy covers you for loss of "personal property of others" left in your possession—and that the amount of coverage is adequate. Getting full reimbursement for the selling price of consigned goods may require an added supplement (called an endorsement) to your insurance policy. Check with your insurance agent or broker.

For a consignment contract, including detailed instructions and guidance, as well as small business forms and contracts, see Nolo's website for it's Online Legal Forms and business software, *Quicken Legal Business Pro.*

What is a business plan, and do I need to write one?

A business plan is a written document that describes the business you want to start and how it will become profitable. The document usually starts with a statement outlining the purpose and goals of your business and how you plan to realize them, including a detailed marketing plan. It should also contain a formal profit and loss projection and cash flow analysis designed to show that the business will be profitable if it develops as expected.

Your business plan enables you to explain your business prospects to potential lenders and investors in a language they can understand. Even more important, the work of creating a thorough business plan will help you see whether the business you hope to start is likely to meet your personal and financial goals. Many budding entrepreneurs who take an honest look at their financial numbers see that hoped-for profits are unlikely to materialize. One of the most important purposes of writing a good business plan is to talk yourself out of starting a bad business.

I plan to sell products and services directly to the public. What do I need to know to comply with consumer protection laws?

Many federal and state laws regulate the relationship between a business and its customers. These laws cover such things as advertising, pricing, door-to-door sales, written and implied warranties, and, in a few states, layaway plans and refund policies. You can find out more about consumer protection laws at the website of the Federal Trade Commission, www.ftc.gov, and by contacting your state's consumer protection agency.

Although it's essential to understand and follow the rules that protect consumers, most successful businesses regard them as only a foundation for building friendly customer service policies designed to produce a high level of customer satisfaction.

RESOURCE

For more information about starting your small business, see these Nolo books:

- *The Small Business Start-Up Kit,* by Peri H. Pakroo. Shows you how to choose from among the basic types of business organizations, write an effective business plan, file the right forms in the right place, acquire good bookkeeping and accounting habits, get the proper licenses and permits, market your business, and create a website. Nolo also publishes two other business start-up books by Peri Pakroo that cover the same topics, but for a defined audience: *The Women's Small Business Start-Up Kit* and *The Small Business Start-Up Kit for California.*

- *Legal Guide for Starting & Running a Small Business*, by Fred S. Steingold. Provides clear, plain-English explanations of the laws that affect business owners every day. It covers partnerships, corporations, limited liability companies, leases, trademarks, contracts, franchises, insurance, hiring and firing, and much more.
- *Legal Forms for Starting & Running a Small Business*, by Fred S. Steingold. Contains the forms and instructions you need to accomplish many routine legal tasks, such as borrowing money, leasing property, and contracting for goods and services.
- *Negotiate the Best Lease for Your Business*, by Janet Portman and Fred S. Steingold. Gives you all the information you need to choose the right spot and negotiate a commercial lease.
- *Working for Yourself: Law & Taxes for Independent Contractors, Freelancers & Consultants*, by Stephen Fishman. Covers every aspect of starting your own business, including information on taxes, choosing the right location, bookkeeping, and more.
- *Quicken Legal Business Pro* software. Contains over 100 forms, contracts, and worksheets that all small businesses should have, plus the text of six best-selling Nolo business titles.
- *How to Write a Business Plan*, by Mike McKeever. Shows you how to write the business plan necessary to finance your business and make it work.

ONLINE HELP

The following sites are great resources for information on starting a business:

- **www.nolo.com** Nolo's website provides a wide variety of articles on starting a business, including choosing and registering a business name, ecommerce, dealing with licenses, permits, taxes, and much more.
- **www.sba.gov** The U.S. Small Business Administration includes extensive resources for starting a small business, from creating a business plan and raising money to choosing a business location and hiring employees, with links to local resources, such as Women's Business Centers.
- **www.usa.gov** The federal government website includes a special section of resources on starting a business, links to secretary of state offices, consumer protection agencies, and more.
- **www.bplans.com** Palo Alto Software provides over 500 sample business plans with step-by-step advice on creating a plan for your business, from restaurants to online stores.

Legal Structures for Small Businesses

There is no one legal structure that's best for all small businesses. Whether you're better off starting as a sole proprietor or choosing one of the more complicated organizational structures, such as a partnership, corporation, or limited liability company (LLC), usually depends on several factors, including the size and profitability of your business, how many people will own it, and whether it will face liability risks not covered by insurance.

If I'm the only owner, what's the easiest way to structure my business?

The vast majority of small business people begin as sole proprietors, because it's cheap, easy, and fast. With a sole proprietorship, there's no need to draft an agreement or go to the trouble and expense of registering a corporation or limited liability company (LLC) with your state regulatory agency. Usually, all you have to do is get a local business license and, unless you are doing business under your own name, file and possibly publish a fictitious name statement.

If it's so simple, why aren't all businesses sole proprietorships?

There are several reasons why doing business as a sole proprietor is not right for everyone. First, a sole proprietorship is possible only when a business is owned by one person. (The only exception to the sole owner rules is for spouses. Spouses can share ownership of a business and still be treated as sole proprietors for tax purposes.) Second, the owner of a sole proprietorship is personally responsible for all business debts, whereas limited liability companies and corporations normally shield their owners' assets from such debts. And finally, unlike a corporation that is taxed separately from its owners (or an LLC that elects to be taxed as a corporation), a sole proprietor and the business are considered to be the same legal entity for tax purposes. This means you'll report all of the business's income, expenses, and deductions on your individual tax return.

I'm starting my business with several other people. What are the advantages and disadvantages of forming a general partnership?

One big advantage of a general partnership is that you usually don't have to register it with your state and pay a fee, as you do to establish a corporation or limited liability company. And because a partnership is a pass-through tax entity (the partners, not the partnership, are taxed on the partnership's profits), filing income tax returns is easier than it is for a regular corporation, where separate tax returns must be filed for the corporate entity and its owners. But because the business-related acts of one partner legally bind all others, it is essential that you only go into business with a partner or partners you completely trust. It is also essential that you prepare a written partnership agreement establishing, among other things, each partner's share of profits or losses and day-to-day duties as well as what happens if one partner dies or retires.

Finally, a major disadvantage of doing business as a partnership is that all partners are personally liable for business debts and liabilities (for example, a judgment in a lawsuit). Of course, a good insurance policy can do much to reduce lawsuit worries, and many small, savvy businesses do not face debt problems. However, a business that anticipates significant risks in either of these areas should probably organize itself as a corporation or LLC in order to benefit from the limited liability these business structures provide.

What exactly is limited liability—and why is it so important?

Some types of businesses—corporations and limited liability companies are the most common—shield their owners from personal responsibility for business debts. For instance, if the business goes bankrupt, its owners are not usually required to use their personal assets to make good on business losses—unless they voluntarily assume responsibility. Other types of businesses—sole proprietorships and general partnerships—do not provide this shield, which means their owners are personally responsible for business liabilities. To see how this works, assume someone obtains a large court judgment against an incorporated business. Because corporate stockholders are not personally liable for business debts, their houses and other personal assets can't be taken to pay the judgment, even if the corporation files for bankruptcy. By comparison, if a sole proprietorship or partnership gets into the same kind of trouble, the houses, bank accounts, and other valuable personal assets of the business's owners (and possibly their spouses) can be attached and used to satisfy the debt.

Why do so many small business owners choose not to take advantage of limited liability protection?

Many small businesses simply don't have major debt or lawsuit worries, so they don't need limited liability protection. For example, if you run a small service business (perhaps you are a graphic artist, management consultant, or music teacher), your chances of being sued or running up big debts are low. And when it comes to liability for many types of debts, creating a limited liability entity makes little practical difference for new businesses. Often, if you want to borrow money from a commercial lender or establish credit with a vendor, you will be required to pledge your personal assets or personally guarantee payment of the debt, even if you've chosen a limited liability business structure.

Finally, organizing your business to achieve limited liability status is no substitute for purchasing a good business insurance policy, especially if your business faces serious and predictable financial risks (for instance, the risk that a customer may trip and fall on your premises or that your products may malfunction). After all, if a serious injury occurs and you don't have insurance, all the assets of your business—which will probably amount to a large portion of your net worth—can be grabbed to satisfy any resulting court judgment. If you purchase comprehensive business insurance, your personal assets may not be at significant risk, and you may therefore conclude you don't need limited liability status.

Given all its limitations, when is it wise for a small business person to seek limited liability status?

You should consider forming a business that offers its owners limited liability if:

- your business subjects you to a risk of lawsuits in an area where insurance coverage is unaffordable or incomplete, or
- your business will incur significant debts, is well established, and has a good credit rating so that you no longer need to personally guarantee every loan or credit application.

The easiest and most popular way to gain limited liability status is to form a corporation or a limited liability company (LLC).

Is forming a corporation difficult?

No. As long as you and close associates and family members will own all of the stock, and none of the stock will be sold to the public, the necessary documents—principally your articles of incorporation and corporate bylaws—can usually be prepared in a few hours.

While most states use the term articles of incorporation to refer to the basic document creating the corporation, some states use the term certificate of incorporation, certificate of formation, or charter.

The first step in forming a corporation is to check with your state's corporate filing office (usually either the secretary of state or department of corporations) and conduct a trademark search to be sure the name you want to use is legally available. Chapter 8 covers trademark searches.

You then fill in the blanks in a preprinted form (available from most states' corporate filing offices or websites) listing the purpose of your corporation, its principal place of business, and the number and type of shares of stock. You'll file these documents with the appropriate office, along with a registration fee that usually will be between $200 and $1,000, depending on the state.

You'll also need to complete, but not file, corporate bylaws. These will outline a number of important corporate housekeeping details, such as when annual shareholder meetings will be held, who can vote, and how shareholders will be notified if there is need for an additional special meeting.

Fortunately, good self-help resources (see the list below) can make it easy and safe to incorporate your business without a lawyer.

What about operating my corporation? Aren't ongoing legal formalities involved?

Assuming your corporation has not sold stock to the public, conducting corporate business is remarkably straightforward and uncomplicated. Often it amounts to little more than recording key corporate decisions (for example, borrowing money or buying real estate) and holding an annual meeting. Even these formalities can often be done by written agreement and don't necessarily require a face-to-face meeting between the directors.

How are corporations taxed?

Corporate taxation is complicated; we'll be able to cover only the main points here. Most types of businesses—sole proprietorships, partnerships, corporations that have qualified for subchapter S status, and limited liability companies that have not elected to be taxed as regular, or C, corporations—are pass-through tax entities. This means that all business profits and losses pass through the business and are reported on the individual tax returns of the owners. For example, if a sole proprietor's convenience store turns a yearly profit of $85,000, this amount goes right on the owner's personal tax return. By contrast, a regular for-profit corporation (and any LLC that elects to be taxed like a corporation) is a separate tax entity—meaning that the business files a tax return and pays its own taxes.

This corporate tax structure creates the possibility of double taxation—the corporation pays tax on its profit, then the owners pay tax again when those profits are paid to them as dividends. But corporate profits won't always be taxed twice. That's because owners of most incorporated small businesses are also employees of those businesses; the money they receive in the form of salaries and bonuses is tax deductible to the corporation as an ordinary and necessary business expense. If the corporation pays surplus money to owners in the form of reasonable salaries, along with bonuses and other fringe benefits, a corporation does not have to show a profit, and therefore will pay no corporate income tax. In addition, most small corporations don't pay dividends, so there's no double taxation.

Are there tax advantages to forming a corporation?

Frequently, yes. Corporations pay federal income tax at a lower rate than most individuals for the first $75,000 of their profits—15% of the first $50,000 of profit and 25% of the next $25,000. (Professional corporations are charged a flat 35% tax rate.) By contrast, in a sole proprietorship or partnership, where the business owner(s) pay taxes on all profits at their personal income tax rates, they could pay more.

A corporation can often reduce taxes by paying its owner-employees a decent

Small Business Structures: An Overview		
Type of Entity	**Main Advantages**	**Main Drawbacks**
Sole Proprietorship	Simple and inexpensive to create and operate Owner reports profit or loss on his or her personal tax return	Owner personally liable for business debts and liabilities
General Partnership	Relatively easy and inexpensive to create and operate Owners (partners) report their share of profit or loss on their personal tax returns	Owners (partners) personally liable for business debts Must prepare and file separate partnership tax return
Limited Partnership	Limited partners have limited personal liability for business debts as long as they don't participate in management General partners can raise cash without involving outside investors in management of business	General partners personally liable for business debts More expensive to create than a general partnership Suitable mainly for companies that invest in real estate or other businesses
Regular Corporation	Owners have limited personal liability for business debts Owners' fringe benefits (such as health insurance and pension plans) can be deducted as business expenses Owners can split corporate profit among owners and corporation, sometimes paying a lower overall tax rate	More expensive to create than partnership or sole proprietorship Paperwork can seem burdensome to some owners Separate taxable entity that must prepare and file a separate corporate tax return
S Corporation	Owners have limited personal liability for business debts Owners report their share of corporate profit or loss on their personal tax returns Owners can use corporate loss to offset personal income	More expensive to create than partnership or sole proprietorship More paperwork than for a limited liability company, which offers some of the same advantages Income must be allocated to owners in proportion to their ownership interests Fringe benefits deductible only for owners who own more than 2% of shares
Professional Corporation	Owners have no personal liability for malpractice of other owners	More expensive to create than partnership or sole proprietorship Paperwork can seem burdensome to some owners All owners must generally belong to, and often be licensed to practice in, the same profession

Small Business Structures: An Overview (continued)

Type of Entity	Main Advantages	Main Drawbacks
Nonprofit Corporation	Corporation doesn't pay income taxes Contributions to charitable corporations are tax deductible Fringe benefits can be deducted as business expense	Full tax advantages available only to groups organized for charitable, scientific, educational, literary, or religious purposes Property transferred to corporation stays there; if corporation ends, property must go to another nonprofit
Limited Liability Company	LLCs can be organized with one or more members Owners have limited personal liability for business debts even if they participate in management Owners report their share of profit or loss on their personal tax returns IRS rules allow LLCs to choose between being taxed as partnership or corporation	More expensive to create than partnership or sole proprietorship
Professional Limited Liability Company	Same advantages as a regular limited liability company Gives state licensed professionals a way to enjoy those advantages	Same as for a regular limited liability company Members must all belong to the same profession One state (California) does not permit professionals to organize as an LLC
Limited Liability Partnership	Mostly of interest to partners in certain professions such as law, medicine, and accounting Owners (partners) usually aren't personally liable for the malpractice of other partners Owners report their share of profit or loss on their personal tax returns	Owners (partners) are usually personally liable for many business debts Not available in all states Often limited to a short list of professions

salary (which, of course, is tax deductible to the corporation but taxable to the employee), and then retaining additional profits in the business (say, for future expansion). The additional profits will be taxed at the lower corporate tax rates. Under IRS rules, however, the maximum amount of profits most corporations are allowed to retain without an additional tax is $250,000, and some professional corporations are limited to $150,000.

I hear a lot about limited liability companies. How do they work?

For many years, small business people had to choose between operating as a sole proprietor (or, if several people were involved, a partnership) or incorporating. On the one hand, many owners were attracted to the tax reporting simplicity of being a sole proprietor or partner. On the other, they desired the personal liability protection offered by incorporation. Until the mid-1990s, it was possible to safely achieve these dual goals only by forming a corporation and then complying with a number of technical rules to gain S corporation status from the IRS. Then the limited liability company (LLC) was introduced and is now widely used.

LLCs have many of the most popular attributes of both partnerships (pass-through tax status) and corporations (limited personal liability for the owners). You can form an LLC by filing a document, usually called articles of organization, with your state's corporate filing office (often the secretary of state).

Can any small business register as a limited liability company?

Most small businesses can be run as LLCs because limited liability companies are recognized by all states. And all states permit one-owner LLCs, which means that sole proprietors can easily organize their businesses as LLCs to obtain both limited liability and pass-through tax status.

Are there any drawbacks to forming a limited liability company?

Very few, beyond the fact that LLCs require a moderate amount of paperwork at the outset and a filing fee. You must file articles of organization with your state's secretary of state, along with a filing fee that will range from a few hundred dollars in some states to almost $1,000 in others.

RESOURCE

For more about choosing a structure for your small business, see these Nolo books:

- *LLC or Corporation?* by Anthony Mancuso. Explains everything you need to know to choose the best legal structure for your business.
- *Legal Guide for Starting & Running a Small Business,* by Fred S. Steingold. Explains what you need to know to choose the right form for your business and shows you what to do to get started.
- *Form Your Own Limited Liability Company,* by Anthony Mancuso. Explains how to set up an LLC in any state, without the aid of an attorney.
- *Incorporate Your Business,* by Anthony Mancuso. Explains how to set up a corporation in any state.
- *Form a Partnership,* by Denis Clifford and Ralph Warner. Explains how to create a partnership for your business.

ONLINE HELP

The following sites offer useful resources on business entities:

- **www.nolo.com** Nolo offers many online resources for small businesses, including an LLC online formation service, ebooks, online business forms, and software that can help you start your business. The Business Formation section of Nolo's website includes articles on the various types of business structures and how to choose (or change) a business structure.
- **www.usa.gov** The federal government website links to state business entity filing websites, such as secretary of state offices.

Nonprofit Corporations

In the long run you hit only what you aim at. Therefore, though you should fail immediately, you had better aim at something high.

—Henry David Thoreau

A nonprofit corporation is a group of people who join together to do some activity that benefits the public, such as running a homeless shelter, an artists' performance group, or a low-cost medical clinic. Making an incidental profit from these activities is allowed under legal and tax rules, but the primary purpose of the organization should be to do good work, not to make money. Nonprofit goals are typically educational, charitable, or religious.

How do nonprofit organizations begin?

Most nonprofits start out as small, informal, loosely structured organizations. Volunteers perform the work, and the group spends what little money it earns to keep the organization afloat. Formal legal papers (such as a nonprofit charter or bylaws) are rarely prepared in the beginning. Legally, groups of this sort are considered nonprofit associations, and each member can be held personally liable for organizational debts and liabilities.

Once a nonprofit association gets going and starts to make money, or wishes to obtain a tax exemption to attract public donations and qualify for grant funds, the members will formalize its structure. Usually the members decide to incorporate, but forming an unincorporated nonprofit association by adopting a formal association charter and operating bylaws is an alternative.

Most groups form a nonprofit corporation because it is the traditional form—the IRS and grant agencies are very familiar with it. Also, once incorporated, the individual members of the nonprofit are not personally liable for debts of the organization—a big legal advantage over the unincorporated association.

Will my association benefit from becoming a nonprofit corporation?

Here are some circumstances that might make it worth your while to incorporate and get tax-exempt status:

- **You want to solicit tax deductible contributions.** Contributions to nonprofits are generally tax deductible for those who make them. If you want to solicit money to fund your venture, you'll make it more attractive to potential donors if their contributions are tax deductible.
- **Your association makes a taxable profit from its activities.** If your association will generate any kind of income from its activities, it's wise to incorporate so that you and your associates don't have to pay income tax on this money.
- **You want to apply for public or private grant money.** Without federal tax-exempt status, your group is unlikely to qualify for grants.
- **Your members want some protection from legal liability.** By incorporating your association, you can generally insulate your officers, directors, and members from liability for the activities they engage in on behalf of the corporation.
- **Your advocacy efforts might provoke legal quarrels.** If, for instance, your association is taking aim at a powerful industry (such as tobacco companies), it might be worth incorporating so that your association's officers and directors will have some protection from the spurious lawsuits that may come—and will also receive compensation for their legal fees.

Forming a nonprofit corporation brings other benefits as well, such as lower nonprofit mailing rates and local real estate and personal property tax exemptions.

Is forming a nonprofit corporation difficult?

Legally, no. To form a nonprofit corporation, one of the organization's founders prepares and files standard articles of incorporation—a short legal document that lists the name and the directors of the nonprofit plus certain other basic required information. The articles are filed with the secretary of state (or your state's corporate filing office) for a modest filing fee. After the articles are filed, the group is a legally recognized nonprofit corporation.

Is there more to forming a nonprofit than this simple legal task?

Taxwise, there is more. In addition to filing your articles, you will want to apply for and obtain federal and state nonprofit tax exemptions. Many groups don't want to form a nonprofit unless they can qualify for tax-exempt status. Unfortunately, you must form your corporation before you submit your federal tax exemption application. Why? Because the IRS requires that you submit a copy of your filed articles with the exemption application. Still, you should carefully review the tax exemption application before you submit your corporation papers. Doing so will give you an idea of whether your organization will qualify for a tax exemption or not.

What type of tax exemption do most nonprofits get?

Most organizations obtain a federal tax exemption under Section 501(c)(3) of the Internal Revenue Code, for charitable, educational, religious, scientific, or literary purposes. States typically follow the federal lead and grant state tax-exempt status to nonprofits recognized by the IRS as 501(c)(3) organizations.

How can my organization get a 501(c)(3) tax exemption?

You'll need to file the IRS Form 1023 exemption application. This is a lengthy and technical application with many references to the federal tax code. Smaller nonprofits may be eligible to use the shorter, streamlined Form 1023-EZ that is much easier to complete. For help creating your nonprofit in any state, see Nolo's *How to Form a Nonprofit Corporation,* by Anthony Mancuso.

Are there any restrictions imposed on 501(c)(3) nonprofits?

You must meet the following conditions to qualify for a 501(c)(3) IRS tax exemption:

- The assets of your nonprofit must be irrevocably dedicated to charitable, educational, religious, or similar purposes. If your 501(c)(3) nonprofit dissolves, any assets it owns must be transferred to another 501(c)(3) organization. (In your organizational papers, you don't have to name the specific organization that will receive your assets—a broad dedication clause will do.)
- Your organization cannot campaign for or against candidates for public office, and political lobbying activity is restricted.
- If your nonprofit makes a profit from activities unrelated to its nonprofit purpose, it must pay taxes on the profit (but up to $1,000 of unrelated income can be earned tax-free).

RESOURCE

For more information about nonprofit organizations, see these Nolo books:

- *How to Form a Nonprofit Corporation,* by Anthony Mancuso. Shows you how to form a tax-exempt corporation in all 50 states. In California, look for *How to Form a Nonprofit Corporation in California,* also by Anthony Mancuso.
- *Every Nonprofit's Tax Guide,* by Stephen Fishman. A comprehensive guide to the legal and tax requirements for maintaining tax-exempt status and avoiding problems with the IRS.

- *Starting & Building a Nonprofit*, by Peri Pakroo. A practical guide to getting a nonprofit up and running, with useful advice on developing strategic plans and budgets, fundraising, and using social media.

ONLINE HELP

The Nonprofits section of Nolo's website (www.nolo.com) offers many articles of interest to nonprofits, such as how to build a nonprofit board and use volunteers, as well as books on fundraising and human resources, in addition to the titles listed above.

Small Business Taxes

Taxes are a fact of life for every small business. Those who take the time to understand and follow the rules will have little trouble with tax authorities. By contrast, those who are sloppy or dishonest are likely to be dogged by tax bills, audits, and penalties. The moral is simple: Meeting your obligations to report business information and pay taxes is one of the cornerstones of operating a successful business.

I want to start my own small business. What do I have to do to keep out of trouble with the IRS?

Start by learning a new set of "3 Rs"—record keeping, record keeping, and (you guessed it) record keeping. IRS studies show that poor records—not dishonesty—cause most small business people to lose at audits or fail to comply with their tax reporting obligations, with resulting fines and penalties. Even if you hire someone to keep your records, you need to know your obligations—if your bookkeeper or accountant messes up, you'll be held responsible.

I don't have enough money in my budget to hire a business accountant or tax preparer. Is it safe and sensible for me to keep my own books?

Yes, if you remember to keep thorough, current records. Consider using accounting and checkbook register software to track your expenses and help with your tax return. To ensure that you're on the right track, it's a good idea to run your bookkeeping system by a savvy small business tax professional, such as a CPA. With just a few hours of work, a tax pro can help you avoid the most common mistakes and show you how to dovetail your bookkeeping system with tax filing requirements.

When your business is firmly in the black and your budget allows for it, consider hiring a bookkeeper to do your day-to-day payables and receivables. And hire an outside tax pro to handle your heavy-duty tax work—not only are the fees a tax deductible business expense, but chances are your business will benefit if you put more of your time into running it and less into completing paperwork.

Record-Keeping Basics

Keep all receipts and canceled checks for business expenses. It will help if you separate your documents by category, such as:

- auto expenses
- rent
- utilities
- advertising
- travel
- entertainment, and
- professional fees.

Organize your documents by putting them into individual folders or envelopes, and keep them in a safe place. If you are ever audited, the IRS is most likely to zero in on business deductions for travel and entertainment, and car expenses. Remember that the burden will be on you to explain your deductions. If you're feeling unsure about how to get started or what documents you need to keep, consult a tax professional familiar with record keeping for small businesses.

What is—and isn't—a tax deductible business expense?

Just about any "ordinary, necessary and reasonable" expense that helps you earn business income is deductible. These terms reflect the purpose for which the expense is made. For example, buying a computer, or even a sound system, for your office or store is an ordinary and necessary business expense, but buying the same items for your family room obviously isn't. The property must be used in a trade or business, which means it is used with the expectation of generating income.

In addition to the "ordinary and necessary" rule, a few expenses are specifically prohibited by law from being tax deductible —for instance, you can't deduct a bribe paid to a public official. Other deduction no-nos are traffic tickets and clothing you wear on the job, unless it is a required uniform. As a rule, if you think it is necessary for your business, it probably is deductible. Just be ready to explain it to an auditor.

If I use my car for business, how much of that expense can I write off?

You must keep track of how much you use your car for business in order to figure out your deduction. (You'll also need to produce these records if you're ever audited.) Start by keeping a log showing the miles for each business use, always noting the purpose of the trip. Then, at the end of the year, you will usually be able to figure your deduction by using either the mileage method (an annual per-mile amount set by the IRS) or the actual expense method (you can take the total you pay for gas and repairs plus depreciation according to a tax code schedule, multiplied by the percentage of business use). Figure the deduction both ways and use the method that benefits you most.

Business Costs That Are Never Deductible

A few expenses are not deductible even if they are business-related, because they violate public policy (IRC § 162). These expenses include:

- any type of government fine, such as a tax penalty paid to the IRS, or even a parking ticket
- bribes and kickbacks
- any kind of payment made for referring a client, patient, or customer, if it is contrary to a state or federal law, and
- expenses for lobbying and social club dues.

Thankfully, very few other business expenses are affected by these rules.

Can I claim a deduction for business-related entertainment?

You may deduct only 50% of expenses for entertaining clients, customers, or employees. The entertainment must be either directly related to the business (such as a catered business lunch) or associated with the business, meaning that the entertainment took place immediately before or immediately after a business discussion. As a general rule, you can't claim an entertainment deduction for activities other than a meal. The IRS doesn't believe it's possible to engage in serious business discussions at a ball game, concert, golf outing, or other large social gathering. For those types of entertainment activities to qualify for a deduction, you will need to show that you discussed business before or after the activity.

Parties and other social events you put on for your employees and their families are an exception to the 50% rule—such events are 100% deductible. Keep in mind that if you are audited, you must be able to show some proof that it was a legitimate business expense. So, keep a guest list and note the business (or potential business) relationship of each person entertained.

Must some types of business supplies and equipment be deducted over several years?

Current expenses, which include the everyday costs of keeping your business going, such as office supplies, rent, and electricity, can be deducted from your business's total income in the year you incur them. But expenditures for things that will generate revenue in future years—for example, a desk, copier, or car—must be capitalized, that is, written off or amortized over their useful life (usually three, five, or seven years, according to IRS rules). There is one important exception to this rule—Section 179 (discussed below).

If I buy business equipment this year, can I take the whole deduction at once?

Normally the cost of capital equipment—equipment that has a useful life of more than one year—must be deducted over a number of years. There is one major exception. Section 179 of the Internal Revenue Code allows you to deduct a certain amount up to $500,000 each year against your business income, subject to a phase-out if capital expenditures exceed $2 million. Even if you buy the equipment on credit, with no money down, you can still qualify for this deduction.

Business Assets That Must Be Capitalized

- Buildings
- Computer components and software
- Copyrights and patents
- Equipment
- Improvements to business property
- Inventory
- Office furnishings and decorations
- Small tools and equipment
- Vehicles
- Window coverings.

A friend told me that corporations get the best tax breaks of any type of business, so I am thinking of incorporating my start-up. What do you recommend?

There's a seed of truth in what your friend told you, but keep in mind that most tax benefits flow to profitable, established businesses, not to start-ups in their first few years. For example, corporations can offer more tax-flexible pension plans and greater medical deductions than sole proprietors, partnerships, or LLCs, but few start-ups have the cash flow needed to take full advantage of this tax break. Similarly, the ability to split income between a corporation and its owners—thereby keeping income in lower tax brackets—is effective only if the business is solidly profitable. And incorporating adds state fees, as well as legal and accounting charges, to your expense load. So unless you are sure that substantial profits will begin to roll in immediately, hold off.

For more information about choosing the right structure for your business, see "Legal Structures for Small Businesses," above.

I am thinking about setting up a consulting business with two of my business associates. Do we need to have partnership papers drawn up? Does it make any difference taxwise?

If you go into business with other people and split the expenses and profits, under the tax code you are in partnership whether you have signed a written agreement or not. This means that you will have to file a partnership tax return every year, in addition to your individual tax return.

Even though a formal partnership agreement doesn't affect your tax status, it's essential to prepare one to establish all partners' rights and responsibilities vis-à-vis each other, and to provide for how profits and losses will be allocated to each partner. For more information about partnerships, see "Legal Structures for Small Businesses," above.

I am a building contractor with a chance to land a big job. If I get it, I'll need to hire people quickly. Should I hire independent contractors or employees?

If you will be telling your workers where, when, and how to do their jobs, you should treat them as employees, because that's how the IRS will classify them. Generally, you can treat workers as independent contractors only if they have their own businesses and offer their services to several clients—for example, a specialty sign painter with his own shop.

When in doubt, err on the side of treating workers as employees. While classifying your workers as independent contractors might save you money in the short run (you wouldn't have to pay the employer's share of payroll taxes or have an accountant keep records and file payroll tax forms), it may get you into big trouble if the IRS later audits you. The IRS is very aware of the tax benefits of misclassifying an employee as an independent contractor and regularly audits companies that hire large numbers of independent contractors. If your company is audited, the IRS may reclassify your so-called independent contractors as employees—and slap you with hefty back taxes, penalties, and interest.

Commonly Overlooked Deductible Business Expenses

Despite the fact that most people keep a sharp eye out for deductible expenses, it's not uncommon to miss a few. Some overlooked routine deductions include:

- advertising giveaways and promotions
- audios and videos related to business skills
- bank service charges
- business association dues
- business gifts
- business-related magazines and books (like this one)
- casual labor and tips
- casualty and theft losses
- charitable contributions
- coffee service
- commissions
- consultant fees
- credit bureau fees
- education to improve business skills
- interest on credit cards for business expenses
- interest on personal loans used for business purposes
- office supplies
- online computer services related to business
- parking and meters
- petty cash funds
- postage
- promotion and publicity
- seminars and trade shows
- taxi and bus fare, and
- telephone calls away from the business.

I am planning a trip to attend a trade show. Can I take my family along for a vacation and still deduct the expenses?

If you take others with you on a business trip, you can deduct business expenses for the trip no greater than if you were traveling alone. If your family rides in the backseat of the car and stays with you in one standard motel room, then you can fully deduct your automobile and hotel expenses. You can also fully deduct the cost of your air ticket, but not the tickets of family members even if the tickets featured a two-for-one or bring-along-the-family discount. You can't claim a deduction for your family's meals or jaunts to Disneyland or Universal Studios, however. And if you extend your stay and partake in some of the fun after the business is over, the expenses attributed to the nonbusiness days aren't deductible, unless you extended your stay to get discounted airfare (the Saturday overnight requirement, for example). In this case, your hotel room and your meals would be deductible.

RESOURCE

For more information about small business taxes, see these Nolo books:

- *Tax Savvy for Small Business,* by Frederick W. Daily and Jeffrey A. Quinn. Tells small business owners what they need to know about federal taxes and shows them how to make the right tax decisions.
- *Deduct It! Lower Your Small Business Taxes,* by Stephen Fishman. Provides invaluable information on business deductions for small business owners.
- *Working With Independent Contractors,* by Stephen Fishman. Explains who qualifies as an independent contractor, describes applicable tax rules, and shows employers how to set up effective working agreements with independent contractors.
- *Working for Yourself: Law & Taxes for Independent Contractors, Freelancers & Consultants,* by Stephen Fishman. Designed for the tens of millions of Americans who are self-employed and offer their services on a contract basis.

ONLINE HELP

The following sites are good resources for information on tax issues of interest to small businesses:

- **www.nolo.com** The Taxes section of Nolo's website offers many articles of interest to small businesses on topics such as paying estimated taxes, state laws on Internet sales tax, and how to survive a tax audit.
- **www.irs.gov** The IRS website has lots of information and resources for small businesses, such as IRS Publication 535, *Business Expenses,* plus links to state government tax agencies.

Home-Based Businesses

With technology advances, it is convenient and economical to operate a business from home. Depending on local zoning rules, as long as the business is small, quiet, and doesn't create traffic or parking problems, it's usually legal to do so. But as with any other business endeavor, it pays to know the rules before you begin.

Is a home-based business legally different from other businesses?

No. The basic legal issues, such as picking a name for your business and deciding whether to operate as a sole proprietorship, partnership, limited liability company, or corporation, are the same. Similarly, when it comes to signing contracts, hiring employees, and collecting from your customers, the laws are identical whether you run your business from home or the top floor of a high-rise.

Are there laws that restrict a person's right to operate a business from home?

Municipalities have the legal right to establish rules about what types of activities can be carried out in different geographic areas. For example, laws and ordinances often establish zones for stores and offices (commercial zones), factories (industrial zones), and houses (residential zones). In some residential areas—especially in affluent communities—local zoning ordinances absolutely prohibit all types of business. In the great majority of municipalities, however, residential zoning rules allow small nonpolluting home businesses, as long as the home is used primarily as a residence and the business activities don't negatively affect neighbors.

How can I find out whether residential zoning rules allow the home-based business I have in mind?

Get a copy of your local ordinance from your city or county clerk's office, the city attorney's office, or your public library, and read it carefully. Many local ordinances are available online at www.statelocalgov.net or www.municode.com.

Zoning ordinances are worded in many different ways to limit business activities in residential areas. Some are extremely vague, allowing "customary home-based occupations." Others allow homeowners to use their houses for a broad—but, unfortunately, not very specific—list of business purposes (for example, "professions and domestic occupations, crafts, or services"). Still others contain a detailed list of approved occupations, such as "law, dentistry, medicine, music lessons, photography, cabinetmaking."

If you read your ordinance and still aren't sure whether your business is okay, you may be tempted to talk to zoning or planning officials. But until you figure out what the rules and politics of your locality are, it may be best to do this without identifying and calling attention to yourself. (For example, have a friend who lives nearby make inquiries.)

The business I want to run from home is not specifically allowed or prohibited by my local ordinance. What should I do to avoid trouble?

Start by understanding that in most areas zoning and building officials don't actively search for violations. The great majority of home-based businesses that run into trouble do so when a neighbor complains—often because of noise or parking problems, or even because of the unfounded fear that your business is doing something illegal, such as selling drugs.

It follows that your best approach is often to explain your business activities to your neighbors and make sure that your activities are not worrying or inconveniencing them. For example, if you teach piano lessons or do physical therapy from your home and your students or clients will often come and go, make sure your neighbors are not bothered by noise or losing customary on-street parking spaces.

Do zoning ordinances include rules about specific activities, such as making noise, putting up signs, or having employees?

Many ordinances—especially those that are fairly vague about what types of businesses you can run from your home—restrict how you can carry out your business. The most typical rules limit your use of on-street parking, prohibit outside signs, limit car and truck traffic, and restrict the number of employees who can work at your house on a regular basis (some prohibit employees altogether). In addition, some zoning ordinances limit the percentage of your home's floor space that can be devoted to the business. Again, you'll need to study your local ordinance carefully to see how these rules will affect you.

I live in a planned development that has its own rules for home-based businesses. Do these control my business activities, or can I rely on my city's home-based business ordinance, which is less restrictive?

In an effort to protect residential property values, most subdivisions, condos, and planned unit developments create special rules—typically called covenants, conditions, and restrictions (CC&Rs)—that govern many aspects of property use. Rules pertaining to home-based businesses are often significantly stricter than those found in city ordinances. As long as the rules of your planned development are reasonably clear and consistently enforced, you must follow them.

Will maintaining a home office help me show the IRS that I'm an independent contractor?

No. An independent contractor is a person who controls both the outcome of a project and the means of accomplishing it, and who offers services to a number of businesses or individual purchasers. Although having an office or place of business is one factor the IRS looks at in determining whether an individual qualifies as an independent contractor, it makes no difference where your office is located.

Insuring Your Home-Based Business

Don't rely on a standard homeowners' or renters' insurance policy to cover your home-based business. These policies often exclude or strictly limit coverage for business equipment and injuries to business visitors. For example, if your computer is stolen or a client or business associate trips and falls on your steps, you may not be covered.

Fortunately, it's easy to avoid these nasty surprises. Sit down with your insurance agent and fully disclose your planned business operation. You'll find that it's relatively inexpensive to add business coverage to your homeowners' policy—and it's a tax deductible expense. But be sure to check prices—some insurance companies provide special, cost effective policies designed to protect both your home and your home-based business.

Are there tax advantages to working from home?

Almost all ordinary and necessary business expenses (everything from wages to computers to paper clips) are tax deductible, no matter where they are incurred—in a factory or office, while traveling or at home.

But if you operate your business from home and qualify under IRS rules, you may be able to deduct part of your rent from your income taxes—or if you own your home, to take a depreciation deduction.

You may also be eligible to deduct a portion of your total utility, home repair and maintenance, property tax, and house insurance costs, based on the percentage of your residence you use for business purposes.

To qualify for home office deductions, the IRS requires you to meet two legal tests:

- you must use your business space regularly and exclusively for business purposes, and
- your home office must be the principal place where you conduct your business. This rule is satisfied if your office is used for administrative or managerial activities, as long as these activities aren't often conducted at another business location. Alternatively, you must meet clients at home or use a separate structure on your property exclusively for business purposes.

The amount of your deduction can't exceed your home-based business's total profit.

How big will my home office tax deduction be if my business qualifies under IRS rules?

To determine your deduction, you first need to figure out how much of your home you use for business as compared to other purposes. Do this by dividing the number of square feet used for your home business by the total square footage of your home. The resulting percentage determines how much of your rent (or, if you are a homeowner, depreciation), insurance, utilities, and other expenses are deductible. There is also an alternative simplified method of calculating the home office deduction, but the deduction using that method is capped at $1,500 per year.

Remember, you can't deduct more than the profit your home-based business generates. Additional technical rules apply to calculating depreciation on houses you own to allow for the fact that the structure, but not the land, depreciates. For more information on the home office deduction, see IRS Publication 587, *Business Use of Your Home* (available on the IRS website).

Do I need to watch out for any tax traps when claiming deductions for my home office?

Claiming a home office deduction should not increase your audit risk, especially if you carefully follow the rules.

Keep in mind that if you sell your house, you will have to pay a 25% tax on the depreciation portion of the home-based office deductions you have previously taken, whether you made a profit or not. And you can't use the $250,000 per person capital gains exclusion on the sale of a home to offset this tax. For example, if your depreciation deductions total $5,000 for the last seven years, you have to pay capital gains tax of 25% on this amount in the year you sell your house. Despite this tax, it's generally wise to continue to take your home office deductions each year. Especially for people who don't plan to sell their houses anytime soon, it's usually beneficial to receive a tax break today that you won't have to repay for many years. You can use your tax savings to help your business grow.

I have a full-time job, but I also operate a separate part-time business from home. Can I claim a tax deduction for my home-based business expenses?

Yes, as long as your business meets certain IRS rules. It makes no difference that you work only part-time at your home-based business or that you have another occupation. But your business must be more than a disguised hobby—it has to pass muster with the IRS as a real business.

The IRS defines a business as "any activity engaged in to make a profit." If a venture makes money—even a small amount—in three of five consecutive years, it is presumed to possess a profit motive. (IRC § 183(d).) However, courts have held that some activities that don't meet this three profitable years out of five test still qualify as a business if they are run in a businesslike manner. When determining whether an unprofitable venture qualifies for a deduction, courts may look at whether you kept thorough business records, had a separate business bank account, prepared advertising or other marketing materials, and obtained any necessary licenses and permits (a business license from your city, for example).

RESOURCE

For more information about home-based business, see these Nolo books:

- *Home Business Tax Deductions: Keep What You Earn,* by Stephen Fishman. Explains how to take advantage of the many tax write-offs available to those who run a business from home.
- *Tax Savvy for Small Business,* by Frederick W. Daily and Jeffrey A. Quinn. Shows you how to take the home office deduction, including depreciation and household expenses.
- *Working for Yourself: Law & Taxes for Independent Contractors, Freelancers & Consultants,* by Stephen Fishman. Shows independent contractors how to meet business start-up requirements, comply with strict IRS rules, and make sure they get paid in full and on time.
- *The Women's Small Business Start-Up Kit,* by Peri Pakroo. Includes a useful chapter on choosing among different business locations: home, shared office space, or separate office or commercial space.

Employers' Rights & Responsibilities

At some point during your business venture, you may need to hire people to help you manage your workload. When you do, you'll have to follow a host of federal, state, and local laws that regulate your relationship with your employees. Among the things you'll need to know and understand are:

- proper hiring practices, including how to write appropriate job descriptions, conduct interviews, and respect applicants' privacy rights
- paperwork requirements, including tax obligations, verifying your employees' authorization to work in the U.S., and more
- wage and hour laws, such as minimum wage and overtime, as well as the laws that govern retirement plans, and health care benefits
- workplace safety rules and regulations
- how to write an employee handbook, conduct performance reviews, and maintain employee personnel files
- how to avoid discrimination and harassment based on protected characteristics, such as age, gender, race, pregnancy, religion, disability, and national origin, and
- how to avoid legal trouble if you need to fire an employee.

This section provides you with an overview of your role as an employer. You can find more guidance on employees' rights—including questions and answers about wages, hours, and workplace safety—in Chapter 4; retirement plans are covered in Chapter 13.

First things first. How can I write job advertisements that will attract the best pool of potential employees, without getting in legal hot water?

The best way to write an ad that meets legal requirements is to stick to the job skills and qualifications needed and the basic responsibilities of the position. Some examples:

"Fifty-unit apartment complex seeks experienced manager with general maintenance skills."

"Midsized manufacturing company has opening for accountant with tax experience to oversee interstate accounts."

"Cook trainee position available in new vegetarian restaurant. Flexible hours."

Many small employers get tripped up when summarizing a job in an advertisement. This can easily happen if you're not familiar with the legal guidelines. Nuances in an ad can be used as evidence of discrimination against applicants based on gender or age, for example.

Help Wanted ads placed by federal contractors must state that all qualified applicants will receive consideration for employment without regard to race, color, religion, sex, or national origin. Ads often express this with the phrase, "An Equal Opportunity Employer." To show your intent to be fair, you may want to include this phrase in your ad even if you're not a federal contractor.

Pitfalls to Avoid in Job Ads

Don't Use	Use
Salesman	Salesperson
College Student	Part-time Worker
Handyman	General Repairperson
Gal Friday	Office Manager
Married Couple	Two-Person Job
Counter Girl	Retail Clerk
Waiter	Wait Staff
Young	Energetic

Any tips on how to conduct a good interview that gets me the information I need, while avoiding questions that cause legal trouble?

Good preparation is your best ally. Before you begin to interview applicants for a job opening, write down a set of questions focusing on the job duties and the applicant's skills and experience. For example:

"Tell me about your experience in running a mailroom."

"How much experience did you have making cold calls on your last job?"

"Explain how you typically go about organizing your workday."

"Have any of your jobs required strong leadership skills?"

By writing down the questions and sticking to the same format at all interviews for the position, you reduce the risk that a rejected applicant will later complain about unequal treatment. It's also smart to summarize the applicant's answers for your files, but don't get so involved in documenting the interview that you forget to listen closely to the applicant. And don't be so locked in to your list of questions that you don't follow up on something significant that an applicant has said or pin down an ambiguous or evasive response.

To break the ice, you might start by giving the applicant some information about the job, such as the duties, hours, pay range, benefits, and career opportunities. Questions about the applicant's work history and experience that may be relevant to the job opening are always appropriate. But don't encourage the applicant to divulge the trade secrets of a present or former employer, especially a competitor. That can lead to a lawsuit. And be cautious about an applicant who volunteers such information or promises to bring secrets to the new position; that person will probably play fast and loose with your own company's secrets, given the chance.

Can an applicant who doesn't get the job sue for discrimination?

Federal and state laws prohibit many employers from discriminating against an employee or applicant because of race, color, gender, religious beliefs, national origin, disability, genetic information, or age (if the person is at least 40 years old). Also, many states and cities have laws prohibiting employment discrimination based on other characteristics, such as marital status, sexual orientation, or gender identity. Often, these laws apply only if you have a minimum number of employees; for example, most federal antidiscrimination laws apply to private employers with 15 or more employees.

A particular form of discrimination becomes illegal when Congress, a state legislature, or a city council decides that a characteristic—race, for example—bears no legitimate relationship to employment decisions. As an employer, that means you must be prepared to show that your hiring and promotion decisions have been based on objective, job-related criteria.

Still, when hiring, you can exercise a wide range of discretion based on business considerations. You remain free to hire, promote, discipline, and fire employees and to set their duties and salaries based on their skills, experience, performance, and reliability—all factors that are logically tied to valid business purposes.

The law also prohibits employer practices that seem neutral but have a disproportionate impact on a protected class. If one of your policies is challenged on these grounds, you will need to show a valid business reason for its existence. For example, refusing to hire people who can't meet a strength or lifting requirement is permissible if it's clearly related to the physical demands of the particular job, such as felling and hauling huge trees. But applying such a requirement to exclude applicants for a job as a cook or receptionist wouldn't pass legal muster.

Can I run a background check on a prospective employee?

As an employer, you likely believe that the more information you have about job applicants, the better your hiring decisions will be. But make sure any information you seek is actually related to the job. It's often not necessary to order school transcripts and credit reports for every position. If you're hiring a bookkeeper, for example, previous job experience is much more important than the grades the applicant received in a community college bookkeeping program ten years ago. On the other hand, if the applicant is fresh out of school and has never held a bookkeeping job, a transcript may yield some insights.

If you pay someone outside of your company (such as a private investigator or background search company) to look into an applicant's background, or if you request a report from a credit agency about an applicant, you must comply with a federal law called the Fair Credit Reporting Act or FCRA. (15 U.S.C. § 1681.) Among other things, this law requires you to get the applicant's consent in writing beforehand and to give the applicant a copy of the background check or investigative report if you decide not to hire the applicant based on its contents. You can find a summary of the FCRA and tips for compliance in *The Essential Guide to Federal Employment Laws*, by Lisa Guerin and Sachi Barreiro (Nolo).

Make sure you follow your state's rules for background checks, too. Some states, for example, don't allow employers to consider credit reports in hiring for most positions.

Can I require job applicants to pass a drug test?

It depends on the laws of your state. Although many states allow employers to test all applicants for illegal drug use, some states allow testing only for certain jobs (those that require driving, carrying a weapon, or operating heavy machinery, for example). Even states that allow applicant testing often impose procedural rules—that employers give written notice of the drug test and an opportunity to challenge a positive result for example. Before requiring any applicant to take a drug test, you should check with your state's department of labor to find out what the law allows; find your state department of labor at www.dol.gov/whd/state/state.htm.

In general, you will be on safest legal ground if you have a strong, legitimate reason for testing applicants—such as protecting the safety of other employees or the public. Be careful when testing current employees, however: The rules are usually stricter and include more procedural safeguards.

Is illegal drug use a disability?

When it passed the Americans with Disabilities Act (ADA), Congress refused to recognize current illegal drug use as a disability. Therefore, if an applicant fails a legally administered drug test, you will not violate the ADA by refusing to hire that applicant.

However, the ADA does protect applicants with a history of drug addiction and those who have successfully completed (or are currently attending) a supervised drug rehabilitation program, as long as they are not currently using illegal drugs. Although you can require these applicants to take a drug test or show you proof of their participation in a rehabilitation program, you cannot refuse to hire them solely because they have a history of illegal drug use.

What paperwork do I have to complete when I hire a new employee?

There are a few steps you are legally obligated to take when you hire someone new. Federal and state laws impose these requirements:

- **Report the employee to your state's new hire reporting agency.** The new hire reporting program requires employers to report basic identifying information on new employees for the purpose of locating parents who owe child support. For more information, go to the Administration for Children & Families website at www.acf.hhs.gov/programs/css/employers, where you can find the name and address of your state's new hire reporting agency. Most states provide a form you can use to provide the necessary information.
- **Fill out Form I-9, *Employment Eligibility Verification*.** U.S. Citizenship and Immigration Services (USCIS, formerly known as the INS) requires employers to use this form to verify that every employee they hire is eligible to work in the United States. You don't have to file this form with the USCIS, but you must keep it in your files and make it available for inspection by officials of the USCIS. You can obtain the form online at www.uscis.gov.
- **Have the employee fill out IRS Form W-4, *Withholding Allowance Certificate*.** On this form, employees tell you how many allowances they are claiming for tax purposes, so that you can withhold the correct amount of tax from their paychecks. (You don't have to file the form with the IRS.) You can find this form at www.irs.gov.
- **Provide required notices and posters.** The Affordable Care Act requires employers to give employees notice

of their health insurance coverage options within two weeks of their hire. A model notice is available at the Department of Labor's website, www.dol.gov/ebsa/healthreform. Your state or city might also require you to provide employees with certain notices, or to display certain posters at the workplace, regarding employees' rights.

You may choose to have a new employee fill out additional paperwork—for example, to acknowledge receipt of your company's employee handbook—but such documents aren't legally required.

How do I avoid legal problems when giving employee evaluations?

Be honest and objective in employee evaluations. If a fired employee initiates a legal action against you, a judge or jury will probably see those evaluations. If your statements in the evaluations are inconsistent with your reasons for firing the employee, it will create problems for you. For example, a jury will sense that something is wrong if you consistently rate a worker's performance as poor or mediocre, but continue to hand out generous raises or perhaps even promote the employee. The logical conclusion: You didn't take the criticisms in your evaluation report seriously, so you shouldn't expect the employee (or the jury) to take them seriously, either.

It can also be damaging to include only positive remarks or praise in report after report if that isn't the full picture. Even if your intentions are good, if all your written accounts suggest the employee is doing a great job and you later discipline or fire the employee, your actions will look unfair to both the employee and an objective outsider. Or worse, your glowing performance reviews will serve as evidence that you really fired the employee for discriminatory reasons.

Finally, make sure your evaluation is tied to the employee's job performance. Avoid expressing general thoughts or opinions and, whenever possible, cite verifiable facts instead. For example, if an employee is chronically late, write "you were late seven times in the last month (time records attached)" instead of "you're late all the time."

If your system is working, employees with excellent evaluations should not need to be fired for poor performance. And employees with poor performance shouldn't be surprised when you impose discipline.

As a small employer, what should I keep in personnel files and what right do employees have to see what's inside?

Create a file for each employee in which you keep all job-related information, including:

- job description
- job application
- offer of employment
- IRS form W-4, *Employee's Withholding Allowance Certificate*

- receipt or acknowledgment form for employee handbook
- performance evaluations
- sign-up forms for employee benefits
- complaints from customers and coworkers
- awards or citations for excellent performance
- warnings and disciplinary actions, and
- notes on an employee's attendance or tardiness.

Experts recommend keeping one separate file for all of your employees' USCIS I-9 *Employment Eligibility Verification* forms. There are two practical reasons for keeping these forms in their own file (and out of your employees' personnel files). First, this will limit the number of people who know an employee's immigration status. If the I-9 is in the employee's personnel file, anyone who reviews that file (a supervisor, human resources employee, or payroll administrator) will know whether or not the employee is a citizen. This could lead to problems later, if the employee claims to have been discriminated against based on citizenship status. If you keep the forms in a separate file, fewer people will be aware of the employee's citizenship status, and the employee will have a much tougher time trying to prove that important employment decisions were made on that basis.

Second, if the U.S. Citizenship and Immigration Service (formerly the INS) decides to audit you, it is entitled to see I-9 forms kept in the normal course of business. If you keep these forms in each employee's personnel file, that means the government will rummage through all of these files, causing privacy concerns for your employees and opening your company up to questions about your other employment practices. On the other hand, if you keep your forms in a single folder, you can simply hand over that folder if the USCIS comes knocking.

Many states have laws giving employees—and former employees—the right to see their own personnel files. The rules vary from state to state. Typically, if your state allows employees to see their files, you can insist that a supervisor be present to make sure nothing is taken, added, or changed. Some state laws allow employees to obtain copies of items in their files, but not necessarily all items. For example, the employee may only be entitled to copies of documents that he or she has signed. If an employee is entitled to a copy of an item in the file or if you're inclined to let the employee have a copy of the entire file, you—rather than the employee—should make the copy.

Usually, you won't have to let the employee see sensitive items such as information assembled for a criminal investigation, reference letters, and information that might violate the privacy of other people. In a few states, employees have the right to insert rebuttals in their personnel files if they disagree with any of the file's contents.

Special Rules for Medical Records

The Americans with Disabilities Act (ADA) and the Family and Medical Leave Act (FMLA) impose very strict limitations on how you must handle information from medical examinations and inquiries. You must keep the medical information in files that are separate from nonmedical records and keep them in a locked cabinet. To further guarantee the confidentiality of medical records, designate one person to be in charge of those files.

The ADA and FMLA allow very limited disclosure of medical information. You may:

- inform supervisors about necessary restrictions on an employee's duties and about necessary accommodations
- inform first aid and safety workers about a disability that may require emergency treatment or special evacuation procedures, or
- provide medical information required by government officials.

Otherwise, don't disclose medical information about employees. The best policy is to treat all employee medical information as confidential.

Am I required to offer my employees paid vacation, disability, maternity, or sick leave?

No federal law requires you to offer paid vacation, sick leave, disability leave, or maternity leave to your employees. Some states and local governments have different rules, however. A handful of states and cities have passed paid sick leave laws, requiring employers of a certain size to provide at least a few days of paid sick leave per year. A handful of states also have temporary disability insurance programs, which provide employees with some compensation while they are unable to work because of a disability (including pregnancy). A few states also use these programs to provide paid family leave to employees who need time off to bond with a new child or to care for a sick family member.

Many employers choose to offer some paid vacation or sick leave to their employees as a benefit of employment. If you decide to do this, you must apply the policy consistently to all employees. If you offer some employees a more attractive package than others without a legitimate reason, you are opening yourself up to claims of discrimination.

And, while no state requires paid vacation, some states impose rules on employers that choose to do so—for example, that accrued vacation must roll over from year to year and must be paid out at the time of separation.

Must I offer my employees unpaid leave for illness or caretaking repsonsibilities?

Under federal law, there are two situations in which you might be legally required to offer unpaid leave to your employees.

First, if the employee requesting leave has a disability under the Americans with Disabilities Act (see below) and requests the leave as a reasonable accommodation, you may be required to grant the leave request. For example, an employee who needs time off to undergo surgery or treatment for a disabling condition is probably entitled to unpaid leave, unless you can show that providing the leave would be an undue hardship to your business.

Second, your employees might be entitled to unpaid leave under the Family and Medical Leave Act (FMLA). The FMLA requires employers with 50 or more employees to provide unpaid leave to employees for their own serious health conditions, to care for a family member with a serious health condition, or to bond with a new child, among other things. Some states have similar laws that apply to smaller employers or provide leave for additional purposes, such as pregnancy disability leave. See Chapter 4 for an explanation of when you must provide leave under the FMLA.

What am I legally required to do for my employees who have disabilities?

The Americans with Disabilities Act (ADA) prohibits employers from discriminating against applicants or employees with disabilities. However, the ADA does not require employers to hire or retain workers who can't do their jobs. Only "qualified workers with disabilities"—employees who can perform all the essential elements of the job, with or without some form of accommodation from their employers—are protected by the law.

An employee is legally disabled if any one of the following is true:

- The employee has a physical or mental impairment that substantially limits a major life activity (such as the ability to walk, talk, see, hear, breathe, reason, or take care of oneself) or a major bodily function (such as cell growth or the proper working of the immune or respiratory system). Courts tend not to categorically label certain conditions as disabilities. Instead, they consider the effect of the particular condition on the particular employee. An episodic condition or disease in remission that limits a major life activity or bodily function when active qualifies as a disability.
- The employee has a record or history of such impairment.
- The employee is regarded by the employer as having such an impairment, even if the employer is incorrect.

The ADA also requires employers to make reasonable accommodations for employees with disabilities. This means you may have to provide some assistance or make some changes in the job or workplace to enable the worker to do the job. For example, an employer might lower the height of a workspace or install ramps to accommodate a worker in a wheelchair, provide voice-recognition software for a worker with cerebral palsy, or provide TDD telephone equipment for a worker with impaired hearing.

Employees With Mental Disabilities

The ADA applies equally to employees with physical disabilities and employees with mental or psychiatric disabilities. Therefore, workers who suffer from severe depression, bipolar disorder, schizophrenia, attention deficit disorder, and other mental conditions may be covered by the ADA, if the condition meets the ADA's definition of a disability.

Workers with mental disabilities are also entitled to reasonable accommodations. For example, you might allow an employee whose antidepressant medication causes drowsiness in the morning to come in a few hours late, or provide an office with soundproofed walls to reduce distractions for an employee who suffers from attention deficit disorder.

It is the employee's responsibility to inform the employer of any disability that affects the employee's work and to request a reasonable accommodation. Once an employee raises the issue, you must engage in a dialog with the worker to try to figure out what kinds of accommodations might be effective and practical. Although you don't have to provide the precise accommodation your worker requests, you do have to work together to come up with a reasonable solution.

Employers don't have to provide an accommodation if it would cause their business to suffer "undue hardship": significant cost or difficulty, given the size, resources, and structure of the business. There are no hard and fast rules about when an accommodation poses an undue hardship. When faced with this issue, courts consider a number of factors, including:

- the cost of the accommodation
- the size and financial resources of the employer
- the structure of the employer's business, and
- the effect the accommodation would have on the business.

One of my employees just told me that she was sexually harassed by a coworker. What should I do?

Most employers feel anxious when faced with complaints of sexual harassment. And with good reason: Such complaints can lead to workplace tension, government investigations, and even costly legal battles. If the complaint is mishandled, even unintentionally, an employer may unwittingly put itself out of business.

Here are some basics to keep in mind if you receive a complaint:

- **Educate yourself.** Do some research on the law of sexual harassment, including what sexual harassment is, how it is proven in court, and what your responsibilities are as an employer. An excellent place to start is the website for the Equal Employment Opportunity Commission (www.eeoc.gov), the federal agency responsible for administering laws prohibiting discrimination and harassment.
- **Follow established procedures.** If you have an employee handbook or other documented policies relating to sexual harassment, follow those policies. Don't open yourself up to claims of discrimination by acting inconsistently.
- **Interview the people involved.** Start by talking to the person who complained. Then talk to the employee accused of harassment, followed by any witnesses. Get details: what was said or done, when, where, and who else was there.
- **Look for corroboration or contradiction.** Usually, the accuser and accused offer different versions of the incident, leaving you with no way of knowing who's telling the truth. Turn to other sources for clues. For example, schedules, time cards, and other attendance records (for trainings, meetings, and so on) may help you determine if each party was where he or she claimed to be. Witnesses may have seen part of the incident. And in some cases, documents will prove one side right. After all, it's hard to argue with an X-rated email.
- **Keep it confidential.** A sexual harassment complaint can polarize a workplace. Workers will likely side with either the complaining employee or the accused employee, and the rumor mill will start working overtime. Worse, if too many details about the complaint are leaked, you may be accused of damaging the reputation of the alleged victim or alleged harasser and get slapped with a defamation lawsuit. Avoid these problems by sharing information on a need-to-know basis only. But don't promise the complaining employee that you'll keep the complaint entirely confidential. After all, you will probably have to discuss it with the accused employee, and perhaps with witnesses or your superiors.
- **Document everything.** Take notes during your interviews, including important and objective information like the person's full name, the date, and what the person said. Before the interview is over, go back through your notes with the interviewee to make sure you got it right. Write down the steps you have taken to

learn the truth, including interviews you have conducted and documents you have reviewed. Document any action taken against the accused, or the reasons for deciding not to take action. This written record will protect you later if your employee claims that you ignored a complaint or conducted a one-sided investigation.

- **Cooperate with government agencies.** If the accuser files a complaint with a government agency (either the federal Equal Employment Opportunity Commission (EEOC) or an equivalent state agency), that agency may investigate. Try to provide the agency with the materials it requests, but remember that the agency is gathering evidence that could be used against you later. This is a good time to consider hiring a lawyer to advise you.
- **Don't retaliate.** It is against the law to punish someone for making a sexual harassment complaint. The most obvious forms of retaliation are termination, discipline, demotion, pay cuts, or threats of any of these actions. More subtle forms of retaliation may include changing the shift hours or work area of the accuser, changing the accuser's job responsibilities or reporting relationships, or leaving the accuser out of meetings and other office functions.
- **Take appropriate action against the harasser.** Once you have gathered all the information available, sit down and figure out what really happened. If you conclude that some form of sexual harassment occurred, decide how to discipline the harasser appropriately. Once you have decided on an appropriate action, take it quickly, document it, and notify the accuser.

My employees' religious differences are causing strife in the workplace. What am I required to do?

This is a tricky area. An increasing number of employees are claiming religious discrimination. And unfortunately, the law in this delicate area is unclear.

First, make sure you aren't imposing your religious beliefs on your employees. You have the legal right to discuss your own religious beliefs with an employee, if you're so inclined, but you can't persist to the point that the employee feels you're being hostile, intimidating, or offensive. So if an employee objects to your discussion of religious subjects or you get even an inkling that your religious advances are unwelcome, back off. Otherwise, you may find yourself embroiled in a lawsuit or administrative proceeding.

If employees complain to you that a coworker is badgering them with religious views, you have a right—if not a duty—to intervene, although you must, of course, use the utmost tact and sensitivity.

While you may feel that the best way to resolve these knotty problems is to simply banish religion from the workplace, that's generally not a viable alternative. You're legally required to accommodate the religious needs of employees by, for example, allowing employees to wear religious attire to work or giving employees time off for religious holidays. You don't, however, have to make an accommodation that would impose an undue hardship, such as those requiring more than ordinary administrative costs or diminishing efficiency in other jobs.

Can I read employee messages sent on the company email system?

Unless you actively take steps to assure employees that you won't read their email, you are on fairly safe legal ground looking at employees' emails sent on your system, as long as you have a legitimate business reason for doing so. Courts have consistently held that employees don't have a reasonable expectation of privacy in email sent on company equipment.

But savvy employers don't rely on this legal trend alone to protect themselves. They go a step further and create a written policy, usually in an employee handbook, notifying employees that emails sent on company systems are not private. Some companies also ask employees to acknowledge, in writing, that they received and understood the policy. A signed acknowledgment statement like this will make it next to impossible for an employee to argue that you violated his or her privacy rights by monitoring emails.

It's been a bad year for my business, and it looks as though I may have to lay off some workers. Are there legal problems to avoid?

As long as your employees work at will, you're free to lay off or terminate employees because business conditions require it. But if you do cut back, don't leave your business open to claims that the layoffs were really a pretext for getting rid of employees for illegal reasons, such as discrimination.

Be sensitive to how your actions may be perceived. If the layoff primarily affects workers of a particular race, women, or older employees, someone may well question your motives. Make sure that you have sound business reasons for laying off each employee.

Larger employers—those with at least 100 employees—are legally required to give employees 60 days' notice before a plant closing or mass layoff. This requirement is set out in the federal Workers Adjustment and Retraining Notification Act (WARN Act). There are plenty of exceptions to the WARN Act, however. Most notably, it applies only if a large number of employees are being let go. Many states have passed similar laws, some of which apply to smaller employers and/or layoffs involving fewer employees. In a few states, employers are required to give more than notice; for example, they may have to pay a small severance or continue paying for health insurance coverage for laid-off workers.

Can I fire employees for criticizing the company on Facebook?

As some employers have learned the hard way, firing or disciplining employees for posting statements that are critical of the company, their supervisors, or workplace rules might violate the National Labor Relations Act (NLRA), the primary federal law that governs labor issues and unions. What do employee posts have to do with labor relations? The NLRA protects the rights of employees to communicate with each other about the terms and conditions of employment and join together to bring their concerns to their employer (called "protected concerted activity" or simply "Section 7 activity"), whether or not a union represents them. This includes communications through social media.

To be protected activity, more than one employee must be involved. Employees who are engaged in solitary griping or name-calling are not protected. However, it can be tough to tell whether a complaint has crossed the line into protected territory. Is it enough if one coworker hits the "like" button? Or if an angry rant filled with curse words includes a sentence challenging a workplace rule or practice? These issues are still very much in play. For now, the best practice is to double-check with a lawyer before you fire an employee for online posts about work, no matter how angry or uncivil the post.

How can I make sure that my employees don't reveal my company's trade secrets to a competitor, especially after they leave the company?

You should take two steps to protect your trade secrets from disclosure by former employees. First, always treat your trade secrets as confidential. Second, require any employee who will learn your trade secrets to sign a nondisclosure agreement.

A trade secret is any information that is treated as secret and that provides its owner with a competitive advantage in the market. In other words, the information must be handled in a manner that can reasonably be expected to prevent others from learning about it. Examples of trade secrets might include recipes, manufacturing processes, customer or pricing lists, and ideas for new products. If you own a trade secret, you have the legal right to prevent anyone from disclosing, copying, or using it, and you can sue anyone who violates these rights to your disadvantage.

Always keep your trade secrets confidential. For example, you should mark documents containing trade secrets "confidential" and limit their circulation, disclose trade secret material only to those employees with a real need to know, keep trade secret materials in a safe place, and have a written policy stating that trade secrets are not to be revealed to outsiders.

In addition to taking steps to keep your trade secrets confidential, you should also require any employee who will have access to your trade secrets to sign a nondisclosure agreement (NDA) promising not to reveal your secrets.

What are my legal obligations to an employee who is leaving the company?

Surprisingly, your responsibility to your employees doesn't necessarily end when the employment relationship ends. Even after an employee quits or is fired, you may have to:

- **Provide the employee's final paycheck in accordance with state law.** Most states require that an employee receive this check fairly quickly, sometimes immediately after getting fired.
- **Provide severance pay.** No law requires employers to provide severance pay (although a few states require employers to pay severance to workers fired in a plant closure). But if you promised to pay severance orally or in writing (for example, in a written contract or company policy), you must do so.
- **Give information on continuation of health insurance, under a federal law called the Consolidated Omnibus Budget Reconciliation Act (COBRA).** If you offer your employees health insurance, and your company has 20 or more employees, you must notify departing employees of their right to continue their coverage under the company's group health insurance plan for a specified period. You aren't required to pay for the coverage, however.
- **Allow former employees to view their personnel files.** Most states give employees and former employees the legal right to see their personnel files, and to receive copies of at least some of the documents relating to their jobs. State laws vary as to how long employers must keep these records for former employees.

I've been asked to give a reference for a former employee I had to fire. I don't want to be too positive about him, but I am also afraid he might sue me for unflattering remarks. Advice?

The key to protecting yourself is to stick to the facts and act in good faith. You'll get in trouble only if you exaggerate or cover up the truth, or if you are motivated by a desire to harm your former employee.

Former employees who feel maligned can sue for defamation. However, to win a defamation case, the employee must prove that you intentionally gave out false information and that the information harmed the employee's reputation. If you can show that the information you provided was true, the lawsuit will be dismissed.

And even if it turns out that the information you provided is untrue, employers in most states are entitled to protection based on a legal doctrine called "qualified privilege." To receive protection, you will probably have to show all of the following:

- that either a former employee or that employee's prospective employer asked you to provide a reference
- that you limited your comments to truthful, job-related statements, and
- that your comments weren't motivated by ill will or malice toward the employee.

A practical policy—and one that gives you a high degree of legal protection—is simply not to discuss an employee with prospective employers if you can't say something positive. Just tell the person inquiring that your policy is to only provide dates of employment, job title, and salary. And warn former employees not to list you as a reference if you won't be able to give a positive one.

Where an employee's record is truly mixed, it's usually possible to accent the positive while you try to put negative information into a more favorable perspective. If you do choose to go into detail, don't hide the bad news. In very extreme cases, you could be sued by the new employer for concealing this information (for example, where the employee goes on to commit a serious crime or engage in dangerous conduct that you could have warned about).

Do I have the same legal obligations to independent contractors as I do to employees?

Generally, an employer has more obligations, both legally and financially, to employees than to independent contractors. The workplace rights guaranteed to employees do not protect independent contractors, for the most part. And an employer must make certain contributions to the government on behalf of its employees, while independent contractors are expected to make these payments themselves.

Here are a number of rules that apply only to employees:

- **Antidiscrimination laws.** Most laws prohibiting employers from discriminating against employees or applicants based on such characteristics as race, gender, national origin, religion, age, or disability do not protect independent contractors.
- **Wage and hour laws.** Independent contractors are not covered by laws governing the minimum wage, overtime pay, and the like.
- **Medical and parental leave laws.** You are not required to offer independent contractors medical or parental leave.
- **Workers' compensation laws.** You do not have to provide workers' compensation for independent contractors.
- **Unemployment insurance.** You do not have to contribute to your state's unemployment insurance fund for independent contractors.
- **Social Security taxes.** You are not required to make any Social Security or Medicare payments on behalf of independent contractors.
- **Wage withholding.** You are not required to withhold state or federal income tax, or state disability insurance

payments (where applicable) from the paychecks of independent contractors.

See Chapter 4 for details on employee rights regarding wage and hour laws, discrimination, and other issues.

When can I classify a worker as an independent contractor?

Different government agencies use different tests to decide whether workers should be classified as independent contractors or employees. Generally, these tests are intended to figure out whether an independent contractor is truly a self-employed businessperson offering services to the general public. The more discretion a worker has to decide how, when, and for whom to perform work, the more likely that the worker is an independent contractor. For example, an independent contractor might do similar work for other companies, provide the tools and equipment to do the job, decide how to do the job (including when, where, and in what order to do the work), and hire employees or assistants to help out with big projects. On the other hand, a worker who works only for you, under conditions determined by you, is more likely to be classified as an employee.

Employers that misclassify employees as independent contractors, even unintentionally, can be required to pay large sums in unpaid minimum wages, overtime, and penalties.

RESOURCE

For more about employers' rights and responsibilities, see these Nolo books:

- *The Employer's Legal Handbook,* by Fred S. Steingold. Explains employers' legal rights and responsibilities in detail.
- *The Job Description Handbook,* by Margie Mader-Clark. Helps you write job descriptions that are effective and legal.
- *Dealing With Problem Employees,* by Amy DelPo and Lisa Guerin. Offers employers step-by-step instructions for handling problems in the workplace, from giving effective performance evaluations to terminating employment when things don't work out.
- *The Essential Guide to Federal Employment Laws,* by Lisa Guerin and Sachi Barreiro. Summarizes every major federal workplace law and provides compliance tips, resources, record-keeping requirements, and more.
- *The Manager's Legal Handbook,* by Lisa Guerin and Sachi Barreiro. Provides all the basic information, tips, and real-world examples managers need to answer their employment law questions.
- *The Performance Appraisal Handbook,* by Amy DelPo. Gives information, advice, and instructions on how to give legal, effective performance evaluations.
- *Create Your Own Employee Handbook,* by Lisa Guerin and Amy DelPo. Shows you all the practical information, sample policies, and forms you need to make an employee handbook that works for your company.

- *The Essential Guide to Handling Workplace Harassment & Discrimination,* by Deborah C. England. Explains how to recognize, prevent, investigate, and remedy harassment and discrimination in the workplace.
- *The Essential Guide to Workplace Investigations,* by Lisa Guerin. Provides step-by-step instructions for investigating common problems—and taking effective action to stop them.
- *Smart Policies for Workplace Technologies,* by Lisa Guerin. Provides sensible information and sample policies for employee use of email, cellphones, instant messaging, and more.
- *The Employee Perfomrnace Handbook,* by Margie Mader-Clark and Lisa Guerin. Gives in-depth information on how to effectively discipline employees while avoiding legal pitfalls.
- *The Essential Guide to Family & Medical Leave,* by Lisa Guerin and Deborah C. England. Covers the ins and outs of the Family and Medical Leave Act (FMLA).
- Information on independent contractors can be found in *Working With Independent Contractors,* by Stephen Fishman.
- *Consultant and Independent Contractor Agreements,* by Stephen Fishman. Helps you draft legal agreements with independent contractors after you've decided to hire them.

ONLINE HELP

The following sites are good resources for general small business information:

- **www.nolo.com** Nolo offers free information and books, software, and forms for small businesses and employers on a wide variety of subjects, including starting and running your small business and hiring employees.
- **www.nfib.com** The National Federation of Independent Business provides news, workshops, and action alerts for small business owners. The NFIB is the nation's largest advocacy organization for small and independent businesses.
- **www.sba.gov** The Small Business Administration provides information about starting, financing, and expanding your small business.
- **www.eeoc.gov** The Equal Employment Opportunity Commission provides information on federal discrimination laws and lists of state resources.
- **www.dol.gov** The U.S. Department of Labor website includes information on wage and hour laws, workers' compensation, family and medical leave, links to state labor offices, and much more.

CHAPTER

6

Patents

To invent, you need a good imagination and a pile of junk.

—**Thomas Edison**

Many of us muse about the million-dollar idea: the invention that will make life easier for others and more lucrative for us. Most of these ideas never get off the ground, however; we decide it's not really worth the time and effort to create the perfect dog toothbrush, clothes hanger, or juice squeezer. But every now and then we may hit on a winner—an idea worth developing, marketing, and protecting. In these situations, we must turn to the patent laws for help.

This chapter addresses the basic legal issues that arise in the patent area, answering questions such as:

- What is a patent?
- When does a particular invention qualify for a patent?
- How do you get a patent in the United States or abroad?
- How are patent rights enforced?
- How can you profit from your patent?

Qualifying for a Patent

There is nothing which persevering effort and unceasing and diligent care cannot accomplish.

—**Seneca**

A patent is a document issued by the U.S. Patent and Trademark Office (PTO) that grants a monopoly for a limited period of time on the right to manufacture, use, and sell an invention.

What types of inventions can be patented?

The PTO issues three different kinds of patents: utility patents, design patents, and plant patents.

Design patents filed on or after May 13, 2015 last for 15 years from the date the patent issues. Plant and utility patents last for 20 years from the date of filing.

To qualify for a utility patent—by far the most common type of patent—an invention must be:

- a process or method for producing a useful, concrete, and tangible result (such as a genetic engineering procedure, an investment strategy, or computer software)
- a machine (usually something with moving parts or circuitry, such as a cigarette lighter, sewage treatment system, laser, or photocopier)
- an article of manufacture (such as an eraser, tire, transistor, or hand tool)
- a composition of matter (such as a chemical composition, drug, soap, or genetically altered life form), or
- an improvement of an invention that fits within one of the first four categories.

Often, an invention will fall into more than one category. For instance, a laser can usually be described both as a process (the steps necessary to produce the laser beam) and a machine (a device that implements the steps to produce the laser beam). Regardless of the number of categories into which a particular invention fits, it can receive only one utility patent.

If an invention fits into one of the categories described above, it is known as "statutory subject matter" and has passed the first test in qualifying for a patent. But an inventor's creation must overcome several additional hurdles before the PTO will issue a patent. The invention must also:

- have some utility, no matter how trivial
- be novel (that is, it must be different from all previous inventions in some important way), and
- be nonobvious (a surprising and significant development) to somebody who understands the technical field of the invention.

For design patents, the law requires that the design be novel, nonobvious, and nonfunctional. For example, a new shape for a car fender, bottle, or flashlight that doesn't improve how it functions would qualify.

Finally, plants may qualify for a patent if they are both novel and nonobvious. Plant patents are issued less frequently than any other type of patent.

More Examples of Patentable Subject Matter

The following items are just some of the things that might qualify for patent protection: biological inventions; carpet designs; new chemical formulas, processes, or procedures; clothing accessories and designs; computer hardware and peripherals; computer software; containers; cosmetics; decorative hardware; electrical inventions; electronic circuits; fabrics and fabric designs; food inventions; furniture design; games (board, box, and instructions); housewares; jewelry; laser light shows; machines; magic tricks or techniques; mechanical inventions; medical accessories and devices; medicines; methods of doing business; musical instruments; odors; plants; recreational gear; and sporting goods (designs and equipment).

What types of inventions cannot be patented?

Some types of inventions will not qualify for a patent, no matter how interesting or important they are. For example, mathematical formulas, laws of nature, newly discovered substances that occur naturally in the world, and purely theoretical phenomena—for instance, a scientific principle like superconductivity without regard to its use in the real world—have long been considered unpatentable. This means, for example, that you can't patent a general mathematical approach to problem solving or a newly discovered painkiller in its natural state.

In addition, the following categories of inventions don't qualify for patents:

- human genes and isolated DNA, (although *synthetic* DNA created in a laboratory can be patented)
- processes done entirely by human motor coordination, such as choreographed dance routines or a method for meditation
- most protocols and methods used to perform surgery on humans
- printed matter that has no unique physical shape or structure associated with it
- unsafe new drugs
- inventions useful only for illegal purposes, and
- nonoperable inventions, including "perpetual motion" machines (which are presumed to be nonoperable because to operate they would have to violate certain bedrock scientific principles).

Can computer software qualify for patent protection?

Patents don't issue on software itself. Rather, they issue on inventions that use innovative software to produce a useful, concrete, and tangible result. Such inventions are "software-based." Patentable software-based inventions often involve software that connects to and runs hardware components. An example is a device that monitors a patient's heart functions, feeds the raw information into a computer where a program analyzes the information according to a set of algorithms, and causes the results to be displayed on a monitor in a format that shows whether a person is at risk for a heart attack. None of the components of this invention qualify for a patent individually—the physical items have already been invented and the algorithm itself is not patentable. But the overall invention did qualify for a U.S. patent, and the software was the key aspect of the invention.

In 2014, the Supreme Court's decision in *Alice Corp. v. CLS Bank International* cast a cloud over many existing software-based patents. In this case, the Supreme Court invalidated a software patent because the method—one that employed a computer-assisted process for exchanging financial obligations—was an abstract idea, ineligible for patent protection. This court decision set the stage for invalidation of many software patents that simply applied an existing obvious idea to a software or computer setting.

In any event, most software-based inventions do not qualify for patents because they are considered obvious over the prior art. They must be protected another way—usually under trade secret or copyright laws (discussed in Chapters 7 and 8).

Can a business method qualify for a utility patent?

A business method is a series of steps that express some business activity. Examples include a method of calculating an interest rate or a system for evaluating employee performance. Before 1988, the PTO rarely granted patents for methods of doing business. Then, in 1988, the United States Court of Appeals for the Federal Circuit changed this. (*State Street Bank & Trust Co. v. Signal Financial Group, Inc.* 149 F.3d 1368 (Fed. Cir. 1998).) The court ruled that patent laws were intended to protect business methods, so long as the method produced a "useful, concrete and tangible result."

However, in 2014, the future of business method patents became murkier when the Supreme Court declared a software patent invalid because the method employed—a computer-assisted process for exchanging financial obligations—was an abstract idea, ineligible for patent protection. The Supreme Court ruling may have jeopardized hundreds of existing business method patents because it held that an innovator couldn't simply port an existing process—for example, auction bidding—to the Internet and claim that the resulting combination was patentable subject matter. (*Alice Corporation v. CLS Bank International,* 134 S.Ct. 2347 (2014).)

Is it possible to obtain a patent on forms of life?

In *Association for Molecular Pathology v. Myriad Genetics*, 569 U.S. ___ (2013), the Supreme Court ruled that human genes and their associated isolated DNA sequences cannot be patented. However, synthetic DNA—DNA sequences created by humans—can be patented. In addition, genetically altered life forms, from bacteria to corn to cows, may be patented.

What changes resulted from passage of the America Invents Act?

The Leahy-Smith America Invents Act (AIA) made major modifications to the patent law, all of which went into effect in March, 2013. The major change resulting from passage of the Act was that the United States (like almost all other nations) now used a first-to-file system. In other words, after March, 2013, U.S. patents are issued based on which inventor gets to the patent office first, not the date of invention. The new law also eliminates the previous one-year on-sale bar which permitted inventors to sell or publish their invention within a one-year window of the filing. An exception: If the actual inventor-applicant created the publication and it was made up to one year before the filing date, it will not bar the application. In addition, if an inventor is sued for infringement

Are You the First?

As discussed above, patents are awarded only on new and nonobvious inventions. How can an inventor find out whether an invention is really new? Start by finding out whether it has ever been patented. Although a number of great inventions have never received a patent, most have. A quick spin through the patent database can provide a good head start on finding out just how innovative an invention really is.

The Internet can be used for free access to patents. The U.S. Patent and Trademark Office (www.uspto.gov), Google patents (www.google.com/patents), and the European Patent Office, or EPO (www.epo. org) provide free online databases where you simply type in keywords that describe your invention.

Commercial, fee-based databases often offer more choices than the free USPTO site. Below are some fee-based patent databases:

- Thomson Innovation (http://info.thomsoninnovation.com)
- LexisNexis (www.lexis-nexis.com)
- IP.com (www.ip.com), and
- PatBase (www.patbase.com).

Another great resource for complete patent searching is a network of approximately 25 special libraries called Patent and Trademark Resource Centers (PTRCs). While a complete patent search can be done for free in these libraries, many of them also offer computer searches for a reasonable fee. Consult the PTO website at www.uspto.gov to find the PTRC nearest you.

but was commercially using the patented technology more than one year before the filing date of the claimed invention, the inventor has a defense (although that defense doesn't invalidate the patent).

What makes an invention novel?

In the context of a patent application, an invention is considered novel when it is different from all previous inventions (called "prior art") in one or more of its constituent elements. When deciding whether an invention is novel, the PTO will consider all prior art that existed as of the date the inventor files a patent application on the invention.

An invention will flunk the novelty test if it was described in a published document or put to public use before the patent application was filed.

When is an invention considered nonobvious?

To qualify for a patent, an invention must be nonobvious as well as novel. An invention is considered nonobvious if someone who is skilled in the particular field of the invention would view it as an unexpected or surprising development.

For example, in December 2014, Future Enterprises invents a portable, high-quality wireless scanner that can be worn like eyeglasses. A computer engineer would most likely find this invention to be surprising and unexpected. Even though it isn't generally that surprising when computer-based technology becomes more portable, the specific way in which the portability is accomplished by this invention (placing the scanner at eye level) would be a breakthrough in the field—and thus unobvious. Contrast this with a bicycle developer who uses a new, light but strong metal alloy to build his bicycles. Most people skilled in the art of bicycle manufacturing would consider the use of the new alloy in the bicycle to be obvious, given that low weight is a desirable aspect of high-quality bicycles.

Figuring out whether an invention will be considered nonobvious by the PTO is difficult because it is such a subjective exercise—what one patent examiner considers surprising another may not. In addition, the examiner will usually be asked to make the nonobviousness determination well after the date of the filing, because of delays inherent in the patent process. The danger of this type of retroactive assessment is that the examiner may unconsciously be affected by intervening technical improvements. To avoid this, the examiner generally relies only on the prior-art references (documents describing previous inventions) that existed as of the date of filing.

As an example, assume that in 2016, Future Enterprises' application for a patent on the 2014 invention is being examined in the PTO. Assume further that by 2016 you can find a portable "eyeglass scanner" in any consumer electronics store for under $200. The patent examiner will have to go back to when the scanner was invented to fully appreciate how surprising and unexpected it was when it was first conceived—and ignore the fact that in 2016 the technology of the invention is very common.

What makes an invention useful?

Patents may be granted for inventions that have some type of usefulness (utility), even if the use is humorous. For example, there may not be many people who need a musical condom or a motorized spaghetti fork, but both items have some use. However, the invention must work—at least in theory. Thus, a new approach to manufacturing superconducting materials may qualify for a patent if it has a sound theoretical basis—even if it hasn't yet been shown to work in practice. But a new drug that has no theoretical basis and hasn't been tested will not qualify for a patent.

The inventor need not show utility to qualify for a design or plant patent.

Obtaining a Patent

Many times a day I realize how much my own outer and inner life is built upon the labors of my fellow men, both living and dead, and how earnestly I must exert myself in order to give in return as much as I have received.

—**Albert Einstein**

Because a patent grants the inventor a monopoly on the patented invention for a relatively long period of time, patent applications are rigorously examined by the Patent and Trademark Office (PTO). Typically, a patent application travels back and forth between the applicant and the patent examiner until both sides agree on which aspects of an invention the patent will cover, if any. During this process, the inventor may have to amend some of the patent claims—the descriptions of exactly what the invention is and what it does—to distinguish the invention from the prior art. This process typically takes a year or two.

If an agreement is reached, the PTO "allows" the application and publishes a brief description of the patent in a weekly online publication called the *Official Gazette.* (You can access it on the PTO website at www.uspto.gov.) If no one objects to the patent as published, and the applicant pays the required issuance fee, the PTO provides the applicant with a document called a patent deed, which we colloquially refer to as a patent. The patent deed consists primarily of the information submitted in the patent application, as modified during the patent-examination process.

What information is typically included in a patent application?

There is no such thing as an automatic patent through creation or usage of an invention. To receive patent protection, an inventor must file an application, pay the appropriate fees, and obtain a patent. To apply for a U.S. patent, the inventor must file the application with a branch of the U.S. Department of Commerce known as the U.S. Patent and Trademark Office, or PTO. A U.S. patent application typically consists of:

- an information disclosure statement —that is, an explanation of how the invention differs from all previous and similar developments (the "prior art")
- a detailed description of the structure and operation of the invention (called a patent specification) that explains how to build and use the invention
- a precise description of the aspects of the invention to be covered by the patent (called the patent claims)
- all drawings that are necessary to fully explain the specification and claims
- a patent application declaration—a statement under oath that the information in the application is true, and
- the filing fee.

Understanding the Provisional Patent Application

Often inventors want to have a patent application on file when they show their invention to prospective manufacturers, to discourage rip-offs. Also, inventors like to get their invention on record as early as possible in case someone else comes up with the same invention. To accomplish both of these goals, an inventor may file what is known as a provisional patent application (PPA). The PPA need only contain a complete description of the structure and operation of an invention and any drawings that are necessary to understand it—it need not contain claims, formal drawings, a patent application declaration, or an information disclosure statement.

An inventor who files a regular patent application within one year of filing a PPA can claim the PPA's filing date for the regular patent application. If the regular patent application includes any new matter (technical information about the invention) that wasn't in the PPA, the inventor won't be able to rely on the PPA's filing date for the new matter.

In addition, small inventors often include a declaration asking for a reduction in the filing fee.

How are U.S. patents protected abroad?

Patent rights originate in the U.S. Constitution and are implemented exclusively by federal laws passed by Congress. These laws define the kinds of inventions that are patentable and the procedures that must be followed to apply for, receive, and maintain patent rights for the duration of the patent.

All other industrialized countries offer patent protection as well. Though patent requirements and rules differ from country to country, several international treaties (including the Patent Cooperation Treaty and the Paris Convention) allow U.S. inventors to obtain patent protection in other countries that have adopted the treaties if the inventors take certain required steps, such as filing a patent application in the countries on a timely basis and paying required patent fees.

Enforcing a Patent

Once a patent is issued, it is up to the owner to enforce it. If friendly negotiations fail, enforcement involves two basic steps:

- making a determination that the patent is being illegally violated (infringed), and
- filing a federal court action to enforce the patent.

Because enforcing a patent can be a long and expensive process, many potential patent infringement suits never get filed. Instead, the patent owner often settles with the infringer. Frequently, an infringer will pay a reasonable license fee that allows the infringer to continue using the invention.

What constitutes infringement of a patent?

To decide whether an inventor is violating a patent, you must carefully examine the patent's claims (most patents contain more than one of these terse statements of the scope of the invention) and compare the elements of each claim with the elements of the accused infringer's device or process. If the elements of a patent claim match the elements of the device or process (called "reading on" or "teaching" the device or process), an infringement has occurred. Even if the claims don't literally match the infringing device, it is possible that a court would find an infringement by applying what's known as the "doctrine of equivalents." In these cases, the invention in the patent and the allegedly infringing device or process are sufficiently equivalent in what they do and how they do it to warrant a finding of infringement.

For example, Steve invents a tennis racket with a scorekeeper embedded in the racket handle's end. The invention is claimed as a tennis racket handle that combines grasping and scorekeeping functions. Steve receives a patent on this invention. Later, Megan invents and sells a tennis racket with a transparent handle that provides a more sophisticated scorekeeping device than Steve's racket. Even though Megan's invention improves on Steve's invention in certain respects, it will most likely be held to be an infringement of Steve's invention, for one of two reasons:

- Megan's invention teaches the same elements as those claimed in Steve's patent (a tennis racket handle with two functions), or
- considering what it is and how it works, Megan's invention is the substantial equivalent of Steve's invention (the doctrine of equivalents).

You can't always rely on the doctrine of equivalents to protect your invention from infringers, however. If you amended your patent claims during the application process (something the patent examiner might ask you to do), you cannot use the doctrine of equivalents to go after infringers unless:

- your amendment involved a feature of the invention that was unforeseeable when you originally filed the application, or
- your amendment could not be included in the original claim for some other reason.

These rules are based on a Supreme Court case from 2002 (*Festo v. Shoketsu Kinzoku Kabushiki Co. Ltd.*, 122 S.Ct. 1831).

What remedies are available for patent infringement?

A patent owner may enforce the patent by bringing a patent infringement action (lawsuit) in federal court against anyone who uses the invention without permission. If the lawsuit is successful, the court will take one of two approaches. It may issue a court order (called an injunction) preventing the infringer from any further use or sale of the infringing device and award damages to the patent owner. Or, the court may work with the parties to hammer out an agreement under which the infringing party will pay the patent owner royalties in exchange for permission to use the infringing device.

Bringing a patent infringement action can be tricky, because it is possible for the alleged infringer to defend by proving to the court that the patent is really invalid (most often by showing that the PTO made a mistake in issuing the patent in the first place). In a substantial number of patent infringement cases, the patent is found invalid and the lawsuit dismissed, leaving the patent owner in a worse position than before the lawsuit.

When does patent protection end?

Patent protection usually ends when the patent expires. For all utility patents filed before June 8, 1995, the patent term is 17 years from the date of issuance. For utility patents filed on or after June 8, 1995, the patent term is 20 years from the date of filing. For design patents, the period is 14 years from date of issuance. For plant patents, the period is 17 years from date of issuance.

A patent may expire if its owner fails to pay required maintenance fees. Usually this occurs because attempts to commercially exploit the underlying invention have failed and the patent owner chooses not to throw good money after bad.

Patent protection ends if a patent is found to be invalid. This may happen if someone shows that the patent application was insufficient or that the applicant committed fraud on the PTO, usually by lying or failing to disclose the applicant's knowledge about prior art that would legally prevent issuance of the patent. A patent may also be invalidated if someone shows that the inventor engaged in illegal conduct when using the patent—such as conspiring with a patent licensee to exclude other companies from competing with them.

Once a patent has expired, the invention described by the patent falls into the public domain: It can be used by anyone without permission from the owner of the expired patent. The basic technologies underlying television and personal computers are good examples of valuable inventions that are no longer covered by in-force patents.

The fact that an invention is in the public domain does not mean that subsequent developments based on the original invention are also in the public domain. New inventions that improve public domain technology are constantly being conceived and patented. For example, televisions and personal computers that roll off today's assembly lines employ many recent inventions that are covered by in-force patents.

The Life of an Invention

Although most inventors are concerned with the rights a patent grants during its monopoly or in-force period (from the date the patent issues until it expires), the law actually recognizes five "rights" periods in the life of an invention. These five periods are as follows:

1. **Invention conceived but not yet documented.** When an inventor conceives an invention but hasn't yet made any written, signed, dated, and witnessed record of it, the inventor has no rights whatsoever.
2. **Invention documented but patent application not yet filed.** Even after recording an invention with properly signed and witnessed documentation, the inventor still has no patent rights. The invention may also be treated as a "trade secret"—that is, kept confidential. This gives the inventor the legal right to sue and recover damages from anyone who illegally learns of the invention—for example, through industrial spying.
3. **Patent pending (patent application filed but not yet issued).** During the patent pending period, including the one-year period after a provisional patent application is filed, the inventor's rights are the same as they are in Period 2, above, with one exception. If the patent owner intends to also file for a patent abroad, the PTO will publish the application 18 months after the earliest claimed filing date. An inventor whose application is published before a patent issues may obtain royalties from an infringer from the date of publication, as long as the application later issues as a patent and the infringer had actual notice of the published application. Otherwise, the inventor has no rights whatsoever against infringers—only the hope of a future monopoly, which doesn't commence until a patent issues.

   By law, the PTO must keep all patent applications secret until the application is published or the patent issues, whichever comes first. The patent pending period usually lasts from one to three years.
4. **In-force patent (patent issued but hasn't yet expired).** After the patent issues, the patent owner can bring and maintain a lawsuit for patent infringement against anyone who makes, uses, or sells the invention without permission. The patent's in-force period lasts from the date it issues until it expires. Also, after the patent issues, it becomes a public record or publication that prevents others from getting patents on the same or similar inventions—that is, it becomes "prior art" to anyone who files a subsequent patent application.
5. **Patent expired.** After the patent expires, the patent owner has no further rights, although infringement suits can still be brought for any infringement that occurred during the patent's in-force period as long as the suit is filed within the time required by law. An expired patent remains a valid "prior-art reference" forever.

Putting a Patent to Work

Our aspirations are our possibilities.

—**Robert Browning**

On its own, a patent has no value. A patent becomes valuable only when a patent owner takes action to profit from his or her monopoly position. There are several basic approaches to making money from a patent.

How can an inventor make money with a patent?

Some inventors start new companies to develop and market their patented inventions. This is not typical, however, because the majority of inventors would rather invent things than run a business. More often, an inventor makes arrangements with an existing company to develop and market the invention. This arrangement usually takes the form of a license (contract) authorizing the developer to commercially exploit the invention in exchange for paying the patent owner royalties for each invention sold. Or, in a common variation of this arrangement, the inventor may sell all the rights to the invention for a lump sum.

What does it mean to license an invention?

A license is written permission to use an invention. A license may be exclusive (if only one manufacturer is licensed to develop the invention) or nonexclusive (if a number of manufacturers are licensed to develop it). The license may be for the entire duration of the patent or for a shorter period of time.

The developer itself may license other companies to market or distribute the invention. The extent to which the inventor will benefit from these sublicenses depends on the terms of the agreement between the inventor and the developer. Especially when inventions result from work done in the course of employment, the employer-business usually ends up owning the patent rights and receives all or most of the royalties based on subsequent licensing activity. (See the next question.)

In many cases, a developer will trade licenses with other companies—called cross-licensing—so that companies involved in the trade will benefit from each other's technology. For example, assume that two computer companies each own several patents on newly developed remote-controlled techniques. Because each company would be strengthened by being able to use the other company's inventions as well as its own, the companies might agree to swap permissions to use their respective inventions.

Can inventors who are employed by a company benefit from their inventions?

Typically, inventor-employees who invent in the course of their employment are bound by employment agreements that automatically assign all rights in the invention to the employer. While smart research and development companies give their inventors bonuses for valuable inventions, they aren't legally obligated to do so (unless the contract requires it).

If there is no employment agreement, the employer may still own rights to an employee-created invention under the "employed to invent" rule. If an inventor is employed—even without a written employment agreement—to accomplish a defined task, or is hired or directed to create an invention, the employer will own all rights to the subsequent invention.

If there is no employment agreement and the inventor is not employed to invent, the inventor may retain the right to exploit the invention, but the employer is given a nonexclusive right to use the invention for its internal purposes (this is called a shop right). For example, Robert is a machinist in a machine shop and invents a new process for handling a particular type of metal. If Robert isn't employed to invent and hasn't signed an employment agreement giving the shop all rights to the invention, Robert can patent and exploit the invention for himself. The shop, however, would retain the right to use the new process without having to pay Robert.

How Patents Differ From Copyrights and Trademarks

In some cases, a design may be subject to patent, trademark, and copyright protection all at the same time.

How do patents differ from copyrights?

With the exception of innovative designs, patents are closely associated with things and processes that are useful in the real world. Almost at the opposite end of the spectrum, copyright applies to expressive arts such as novels, fine and graphic arts, music, photography, software, video, cinema, and choreography. While it is possible to get a patent on technologies used in the arts, it is copyright that keeps one artist from stealing another artist's creative work.

An exception to the general rule that patents and copyright don't overlap can be found in product designs. It is possible to get a design patent on the purely ornamental (nonfunctional) aspects of a product design and also claim a copyright in the same design. For example, the stylistic fins of a car's rear fenders may qualify for both a design patent (because they are strictly ornamental) and copyright (as to their expressive elements).

For more information about copyright law, see Chapter 7.

What's the difference between patent and trademark?

Generally speaking, patents allow the creator of certain kinds of inventions that contain new ideas to keep others from making commercial use of those ideas without the creator's permission. Trademark, on the other hand, is not concerned with how a new technology is used. Rather, it applies to the names, logos, and other devices—such as color, sound, and smell—that are used to identify the source of goods or services and distinguish them from their competition.

Generally, patent and trademark laws do not overlap. When it comes to a product design, however—say, jewelry or a distinctively shaped musical instrument—it may be possible to obtain a patent on a design aspect of the device while invoking trademark law to protect the design as a product identifier. For example, a surfboard manufacturer might receive a patent for a surfboard design that mimics the design used in a popular surfing film. If the design is intended to be—and actually is—used to distinguish the particular type of surfboard in the marketplace, trademark law may kick in to protect the appearance of the board.

For more information about trademarks, see Chapter 8.

RESOURCE

For more information about patents, see these Nolo books:

- *Patent It Yourself,* David Pressman and Thomas Tuytschaevers. Takes you step by step through the process of getting a patent without hiring a patent lawyer.
- *Patent Pending in 24 Hours,* by Richard Stim and David Pressman. Explains how to prepare and file a provisional patent application.
- *Patent Searching Made Easy,* by David Hitchcock. Explains the various methods for performing patent research.
- *Profit From Your Idea,* by Richard Stim. Explains how to realize your invention's commercial potential.
- *Patent, Copyright & Trademark,* by Richard Stim. Provides concise definitions and examples of the important words and phrases commonly used in patent law.
- *Nolo's Patents for Beginners,* by David Pressman and Richard Stim. Explains all of the essential patent principles in plain English.

ONLINE HELP

The following sites are good resources about patent law:

- **www.nolo.com** Nolo provides a system for filing a provisional patent online and offers information about a wide variety of legal topics, including patent law.
- **www.uspto.gov** The U.S. Patent and Trademark Office is the place to go for recent policy and statutory changes and transcripts of hearings on various patent law issues. The U.S. Patent and Trademark Office maintains a searchable electronic database of the front page of all patents issued since 1971. This site is an excellent way to initiate a search for relevant patents.

CHAPTER

7

Copyrights

People seldom improve when they have no other model but themselves to copy after.

—Oliver Goldsmith

It has long been recognized that everyone benefits when creative people are encouraged to develop new intellectual and artistic works. When the U.S. Constitution was written in 1787, the framers took care to include a copyright clause (Article I, Section 8) giving Congress the power to "promote the Progress of Science and useful Arts" by passing laws that give creative people exclusive rights in their own artistic works for a limited period of time.

Copyright laws are not designed solely to enrich creative artists but to promote human knowledge and development. These laws encourage artists in their creative efforts by giving them a minimonopoly over their works, called a copyright. But this monopoly is limited when it conflicts with the overriding purpose of encouraging people to create new works of scholarship or art.

This chapter introduces you to copyright law and guides you through the first steps of creating, owning, and protecting a copyright. To learn about how copyrights differ from—and work with—patents and trademarks, see Chapters 6 and 8.

Copyright Basics

It is necessary to any originality to have the courage to be an amateur.

—Wallace Stevens

Copyright is a legal device that gives the creator of a work of art or literature, or a work that conveys information or ideas, the right to control how that work is used. The Copyright Act of 1976—the federal law providing for copyright protection—grants authors a bundle of exclusive rights over their works, including the right to reproduce, distribute, adapt, or perform them.

An author's copyright rights may be exercised only by the author—or by a person or entity to whom the author has transferred all or part of those rights. If someone wrongfully uses the material covered by a copyright, the copyright owner can sue and obtain compensation for any losses suffered.

What types of creative work does copyright protect?

Copyright protects works such as poetry, movies, video games, videos, DVDs, plays, paintings, sheet music, recorded music performances, novels, software code, websites, sculptures, photographs, choreography, and architectural designs.

To qualify for copyright protection, a work must be "fixed in a tangible medium of expression." This means that the work must exist in some physical form for at least some period of time, no matter how brief. Virtually any form of expression will qualify as a tangible medium, including a computer's random access memory (RAM), the recording media that capture all radio and television broadcasts, and the scribbled notes on the back of an envelope that contain the basis for an impromptu speech.

In addition, the work must be original—that is, independently created by the author. It doesn't matter if an author's creation is similar to existing works, or even if it is arguably lacking in quality, ingenuity, or aesthetic merit. As long as the author toils without copying from someone else, the results are protected by copyright.

Finally, to receive copyright protection, a work must be the result of at least some creative effort on the part of its author. There is no hard and fast rule as to how much creativity is enough. As one example, a work must be more creative than a telephone book's white pages, which are simply an alphabetical listing of telephone numbers rather than a creative selection of listings.

Does copyright protect an author's creative ideas?

No. Copyright shelters only fixed, original, and creative expression, not the ideas or facts upon which the expression is based. For example, copyright may protect a particular song, novel, or computer game about a romance in space, but it cannot protect the underlying idea of having a love affair among the stars. Allowing authors to monopolize their ideas would thwart the underlying purpose of copyright law, which is to encourage people to create new work.

For similar reasons, copyright does not protect facts—whether scientific, historical, biographical, or news of the day. Any facts that an author discovers in the course of research are in the public domain, free to all. For instance, anyone is free to use information included in a book about how the brain works, an article about the life and times of Neanderthals, or a TV documentary about the childhood of former President Clinton—as long as later users express the information in their own words.

Facts are not protected even if the author spends considerable time and effort discovering things that were previously unknown. For example, the author of a book on Neanderthals takes ten years to gather all the necessary materials and information for her work. At great expense, she travels to hundreds of museums and excavations around the world. But after the book is published, any reader is free to use the results of this ten-year research project to write their own book on Neanderthals—provided that they don't copy the manner in which the facts were expressed by the original author.

Is the Work Published?

In the complicated scheme of copyright laws, which law applies to a particular work depends on when that work is published. A work is considered published when the author makes it available to the public on an unrestricted basis. This means that it is possible to distribute or display a work without publishing it if there are significant restrictions placed on what can be done with the work and when it can be shown to others. For example, Andres Miczslova writes an essay called "Blood Bath" about the war in Iraq and distributes it to five human rights organizations under a nonexclusive license that places restrictions on their right to disclose the essay's contents. "Blood Bath" has not been "published" in the copyright sense. If Miczslova authorizes the human rights organizations to post the essay on the Internet, however, it would likely be considered published.

How long does a copyright last?

For works published after 1977, the copyright lasts for the life of the author plus 70 years. However, if the work is a work for hire (that is, the work is done in the course of employment or has been specifically commissioned) or is published anonymously or under a pseudonym, the copyright lasts between 95 and 120 years, depending on the date the work is published.

All works published in the United States before 1923 are in the public domain. Works published after 1922, but before 1964, are protected for 95 years from the date of publication, if a renewal was filed with the Copyright Office during the 28th year after publication. If no renewal was filed, such works are in the public domain. Works published from 1964 to 1977 are protected for 95 years whether or not a renewal was filed. If the work was created, but not published, before 1978, the copyright lasts for the life of the author plus 70 years. And if such a work was published before 2003, the copyright lasts until December 31, 2047.

Copyright Ownership

He who can copy, can do.

—Leonardo Da Vinci

A copyright is initially owned by a creative work's author or authors. But under the law, a person need not actually create the work to be its "author" for copyright purposes. A protectible work created by an employee in the course of a job is initially owned by the employer—that is, the employer is considered to be the work's author. Such works are called "works made for hire." Works created by nonemployees (independent contractors) may also be works made for hire if the contractors sign written agreements to that effect and the work falls within one of eight enumerated categories (see below).

Like any other property, a copyright can be bought and sold. Transfers of copyright ownership are unique in one respect, however: Authors or their heirs have the right to terminate any transfer of copyright ownership 35 to 40 years after it is made.

What are the exceptions to the rule that the creator of a work owns the copyright?

Copyrights are generally owned by the people who create the works of expression, with some important exceptions:

- If a work is created by an employee in the course of employment, the employer owns the copyright.
- If the work is created by an independent contractor, and the independent contractor signs a written agreement stating that the work shall be "made for hire," the commissioning person or organization owns the copyright only if the work is (1) a part of a larger literary work, such as an article in a magazine or a poem or story in an anthology; (2) part of a motion picture or other audiovisual work, such as a screenplay; (3) a translation; (4) a supplementary work such as an afterword, an introduction, chart, editorial note, bibliography, appendix, or index; (5) a compilation; (6) an instructional text; (7) a test or answer material for a test; or (8) an atlas. Works that don't fall within one of these eight categories are works made for hire only if created by an employee within the scope of employment.
- If the creator has sold the entire copyright, the purchasing business or person becomes the copyright owner.

Who owns the copyright in a joint work?

When two or more authors prepare a work with the intent to combine their contributions into inseparable or interdependent parts, the work is considered a joint work, and the authors are considered joint copyright owners. The most common example of a joint work is when a book or article has two or more authors. However, if a book is written primarily by one author but another author contributes a specific chapter to the book and is given credit for that chapter, then this probably wouldn't be a joint work because the contributions aren't inseparable or interdependent.

The U.S. Copyright Office considers joint copyright owners to have an equal right to register and enforce the copyright. Unless the joint owners make a written agreement to the contrary, each copyright owner has the right to commercially exploit the copyright, as long as the other copyright owners get an equal share of the proceeds.

Can two or more authors provide contributions to a single work without being considered joint authors?

Yes. If, at the time of creation, the authors did not intend their works to be part of an inseparable whole, combining their works later does not create a joint work. Rather, the result is considered a collective work. In this case, each author owns a copyright in only the material he or she added to the finished product. For example, in 1980, Vladimir writes a book of short stories. In 2000, Vladmir's son writes a book of short stories. In 2015, Vladmir's publisher issues a collection of short stories called *Father and Son* including stories by Vladmir and by Vladmir's son. The 2015 book is a collective work. Vladimir owns the copyright in his stories, and Vladmir's son owns the copyright in his stories.

What rights do copyright owners have?

The Copyright Act of 1976 grants a number of exclusive rights to copyright owners, including:

- reproduction right—the right to make copies of a protected work
- distribution right—the right to sell or otherwise distribute copies to the public
- right to create adaptations (called derivative works)—the right to prepare new works based on the protected work, and
- performance and display rights—the rights to perform a protected work (such as a stageplay) or to display a work in public.

This bundle of rights allows a copyright owner to be flexible when deciding how to realize commercial gain from the underlying work; the owner may sell or license any or all of these rights.

Can a copyright owner transfer rights?

Yes. When a copyright owner wishes to commercially exploit the work covered by the copyright, the owner typically transfers one or more of these rights to the person or entity who will be responsible for getting the work to market, such as a book or software publisher. It is also common for the copyright owner to place some limitations on the exclusive rights being transferred. For example, the owner may limit the transfer to a specific period of time, allow the right to be exercised only in a specific part of the country or world, or require that the right be exercised only through certain media, such as hardcover books, audiotapes, magazines, or online.

If a copyright owner transfers all of these rights unconditionally, it is generally termed an "assignment." When only some of the rights associated with the copyright are transferred, it is known as a "license." An exclusive license exists when the transferred rights can be exercised only by the owner of the license (the licensee) and no one else—including the person who granted the license (the licensor). If the license allows others (including the licensor) to exercise the same rights being transferred in the license, the license is said to be nonexclusive.

The U.S. Copyright Office allows buyers of exclusive and nonexclusive copyright rights to record the transfers in the U.S. Copyright Office. This helps to protect the buyer in case the original copyright owner later tries to transfer the same rights to another party.

Copyright Protection

Copyright protection automatically comes into existence when the protected work is created. However, the degree of protection that copyright laws extend to a protected work can be influenced by later events.

Do I have to include a copyright notice on my work?

Until 1989, a published work had to contain a valid copyright notice to receive protection under the copyright laws. But this requirement is no longer in force—works first published after March 1, 1989, need not include a copyright notice to gain protection under the law.

But even though a copyright notice is not required, it's still important to include one. When a work contains a valid notice, an infringer cannot claim ignorance in court. This makes it much easier to win a copyright infringement case and perhaps collect enough damages to make the cost of the case worthwhile. And the very existence of a notice might discourage infringement.

Including a copyright notice may also make it easier for a potential infringer to track down a copyright owner and legitimately obtain permission to use the work.

International Copyright Protection

Copyright protection rules are fairly similar worldwide, due to several international copyright treaties. The most important international treaty is the Berne Convention. Under this treaty, all member countries must afford copyright protection to authors who are nationals of any member country. This protection must last for at least the life of the author plus 50 years and must be automatic, without the need for the author to take any legal steps to preserve the copyright.

In addition to the Berne Convention, the GATT (General Agreement on Tariffs and Trade) treaty contains a number of provisions that affect copyright protection in signatory countries. Together, the Berne Copyright Convention and the GATT treaty allow U.S. authors to enforce their copyrights in most industrialized nations, and allow the nationals of those countries to enforce their copyrights in the United States.

What is a valid copyright notice?

A copyright notice should contain:

- the word "copyright"
- a "c" in a circle (©)
- the date of publication, and
- the name of either the author or the owner of all the copyright rights in the published work.

For example, the correct copyright for the 12th edition of *The Copyright Handbook,* by Stephen Fishman (Nolo), is *Copyright © 2014 by Stephen Fishman.*

When can I use a work without the author's permission?

When a work becomes available for use without permission from a copyright owner,

If You Want to Use Material on the Internet

Each day, people post vast quantities of creative material on the Internet—material that is available for downloading by anyone who has the right computer equipment. Because the information is stored somewhere on an Internet server, it is fixed in a tangible medium and potentially qualifies for copyright protection. Whether it does, in fact, qualify depends on other factors that you would have no way of knowing about, such as when the work was first published (which affects the need for a copyright notice), whether the copyright in the work has been renewed (for works published before 1964), whether the work is a work made for hire (which affects the length of the copyright), and whether the copyright owner intends to dedicate the work to the public domain.

As a general rule, it is wise to operate under the assumption that all materials are protected by either copyright or trademark law unless conclusive information indicates otherwise. A work is not in the public domain simply because it has been posted on the Internet (a popular fallacy) or because it lacks a copyright notice (another fallacy). As a general rule, you need permission to reproduce copyrighted materials, including photos, text, music, and artwork. It's best to track down the author of the material and ask for permission.

The most useful sources for finding information and obtaining permission are copyright collectives or clearinghouses. These are organizations that organize and license works by their members. For example, the Copyright Clearance Center (www.copyright.com) and iCopyright (www.icopyright.com) provide permissions for written materials. You can use an Internet search engine to locate other collectives for music, photos, and artwork.

If you want to use only a very small portion of text for educational or nonprofit purposes, the fair use rule may apply (see below).

it is said to be "in the public domain." Most works enter the public domain because their copyrights have expired.

To determine whether a work is in the public domain and available for use without the author's permission, you first have to find out when it was published. Then you can apply the periods of time set out earlier in this chapter. (See "How long does a copyright last?" above.) If the work was published between 1923 and 1963, however, you must check the U.S. Copyright Office records to see whether the copyright was properly renewed. If the author didn't renew the copyright, the work has fallen into the public domain and you may use it.

The Copyright Office (www.copyright.gov) will check renewal information for you, for a fee. You can also hire a private copyright search firm to see whether a renewal was filed. Finally, you may be able to conduct a renewal search yourself. The renewal records for works published from 1950 to the present are available online at www.copyright.gov. Renewal searches for earlier works can be conducted online at https://archive.org/details/copyrightrecords, or at the Copyright Office in Washington, DC, or at one of the many government depository libraries throughout the country. Contact the Copyright Office for more information.

With one important exception, you should assume that every work is protected by copyright (and therefore off limits) unless you can establish otherwise. As mentioned above, you can't rely on the presence or absence of a copyright notice (©) to make this determination, because a notice is not required for works published after March 1, 1989. And even for works published before 1989, the absence of a copyright notice doesn't mean the copyright isn't valid—for example, if the author made diligent attempts to correct the situation, the copyright may still be in force.

The exception to the general rule that you can't use a copyrighted work without the author's permission is called the "fair use rule." This rule recognizes that society can often benefit from the unauthorized use of copyrighted materials when the purpose of the use serves the ends of scholarship, education, or an informed public. For example, scholars must be free to quote from their research resources in order to comment on the material. To strike a balance between the public's need to be well informed and the rights of copyright owners to profit from their creativity, Congress passed a law authorizing the use of copyrighted materials in certain circumstances deemed to be "fair"—even if the copyright owner doesn't give permission.

Often, it's difficult to know whether a court will consider a proposed use to be fair. The fair use statute requires the courts to consider the following questions in deciding this issue:

- Is it a competitive use? If the use potentially affects the sales of the copied material, it's probably not fair.

- How much material was taken compared to the entire work of which the material was a part? The more someone takes, the less likely that the use is fair.
- How was the material used? Did the defendant change the original by adding new expression or meaning? Did the defendant add value to the original by creating new information, new aesthetics, new insights, and understandings? If the use was transformative, this weighs in favor of a fair use finding. Criticism, comment, news reporting, research, scholarship, and nonprofit educational uses are also likely to be judged fair uses. Uses motivated primarily by a desire for a commercial gain are less likely to be fair use.

As a general rule, if you are using a small portion of somebody else's work in a noncompetitive way for the purpose of benefitting the public, you're on pretty safe ground. On the other hand, if you take large portions of someone else's expression for your own purely commercial reasons, the rule usually won't apply.

Copyright Registration and Enforcement

Although every work published after 1989 is automatically protected by copyright, you can strengthen your rights by registering your work with the U.S. Copyright Office. This registration makes it possible to bring a lawsuit to protect your copyright if someone violates (infringes) it. The registration process is straightforward and inexpensive, and can be done without a lawyer.

Why should I register my work with the U.S. Copyright Office?

You must register your copyright with the U.S. Copyright Office before you are legally permitted to bring a lawsuit to enforce it.

You can register a copyright at any time, but filing promptly may pay off in the long run. "Timely registration"—that is, registration within three months of the work's publication date or before any copyright infringement actually begins—makes it much easier to sue and recover money from an infringer. Timely registration creates a legal presumption that your copyright is valid and allows you to recover up to $100,000 (and possibly lawyer's fees) without having to prove that you suffered actual monetary losses because of the infringement.

How do I register a copyright?

You can register your copyright by filling out a simple online form and depositing one or two samples of the work (depending on what it is) with the U.S. Copyright Office. You can register online using the Copyright Office's eCO system. Registration currently costs $35 per work for electronic filing, of a single work by a single author (not made for hire); other electronic filings cost $85.

(Paper forms can be filed for a fee of $85.) If you're registering several works that are part of one series, you may be able to save money by registering the works together (called "group registration").

The Copyright Office also has a preregistration procedure for certain works that have a history of prerelease infringement—for example, movies, music, books, computer programs, and advertising photographs. Preregistration offers protection under limited circumstances, primarily when a copyright owner needs to sue for infringement while a work is still being prepared for commercial release. It is not a substitute for registration; it simply indicates that you intend to register the work after you have completed and/or published it. To find out whether your work is eligible for preregistration, contact the U.S. Copyright Office using the information above.

How are copyrights enforced?

If someone violates the rights of a copyright owner, the owner is entitled to file a lawsuit in federal court asking the court to:

- issue orders (restraining orders and injunctions) to prevent further violations
- award money damages if appropriate, and
- in some circumstances, award attorneys' fees.

Whether the lawsuit will be successful and whether damages will be awarded depends on whether the alleged infringer can raise one or more legal defenses to the charge. Common legal defenses to copyright infringement are:

- too much time has elapsed between the infringing act and the lawsuit (the statute of limitations defense)
- the infringement is allowed under the fair use doctrine (discussed above)
- the infringement was innocent (the infringer had no reason to know the work was protected by copyright)
- the infringing work was independently created (that is, it wasn't copied from the original), or
- the copyright owner authorized the use in a license.

Someone who has good reason to believe that a use is fair—but later ends up on the wrong end of a court order—is likely to be considered an innocent infringer at worst. Innocent infringers usually don't have to pay any damages to the copyright owner, but they do have to cease the infringing activity or pay the owner for the reasonable commercial value of that use.

RELATED TOPIC

For more information about copyrights, see these Nolo books:

- *The Copyright Handbook: What Every Writer Needs to Know,* by Stephen Fishman. A complete guide to the law of copyright with forms for registering a copyright.

- *Patent, Copyright & Trademark: An Intellectual Property Desk Reference*, by Richard Stim. Provides concise definitions and examples of the important words and phrases commonly used in copyright law.
- *Getting Permission: How to License & Clear Copyrighted Materials Online & Off*, by Richard Stim. Spells out how to obtain permission to use art, music, writing, or other copyrighted works and includes a variety of permission and licensing agreements.
- *The Public Domain: How to Find & Use Copyright-Free Writings, Music, Art & More*, by Stephen Fishman. An authoritative book that explains what is protected by copyright law.

ONLINE HELP

The following sites are good resources for copyright information:

- **www.nolo.com** Nolo offers information about a wide variety of legal topics, including copyright law.
- **www.copyright.gov** The U.S. Copyright Office offers regulations, guidelines, forms, and links to other helpful copyright sites.
- **http://fairuse.stanford.edu** This is one of the leading websites for measuring fair use. It provides academic fair use links and guidelines.
- **wwwdearrichblog.com** An intellectual property blog that provides timely copyright information.

CHAPTER

8

Trademarks

A good name lost is seldom regained.

—Joel Hawes

Most of us encounter many trademarks each day; we might stop at Starbucks for coffee then drive our Tesla to work, where we sit down at an Apple computer. But as we go about our daily tasks, we rarely think about the laws behind the familiar words and images that identify the products and services we use.

Trademark law sets the legal rules that govern how businesses may:

- distinguish their products or services in the marketplace to prevent consumer confusion, and
- protect the means they've chosen to identify their products or services against use by competitors.

This chapter will introduce you to trademark law and answer common questions about choosing, using, and protecting a trademark.

Types of Trademarks

The term "trademark" is commonly used to describe many different types of devices that label, identify, and distinguish products or services in the marketplace. The basic purpose of all these devices is to inform potential customers of the origin of the underlying products or services.

What is a trademark?

A trademark is a distinctive word, phrase, logo, graphic symbol, slogan, or other device that is used to identify the source of a product and to distinguish a manufacturer's or merchant's products from others. Some examples are Nike sports apparel, Gatorade beverages, and Angry Birds video games. In the trademark context, "distinctive" means unique enough to help customers recognize a particular product in the marketplace. A mark may either be inherently distinctive (the mark is unusual in and of itself, such as Milky Way candy bars) or may become distinctive over time because customers come to associate the mark with the product or service (for example, Beef & Brew restaurants).

Consumers often make their purchasing choices on the basis of recognizable trademarks. For this reason, the main purpose of trademark law is to make sure that trademarks don't overlap in a manner that causes customers to become confused about the source of a product. However, in the case of trademarks that have become famous—for example, McDonald's—the courts are willing to prohibit a wider range of uses of the trademark (or anything close to it) by anyone other than the famous mark's owner. For instance, McDonald's was able to prevent the use of the mark McSleep by a motel chain because McSleep traded on the McDonald's mark reputation for a particular type of service (quick, inexpensive, standardized). This type of sweeping protection is authorized by federal and state statutes (referred to as antidilution laws) designed to prevent the weakening of a famous mark's reputation for quality.

What is a service mark?

For practical purposes, a service mark is the same as a trademark—but while trademarks promote products, service marks promote services and events. As a general rule, when a business uses its name to market its goods or services on signs or in advertising copy, the name qualifies as a service mark. Some familiar service marks: Jack in the Box (fast food service), FedEx Office (photocopying service), ACLU (legal service), Netflix (movie rental service), CBS's stylized eye in a circle (television network service), and the Olympic Games' multicolored interlocking circles (international sporting event).

What is a certification mark?

A certification mark is a symbol, name, or device used by an organization to vouch for products and services provided by others—for example, the "Good Housekeeping Seal of Approval." This type of mark may cover characteristics such as regional origin, method of manufacture, product quality, and service accuracy. Some other examples of certification marks: Stilton cheese (a product from the Stilton locale in England), Carneros wines (from grapes grown in the Carneros region of Sonoma/Napa counties), and Harris tweeds (a special weave from a specific area in Scotland).

What is a collective mark?

A collective mark is a symbol, label, word, phrase, or other mark used by members of a group or organization to identify goods, members, products, or services they render. Collective marks are often used to show membership in a union, association, or other organization.

The use of a collective mark is restricted to members of the group or organization that owns the mark. Even the group itself —as opposed to its members—cannot use the collective mark on any goods it produces. If the group wants to identify its product or service, it must use its own trademark or service mark.

> EXAMPLE: The letters "ILGWU" on a shirt label are the collective mark that identifies the shirt as a product of a member of the International Ladies' Garment Workers Union. If, however, the ILGWU wanted to start marketing its own products, it could not use the ILGWU collective mark to identify them; the union would have to get a trademark of its own.

What is trade dress?

In addition to a label, logo, or other identifying symbol, a product may come to be known by its distinctive packaging—for example, Kodak film or the Galliano liquor bottle—and a service by its distinctive decor or shape, such as the decor of Gap clothing stores. Collectively, these types of identifying features are commonly termed "trade dress." Because trade dress often serves the same function as a trademark or service mark—the identification of goods and services in the marketplace—trade dress can be protected under the federal trademark laws and in some cases registered as a trademark or service mark with the Patent and Trademark Office.

What kinds of things can be considered trademarks or service marks?

Most often, trademarks are words or phrases that are clever or unique enough to stick in a consumer's mind. Logos and graphics that become strongly associated with a product line or service are also typical. But a trademark or service mark can also consist of letters, numbers, a sound, a smell, a color, a product shape, or any other nonfunctional but distinctive aspect of a product or service that tends to promote and distinguish it in the marketplace. Titles, character names, or other distinctive features of movies, television, and radio programs can also serve as trademarks or service marks when used to promote a service or product. Some examples of unusual trademarks are the pink color of housing insulation manufactured by Owens Corning and the shape of the Absolut vodka bottle.

What's the difference between a business name and a trademark or service mark?

The name that a business uses to identify itself is called a "trade name." This is the name the business uses on its stock certificates, bank accounts, invoices, and letterhead. When used to identify a business in this way—as an entity for nonmarketing purposes—the business name is given some protection under state and local corporate and fictitious business name registration laws, but it is not considered a trademark or entitled to protection under trademark laws.

If, however, a business uses its name to identify a product or service produced by the business, the name will then be considered a trademark or service mark and will be entitled to protection if it is distinctive enough. For instance, Apple Computer Corporation uses the trade name Apple as a trademark on its line of computer products.

Although trade names by themselves are not considered trademarks for purposes of legal protection, they may still be protected under federal and state unfair competition laws against a confusing use by a competing business.

If my trade name is registered with the secretary of state as a corporate name, or placed on a fictitious business name list, can I use it as a trademark?

Not necessarily. When you register a corporate name with a state agency or place your name on a local fictitious business name register, there is no guarantee that the name has not already been taken by another business as a trademark. This means that before you start using your business name as a trademark, you will need to make sure it isn't already being used as a trademark by another company in a way that prevents you from using it. For more information about trademark searches, see "Conducting a Trademark Search," below.

Trademark Protection

If a trademark or service mark is protected, the owner of the mark can:

- prevent others from using it in a context where it might confuse consumers, and
- recover money damages from someone who used the mark knowing that it was already owned by someone else.

Trademark law also protects famous marks by allowing owners to sue to prevent others from using the same or a similar mark, even if customer confusion is unlikely.

Not all marks are entitled to an equal amount of protection, however—and some aren't entitled to any protection at all.

What laws offer protection to trademark owners?

The basic rules for resolving disputes over who is entitled to use a trademark come from decisions by federal and state courts (the common law). These rules usually favor the business that first used the mark when the second use would be likely to cause customer confusion. A number of additional legal principles that protect owners against improper use of their marks derive from federal statutes known collectively as the Lanham Act (Title 15 U.S.C. §§ 1051 to 1127). And all states have statutes that govern the use and protection of marks within the state's boundaries.

Inherently Distinctive Marks

Trademarks that are unusually creative are known as inherently distinctive marks. Typically, these marks consist of:

- unique logos or symbols (such as the McDonald's Golden Arch and the Nike swoosh)
- made-up words or words that have no dictionary meaning, such as Exxon or Kodak (called "fanciful" or "coined" marks)
- words that are surprising or unexpected in the context of their usage, such as Apple Computer or Diesel Bookstore (called "arbitrary marks"), and
- words that cleverly connote qualities about the product or service, such as Coppertone Suntan lotion (called "suggestive or evocative marks").

In addition to laws that specifically protect trademark owners, all states have laws that protect one business against unfair competition by another business, including the use by one business of a name already used by another business in a context that's likely to confuse customers.

What types of marks are entitled to the most legal protection?

Trademark law grants the most legal protection to the owners of names, logos, and other marketing devices that are distinctive—that is, memorable because they are creative or out of the ordinary, or because they have become well known to the public through their use over time or because of a marketing blitz.

Which marks receive the least protection?

Trademarks and service marks consisting of common or ordinary words are not considered inherently distinctive and receive less protection under federal and state laws. Typical examples of trademarks using common or ordinary words are:

- people's names, such as Pete's Muffins or Smith Graphics
- geographic terms, such as Northern Dairy or Central Insect Control, and
- descriptive terms—that is, words that attempt to literally describe the product or some characteristic of the product, such as Rapid Computers, Clarity Video Monitors, or Ice Cold Ice Cream.

However, nondistinctive marks may become distinctive through use over time or through intensive marketing efforts.

What about Ben & Jerry's Ice Cream? Even though Ben and Jerry are common names, isn't the Ben & Jerry's trademark entitled to maximum protection?

Absolutely. Even if a mark is not inherently distinctive, it may become distinctive if it develops great public recognition through long use and exposure in the marketplace. A mark that becomes protected in this way is said to have acquired a "secondary meaning." In addition to Ben & Jerry's, examples of otherwise common marks that have acquired a secondary meaning and are now considered to be distinctive include ChapStick (lip balm) and Park 'n Fly (airport parking services.)

What cannot be protected under trademark law?

There are five common situations in which there is no trademark protection. In any of these situations, the intended trademark cannot be registered, and the owner has no right to stop others from using a similar name. Generally, when speaking of what *cannot* be protected under trademark law, we are referring to the standards established under the Lanham Act (the federal statute that provides for registration of marks and federal court remedies in case a mark is infringed).

- **Nonuse.** An owner may lose trademark protection by "abandoning" a trademark. This can happen in many ways. The most common is when the mark is no longer used in commerce and there is sufficient evidence that the owner intends to discontinue its use. Under the Lanham Act, a trademark is presumed to be abandoned after three years of nonuse. But an owner who can prove an intent to resume commercial use of the mark will not lose trademark protection.
- **Generics and genericide.** A generic term describes a type of goods or services; it is not a brand name. Examples of generic terms are "computer," "eyeglasses," and "eBook." Consumers are used to seeing a generic term used in conjunction with a trademark (for example, Avery labels or Hewlett-Packard printers). On some occasions, a company invents a new word for a product (for example, Kleenex for a tissue) that functions so successfully as a trademark that the public eventually comes to believe that it is the name of the item. This is called genericide. When that happens, the term loses its trademark protection. Other famous examples of genericide are "aspirin," "yo-yo," "escalator," "thermos," and "kerosene."
- **Confusingly similar marks.** A mark will not receive trademark protection if it is so similar to another existing trademark that it causes confusion among consumers. This standard, known as likelihood of confusion, is a foundation of trademark law. Many factors are weighed when considering "likelihood of confusion." The most important are: the similarity of the marks, the similarity of the goods, the degree of care exercised by the consumer when making the purchase, the intent of the person using the similar mark, and any actual confusion that has occurred.
- **Weak marks.** A weak trademark will not be protected unless the owner can prove that consumers are aware of the mark. There are three types of weak marks: descriptive marks, geographic marks that describe a location, and marks that are primarily surnames (last names). When an applicant attempts to register a weak mark, the PTO will permit the applicant to submit proof of distinctiveness or to move the application from the Principal Register to the Supplemental Register. (See "Registering a Trademark," below, for more information about the different benefits these registers offer.)
- **Functional features.** Trademark law, like copyright law, will not protect functional features. Generally, a functional feature is something that is necessary for the item to work.

The issue usually arises with product packaging or shapes. For instance, the unique shape of the Mrs. Butterworth syrup bottle is not a functional feature because it is not necessary for the bottle to work. Therefore, it is eligible for trademark protection.

Are Internet domain names—names for sites on the World Wide Web—protected by trademark law?

Domain name registration, by itself, does not give you the power to stop another business from using the same name for its business or product. Instead, it gives you only the right to use that specific Internet address. To protect your domain name as a trademark, the name must meet the usual trademark standards. That is, the domain name must be distinctive or must achieve distinction through customer awareness, and you must be the first to use the name in connection with your type of service or product. An example of a domain name that meets these criteria and has trademark protection is Amazon.com. Amazon.com was the first to use this distinctive name for online retail sales, and the name has been promoted to customers through advertising and sales.

Using and Enforcing a Trademark

Generally, a trademark is owned by the business that first uses it in a commercial context—that is, attaches the mark to a product or uses the mark when marketing a product or service. A business may also obtain trademark protection if it files for trademark registration before anyone else uses the mark. (Trademark registration is discussed in more detail in "Registering a Trademark," below.)

Once a business owns a trademark, it may be able to prevent others from using that mark, or a similar one, on their goods and services.

What does it mean to "use" a trademark?

In trademark law, "use" means that the mark is at work in the marketplace, identifying available goods or services. This doesn't mean that the product or service actually has to be sold, as long as it is legitimately offered to the public under the mark in question—that is, the goods and services can be provided at the time the advertisement is published. For example, Robert creates a website where he offers his new invention—a humane mousetrap—for sale under the trademark MiceFree. Even if Robert doesn't sell any traps, he is still "using" the trademark as long as the traps are available and ready to be shipped at the time the ad is posted (and "MiceFree" appears on the traps or on tags attached to them). Similarly, if Kristin, a trademark attorney, puts up a website to offer her services under the service mark Trademark Queen, her service mark will be in use as long as she is ready to respond to customer requests for her advice at the time her website goes "live."

How can a business reserve a trademark for future use?

It is possible to acquire ownership of a mark by filing an "intent-to-use" (ITU) trademark registration application with the U.S. Patent and Trademark Office before someone else actually uses the mark. The filing date of this application will be considered the date of first use of the mark if the applicant actually uses the mark within the required time limits—six months to three years after the PTO approves the mark, depending on whether the applicant seeks and pays for extensions of time.

For more information about trademark registration, see "Registering a Trademark," below.

When can the owner of a trademark stop others from using it?

Whether the owner of a trademark can stop others from using it depends on such factors as:

- whether the trademark is being used on competing goods or services (goods or services compete if the sale of one is likely to affect the sale of the other)
- whether consumers would likely be confused by the dual use of the trademark, and
- whether the trademark is being used in the same part of the country or is being used on related goods (goods that will probably be noticed by the same customers, even if they don't compete with each other).

In addition, under federal and state laws known as "antidilution statutes," a trademark owner may go to court to prevent its mark from being used by someone else if the mark is famous and the later use would dilute the mark's strength—that is, weaken its reputation for quality (called "tarnishment") or render it common through overuse in different contexts (called "blurring").

Antidilution statutes can apply even if there is no way customers would be likely to confuse the source of the goods or services designated by the later mark with the famous mark's owner. For instance, consumers would not think that Microsoftball (for a sporting device) is associated with Microsoft, the software company, but Microsoftball could still be forced to choose another name under federal and state antidilution laws.

Certain acts are not considered dilution, including comparing goods in an advertisement; parodying, criticizing, or commenting upon a famous mark owner or the owner's goods or services; reporting news; and any noncommercial use of a mark.

TM and ®: What Do They Mean?

Many people like to put a "TM" (or "SM" for service mark) next to their mark to let the world know that they own it. However, it is not legally necessary to provide this type of notice; the use of the mark itself is the act that confers ownership.

The "R" in a circle (®) is a different matter entirely. This notice may not be put on a mark unless it has been registered with the U.S. Patent and Trademark Office—and it should accompany a mark after registration is complete. Failing to put the notice on a registered trademark can greatly reduce your chances of recovering significant damages if you later have to file a lawsuit against an infringer.

How does a trademark owner prevent others from using the mark?

Typically, the owner will begin by sending a letter, called a "cease and desist letter," to the wrongful user, demanding that it stop using the mark. If the wrongful user continues to infringe the mark, the owner can file a lawsuit to stop the improper use. The lawsuit is usually filed in federal court if the mark is used in more than one state or country, and in state court if the dispute is between purely local marks. In addition to preventing further use of the mark, a trademark owner can sometimes obtain money damages from the wrongful user.

When can a trademark owner get money from someone who has infringed the owner's mark?

If a trademark owner proves in federal court that the infringing use is likely to confuse consumers and that the owner suffered economically as a result of the infringement, the competitor may have to pay the owner damages based on the loss. And if the court finds that the competitor intentionally copied the owner's trademark, or at least should have known about the mark, the competitor may have to give up the profits it made by using the mark as well as pay other damages, such as punitive damages, fines, or attorneys' fees. On the other hand, if the trademark's owner has not been damaged, a court can allow the competitor to continue to use the trademark under limited circumstances designed to avoid consumer confusion.

Do I have the right to use my last name as a mark even if someone else is already using it for a similar business?

It depends on the name. A mark that is primarily a surname (last name) does not qualify for protection under federal trademark law unless the name becomes well known as a mark through advertising or long use. If this happens, the mark is said to have acquired a "secondary meaning."

If a surname acquires a secondary meaning, it is off limits for all uses that might cause customer confusion, whether or not the name is registered. Sears, McDonald's, Hyatt, Champion, Howard Johnson's, and Calvin Klein are just a few of the hundreds of surnames that have become effective and protected marks over time.

Also, a business that tries to capitalize on the name of its owner to take advantage of an identical famous name being used as a trademark may be forced, under the state or federal antidilution laws, to stop using the name. This may happen if the trademark owner files a lawsuit.

Conducting a Trademark Search

If you want to find out whether the trademark you've chosen for your products or services is available, you'll need to conduct a trademark search—an investigation to discover potential conflicts between your desired mark and any existing marks. Ideally, the search should be done before you begin to use a mark; this will help you avoid the expensive mistake of infringing a mark belonging to someone else.

Why do I need to conduct a trademark search?

The consequences of failing to conduct a reasonably thorough trademark search may be severe, depending on how widely you intend to use your mark and how much it would cost you to change it if a conflict later develops. If the mark you want to use has been federally registered by someone else, a court will presume that you knew about the registration—even if you did not. You will be precluded from using the mark in any context where customers might become confused. And if you do use the mark improperly, you will be cast in the role of a "willful infringer." Willful infringers can be held liable for large damages and payment of the registered owner's attorneys' fees; they can also be forced to stop using the mark altogether.

My business is local. Why should I care what name or mark someone else in another part of the country is using?

Most small retail or service-oriented business owners well know the mantra for success: location, location, location. With the Internet's firm hold, however, the concept of location takes on a whole new meaning. Instead of being rooted in physical space, businesses are now required to jockey for locations in the virtual or electronic space known as the Internet.

Vast numbers of businesses—even local enterprises—are putting up their own websites, creating a new potential for competition (and confusion) in the marketplace. Because of this, every business owner must pay attention to whether a proposed name or mark has already been taken by another business, regardless of the location or scope of that business.

Can I do my own trademark search?

Yes. Although the most thorough trademark searches are accomplished by professional search firms such as Thomson & CompuMark, it is also possible to conduct a preliminary online trademark search to determine whether a trademark is distinguishable from other federally registered trademarks. You can accomplish this with the PTO's trademark databases (www.uspto.gov), or with Trademarkia (www.trademarkia.com), which provides free access to records of federally registered marks or marks that are pending.

You should also search for marks that have not been registered. This is important because an existing mark, even if it's unregistered, would preclude you from:

- registering the same or a confusingly similar mark in your own name, and
- using the mark in any part of the country or any commercial transaction where customers might be confused.

You can search for unregistered marks on the Internet. In the libraries, use the available product guides and other materials. On the Internet, look for online shopping websites and review the inventory for items similar to yours. For example, go to ToysRUs (www.toysrus.com) to find hundreds of trademarked toys. You can also search for unregistered marks by using an Internet search engine. Enter your proposed name in the search field of an Internet search engine (such as Google or Yahoo). You will get a report of every time that name appears on pages indexed by that engine. Because no search engine is 100% complete, you should do this same search on several different search engines.

How can I find out whether a mark I want to use is already being used as a domain name (the name of a website)?

Every website is identified by a unique phrase known as a "domain name." For example, the domain name for Nolo is Nolo.com. Because so much business is now being done online, most people will want to be able to use their proposed mark as a domain name so that their customers can easily locate them on the Web.

The easiest way to find out whether a domain name is already in use is to check with one of the dozens of online companies that have been approved to register domain names. You can access a listing of these registrars through InterNIC's site at www.internic.net or the site of the Internet Corporation for Assigned Names and Numbers (ICANN) at www.icann.org. ICANN is the organization that oversees the process of approving domain name registrars.

Should I have a professional firm conduct my trademark search?

Many people prefer to pay a professional search firm to handle a trademark search. This makes sense if your financial plans justify an initial outlay of several hundred dollars, the minimum cost for a thorough professional search for both registered and unregistered marks. Depending on the search firm, you may also get a legal opinion as to whether your proposed mark is legally safe to use in light of existing registered and unregistered marks. Obtaining a legal opinion may provide important protection down the road if someone later sues you for using the mark.

How do I find a professional search firm?

There are many trademark search services in the United States. Here are two of the most well known:

TradeMark Express (www.tmexpress.com). TradeMark Express is a private company that, in addition to other trademark-related services, offers a full choice of trademark searches.

Thomson CompuMark (www.trademarks.thomsonreuters.com). Thomson CompuMark is the trademark search service of choice for the legal professional.

If you don't like doing business at a distance, you can find trademark search services in your area by looking in the yellow pages of the nearest good-sized city under "trademark consultants" or "information brokers." If that yields nothing, consult the advertisements in a local legal journal or magazine. You can also find a good list of trademark search firms at www.ggmark.com.

Registering a Trademark

It is possible to register certain types of trademarks and service marks with the U.S. Patent and Trademark Office (PTO). Federal registration puts the rest of the country on notice that the trademark is already taken and makes it easier to protect a mark against would-be copiers.

How does a mark qualify for federal registration?

To register a trademark with the PTO, the mark's owner first must put it into use "in commerce that Congress may regulate." This means the mark must be used on a product or service that crosses state, national, or territorial lines or that affects commerce crossing such lines—for example, a catalog business or a restaurant or motel that caters to interstate or international customers. Even if the owner files an intent-to-use (ITU) trademark application (ITU applications are discussed in "Using and Enforcing a Trademark," above), the mark will not actually be registered until it is used in commerce.

Once the PTO receives a trademark registration application, the office must answer the following questions:

- Is the trademark the same as or similar to an existing mark used on similar or related goods or services?
- Is the trademark on the list of prohibited or reserved names?

- Is the trademark generic—that is, does the mark describe the product itself rather than its source?
- Is the trademark too descriptive (not distinctive enough) to qualify for protection?

If the answer to each question is "no," the trademark is eligible for registration and the PTO will continue to process the application.

I know the PTO won't register a mark if it's not distinctive or already in use. But are there other types of marks that are ineligible for federal registration?

Yes. The PTO won't register any marks that contain:

- names of living persons without their consent
- the U.S. flag
- other federal and local governmental insignias
- the name or likeness of a deceased U.S. president without his widow's consent
- words or symbols that disparage living or deceased persons, institutions, beliefs, or national symbols, or
- marks that are judged immoral, deceptive, or scandalous.

As a general rule the PTO takes a liberal view of the terms "immoral" and "scandalous" and will rarely refuse to register a mark on those grounds.

If the PTO decides that a mark is eligible for federal registration, what happens next?

Next, the PTO publishes the trademark in the *Official Gazette* (an online publication of the U.S. Patent and Trademark Office). The *Gazette* states that the mark is a candidate for registration; this provides existing trademark owners with an opportunity to object to the registration. If someone objects, the PTO will schedule a hearing to resolve the dispute.

Is it possible to federally register a mark made up of common or ordinary words?

Yes, if the combination of the words is distinctive. But even if the entire mark is judged to lack sufficient distinctiveness, it can be placed on a list called the Supplemental Register. (Marks that are considered distinctive—either inherently or because they have become well known—are placed on a list called the Principal Register.) Marks on the Supplemental Register receive far less protection than do those on the Principal Register. The benefits granted by each type of registration are discussed in more detail below.

What are the benefits of federal trademark registration?

It depends on which register carries the mark. Probably the most important benefit of placing a mark on the Principal Register is that anybody who later starts using the same or a confusingly similar trademark may be presumed by the courts to be a "willful infringer" and therefore liable for large money damages.

Placing a trademark on the Supplemental Register produces significantly fewer benefits but still provides notice of ownership. This notice makes it far less likely that someone will use that identical mark; the fear of being sued for damages should keep potential infringers away. Also, if the trademark remains on the Supplemental Register for five years—meaning that the registration isn't canceled for some reason—and the mark remains in use during that time, it may be moved to the Principal Register under the secondary meaning rule (secondary meaning will be presumed).

How to Register Your Trademark

For most trademarks already in use, federal registration is a relatively straightforward process. The PTO, www.uspto.gov, has an excellent online system for filing an application for trademark registration, known as TEAS (Trademark Electronic Application System). In order to encourage applicants to file their trademark using TEAS, the PTO has stopped supplying blank trademark application forms. To further discourage paper applications, the PTO charges more for paper filings: $375, as opposed to $225 for a TEAS PLUS application, $275 for a TEAS RF application, and $325 for a TEAS application. When you complete your registration form online, you will have to:

- describe your mark
- state when it was first used
- describe the products or services on which the mark will be used, and
- suggest the classification under which the mark should be registered (there are approximately 40 classifications for goods and services; the PTO can help you figure out which one is right for your mark).

In addition, you must submit:

- a "drawing" of your mark (for word marks, this simply involves setting the mark out in the middle of a page in capital letters)
- a sample of how your proposed mark is being used, and
- the registration fee.

If you are applying to register your mark on the basis of its intended use, then you needn't provide the samples or the date of first use, but you can't complete your registration until you put your mark into actual use and file some additional paperwork with the PTO.

The PTO website also offers plain-English instructions for completing the online application. For more information about registering your trademark, see the resource list at the end of this chapter.

Even if a mark is not registered, it is still possible for the owner to sue the infringer under a federal statute that forbids use of a "false designation of origin" (Title 15 U.S.C. § 1125). It is usually much easier to prove the case and collect large damages, however, if the mark has been registered.

How long does federal registration last?

Once a trademark or service mark is placed on the Principal Register, the owner receives a certificate of registration good for an initial term of ten years. The registration may lapse before the ten-year period expires, however, unless the owner files a form within six years of the registration date (called the Section 8 Declaration) stating that the mark is either still in use in commerce or that the mark is not in use for legitimate reasons.

The Section 8 Declaration is usually combined with a Section 15 Declaration, which effectively renders the trademark incontestable except for limited reasons.

The original registration may be renewed indefinitely for additional ten-year periods if the owner files the required renewal applications (called a Section 9 Declaration) with the U.S. Patent and Trademark Office. A Section 8 Declaration must also be filed at the time of trademark renewal. Failure to renew a registration does not void all rights to the mark, but if the owner fails to reregister, the special benefits of federal registration will be lost.

What happens if there is a conflict between an Internet domain name and an existing trademark?

The answer depends on the nature of the conflict. There are three reasons a conflict may develop between the owner of a trademark and the owner of a domain name:

The domain name registrant is a cybersquatter. If a domain name is registered in bad faith—for example, someone registers the name with the intent of selling it back to a company with the same name—the domain name can be taken away under federal law or under international arbitration rules for domain name owners. A victim of cybersquatting in the United States can now sue under the provisions of the Anticybersquatting Consumer Protection Act (ACPA) or can fight the cybersquatter using an international arbitration system created by ICANN. The ICANN arbitration system is usually faster and less expensive than suing under the ACPA. In addition, it does not require an attorney. For information on the ICANN policy, visit the organization's website at www.icann.org.

The domain name infringes an existing trademark. If a domain name is likely to confuse consumers because it is similar to an existing trademark, the owner of the federally owned trademark can sue for infringement in federal court. For example, it's likely that the Adobe company, makers of graphics software, would be able to prevent another software company from using the domain name of www.adoobie.com.

The domain name dilutes a famous trademark. If a domain name dilutes the power of a famous trademark, the trademark owner can sue under federal laws to stop the continued use. Dilution occurs when the domain name blurs or tarnishes the reputation of a famous trademark. For example, Gucci could probably prevent a company from using the domain name "guccigoo.com" for the purpose of selling baby diapers.

Can a business register its mark at the state level?

It is possible to register a mark with the state trademark agency, although the state registration does not offer the same level of protection provided by federal law. The main benefit of state registration is that it notifies anyone who checks the list that the mark is owned by the registrant. This will lead most would-be users of the same mark to choose another one rather than risk a legal dispute with the registered mark's owner. If the mark is also federally registered, this notice is presumed, and state registration isn't necessary. If, however, the mark is used only within the state and doesn't qualify for federal registration, state registration is a good idea.

How Trademarks Differ From Patents and Copyrights

Trademarks are often mentioned in the same breath as copyrights and patents. Though these terms do sometimes apply to the same thing, they're more often defined by their differences. It's important to understand how trademark law differs from other laws protecting creative works (collectively called "intellectual property laws").

How does trademark differ from copyright?

Copyright protects original works of expression, such as novels, fine and graphic arts, music, photography, software, video, cinema, and choreography by preventing people from copying or commercially exploiting them without the copyright owner's permission. But the copyright laws do not protect names, titles, or short phrases. That's where trademark law comes in. Trademark protects distinctive words, phrases, logos, symbols, slogans, and any other devices used to identify and distinguish products or services in the marketplace.

There are, however, areas where both trademark and copyright law may be used to protect different aspects of the same product. For example, copyright laws may protect the artistic aspects of a graphic or logo used by a business to identify its goods or services, while trademark may protect the graphic or logo from use by others in a confusing manner in the marketplace.

Similarly, trademark laws are often used in conjunction with copyright laws to protect advertising copy. The trademark laws protect the product or service name and any slogans used in the advertising, while the copyright laws protect the additional creative written expression contained in the ad.

For more information about copyright law, see Chapter 7.

What's the difference between patent and trademark?

Patents allow the creator of certain kinds of inventions that contain new ideas to keep others from making commercial use of those ideas without the creator's permission. For example, Tom invents a new type of hammer that makes it very difficult to miss the nail. Not only can Tom keep others from making, selling, or using the precise type of hammer he invented, but he may also be able to apply his patent monopoly rights to prevent people from making commercial use of any similar type of hammer during the time the patent is in effect (20 years from the date the patent application is filed).

Generally, patent and trademark laws do not overlap. When it comes to a product design, however—say, jewelry or a distinctively shaped musical instrument—it may be possible to obtain a patent on a design aspect of the device while invoking trademark law to protect the design as a product identifier. For instance, an auto manufacturer might receive a design patent for the stylistic fins that are part of a car's rear fenders. Then, if the fins were intended to be—and actually are—used to distinguish the particular model car in the marketplace, trademark law may kick in to protect the appearance of the fins.

For more information about patent law, see Chapter 6.

RESOURCE

For more information about trademarks, see these Nolo books:

- *Trademark: Legal Care for Your Business & Product Name,* by Stephen Fishman. Shows you how to choose a legally strong business and product name, register the name with state and federal agencies, and sort out any name disputes that arise.
- *Patent, Copyright & Trademark: An Intellectual Property Desk Reference,* by Richard Stim. Provides concise definitions and examples of the important words and phrases commonly used in trademark law.

The following associations of trademark lawyers offer a number of helpful publications. Visit online for a list of available materials.

- International Trademark Association (INTA) www.inta.org
- American Intellectual Property Law Association (AIPLA) www.aipla.org.

ONLINE HELP

The following sites are good resources for information on trademark law:

- **www.nolo.com** Nolo provides a system for filing a trademark application online and offers information about a wide variety of legal topics, including trademarks.
- **www.inta.org** The International Trademark Association (INTA) provides trademark services, publications, and online resources.
- **www.uspto.gov** The U.S. Patent and Trademark Office provides new trademark rules and regulations, free trademark searching, and lots of useful links to trademark-related sites.
- **www.schwimmerlegal.com** Martin Schwimmer's trademark blog is one of the most interesting (and popular) sources of daily trademark news.
- **www.ggmark.com** This site, maintained by a trademark lawyer, provides basic trademark information and a fine collection of links to other trademark resources.

CHAPTER

9

Your Money

Too many people spend money they haven't earned, to buy things they don't want, to impress people they don't like.

—Will Rogers

America's economy is driven by consumer spending. When we open a newspaper or magazine, turn on the radio or television, or take a drive across town, we're bombarded with ads urging us to spend our hard-earned dollars. And we respond by pulling out our cash, checks, credit cards, and debit cards.

What the ads don't tell you is what to do when things go wrong—for example, when the item you buy is defective, you lose your credit card, you need extra time to pay, or you fall behind and the debt collectors start calling.

Fortunately, many federal (and some state) laws provide some protections to consumers; this chapter describes some of the most important ones. While no law substitutes for common sense, comparison shopping, and avoiding offers that sound too good to be true, many laws can help you if you run into trouble.

Purchasing Goods and Services

I did not have three thousand pairs of shoes: I had one thousand and sixty.

—Imelda Marcos

While 19th-century business relationships were governed by the doctrine "caveat emptor" or "let the buyer beware," the notion that a buyer–seller arrangement should be fair gained ground in the 20th century. As a result, you now have a right to receive goods and services that meet certain minimum standards.

When I buy something, is it covered by a warranty?

Generally, yes. A warranty (also called a guarantee) is an assurance about the quality of goods or services you buy and is intended to protect you if something you purchase fails to live up to what you were promised.

An express warranty is one that is explicitly stated, usually in writing. Most express warranties state something such as "this product is warranted against defects in materials or workmanship" for a specified time. Most either come directly from the manufacturer or are included in the sales contract you sign with the seller. But an express warranty may also be in an advertisement or on a sign in a store ("all dresses are 100% silk"), or in a salesperson's oral description of a product's features.

An implied warranty is not spoken or written but is based on reasonable consumer expectations. There are two implied warranties—one for "merchantability" and one for "fitness." The implied warranty of merchantability is an assurance that a new item will work if you use it for a reasonably expected purpose (for example, that a toaster will toast bread or a power drill will drill holes). This warranty applies only to the product's ability to perform its basic purpose, not to everything that could possibly go wrong with the product. For used items, the warranty of merchantability is a promise that the product will work as expected, given its age and condition.

The implied warranty of fitness applies when you buy an item with a specific (even unusual) purpose in mind. If you communicated your specific needs to the seller, the implied warranty of fitness assures you that the item will meet these needs.

How long does a warranty last?

An express warranty lasts for the term stated in the language of the warranty—for example, "three years after the date of purchase." The lifespan of an implied warranty depends on state law. Some states limit an implied warranty to a period of time—one or two years, for example. Others say that an implied warranty lasts only as long as any express warranty made about a product.

Can a seller avoid a warranty by selling a product "as is"?

The answer depends on whether the warranty is express or implied and on the laws of the state where you live. Sellers cannot avoid express warranties by claiming the product is sold "as is." On the other hand, if there is no express warranty, sellers can sometimes avoid an implied warranty by selling the item "as is." Some states prohibit all "as is" sales. And in all states, the buyer must know that the item is sold "as is" in order for the seller to avoid an implied warranty.

How do I enforce a warranty if something is wrong with the product I bought?

Most of the time, a defect in an item will show up immediately, and you can ask the seller or manufacturer to fix or replace it. It's best to make this request in a letter that states when you purchased the item, what you paid for it, and what's wrong with it. If the seller refuses, try to mediate the dispute through a community or Better Business Bureau mediation program. (For more information about mediation, see Chapter 16.) You can also contact your state or local consumer protection agency.

If all else fails, you can sue. If the seller or manufacturer won't make good under a warranty, you must sue within one to four years of when you discovered the defect, depending on your state's laws.

Do I have any recourse if the item breaks after the warranty expires?

Usually not. But in most states, if the item gave you some trouble while it was under the warranty and you had it repaired by someone authorized by the manufacturer to make repairs, the manufacturer must extend your original warranty for the amount of time the item sat in the shop. If you think you're entitled to an extension, call the manufacturer and ask to speak to the department that handles warranties.

You may have other options as well. If your product was trouble-free during the warranty period, the manufacturer may offer a free repair for a problem that arose after the warranty expired if the problem is widespread. Many manufacturers have secret "fix-it" lists—items with defects that don't affect safety and therefore don't require a recall but that the manufacturer will repair for free. It can't hurt to call and ask.

Is paying for an extended warranty contract a good idea?

Usually not. Merchants encourage you to buy extended warranties (also called service contracts) because they are a source of big profits for stores, which pocket up to 50% of the amount you pay.

Rarely will you have the chance to exercise your rights under an extended warranty, however. Name-brand electronic equipment and appliances usually don't break down during the first few years (and if they do, they're covered by the original warranty), and they often have a lifespan well beyond the length of the extended warranty.

I think I was the victim of a scam. Can I get my money back?

Federal and state laws prohibit "unfair or deceptive trade acts or practices." If you think you've been cheated, *immediately* let the appropriate government offices know. Although any government investigation will take some time, these agencies often have the resources to go after unscrupulous merchants. And the more agencies you notify, the more likely someone will take notice of your complaint and act on it.

Unfortunately, government agencies are rarely able to get your money back. If the business is a reputable one, however, it may refund your money when a consumer fraud law enforcement investigator shows up. It certainly can't hurt to complain.

If you can't get relief from a government agency, consider suing the company in small claims court. *Everybody's Guide to Small Claims Court,* by Ralph Warner (Nolo), provides extensive information on how to sue in small claims court. (See Chapter 16.)

I received some unordered merchandise in the mail, and now I'm getting billed. Do I have to pay?

You don't owe any money if you receive an item you never ordered. It's considered a gift. If you get bills or collection letters from a seller who sent you something you never ordered, write to the seller stating your intention to treat the item as a gift. If the bills continue, insist that the seller send you proof of your order. If this doesn't stop the bills, notify the Federal Trade Commission or the state consumer protection agency in the state where the merchant is located.

If you sent for something in response to an advertisement claiming a "free" gift or "trial" period, and are now being billed, be sure to read the fine print of the ad. It may say something about charging shipping and handling; or worse, you may have inadvertently joined a club or subscribed to a magazine. Write the seller, cancel your membership or subscription, offer to return the merchandise, and state that you believe the ad was misleading.

I just signed a contract to have carpeting installed in my house, and I changed my mind. Can I cancel?

Possibly. Under the Federal Trade Commission's "cooling-off rule," you have until midnight of the third day (not including Sundays and federal holidays) after a contract was signed to cancel either of the following:

- door-to-door sales contracts for more than $25, or
- a contract for more than $130 made anywhere other than the seller's normal place of business—for instance, at a sales presentation at a hotel or restaurant, outdoor exhibit, computer show, or trade show. Public car auctions, craft fairs, and sales made by mail, Internet, or telephone are not included. Your state may provide more rights.

These (door-to-door sales and contracts made at a trade show and the like) are situations where you are especially vulnerable to deception and high-pressure sales tactics.

This cooling-off period does not apply to contracts to buy a car, truck, van, or camper. If your dealer says otherwise, be sure to get it in writing.

How to File a Complaint for Fraud

Fraud.org, a project of the National Consumers League, can help if you've been defrauded. Fraud.org provides:

- assistance in filing a complaint with appropriate federal agencies, and
- tips on how to avoid becoming a fraud victim.

See www.fraud.org for details.

Also contact your local prosecutor (such as the District Attorney's office) to find out whether it investigates consumer fraud complaints. Finally, contact any local newspaper, radio station, or television station "action line." Especially in metropolitan areas, these folks often have an army of volunteers ready to pursue consumer complaints.

Do I have the right to cancel any other kinds of contracts?

The federal Truth in Lending Act lets you cancel some loans up until midnight of the third day (not including Sundays or federal holidays) after you signed the contract. It applies only to loans for which you pledged your home as security, as long as the loan is not a first mortgage (some other restrictions apply). For example, the Act applies to home improvement loans, home equity loans, and second mortgages. If the lender never notified you of the three-day right to cancel, you have even longer to cancel your loan.

The federal Credit Repair Organization Act gives you three days to cancel a contract with a credit repair organization.

In addition, many states have laws that allow you to cancel written contracts covering the purchase of certain goods or services within a few days of signing, including contracts for dance or martial arts lessons, credit repair services, health club memberships, dating services, weight loss programs, time-share properties, and hearing aids. In a few states, you can also cancel a contract if you negotiated the transaction in a language other than English but the seller did not give you a copy of the contract in that language. Contact your state consumer protection agency to find out what contracts, if any, are covered in your state.

Do I have the right to a cash refund after I make a purchase?

Generally, no. A seller isn't required to offer refunds or exchanges, though many do.

But some states (including California and Florida) require merchants to post their refund or exchange policies, particularly if the seller doesn't offer a full cash refund. Merchants that don't follow these rules have to allow customers to return items for a full refund, as long as the customer does so within the time limits set by state law.

RESOURCE

For more information about purchasing goods and services, see these Nolo books:

- *Everybody's Guide to Small Claims Court,* by Ralph Warner. Extensive information on pursuing your rights in the event a seller or manufacturer won't make good on a warranty.
- *Solve Your Money Troubles,* by Robin Leonard. Explains how to handle debts for defective goods or services.

ONLINE HELP

The following sites are good resources for consumer information on purchasing goods and services:

- **www.consumer.ftc.gov** The Federal Trade Commission has lots of information about goods and services, including fact sheets and links to consumer groups.
- **www.dmaconsumers.org** The Direct Marketing Association is a membership organization made up of mail-order companies and other direct marketers. If you have a complaint about a particular company, contact The Corporate & Social Responsibility Department, c/o DMA, 1615 L Street, NW, Suite 1100, Washington, DC 20036. You can also fill out an online complaint form at www.thedma.org/resources/

consumer-resources/#file-a-complaint. The DMA may contact the mail-order company and try to resolve your problem.

- **www.usa.gov** Your state consumer protection agency is a great resource for all types of consumer problems. Find yours at this website.

Using Credit and Charge Cards

Today, most Americans have two or three credit cards. But using credit cards can be very expensive—the interest rate charged by bank credit card companies averages more than 15%; on gasoline company and department store cards, it's significantly higher.

My credit card debt is consuming my life. How can I cut credit card costs?

If you have more than one card, pay down the balances with the highest interest rates and then use (or obtain) a card with a low rate. Because there is great competition among credit card issuers, you might get a rate reduction simply by asking for one from your current credit card company.

I'm always getting credit card offers with low interest rates in the mail. Should I sign up and transfer the balance from my current card to the new card?

It depends. Check the fine print of the offer. Many credit card companies offer a "teaser" rate—a low rate that lasts for a short period of time. Once the "teaser" period is over, a much higher rate kicks in. Also be sure to consider any annual fees, grace periods, and nuisance fees before you switch.

What are over-the-limit fees and how can I avoid them?

Banks assess high fees if you charge an amount that puts your credit card account over your credit limit (for example, your credit limit is $5,000 and your outstanding balance is $5,500). These are called over-the-limit fees. In the past, people often had no idea that they were making purchases that put their account over the limit until they got their credit card statement listing hefty fees.

In order for a credit card company to charge these fees, you must opt in (agree in advance). To avoid over-the-limit fees, don't opt in (or call and cancel if you already have opted in). That way, transactions that would put your account over your credit limit will be rejected, and you'll avoid unwelcome surprises on your credit card statement.

Is there a way to figure out how much I'm paying in interest each year when I carry a balance on my credit card?

Check your credit card statement.

Federal law requires monthly credit card statements to:

- include a box showing cardholders how much interest and fees they have paid in the current year
- show the due date for the next payment (and the fee for late payment)
- display how long it will take to pay off the existing balance (and the total cost of interest) if the consumer makes only the minimum payment due, and
- show the monthly payment required (and the total cost of interest) for the consumer to pay off the balance within 36 months.

I can't afford the minimum payment required on my statement. Can I pay less?

Most card companies insist that you make the monthly minimum payment, which is usually 2% to 2.5% of the outstanding balance. If you can't make the minimum payment, you can try to negotiate a temporary reduction in the minimum payment or interest rate, or a waiver of payments for a few months.

Bear in mind that paying nothing or very little on your credit card should be a temporary solution only. The longer you pay only a small amount, the quicker your balance will increase due to interest charges.

My wallet was stolen. Will I have to pay charges that the thief made using my credit cards?

No. Federal law limits your liability for unauthorized charges made on your credit or charge card after it has been lost or stolen if you are reasonably prompt about notifying the card issuer. If the fraudulent charge was made in person, you are liable for no more than $50. Many card issuers don't even charge the $50. If the thief used your card over the phone or Internet, you have no liability.

I purchased an item using my credit card and the item fell apart. Can I refuse to pay?

Maybe. Under federal law, you must first attempt in good faith to resolve the dispute with the merchant. If that fails, you must explain to the credit card company, in writing, why you are withholding payment. If you used a VISA, MasterCard, or other non–seller-issued card, you may withhold payment only if the purchase was for more than $50 and was made within your home state or within 100 miles of your home. These limitations don't apply if you use a seller's card, such as your Sears card.

If you made the purchase by phone or Internet, state law determines whether the purchase is considered to be made in your home state or not.

My credit card billing statement contains an error. What should I do?

Immediately write a letter to the customer service department of the card issuer. Give your name, account number, an explanation of the error, and the amount involved. Enclose copies of supporting documents, such as receipts showing the correct amount of the charge. You must act quickly—the issuer must receive your letter within 60 days after it mailed the bill to you.

Be sure to use the correct "billing error" address (you can find it in the tiny print on the back of your statement), not the address where you send your regular payments.

Under the federal Fair Credit Billing Act, the issuer must acknowledge receipt of your letter within 30 days, unless it corrects the bill within that time. Furthermore, the issuer must, within two billing cycles (but in no event more than 90 days), correct the error or explain why it believes the amount to be correct.

During the two-billing-cycle/90-day period, the issuer cannot report the amount to credit reporting agencies or other creditors as delinquent. The issuer can charge you interest on the amount you dispute during this period, but if it later agrees that you were correct, it must drop the interest accrued.

I took out a cash advance using my credit card and feel I was gouged. What are all those fees?

Cash advances usually come with the following fees:

- **Transaction fees.** Most banks charge a transaction fee of up to 4% for taking a cash advance.
- **No grace period.** Most banks charge interest from the date the cash advance is posted, even if you pay it back in full when your bill comes.
- **Interest rates.** The interest rate is often higher on cash advances than it is on ordinary credit card charges.

Which Cards Should You Keep?

When you think about the costs of using your credit cards, you may decide that you're better off canceling most of them. If so, you'll have to decide which cards to keep. If you don't carry a monthly balance, keep a card with no annual fee, but make sure it has a grace period. If you carry a balance each month, consider getting rid of cards that have these features:

- **High interest rates.**
- **Nuisance fees** (such as late-payment fees, over-the-limit fees, inactivity fees, fees for carrying a balance under a certain amount, or a flat monthly fee that's a percentage of your credit limit).

Keep in mind, however, that closing accounts may negatively affect your credit score. This is because closing accounts may increase the ratio of your overall debt to available credit. For more on credit scores, see the "Buying a House" section in Chapter 1.

Using an ATM or Debit Card

A bank is a place where they lend you an umbrella in fair weather and ask for it back when it begins to rain.

—**Robert Frost**

Banks issue ATM cards to allow customers to withdraw money, make deposits, transfer money between accounts, find out their balances, get cash advances, and even make loan payments at all hours of the day or night.

Debit cards combine the functions of ATM cards and checks. Debit cards are issued by banks but can be used at stores. When you pay with a debit card, the money is automatically deducted from your checking account.

What are the advantages of using an ATM or debit card?

There are generally two advantages:

- You don't have to carry your check-book and identification, but you can make purchases directly from your checking account.
- You pay immediately—without running up interest charges on a credit card bill.

Are there disadvantages?

Yes. You don't have 21 to 25 days to pay the bill, as you would if you paid by credit card.

If Your ATM Card Is Lost or Stolen

If your ATM or debit card is lost or stolen (never, never, never keep your personal identification number—PIN—near your card), call your bank immediately and follow up with a confirming letter. Under federal law, your liability is:

- $0 for charges made after you report the card missing
- up to $50 if you notify the bank within two business days after you realize the card is missing (unless you were on extended travel or in the hospital)
- up to $500 if you fail to notify the bank within two business days after you realize the card is missing (unless you were on extended travel or in the hospital), but do notify the bank within 60 days after your bank statement is mailed to you listing the unauthorized withdrawals, and
- unlimited if you fail to notify the bank within 60 days after your bank statement is mailed to you listing the unauthorized withdrawals (unless you were on extended travel, in the hospital, or had similar good reasons for the delay).

In response to consumer complaints about the possibility of unlimited liability, VISA and MasterCard now cap the liability on debit cards at $50. A few states have capped the liability for unauthorized withdrawals on an ATM or debit card at $50 as well. And some large debit card issuers won't charge you anything if unauthorized withdrawals appear on your statement.

You don't have the right to withhold payment (the money is immediately removed from the account) in the event of a dispute with the merchant over goods or services. You have less protection (as compared to credit cards) if your card is stolen. Finally, many banks charge transaction fees when you use an ATM or debit card at locations other than those owned by the bank.

Do I have to pay if there's a mistake on my statement or receipt?

Although ATM statements and debit receipts don't usually contain errors, mistakes do happen. If you find an error, you have 60 days from the date of the statement or receipt to notify the bank. Always call first and follow up with a letter. If you don't notify the bank within 60 days, it has no obligation to investigate the error, and you're out of luck.

The bank has ten business days from the date of your notification to investigate the problem and tell you the result. If the bank needs more time, it can take up to 45 days, but only if it deposits or recredits the disputed amount of money into your account. If the bank later determines that there was no error, it can take the money back, but it must first send you a written explanation.

RESOURCE

For more information about credit, charge, ATM, and debit cards, see:

- *Solve Your Money Troubles,* by Robin Leonard (Nolo). Contains extensive information on credit, charge, ATM, and debit card laws, and practical usage tips.
- The Federal Deposit Insurance Corporation, 877-275-3342, www.fdic.gov. Publishes free pamphlets.
- The Federal Trade Commission Consumer Response Center, 877-FTC-HELP (382-4357), www.consumer.ftc.gov. Offers lots of consumer information on billing errors, credit problems, and credit and ATM cards.

Strategies for Repaying Debts, House Payments, and Student Loans

If you think nobody cares if you're alive, try missing a couple of car payments.

—Earl Wilson

Today, many people are either unemployed or forced to work harder than ever (often in more than one job), earning less, saving little, and struggling with debt. If this story sounds familiar to you, you're not alone. Here are some specific suggestions for dealing with debts.

I feel completely overwhelmed by my debts and don't know where to begin. What should I do?

Take a deep breath and realize that for the most part your creditors want to help you pay them. Whether you're behind on your bills or are afraid of getting behind, call your creditors. Let them know what's going on—job loss, reduction in hours, medical problem, or other issues—and ask for help. Suggest possible solutions such as a temporary reduction of your payments, skipping a few payments and tacking them on at the end of a loan or paying them off over a few months, dropping late fees and other charges, or even rewriting a loan.

If you need help negotiating with your creditors, consider contacting a nonprofit debt counseling organization. To find an agency in your area, go to the website of the U.S. Trustee (www.justice.gov/ust) and click "Credit Counseling & Debtor Education"; you'll find a list of agencies the Trustee's office has approved to provide the counseling debtors must now complete before filing for bankruptcy.

I'm afraid I might miss a car payment—should I just let the lender repossess?

No. Before your car payment is due, call the lender and ask for extra time. If you're at least six months into the loan and haven't missed any payments, the lender may let you miss one or two months' payments and tack them on at the end. If you don't pay or make arrangements with the lender, the lender can repossess without warning, although many lenders will warn you and give you a chance to pay what's due.

If your car is repossessed, you can get it back by paying the entire balance due and the cost of repossession or, in some cases, by paying the cost of the repossession and the missed payments, then making payments under your contract. If you don't get the car back, the lender will sell it at an auction for far less than it's worth. You'll owe the lender the difference between the balance of your loan and what the sale brings in.

If you are far behind on your car payments and can't catch up, think hard about whether you can really afford the car. If you decide to give up your car, there are two options that are almost always better than waiting for the dealer to repossess it. First, you can sell the car yourself and use the proceeds to pay off the loan (or most of the loan). You'll get more for the car if you sell it yourself than the dealer will by selling it at an auction after repossession—which means you'll be able to pay off more of the loan. Or, you can voluntarily "surrender" your car to the dealer before repossession. This will save you repossession costs and attorneys' fees. Because it also makes life easier for dealers, some might agree to waive any deficiency balance or promise not to report the default or repossession to credit bureaus if you work out a deal.

I am behind on my house payments. What should I do?

If you are struggling to pay your mortgage or are facing foreclosure, take immediate action. A foreclosure will hurt your credit rating and make it difficult, if not impossible, to buy another home anytime soon. (Although if you've already defaulted on payments, your credit has already taken a big hit.) In addition, if the profits from selling your home don't cover the unpaid portion of your loan, your lender might be able to sue you for the rest.

Options if you're having trouble making mortgage payments include: negotiating with your lender, applying for government loan modification or mortgage payment assistance programs, filing for bankruptcy, selling your home yourself, or giving your home deed to the lender.

If I am facing foreclosure, can I work something out with my lender?

It's definitely worth a try. As soon as you realize you'll have trouble paying your mortgage—ideally, before you've missed any payments—contact your lender.

The lender may accept partial payments or no payments for a few months (although you may have to agree to make up the difference later). This is called forbearance. The lender may also allow you to reinstate your loan by making up missed payments by a specific date. Or, the lender may agree to a loan modification—altering the terms of the loan so you can better afford the payments.

Are there government programs to help with foreclosure?

Yes. The federal Making Home Affordable initiative has many programs to assist struggling homeowners. Under these programs you may be able to get a loan modification (under the Home Affordable Modification Program, or HAMP), refinance your mortgage, obtain relocation assistance, and more. Learn more at www.makinghomeaffordable.gov. The deadline to apply for most programs is December 31, 2016, but this date might be extended.

Some states have programs as well; many of them were set up to administer funds received from the federal Hardest Hit Fund. These programs often provide mortgage payment assistance or relocation assistance to unemployed or underemployed homeowners. To learn more, visit the U.S. Treasury's website at www.treasury.gov and type "Hardest Hit Fund" into the search box. In addition, some states have implemented foreclosure prevention mediation programs to help homeowners and mortgage lenders negotiate an alternative to foreclosure. You can find information about these programs on www.nolo.com: choose "Foreclosure" and "Government Foreclosure Prevention Programs."

Might I be better off just selling my house?

You're often better off selling the house than having it go to foreclosure. If you can find a buyer who will offer to pay at least what you owe your lender, take the offer. If the offer is for less than you owe your lender, your lender can block the sale. But many lenders will agree to a "short sale"—one that brings in less than you owe the lender. Some lenders require documentation that you are experiencing financial or medical hardship before they will agree to a short sale. If your lender agrees to a short sale, ask it to agree, in writing, to waive the deficiency (the difference between the sale price and what you owe on the loan). If your lender doesn't waive the deficiency, it might be able to sue you for that amount later.

Can I just walk away from the house?

If you get no offers for your house or the lender won't approve a short sale, you can

Beware of the IRS

IRS regulations might require you to pay higher taxes if you settle a debt or a creditor writes off money you owe. The rules state that if a creditor agrees to forgo a debt you owe, you must treat the amount you didn't pay as income. Similarly, if a creditor ceases collection efforts, declares a debt uncollectible, and reports it as a tax loss to the IRS, you must treat this amount as income. This includes any amount owed after a house foreclosure or property repossession, or on a credit card bill.

The rule applies to a debt or part of a debt for $600 or more forgiven by any bank, credit union, savings and loan, or other financial institution. The institution must send you and the IRS a Form 1099-C at the end of the tax year. These forms report that income, which means that when you file your tax return for the tax year in which your debt was forgiven, the IRS will check to make sure that you report the amount on the Form 1099-C as income.

There are some exceptions to this rule, however. Even if you receive a Form 1099-C, you don't have to report the amount in these situations:

- The debt was a student loan and was canceled because you worked in a profession and for an employer as promised when you took out the loan.
- The debt would have been deductible had you paid it.
- The cancellation of the debt is intended as a gift (this would be unusual).
- You discharge the debt in bankruptcy.
- You were insolvent before the creditor agreed to waive the debt. (You are insolvent if your debts exceed the value of your assets.)

In addition, you don't have to repeat certain qualified price reductions made by a property seller, or certain principle mortgage "Pay-for-Performance Payments" under the Home Affordable Modification Program.

walk away from your house. To do this, you transfer your ownership interest in your home to the lender using a deed in lieu of foreclosure. Keep in mind that with a deed in lieu, you won't get any cash back, even if you have lots of equity in your home. The deed in lieu may also appear on your credit report as a negative mark. If you opt for a deed in lieu, try to get concessions from the lender—after all, you are saving it the expense and hassle of foreclosing on your home. For example, ask the lender to eliminate negative references on your credit report or give you more time to stay in the house.

My utility bill was huge because of a very cold winter. Do I have to pay it all at once?

Maybe not. Many energy utilities offer programs that average your periods of high and low usage and allow you to make uniform monthly payments all year long. This means you can spread out utility payments for the high-use months. If you are elderly, disabled, or earn a low income, you may be eligible for reduced rates—ask your utility company. In addition, the federal Low-Income Home Energy Assistance Program (LIHEAP) helps low income customers pay their utility bills. For more information, contact your state's LIHEAP office for assistance (you can find it on the LIHEAP website at www.acf.hhs.gov/ocs/programs/liheap).

I'm swamped with student loans and can't afford my payments. What can I do to avoid default?

Contact the companies that service your student loans and tell them why you can't make your payments. You may be eligible for a deferment or forbearance—ways of postponing repayment. In very limited circumstances, you may be able to cancel a loan. Also talk to your loan holders about flexible payment options—many now offer payments geared to borrowers' incomes.

Another option is consolidating your student loans. With loan consolidation, you can lower your monthly payments by extending your repayment period; you may also be able to lower your interest rate. Consolidation terms and eligibility vary slightly from lender to lender. For information on consolidation, including potential disadvantages, go to www.studentloanborrowerassistance.org.

Finally, if you can prove that repayment would cause you extreme hardship, you may be able to discharge your student loans in bankruptcy. This is very tough to do, however.

I defaulted on a student loan a long time ago, and I just received collection letters. I can't afford very much, but I can pay something. Any suggestions?

Federal law allows you to rehabilitate your student loan by agreeing with your lender to a "reasonable and affordable" payment plan based on your income and expenses. Once you've made nine consecutive monthly payments, your loan will come out of default.

After you make the nine consecutive payments, the holder of your loan will sell it back to a regular loan-servicing company. (This is called loan rehabilitation.) Your new loan servicer will put you on a standard ten-year repayment plan, which may cause your monthly payments to increase dramatically. If you can't afford them, you will need to apply for a deferment (if you are eligible) or request a flexible repayment option.

I paid off my student loan a long time ago, but the Department of Education recently wrote me saying I still owe it. Help!

You need documentation. First, contact your school and ask for the Department of Education report showing the loan's status. Then, think about ways you can show that you paid the loan: Do you have canceled checks or old bank statements? Can you get copies of checks from your bank or a government regulatory agency if your bank is out of business? Does an old roommate remember seeing you write a check every month? Can you get old credit reports (check with lenders from whom you've borrowed in years past) that may show a payment status on an old loan? Get old tax returns (from the IRS, if necessary) showing that you itemized the interest deduction on student loan payments back when that was permitted. The last holder of the loan might have a copy of the signed promissory note. Any of these things will help you prove to the Department of Education that you paid your loan.

To find out more about the status of your loan, visit the Department of Education's website at www.studentaid.ed.gov or the National Student Loan Data System's website at www.nslds.ed.gov. Or contact the student loan ombudsman at 877-557-2575 or go to www.studentaid.ed.gov and under "How to Repay Your Loans," search "contact the ombudsman."

When can a creditor garnish my wages, place a lien on my house, or seize my bank account?

For the most part, a creditor must sue you, obtain a court judgment, and then solicit the help of a sheriff or other law enforcement officer to garnish wages. Even then, the maximum the creditor can take is 25% of your net pay or the amount by which your weekly net earnings exceed 30 times the federal minimum wage, whichever is less. Some states protect even more of your wages.

In two situations your wages may be garnished without your being sued:

- Most federal administrative agencies (including the IRS and the Department of Education) can garnish your wages to collect debts owed to that agency.
- Up to 50% of your wages can be garnished to pay child support or alimony (even more if you don't currently support any dependents or if you are in arrears).

To place a lien on your house or empty your bank account, almost all creditors must first sue you, get a judgment, and then use a law enforcement officer. A few creditors, such as an unpaid contractor who worked on your house, can put a lien on your house without suing. And again, the IRS is an exception—it can place a lien or empty your bank account without suing first.

I bounced a check. Can I get in trouble?

If you write a bad check, you will be on the hook for hefty bad-check processing fees from your bank. And if you don't make good on the check, the person to whom you wrote the check can sue you for damages. Finally, writing a bad check is a crime in every state if, when you wrote the check, you knew you didn't have money to cover it. If you are prosecuted, you may be able to avoid a trial if your county has a "diversion" program, where you attend classes for bad check writers. You must pay the tuition and make good on the bad checks you wrote.

RESOURCE

For more information about repaying debts, see:

- *Solve Your Money Troubles,* by Robin Leonard (Nolo). Explains your legal rights and offers practical strategies for dealing with debts and creditors.
- *Guide to Surviving Debt,* published by the National Consumer Law Center. Contains tips on dealing with debt collectors and repaying debts.

ONLINE HELP

The websites of the following organizations are good resources for information on repaying student loans and other debts:

- **www.studentloanborrowerassistance.org** The Student Loan Borrower Assistance Project offers free, detailed information on student loan consolidation, repayment options, defaults, and much more.
- **www.nfcc.org** National Foundation for Credit Counseling can put you in contact with the consumer credit counseling service office located nearest you and has budget worksheets, tips for consumers, and lots of helpful information. You can also phone the NFCC at 800-388-2227.
- **www.studentaid.ed.gov** The Federal Student Aid Center provides information about federal student loan repayment programs. You can also phone this Center at 800-433-3243.
- **www.consumer.ftc.gov** The Consumer Information Section of the Federal Trade Commission includes extensive articles and resources on debt and credit. You can also phone the FTC at 877-FTC-HELP.

Dealing With the IRS

Of all debts men are least willing to pay the taxes.

—Ralph Waldo Emerson

No three letters bring more fear to the average American than IRS. Yet, at one time or another in our lives, nearly everyone will owe a tax bill they can't pay, need extra time to file a tax return, or even get audited. This section suggests several strategies for dealing with the government's tax collectors.

How long should I keep my tax papers?

Keep anything related to your tax return—W-2 and 1099 forms, receipts and canceled checks for deductible items—for at least three years after you file. The IRS usually has three years from the day you file your return to audit you. For example, if you filed your 2015 tax return on April 15, 2016, keep those records until at least April 16, 2019. To be completely safe, you should keep your records for six years. The reason is that the IRS can audit you up to six years after you file if the IRS believes you underreported your income by 25% or more. Some experts say that you should never discard tax returns.

One last caution: Keep records showing purchase costs and sales figures for real estate, stocks, or other investments for at least three years after you sell these assets. You must be able to show your taxable gain or loss to an auditor.

If I can't pay my taxes, should I file a return anyway?

Absolutely. The consequences of filing and not paying are less severe than those for simply not filing. If you don't file a tax return, the IRS will assess a penalty of up to 25% of the tax due, plus interest. In addition, the IRS could criminally charge you for failing to file a return (although it isn't likely to). By contrast, if you file a return but can't pay, you'll only be on the hook for interest and penalties of ½% per month of the tax you owe.

Who has access to my IRS files?

Under federal law, tax files are confidential. Even IRS officials cannot rummage willy-nilly through your tax files unless they are involved in some kind of case regarding you and your taxes. Consequently, individuals, businesses, and credit reporting agencies do not have access to your tax information unless you authorize its release to the IRS in writing.

The privacy law has exceptions, however, and IRS security is sometimes lax. Your IRS files are shared with other federal and state agencies that can demonstrate a "need to know." This usually occurs when your affairs are being investigated by a law enforcement agency. In fairness to the IRS, many leaks are the result of sloppiness by other federal or state agencies granted access to IRS files. Furthermore, computer hackers have broken into IRS and government databases and retrieved private tax information.

Do many people cheat on their taxes? And what will happen to me if I cheat on mine?

No one really knows how many people cheat the IRS, but several years ago an independent poll found that 20% of Americans admitted to cheating. This is somewhat in line with government studies showing that 82% of us faithfully file and pay our taxes every year. The IRS claims that most cheating is by self-employed small business people who do not have taxes withheld by their employers.

If you are caught in some major cheating, the government can (but rarely does) throw you in jail. Very few people are jailed in the United States for tax crimes—and many of those who are also are charged with drug crimes.

The IRS would much rather collect money than put anyone in prison. More likely, if you're caught cheating, you'll be assessed heavy penalties and will probably be audited for several years.

I am faced with a tax bill that I can't pay. Am I completely at the IRS's mercy, or do I have some options?

There are six ways to deal with a tax bill you can't pay:

- Borrow from a financial institution, family, or friends and pay the tax bill in full.
- Negotiate a monthly payment plan with the IRS. Your payments will include interest and penalty charges. (See IRS Form 9465, *Installment Agreement Request;* these and other IRS forms are available at www.irs.gov.)
- File for Chapter 13 bankruptcy to set up a payment plan for your debts, including your taxes.
- Find out whether you can wipe out the debt in a Chapter 7 bankruptcy (only certain tax debts are dischargeable).
- Make an offer in compromise—that is, ask the IRS to accept less than the full amount due—by filing IRS Form 656, *Offer in Compromise.*
- Ask the IRS to designate your debt temporarily uncollectible if you are out of work or your income is very low. This will buy you time to get back on your feet before dealing with the IRS. But interest and penalties will continue to accrue.

I made a mistake on my tax return and am now being billed for the taxes, plus interest and penalties. Do I have to pay it all?

Maybe not. The IRS must charge you interest on your tax bill, but penalties are discretionary. The IRS abates (cancels) about one-third of all penalties it charges. The trick is to convince the IRS that you had "reasonable cause" (a good excuse) for failing to observe the tax law. Here are some reasons that might work:

- serious illness or a death in the family
- destruction of your records by a flood, fire, or other catastrophe
- wrong advice from the IRS over the phone
- bookkeeper or accountant error, or
- your being in jail or out of the country at the time the tax return was due.

You can ask anyone at the IRS to cancel a penalty, in person or over the phone. And you can ask for a penalty to be canceled even if you already paid it. The best way to get the IRS's attention is to use IRS Form 843, *Claim for Refund and Request for Abatement.* Send this form to your IRS Service Center.

Can the IRS take my house if I owe back taxes?

The IRS can seize just about anything you own—including your home and pension plans. There is a list of items exempt by federal law from IRS seizures, but it is hardly generous, and it doesn't include your residence. Moreover, state homestead-protection laws don't apply to the IRS. With that said, the good news is that the federal Taxpayer Bill of Rights discourages the IRS from taking homes of people who owe back taxes. In addition, the IRS doesn't like the negative publicity generated when it takes a home, unless of course it is the home of a notorious public enemy.

Nevertheless, if the IRS collection division has tried—and failed—to get any cooperation from a tax debtor (for example, if the debtor has not answered correspondence or returned phone calls, or has made threats, lied about income, or hidden assets), the IRS may go after a residence as a last resort. An IRS tax collector isn't authorized to make the decision—it must come from top IRS personnel.

If the IRS lets you know that it plans to take your house, your Congressperson may be able to intervene and put some pressure on the IRS to stop the seizure. And if the seizure would add you and your family to the ranks of the homeless, you can plead that the seizure would create a substantial hardship.

Tax-Avoidance Schemes Don't Work

Dozens of tax-avoidance schemes emerge every decade. Some promoters are very persuasive, particularly if you are predisposed to believing that it's possible to opt out of the tax system. Sad to say, these promoters are all snake-oil salesmen, the most successful of whom make millions peddling their products at expensive seminars and through underground publications. One recent scheme involves holding your assets in multiple family trusts, limited partnerships, and offshore banks. While these artifices may put your assets beyond the reach of your creditors, they won't beat the IRS.

In the unhappy event the IRS does seize your home, all may not be lost. The IRS must sell the home at public auction, usually held about 45 days after the seizure. Then, the high bidder at auction must wait 180 days to get clear title. In this interim period, you have the right to redeem (buy back) the home by coming up with the bid price plus interest.

What are my chances of getting through an audit without owing additional taxes?

Although only about 1% of all tax returns are audited (the percentage is higher for higher income earners and those who own a small business), the IRS has a pretty high success rate. Fewer than 15% of all IRS audit victims make a clean getaway. This is primarily because the IRS's sophisticated computer selection process makes it likely that the agency will audit returns in which adjustments are almost a certainty.

If you receive an audit notice, focus on limiting the damage rather than getting off scot-free. Most adjustments made following an audit result from poor taxpayer records, so make sure you have organized documentation to back up your deductions, exemptions, and other claims. Ignore the tales about dumping a box of receipts on the auditor's desk in the hope that the auditor will let you off rather than go through the mess. It doesn't work like that. If you have any significant worries, get a tax pro to represent you or help you navigate through the perilous audit waters.

Can I challenge the IRS if I get audited and don't agree with the result?

Yes, you do not have to accept any audit report. In most cases, you can appeal by sending a protest letter to the IRS within 30 days after receiving the audit report. If you request an appeals consideration, you will be granted a meeting with an appeals officer who is not part of the IRS division that performed your audit. See IRS Publication 5, *Your Appeal Rights and How to Prepare a Protest If You Don't Agree.*

If your appeal fails, you still can file a petition in tax court. This is a fairly inexpensive and simple process if the audit bill is for less than $50,000. If it's for more, you will most likely need the help of a tax attorney.

Generally, it pays to contest an audit report by appealing and going to court. About half the people who challenge their audit report succeed in lowering their tax bill.

RESOURCE

For more information about dealing with the IRS, see *Stand Up to the IRS,* by Frederick W. Daily (Nolo). This book explains your legal rights and offers practical strategies for dealing with the IRS.

Debt Collections

Laws prohibit debt collectors from using abusive or deceptive tactics to collect a debt. Unfortunately, many collectors ignore the rules. In addition, creditors and debt collectors have powerful collection tools once they have won a lawsuit for the debt. Here are some frequently asked questions and answers to help you deal with debt collectors.

Collection agencies have been calling me all hours of the day and night. Can I get them to stop contacting me?

It's against the law for a debt collector who works for a collection agency (as opposed to working in the collections department of the creditor itself) to call you at an unreasonable time. The law presumes that calls before 8 a.m. or after 9 p.m. are unreasonable. But other hours may be unreasonable too, such as daytime hours for a person who works nights. The law, the federal Fair Debt Collection Practices Act (FDCPA), also bars collectors from calling you at work if you ask them not to, harassing you, using abusive language, making false or misleading statements, adding unauthorized charges to the bill, and many other practices. Under the FDCPA, you can demand that the collection agency stop contacting you, except to tell you that collection efforts have ended or that the creditor or collection agency will sue you. You must put your request in writing.

I'm getting calls from the collections department of a local merchant I did business with. Can I tell that collector to stop contacting me?

Maybe. The FDCPA applies only to debt collectors who work for collection agencies. However, some states have fair debt collection laws that do cover creditors' collection departments. Check with your state consumer protection office to see whether your state law applies to in-house collectors and if so, what types of collection practices it prohibits. Find your state consumer protection agency at www.usa.gov.

A debt collector insists that I wire the money I owe through Western Union. Am I required to do so?

No, and it could be expensive if you do. Many collectors, especially when a debt is more than 90 days past due, will suggest several "urgency payment" options, including:

- **Sending money by express or overnight mail.** This will add at least $10 to your bill; a first-class stamp is fine.
- **Wiring money through Western Union's Quick Collect or American Express's Moneygram.** This is another $10 down the drain.
- **Putting your payment on a credit card.** You'll never get out of debt if you do this.

You Can Run, But You Can't Hide

In this technological age, it's easy to run from collectors—but hard to hide. Collectors use many different resources to find debtors. They may contact relatives, friends, neighbors, and employers to get your new whereabouts. In addition, collectors often get information from post office change of address forms, state motor vehicle registration information, voter registration records, former landlords, and banks.

Can a collection agency add interest to my debt?

In most cases, yes. But only if:

- the original agreement allows for additional interest to accrue during collection proceedings, or
- state law authorizes the addition of interest.

A collection agency sued me and won. Will I still get calls and letters demanding payment?

Probably not. Before obtaining a court judgment, a debt collector generally has only one way of getting paid: to demand payment. This is done with calls and letters. Once the collector (or creditor) sues and gets a judgment, however, you can expect more aggressive collection actions.

If you have a job, the collector will try to garnish a portion of your wages. The collector may also try to seize any bank or other deposit accounts you have. If you own real property, the collector will probably record a lien, which will have to be paid when you sell or refinance your property. Even if you're not currently working or have no property, you're not home free. Depending on the state, court judgments can last up to 20 years and, in many states, can be renewed so they last even longer.

What can I do if a bill collector violates the FDCPA?

Document the violation as soon as it occurs. Write down what happened, when it happened, and who witnessed it. Try to have a witness present the next time you talk to the collector.

Then file a complaint with the Federal Trade Commission and the agency that regulates collection agencies in your state. Send a copy of your complaint to the creditor who hired the collection agency. If the violations are severe enough, the creditor may stop the collection efforts.

Also, you can sue a collection agency (and the creditor that hired the agency) in small claims court for violating the FDCPA. If the violations are outrageous, you can sue the collection agency and creditor in regular civil court. One Texas jury awarded a debtor $11 million when a debt collector made death and bomb threats against her and her husband that frightened them into moving out of the county.

RESOURCE

For more information about debt collections, see:

- *Solve Your Money Troubles,* by Robin Leonard (Nolo). Explains your legal rights and offers practical strategies for dealing with debts and creditors.
- The Federal Trade Commission, 877-FTC-HELP (382-4357), www.consumer.ftc.gov. Publishes free pamphlets on debts and credit, including a few on the Fair Debt Collections Practices Act. Also takes complaints about collection agencies.

Bankruptcy

Where everything is bad it must be good to know the worst.

—Francis Herbert Bradley

If you are seriously in debt, you might consider filing for bankruptcy.

What exactly is bankruptcy?

Bankruptcy is a federal court process designed to help consumers and businesses eliminate their debts or repay them under the protection of the bankruptcy court.

Aren't there different kinds of bankruptcy?

Yes. Bankruptcies can generally be described as "liquidation" or "reorganization."

Liquidation bankruptcy is called Chapter 7. Under Chapter 7 bankruptcy, a consumer or business asks the bankruptcy court to wipe out (discharge) the debts owed. Certain debts cannot be discharged—these are discussed below. In exchange for the discharge of debts, the business assets or the consumer's nonexempt property are sold—that is, liquidated—and the proceeds are used to pay off creditors. The property a consumer might lose is discussed below.

In a reorganization bankruptcy, you file a plan with the bankruptcy court that proposes how you will repay your creditors. Some debts must be repaid in full; others you pay only in part.

There are several types of reorganization bankruptcy. Consumers with secured debts of less than $1,184,200 and unsecured debts of less than $394,725 can file for Chapter 13. Family farmers can file for Chapter 12. Businesses, or consumers with debts in excess of the Chapter 13 debt limits, can file for Chapter 11, which is more time-consuming and expensive.

Who can file for Chapter 7 bankruptcy?

Not everyone is eligible to use Chapter 7. For example, you cannot get a Chapter 7 discharge if your debts were discharged in another Chapter 7 case within the last eight years, or in a Chapter 13 case within the last six years. You also won't be allowed to file if you had a previous Chapter 7 case dismissed within the last 180 days for specified reasons. And, the court may dismiss your Chapter 7 case if you have tried to defraud your creditors.

In order to qualify for Chapter 7 bankruptcy, you must also pass the means test. If the court determines, based on income and expense figures you provide, that you have enough money to pay off a certain portion of your debts, you won't pass the test. Here are the basic steps you have to follow:

1. Calculate your average monthly income in the six months before you file for bankruptcy.
2. Compare your income to your state's median income for a family of your size (you can find median income figures at the website of the U.S. Trustee, www.justice.gov/ust).
3. If your income is equal to or less than the median, you may use Chapter 7. If your income is more than the median, you'll have to add up your expenses—in some cases, using amounts dictated by the IRS rather than what you actually spend—and compare them to your income. If these figures show that you would have enough money left over to pay a portion of your debts, you may not be allowed to use Chapter 7.

How does a Chapter 7 bankruptcy case generally proceed?

You will file a packet of forms with the bankruptcy court listing your income, expenses, assets, debts, and property transactions for the past couple of years. You must also file a certificate showing that you've completed a credit counseling course, and pay a filing fee, currently $335.

Once your case is filed, a bankruptcy trustee will be appointed by the court to oversee your case. Shortly after you file, you must attend a brief "meeting of creditors," where the trustee reviews your forms and asks questions about the information you supplied. (Creditors rarely attend this meeting, despite its name.) If you have any nonexempt property, you must give it (or its cash value) to the trustee.

Three to six months later, after you complete a course on debt management, you will receive a notice from the court that your qualified debts were discharged, and your case will be over.

How does a Chapter 13 bankruptcy case typically proceed?

To file for Chapter 13 bankruptcy, you'll have to file forms listing income, expenses, debts, assets, and property transactions for the past couple of years. You'll also have to file a proposed repayment plan, in which you describe how you intend to repay your debts (or a portion of certain types of debts) over the next three to five years. You'll have to get credit counseling from a nonprofit agency before you file.

The court will appoint a trustee to oversee your case. The trustee will call a meeting of creditors (creditors often attend this meeting, especially if they want something more than you're offering in your repayment plan). Because a creditor or the bankruptcy trustee may challenge certain aspects of your repayment plan, you may have to go back to the drawing board several times. In addition, a creditor or the trustee might challenge the dischargeability of a debt. Eventually, you will attend a hearing before a bankruptcy judge who will either confirm or deny your plan. If your plan is confirmed, and you make all of the payments called for under the plan, any remaining balance on dischargeable debts will be wiped out at the end of your case.

Nondischargeable Debts

Certain debts cannot be discharged—that is, they will not be wiped out if you file for bankruptcy. If you file for Chapter 7, you will still owe these debts even after your bankruptcy case is over. If you file for Chapter 13, you will have to pay these debts in full as part of your repayment plan. Some of the more common nondischargeable debts include:

- tax debts
- debts you owe for child or spousal support
- debts for personal injury or death caused by your drunk operation of a car or other vehicle
- student loans, in many cases
- fines and penalties imposed for breaking the law, and
- certain cash advances and debts for luxury goods incurred shortly before filing for bankruptcy.

What property might I lose if I file for bankruptcy?

You lose no property (other than the income you use to fulfill your repayment plan) in Chapter 13, unless you choose to sell it to pay a debt or give it back to the seller.

In Chapter 7, you select property you are eligible to keep from a list of exemptions provided by your state; in some states, you have the option of instead using exemptions provided in the federal Bankruptcy Code.

Certain kinds of property are exempt in almost every state, while others are almost never exempt. The following are items you can typically keep (exempt property):

- motor vehicles, to a certain value
- reasonably necessary clothing (no mink coats)
- reasonably needed household furnishings and goods (the second TV may have to go)

- household appliances
- jewelry, to a certain value
- personal effects
- life insurance (cash or loan value, or the proceeds of life insurance), to a certain value
- pensions
- part of the equity in your home
- tools of your trade or profession, to a certain value
- portion of unpaid but earned wages, and
- public benefits (welfare, Social Security, unemployment compensation) accumulated in a bank account.

Items you must typically give up (nonexempt property) include:

- expensive musical instruments (unless you're a professional musician)
- stamp, coin, and other collections
- family heirlooms
- cash, bank accounts, stocks, bonds, and other investments
- second car or truck, and
- second or vacation home.

RESOURCE

For more information about bankruptcy, see these Nolo books:

- *How to File for Chapter 7 Bankruptcy,* by Stephen Elias and Albin Renauer. Provides all of the information you need to file for Chapter 7 bankruptcy, including required forms.
- *Chapter 13 Bankruptcy: Keep Your Property & Repay Debts Over Time,* by Stephen Elias and Patricia Dzikowski. Provides detailed information about Chapter 13 bankruptcy.
- *The New Bankruptcy: Will It Work for You?,* by Stephen Elias and Leon Bayer. Helps you decide whether to file for bankruptcy and, if so, which type is best for you.

ONLINE HELP

The following sites are good resources for consumer information on bankruptcy:

- **www.justice.gov/ust** The website of the U.S. Trustee provides lists of approved credit and debt counseling agencies, median income amounts for each state, and means testing.
- **www.uscourts.gov** The website of the U.S. Courts has all of the official bankruptcy forms.

Rebuilding Credit

People who have been through a financial crisis—bankruptcy, repossession, foreclosure, history of late payments, IRS lien or levy, or something similar—may think they will never get credit again. Not true. By following some simple steps, you can rebuild your credit in just a few years.

What is the first step in rebuilding credit?

The first step in rebuilding credit is getting your debts and finances under control. Sit down and make a budget. Determine your expenses, your income, and the amount of your debt. The tricky part comes next—figuring out how to pay your debts and live within your means. There are many ways to do this, and you can get ideas and help from books or online (see the list at the end of this chapter). You can also enlist the help of a consumer credit counselor. The U.S. Trustee's website at www.justice.gov/ust has a list of government-approved debt counselors.

Once you've got a handle on your debts and finances, you can begin cleaning up your credit report and building positive credit for the future.

What is a credit report?

Credit reports are compiled by credit reporting agencies—private, for-profit companies that gather information about your credit history and sell it to banks, mortgage lenders, credit unions, credit card companies, department stores, insurance companies, landlords, and even employers.

Credit reporting agencies get most of their data from creditors. They also search court records for lawsuits, judgments, and bankruptcy filings. And they go through county records to find recorded liens (legal claims against property).

Noncredit data in a credit report usually include names you previously used, past and present addresses, Social Security number, employment history, marriages, and divorces. Your credit history includes the names of your creditors, type and number of each account, when each account was opened, your payment history for the previous 24 to 36 months, your credit limit or the original amount of a loan, and your current balance. The report will show if an account has been turned over to a collection agency or is in dispute.

What should I do if I find mistakes in my credit report?

As you read through your report, make a list of everything out of date. Check for the following:

- lawsuits, paid tax liens, accounts sent out for collection, late payments, and any other adverse information more than seven years old
- bankruptcies more than ten years after the discharge or dismissal (CRAs often list Chapter 13 bankruptcies for only seven years, but they can stay for as many as ten), and
- credit inquiries (requests by companies for a copy of your report) more than two years old.

Next, look for incorrect or misleading information, such as:

- incorrect or incomplete name, address, phone number, Social Security number, or employment information
- bankruptcies not identified by the specific chapter number

- accounts not yours or lawsuits in which you were not involved
- incorrect account histories—such as late payments when you paid on time
- closed accounts listed as open—it may look as if you have too much open credit, and
- any account you closed that doesn't say "closed by consumer."

After reviewing your report, complete a "request for reinvestigation" (you can use the form provided by the credit reporting agencies (CRAs) online). Once the CRA receives your request, it must investigate the items you dispute and contact you within 30–45 days (the exact timeline depends on whether you sent the request after getting your free annual report and whether you send additional information). If you don't hear back within the time limit, send a follow-up letter.

If you are right, or if the creditor who provided the information can no longer verify it, the CRA must remove the information from your report. Credit reporting agencies sometimes remove an item on request without an investigation if rechecking the item is more bother than it's worth.

If you don't get anywhere with the CRA, send a dispute letter directly to the creditor asking that the information be removed. If the information was reported by a collection agency, send the agency a copy of your letter too.

If you still don't get action, file a complaint with the Consumer Financial Protection Bureau (CFPB). The CFPB's contact information is at the end of this chapter.

How to Get Your Credit Report

There are three nationwide credit reporting agencies (CRAs)—Equifax, TransUnion, and Experian. Everyone is entitled to a free report from each of these three CRAs once a year.

If you have already gotten your free report for the year, you are also entitled to a free report if:

- someone has taken adverse action against you because of information contained in your report
- you are on public assistance
- you reasonably believe your report contains errors due to fraud
- you are unemployed and expect to apply for a job within 60 days, or
- you have been the victim of identity theft and have placed a fraud alert on your file.

To get your free report, go to www.annualcreditreport.com, a website created and sponsored by the three CRAs. You can also request your reports by phone at 877-322-8228, or by mailing a form to Annual Credit Report Request Service, P.O. Box 105281, Atlanta, GA 30348-5281 (the form is available online or by phone at the number listed above).

If a CRA is including incorrect information in your report, or you want to explain a particular entry, you have the right to put a brief explanatory statement in your report. The CRA must give a copy of your statement—or a summary—to anyone who requests your report. Be clear and concise; use the fewest words possible.

I've been told that I need to use credit to rebuild my credit. Is this true?

Yes. The one type of positive information creditors most like to see in credit reports is credit payment history. If you have a credit card, use it every month. (Make small purchases and pay them off to avoid interest charges.) If you don't have a credit card, apply for one. Department stores and gasoline companies are more likely to issue accounts with low credit—so this is often a good place to start. Another option is getting a friend or relative to act as cosigner or guarantor. Or, consider a secured credit card (you deposit money with a bank, and the bank issues a credit card with a credit limit that is a percentage of your deposit). Some secured cards don't report to the CRAs, though, so check first—otherwise the card won't help build your credit.

But don't apply for new credit before getting back on your feet. Defaulting on new credit will only make matters worse.

What else can I do to rebuild my credit?

After you've cleaned up your credit report, work on getting positive information into your record. Here are two suggestions:

- If your credit report is missing accounts you pay on time, send the CRAs a recent account statement and copies of canceled checks showing your payment history. Ask that these be added to your report. The CRA doesn't have to add anything, but often will.
- Creditors like to see evidence of stability, so if any of the following information is not in your report, send it to the CRAs and ask that it be added: your current employment, your previous employment (especially if you've been at your current job fewer than two years), your current residence, your date of birth, and your checking account number. Again, the CRA doesn't have to add these, but often will.

RESOURCE

For more information about rebuilding your credit, see these Nolo books:

- *Credit Repair,* by Robin Leonard. A guide to lawfully rebuilding your credit. It contains instructions and forms for cleaning up your credit report, advice on creating a budget and getting your finances under control, strategies for rebuilding credit, and more.

- *Solve Your Money Troubles*, by Robin Leonard. Explains your legal rights and offers practical strategies for dealing with debts and creditors, including rebuilding your credit.

ONLINE HELP

The following sites are good resources for helping you manage your money:

- **www.nolo.com** Nolo offers information about a wide variety of legal topics, including advice about consumer law, bankruptcy, debts, and credit. It also has free online calculators for credit, mortgage, savings, debt, retirement, and more.
- **www.consumerfinance.gov** The Consumer Financial Protection Bureau regulates credit reporting agencies. You can get information about credit discrimination, file a complaint online, and more.
- **www.consumer.ftc.gov** The Federal Trade Commission has dozens of helpful publications on consumer issues, enforcement guidance, tips on spending and using credit wisely, and information on debts and credit, including how to get a free copy of your credit reports and deal with errors in those reports. You can also phone the FTC Consumer Response Center at 877-FTC-HELP (382-4357).
- **www.fraud.org** Fraud.org helps you file a complaint with federal agencies if you've been defrauded. It also offers information on how to avoid becoming the victim of a scam.
- **www.bbb.org** The Better Business Bureau provides general information on its programs and services, including alerts, warnings, and updates about businesses. You can also find information about filing a complaint against a business and using the BBB's dispute resolution program.
- **www.publications.usa.gov** The Federal Citizen Information Center provides the latest in consumer news as well as many publications of interest to consumers, including the *Consumer Information Catalog*.
- **www.irs.gov** The Internal Revenue Service provides tax information, forms, and publications.

CHAPTER

10

Cars and Driving

When Solomon said that there was a time and a place for everything, he had not encountered the problem of parking an automobile.

—**Bob Edwards**

Plainly, Americans love their cars—that's why we own more cars per person than the rest of the world, on average. For the privilege of owning and operating a new vehicle, we pay an average of more than $8,000 per year. We also expend plenty of time and energy figuring out which cars to buy, how to insure and maintain them, and how to keep out of trouble on the road. This chapter provides answers to many common questions about owning a car and driving responsibly.

Buying a New Car

These days, the average new car costs more than $30,000. For that amount of money, you would hope for a hassle-free buying experience and a safe and reliable product. Unfortunately, new car buyers are frequently overwhelmed by the pressure to buy immediately or spend more than planned. What's worse, the product you bring home might be plagued with problems ranging from annoying engine "pings," to frequent stalls, to safety hazards such as poor acceleration or carbon monoxide leaks.

I want to get a good deal on a new car. How do I figure out what make and model I should buy?

There are several good resources to help you comparison shop when you're looking for a new car. *Consumer Reports* magazine publishes an annual car-buying issue that compares price, features, service history, resale value, and reliability. Another helpful source of information is *Motor Trend* magazine. Finally, many websites provide price and feature information. To start, try www.edmunds.com, www.caranddriver.com, or www.jdpower.com.

When deciding what car to buy, resist the urge to buy more car than you can afford—and don't talk yourself into a more expensive car by financing it over four or five years. You'll pay a bundle in interest that way.

Do you have any tips for negotiating with a car dealer?

Negotiating price with a dealer is almost never a pleasant experience. And, if you don't do it well, you are likely to pay hundreds or thousands of dollars more for a car. Here are some tips for getting the best deal.

- Know which car you want (or a few you are interested in), which features you want, and what you can afford to pay before you walk into the dealership. Then, stick to your guns.
- Know the dealer's cost for the car before you start negotiating. Use this figure as the starting point from

which you negotiate up. The dealer invoice price is how much the dealer paid for the car. Many websites list dealer invoice prices. But the dealer's final cost is often even lower, because manufacturers offer dealers behind-the-scenes financial incentives. You can get a better idea of a car's value from websites such as www.consumerreports.org, www.kbb.com, and www.edmunds.com.

- Don't buy in a hurry. Take time to compare prices. And usually, the longer you take and the more times you walk away, the lower the price will fall.
- Contact local dealerships via the Internet and solicit multiple quotes. This forces the dealers to bid against each other. When you get a satisfactory bid, ask the dealer to send you a worksheet showing all prices, taxes, and fees. Bring this to the dealership when you're ready to buy.
- Order your new car if the one you want is not on the lot. Cars on the lot frequently have options you don't want, which jack up the price.
- Don't make a deposit on a vehicle before the dealership has accepted your offer.
- If a rebate is offered, negotiate the price as if the rebate didn't exist. Rebates come from the manufacturer and shouldn't be a reason to pay the dealer more for the car.
- Don't discuss the possibility of a trade-in until you fix the price for your new car.
- Don't trade in your old vehicle without doing your homework. A dealer will give you the low *Kelley Blue Book* value, at most. (The *Kelley Blue Book* lists wholesale and retail prices for cars by year and model. You can find it in libraries, bookstores, or online at www.kbb.com.) Take a look at classified ads to get an idea of how much you could get if you sold your car yourself. Don't accept less than what you can get on the street. If the dealer won't pay you what the car is worth, forget the trade-in and sell your old car yourself.
- Learn about sales tactics dealerships use to get you to pay top dollar. Armed with this information, you will be better able to deflect the tactics and get a good deal. There are lots of books on this subject. One of the best is *Don't Get Taken Every Time,* by Remar Sutton (Penguin Books).

What other information do I need to know before I buy my new car?

Before you sign any contract, find out:

- what the warranty covers and how long it lasts
- how you might lose warranty coverage (such as by driving off-road or installing after-market parts)

- whether an extended warranty is available to you, and if so:
  - what it will cost
  - what it covers
  - how long it lasts
  - whether it duplicates coverage provided by the manufacturer's warranty, and
  - how likely it is that you'll need it (whether the covered parts have a history of problems)
- the vehicle's estimated miles per gallon for city and highway driving, and
- the dealer's suggested maintenance schedule.

Is there anything I should do when my new car is delivered?

Yes. Before signing a receipt and paying for your new vehicle, do the following:

- Check the vehicle against your order, item by item. Make sure all features are included.
- Inspect the vehicle for damage. Some new vehicles are damaged during manufacturing or in transit. Because of this, you should never take delivery of a new vehicle at night or in the rain. Even in good artificial light, it's hard to see nicks and dents. You'll also likely miss subtle changes in paint that may indicate the car was damaged in transit and was repainted. Look especially for chips in the windshield.
- Test drive the vehicle and pay attention to odd noises, smells, and vibrations.
- Make sure the warranty matches what the dealer agreed to.

If I change my mind after I buy a new car, do I have the right to cancel the contract?

No. Unfortunately, many people think they have a right to change their mind, drive the car back to the dealer a day or two after buying, and cancel the contract. But the truth is, the dealer doesn't have to take the car back and probably won't, and you'll be stuck with a car you no longer want or cannot afford.

Soon after I brought my new car home, it started having problems. How do I know if it's a lemon?

Although the precise definition of a lemon varies by state, in general, a new car is a lemon if a number of attempts have been made to repair a "substantial defect" and the car continues to have this defect. A substantial defect is one that impairs the car's use, value, or safety, such as faulty brakes or turn signals. Minor defects, such as loose radio knobs and door handles, don't qualify.

In all states, the defect must occur within a certain period of time (usually one or two years) or within a certain number of miles (usually 12,000 or 24,000). You must allow the dealer or manufacturer to make a "reasonable" number of attempts to fix the defect. Typical state standards for meeting the reasonable repair attempt requirement include:

- the defect is a serious safety defect and remains unfixed after one repair attempt
- the defect is not a serious safety defect and remains unfixed after three or four repair attempts (the number depends on the state), or
- the vehicle is in the shop for a certain number of days (usually 30) in a one-year period.

ONLINE HELP

To find out whether your car qualifies as a lemon in your state, get a copy of your state's lemon law. Both www.lemonlawamerica.com and www.autopedia.com have links to each state's lemon law.

What should I do if my new car is a lemon?

If you think your new car is a lemon, you must notify the manufacturer and give its authorized dealer the opportunity to make repairs. When contacting the manufacturer, follow your state's notice requirements. (These are contained in your state's lemon law, which you can find at www.lemonlaw america.com or www.autopedia.com.) If possible, notify the manufacturer before you bring the car to the dealer. Then, deliver a copy of the notice to the dealer when you bring the car in for repair.

During the repair process, keep detailed records. (If you had your car repaired by a nondealer mechanic before notifying the manufacturer of the problem, keep records of those repairs, too.) Track the number of repair attempts and the time your car is out of service. Each time you bring your car in for repair, prepare a written, dated list of specific problems. Insist on receiving a detailed repair order from the dealer that includes symptoms, repairs done, parts replaced, and time your car was in the shop.

After you have taken the steps above, you can ask the manufacturer for a refund or replacement vehicle. (The dealer may be entitled to a small offset for your use of the car.) In most states, if the manufacturer has established a qualifying arbitration program, it can require you to go to arbitration before it pays you anything.

There are several different types of arbitration programs. If you are given a choice, pick one that is run by a state consumer protection agency rather than an in-house program administered by the manufacturer. Most of the large car manufacturers participate in the Better Business Bureau's Auto Line program—a free mediation and arbitration service to assist consumers with lemon law claims. To find out more, contact the BBB at www.bbb.org/autoline.

What happens at a lemon law arbitration?

At the arbitration hearing, the arbitrator hears both sides of the dispute. The arbitrator has a certain amount of time to decide whether your car is a lemon and whether you're entitled to a refund or a replacement.

Ask for a copy of the arbitration procedures and make sure they are followed.

Consumers who bring substantial documentation to the hearing tend to do better than those with little evidence to back up their claims. The types of documentation that can help include:

- brochures and ads about the vehicle—an arbitration panel is likely to make the manufacturer live up to its claims
- vehicle service records showing how often you took the car into the shop, and
- any other documents showing your attempts to get the dealer to repair your car, including emails and phone records.

It is important to take the arbitration seriously and be as prepared as possible. Although you can usually appeal a bad arbitration decision in court, or sue the manufacturer if the arbitration isn't binding, the arbitration decision could be used against you in court.

If I continue to drive my car while I wait for a decision, will it hurt my case?

Because it often takes a long time to get relief, most lemon laws allow you to keep using your car while pursuing a claim. But keep in mind that some courts may look less favorably on your case if you are able to drive your car. And, of course, you should never drive your car if it is unsafe to do so.

What if I don't like the arbitrator's decision?

If you don't like the ruling and the arbitration wasn't binding, you can usually sue the manufacturer in court. You may want to do this if you have substantial "consequential" damages—that is, damages that resulted from owning the lemon, such as the cost of renting a car while your car was in the shop or time off from work every time your car broke down.

"Secret" Warranty Adjustments

Many automobile manufacturers have "secret warranty," or warranty adjustment, programs. Under these programs, a manufacturer makes repairs for free on defects that occur after a warranty expires in order to avoid a recall and bad press. According to the Center for Auto Safety, at any given time there are about 500 secret adjustment warranty programs available through automobile manufacturers.

Unfortunately, in most states, manufacturers are not required to disclose the existence of a secret warranty program for a particular vehicle defect. This makes it very difficult for consumers to know when a defect may be covered. To learn more about secret warranty programs, including how to find them, see the Center for Auto Safety's website at www.autosafety.org/secret-warranties.

ONLINE HELP

If you think your new car is a lemon. Check out the National Highway Traffic Safety Administration website (www.nhtsa.gov) for consumer complaints about car defects.

Leasing a Car

Many new car drivers lease, rather than purchase, their vehicles. Although leasing isn't for everyone, some people swear by it. Before you sign on the dotted line, be sure you know what you're getting into.

What are the advantages of leasing a new car?

There are three main reasons people lease, rather than buy, a new vehicle:

- People who like to drive a new car every few years will pay much less to lease than to buy. They also don't have to deal with getting rid of their old car—they just turn it in at the end of the lease period.
- Lease payments are lower than loan payments for any given car.
- Leasing gives people the opportunity to drive a more expensive car than they could afford to buy.

Are there any obvious disadvantages to leasing?

Yes—there are many.

- If you continually lease your cars, you will have never-ending car payments. If you look forward to paying off your car and owning it free and clear, don't lease.
- If you decide to buy the car when the lease ends, you'll pay several thousand dollars more than if you had bought initially. For example, if you buy a car, paying $500 a month for four years, you'll pay a total of $24,000. You might be able to lease it for only $400 a month (total payments of $19,200), but you'll probably have to pay another $8,000 to keep it—and if you finance that $8,000, you'll pay even more.
- Most leases charge you as much as 25¢ a mile if you exceed the annual mileage limit—usually between 12,000 and 15,000 miles. If you plan to do extensive driving, leasing probably isn't for you.
- It's very, very expensive to break a lease early. If you no longer want or can't afford to keep your car—for example, because you lost your job or your financial situation changed—you will have to pay a hefty early termination fee.
- If you lease a lemon, in most states the leasing company has to do the complaining (remember, you don't own the car) in order to get redress.
- Leasing companies often require you to buy high levels of insurance, which can be expensive.

Are all leasing costs disclosed up front?

Not necessarily. Although the federal Consumer Leasing Act requires lease agreements to include a statement of costs (such as the number and amount of regular payments), the total amount due, insurance requirements, the penalty for defaulting, and whether you'll have a balloon payment at the end, many lease agreements bury key provisions in the fine print.

If you want to lease, be diligent and read all the fine print. Ask a lot of questions and demand that the answers be put in writing.

Is there any way to find out the interest rate on a lease?

Yes. Ask the dealer for something called the "money factor" or "leasing factor." Multiply that factor by 2,400, and you'll get the approximate interest rate.

Are there any good leasing deals?

Yes—especially those heavily advertised by car manufacturers. Those deals usually offer low monthly payments or a high value for the vehicle at the end (so that you're not paying for a lot of depreciation during the lease term), and offer to lock in the price you'd have to pay at lease-end if you want to keep the vehicle.

To get these good deals, you cannot deviate from the advertised terms. If you want air-conditioning, a larger engine, or any other feature that's not in the ad, the dealer will throw out the entire lease offer and you'll wind up paying a bundle.

Another way to get a good deal is to explore financing through an independent lease company. Look in the yellow pages or on the Internet under "Automotive—Leasing." Also, if you belong to a credit union or the AAA, ask about the possibility of financing your lease through them. Finally, if you are not taking advantage of a specific advertised leasing deal, treat your lease like a vehicle purchase. Shop around, compare lease terms between dealers, and negotiate lease terms before signing the contract. Keep your eye on the agreed-upon value of the vehicle (a lower value means lower monthly payments), upfront costs, lease length, monthly payments, and end-of-lease fees and charges.

I usually shop for a new car in the fall, when dealers are trying to get rid of old inventory. Does this strategy work for leasing?

In general, no. Because dealers lose money on cars sitting in their lots, they often increase the monthly lease payments to make up for lost revenue.

If I lease a vehicle, who pays for maintenance and repairs?

Your lease agreement will specify who must pay. In addition, the agreement should come with a manufacturer's warranty. Ideally, it will cover the entire length of the lease and the number of miles you are likely to drive.

Most lease agreements obligate you to pay for "excessive wear and tear." This means that when you return the vehicle at the end of the lease, the dealer could charge you to fix anything deemed to be beyond what would normally be expected. You should insist that the dealer specify in writing exactly what is meant by "excessive" before you sign the lease contract.

Finally, look for a deal that includes "gap" insurance. If the vehicle is stolen or totaled, gap insurance will pay the difference between what you owe under the lease and what the dealer can recover on the vehicle (assuming it's not stolen)—a difference that could amount to thousands of dollars.

Can I cancel my lease agreement early?

Probably not, unless you're willing to pay a substantial penalty. If you want to cancel your lease, look carefully at the provision describing what happens if you default or terminate the lease early. The provision may state that you'll owe an enormous sum of money, or may use a complex formula to calculate what you owe.

Lease Guide's Lease Kit explains the legal language in your contract regarding early lease termination and includes information on your options if you want to end a lease early. You can purchase the Lease Kit at www.leaseguide.com.

ONLINE HELP

More information about leasing a car. Both the Federal Trade Commission (at www.ftc.gov) and the Federal Reserve Board (at www.federalreserve.gov) publish information to help you understand your rights when leasing a car.

Buying a Used Car

Horsepower was a wonderful thing when only horses had it.

—Anonymous

While buying a used car is often a sound financial decision, the transaction itself has the potential to be a disaster. We probably all know someone who bought a used car—assured that "my grandmother drove it to church once a week"—only to have it fall apart shortly after bringing it home. But, with diligence and caution, you can minimize the risks associated with buying a used car and save a bundle of money in the process.

What are the advantages and disadvantages of buying a used car?

Buying a used car can be a smart financial decision. Not only do used cars cost less, but you also pay less in taxes, registration fees, and insurance. In addition, new cars depreciate rapidly during the first few years of ownership—usually between 25% and 45% in the first three years, depending on the make and model. So when you buy a used car, it has already taken the depreciation "hit." You pay less and your car depreciates more slowly during the years you own it.

But buying a used car has its risks. Most new cars have few problems during the first few years and are covered by warranty. Not so for used cars. Older cars have more problems and, usually, expired warranties. Also, the car could be a lemon or have hidden damage. Following the suggestions below will help you minimize these risks.

How do I go about finding a used car?

It's best to get an idea of the make, model, and year that you want. There are many good sources to help you compare cars. *Consumer Reports* magazine publishes an annual car-buying issue, comparing price, features, service histories, resale values, and reliability. Other sources of information are *Motor Trend* magazine and *The Insider's Guide to Buying a New or Used Car,* by Burke and Stephanie Leon (Betterway Books). The Internet also has lots of information. Try www.carsdirect.com, www.kbb.com, www.edmunds.com, and www.caranddriver.com.

Once you've made a preliminary decision as to what you want and what you can expect to pay, start looking. Here are some places to start:

- **Craigslist (www.craigslist.org).** Most major metropolitan areas have a Craigslist website with listings for cars sold by private owners and dealers.
- **Other websites.** Lots of websites list used cars for sale by geographical area. A few to try include www.carsdirect.com and www.cars.com, but there are many others.
- **The newspaper.** This is the traditional way to look for cars. Check for promotions or dealer sales. For the most part though, anything listed in the classified ads can also be found through Internet sites.
- **Check with new car dealers.** Many sell used cars. They usually list used cars on their websites as well.
- **Check with trusted mechanics.** They may know of reliable used cars for sale.

How much should I spend on a used car?

Check the wholesale and retail values of the cars that interest you. Bookstores and libraries have copies of the *Kelley Blue Book* (which lists wholesale and retail prices), or you can find it online at www.kbb.com.

For a small fee, *Consumer Reports* (www.consumerreports.org or 800-333-0663) will tell you how much a particular car is worth, taking into consideration the car's mileage, condition, and additional equipment (such as power windows or a sunroof).

How do I negotiate a good price?

After you've checked wholesale and retail prices of the car you want and thoroughly explored its condition, you are ready to negotiate. Often, the listed wholesale price of the car is a good opening bid, assuming the car is in decent condition. The seller will probably aim for retail price. The final price will depend on many factors, including the condition of the car, the circumstances of the person from whom you buy it, and your and the seller's negotiating skills.

Obviously, price isn't the only factor to consider when buying a used car. What else do I need to know?

With used cars, reliability is as important as price. Before you buy, you should:

- Have the car checked out by a mechanic you trust, or by a diagnostic center, which will check virtually every aspect and component of a car. Diagnostic centers are generally more expensive—but more thorough—than a mechanic.
- Ask for copies of the maintenance records for the life of the car.
- From your state motor vehicle department, you can often get a printed history of the car's previous ownership. It won't include the names or addresses of previous owners, but it will tell you the mileage each time it was sold and all states (other than where you live) where the car has been registered. You can get similar information from www.carfax.com. CARFAX reports sometimes list maintenance history as well. If this information doesn't match up or looks fishy, don't buy the car. You'll need a car's vehicle identification number (VIN) to get a CARFAX report.
- Do your own visual inspection—you'll want to look for oddities that might indicate damage (such as scratches or new paint).
- Look at the vehicle identification number (VIN) on the lower left-hand side of the front windshield. If it shows any signs of tampering, the car may be stolen.

The Buyers Guide

Federal law requires an automobile dealer to post a Buyers Guide in every used car it offers for sale (motorcycles and most recreational vehicles are exempt from this requirement). Among other things, the Buyers Guide tells you whether the vehicle is sold "as is" or is covered by a warranty. It must describe the warranty. Be sure to get the Buyers Guide when you buy a used car, and make sure it reflects any changes to warranty coverage that you negotiated with the dealer. The Buyers Guide becomes part of the sales contract—if the dealer refuses to make good on the warranty, you'll need it as proof of your original agreement.

If you're buying the car from a private party (as opposed to a car dealer), make sure the person selling the car actually holds title. Ask to see the seller's driver's license (or other form of ID) and the title certificate for the vehicle.

Will a warranty protect me if I get a bad deal on a used car?

If you're buying a used car from a dealer, the dealer will probably offer you an extended warranty. Before buying, be sure you know exactly what is covered and what isn't, and for how long. You'll also need to know the types of problems the car has had in the past, and the types of problems that particular make of car is likely to have in the future. (You can get this kind of information from *Consumer Reports*, at www.consumerreports.org.) It makes no sense to buy an extended warranty that doesn't cover emissions, for example, if the type of car you're buying is likely to have emission problems in a year or so.

Used Car "Lemon Laws"

Some states have lemon laws or warranty coverage for used cars. To find out about your state, contact the state attorney general or department of consumer affairs. Or, you can look up your state's lemon law at www.autopedia.com or www.autosafety.org and check to see whether it covers used cars.

If you're buying a car from a private party, check to see whether the car is still under a factory warranty or whether the original owner purchased an extended warranty—and whether either of these warranties can be transferred to you as the new owner.

Financing a Vehicle Purchase

If you are like most people, you don't have a large sum of cash to plunk down for a new or used car. This means you'll have to finance your purchase. Of course, after you spend time shopping for a car and negotiating a good deal, the last thing you'll want to do is haggle over financing terms. But if you don't shop around for the best financing deal and read the finance contract carefully, you could end up paying lots more for a loan than you should.

I want to buy a car, but I'm not sure how to finance my purchase. Do you have any general advice?

If you can pay for the purchase outright, you'll save money by avoiding interest charges. But if you need to borrow money to buy the car, consider the following sources:

- **The car dealer.** Many offer generous terms—for example, interest at 1.5% or 2%—especially in the early fall when dealers are eager to clear out stock to make room for new models. Be careful that these low-interest loans don't require you to buy upgraded features or credit insurance. And don't assume you are getting the best deal around. Always compare dealer terms to those of banks and credit unions.

- **Banks you do business with.** Dealer financing isn't your only option. Before you buy, contact the banks where you have your savings, checking, credit card, or business accounts. Ask about the going rate for car loans. Also ask about discount rates for loans tied to your other accounts.
- **Credit unions.** If you're a member of a credit union (or are eligible to join one), be sure to investigate its car loans. Historically, credit unions have offered some of the best loan terms.

Regardless of who finances the contract, if you want a good interest rate but have a poor credit history, you'll need to either make a substantial down payment or get a cosigner.

If I borrow money for the purchase, what should the lender tell me about my loan?

If you get a car loan from a bank, credit union, or car dealer, the federal Truth in Lending Act requires that the lender disclose, in writing, important information about your loan, including:

- your right to a written itemization of the amount borrowed
- the total amount of the loan
- the monthly finance charge
- the annual percentage rate (APR)
- the number, amount, and due dates of all payments, and
- whether any late payment fee or penalty may be imposed.

Do You Need Credit Insurance?

Many dealers and lenders will ask you to buy credit insurance—insurance that will pay off your loan if you die or become disabled. (This is just like the dealer asking you to buy an extended warranty—he'd love for you to buy it, but he'll sell you the car without it if you refuse.) Before you add this cost to your contract, consider whether you really need it. Remember, you can always sell the car and use the proceeds to pay off the loan. In fact, most financial experts say credit insurance is unnecessary and advise consumers not to buy it. If you do decide you want this protection, you can almost always buy it from an outside source at a much better price.

Insuring Your Car

Certainly those so inclined can have lots of fun imagining possible needs for insurance.

—Hayden Curry

Most states require every registered vehicle or licensed driver to have some vehicle liability insurance. To find out your state's requirements, check out the Insurance Information Institute's website, at www.iii.org.

Even where it's not required by law, most drivers are wise to have some liability coverage. Before you buy auto insurance, you must decide how much coverage you need and what types of coverage are appropriate for you. And, of course, you'll want to find ways to cut your insurance costs.

What kinds of damage are covered under an auto insurance liability policy?

If you are at fault in a car accident, liability insurance pays for the damages that you cause to someone else. It does not pay for your own damages. There are two kinds of liability insurance: bodily injury and property damage. Bodily injury expenses include medical bills, rehabilitation expenses, and lost wages. Property damage expenses include the repair or replacement of any items belonging to another person that you damage or destroy.

Who is covered under an auto insurance liability policy?

An auto insurance liability policy usually covers the following people no matter what car they are driving:

- **Named insured**—the person or people named in the policy.
- **Spouse**—a spouse not named in the policy, unless he or she does not live with the named insured.
- **Other relative**—anyone living in the household with the named insured who is related by blood, marriage, or adoption, usually including a legal ward or foster child.
- **Anyone driving the insured vehicle with permission.** Someone who steals the car is not covered.

Which vehicles are normally covered under an auto insurance liability policy?

- **Named vehicles**—an accident in a nonnamed vehicle is covered only if a named insured (see above) was driving.
- **Added vehicles**—any vehicle that the named insured uses as a replacement for the original named vehicle, and any additional vehicle the named insured acquires during the policy period (you may be required to notify the company of the new or different vehicle within 30 days after you acquire it).
- **Temporary vehicles**—any vehicle, including a rental vehicle, that substitutes for an insured vehicle that is out of use because it needs repair or service, or has been destroyed.

What is collision coverage?

Collision coverage pays for property damage to your vehicle resulting from a collision with another car or object or from flipping over.

What is comprehensive coverage?

Comprehensive coverage pays for property damage to your vehicle resulting from anything other than a collision, such as a theft or a break-in.

> **When No-Fault Benefits Aren't Enough**
>
> All no-fault laws permit an injured driver to file a liability claim, and a lawsuit if necessary, against another driver who was at fault in an accident. The liability claim permits an injured driver to obtain compensation for medical and income losses above what the no-fault policy paid, as well as compensation for pain, suffering, and other general damages.
>
> Whether and when you can file a liability claim for further damages against the person at fault in your accident depends on the specifics of the no-fault law in your state. In some states, you can always file a liability claim for all damages in excess of your no-fault benefits. In others you must meet a monetary threshold, a serious injury threshold, or both, before you can file a liability claim.

What is uninsured motorist coverage?

If you have an accident with an uninsured vehicle or hit-and-run driver, the place to turn for compensation for your injuries is the uninsured motorist (UM) coverage of your own vehicle insurance policy. Normally, UM covers only bodily injury and not property damage to your vehicle. Vehicle damage would be covered by the collision coverage of your own policy.

What is no-fault automobile insurance?

Under no-fault insurance, each person's own insurance company pays for that person's medical bills and lost wages—up to certain dollar amounts—regardless of who was at fault.

About half of the states have mandatory no-fault laws, often referred to in policies as personal injury protection (PIP). Other states allow you to "add on" no-fault coverage to your existing policy (though it's not required). The advantage of no-fault insurance is prompt payment of medical bills and lost wages without any arguments about who caused the accident. But most no-fault insurance provides extremely limited coverage:

- No-fault pays benefits for medical bills and lost income only. It provides no compensation for pain, suffering, emotional distress, inconvenience, or lost opportunities.
- No-fault coverage does not pay for medical bills and lost income higher than the limits of each person's policy. No-fault benefits often fail to reimburse fully for medical bills and lost income.

- No-fault often does not apply to vehicle damage; those claims are paid under the liability insurance of the person at fault, or by your own collision insurance.

My auto insurance rates keep going up. How can I cut some of the cost?

Here are a few suggestions for ways to reduce your premiums:

- Shop around for insurance. Just because your current company once offered you the best deal doesn't mean it's still competitive.
- Increase your deductibles.
- Reduce your collision or comprehensive coverage on older cars.
- Find out what discounts are available from your company (or from a different company). Discounts are often given to people who:
  - use public transit or carpool to work
  - take a class in defensive driving (especially if you are older)
  - own a car with safety features such as airbags or antilock brakes
  - install antitheft devices
  - are students with good academic records
  - have no accidents or moving violations, or
  - have multiple insurance policies with the same company—such as automobile and homeowners' insurance.
- Find out which vehicles cost more to insure. If you're looking to buy a new car, call your insurance agent and find out which cars are expensive to repair, targeted by thieves, or involved in a higher rate of accidents. These vehicles all have higher insurance rates.
- Consolidate your policies. Most of the time you will pay less if all owners or drivers who live in the same household are on one policy or at least are insured with the same company.

Your Driver's License

To a teenager, a driver's license seems magical—a ticket to freedom. For the rest of us, driver's licenses aren't much more than scraps of paper or plastic bearing bad pictures. But every now and then a question may arise about a license: Is it still good if I move to another state? What if I take a trip to a foreign country? And how do I know if I'm in danger of losing my license?

State laws governing how you can get, use, and lose your driver's license vary tremendously. We can't answer every question here, but we do discuss some of the bigger issues that arise in connection with driving privileges.

Is my driver's license good in every state?

If you have a valid license from one state, you may use it in other states that you visit. But if you make a permanent move to another state, you'll have to get a driver's license there, usually within 30 to 60 days of your move. Most states will issue your new license without requiring tests, though some may ask you to take a vision test and a written exam covering basic driving rules.

If you make frequent business trips to another state, or even if you attend school in a state away from home, there's typically no need to get another driver's license. But when you set up housekeeping and pay taxes in the new state, it's time to apply.

Young Drivers Who Cross State Lines

Adults who visit another state may rely on their driver's licenses, but the same may not be true for young drivers. The driving age varies significantly from state to state (from 15 to 21), and a state that makes young people wait longer to drive may not honor a license from a state that issues licenses to younger folks. A young driver who plans to drive in another state and is younger than the legal limit should contact that state's department of motor vehicles to find out what the rules are.

If I get a ticket in another state, will it affect my license?

Forty-eight states belong either to an agreement called the "Driver's License Compact" or to the "Non-Resident Violator Compact." (The only states that aren't members of either are Michigan and Wisconsin.) When you get a ticket in one of these states, the department of motor vehicles will relay the information to your state—and the violation will affect your driving record as if the ticket had been issued in your home state.

What is a graduated driver's license?

Many states now have different driver's license rules and restrictions for teenagers, intended to promote driving safety among the younger set. These are often called graduated licenses.

Graduated driving programs typically allow teens to get a license prior to age 18, if they participate in a certain number of driver education classes, get lots of hands-on driving training, and hold a permit for a period of time. Once the teen gets the graduated license, restrictions apply, such as not being allowed to drive at night, not being allowed to transport teenage passengers, and the like. Once the teen reaches a certain age, or drives with the restrictions for a certain period of time without any violations, the restrictions are removed.

Can I use my license in a foreign country?

Many countries, including the United States, have signed an international agreement allowing visitors to use their own licenses from other nations. Before traveling to another country, contact its consulate office or embassy to find out whether your license will be sufficient. Find the consulate phone number on the U.S. State

Department's website at http://travel.state.gov. Other good sources of information are foreign government tourism offices and car rental offices in the foreign country.

In addition, you may want to obtain an International Driving Permit, issued by the American Automobile Association. This document translates the information on your driver's license into ten languages. Many countries require the permit, not because it meets their requirements for a license but because it is a ready-made translation of the important information on your American license.

Finally, if you intend to stay in another country for an extended period of time, you should check with the consulate to find out whether you'll need to apply for a license in that country. Every country has its own rules about when a "visit" turns into something more permanent.

When can my driver's license be suspended or revoked?

Driving a car is considered a privilege—and a state won't hesitate to take it away if a driver behaves irresponsibly on the road. A state may temporarily suspend your driving privileges for a number of reasons, including:

- driving under the influence of alcohol or drugs
- refusing to take a blood-alcohol test
- driving without liability insurance
- speeding
- reckless driving
- leaving the scene of an injury accident
- failing to pay a driving-related fine
- failing to answer a traffic summons, or
- failing to file an accident report.

In addition, many states use a point system to keep track of a driver's moving violations. Each moving violation is assigned a certain number of points. If a driver accumulates too many points within a given period of time, the department of motor vehicles suspends the license.

If you have too many serious problems as a driver, your state may take away (revoke) your license altogether. If this happens, you'll have to wait a certain period of time before you can apply for another license. Your state may deny your application if you have a poor driving record or fail to pass required tests.

Finally, a few states revoke or refuse to renew the driver's licenses of parents who owe back child support.

My elderly friend is becoming unsafe behind the wheel. Will her license be taken away?

According to the National Highway Traffic Safety Administration, there are more than 36 million licensed drivers over 65 years old in the U.S.; by the year 2020, there will be more than 40 million drivers in this age group. Studies show that as a group, older drivers drive less than younger drivers, but have more accidents per mile.

Elderly, unsafe drivers often do not come to the attention of the state until the driver is stopped for erratic driving or, worse, is involved in an accident. However, some states impose stricter standards on older drivers in order to spot potential problems. Such measures include:

- issuing licenses with shorter renewal intervals for drivers older than a specified age, typically 65 or 70
- requiring older drivers to renew their licenses in person rather than electronically or by mail, and
- administering tests—such as vision, written, or road tests—that are not routinely required of younger drivers.

The Whole Truth and Nothing but the Truth

Many states will ask you specific questions regarding your health when you renew your driver's license. For example, you might receive a questionnaire that asks whether you have ever had seizures, strokes, heart problems, dizziness, eyesight problems, or other medical troubles. If you have medical problems and answer the questions truthfully, an examiner may question you further and may even deny you a license. If you don't tell the truth, you may get your license—but you're setting yourself up for big legal trouble if you are in an accident caused by one of these impairments. It's not that different from driving a car when you know the brakes are bad: If you go out on the road with defective equipment that you know about (including the driver), you greatly increase the chance that you will be held responsible if the defect causes an accident.

All licensing departments accept information from police officers, families, and physicians about a driver's abilities. If a licensing agency moves to cancel someone's license as the result of an officer's observations, an accident, or the report of family members or a doctor, the driver usually has an opportunity to protest.

What will happen if I'm caught driving with a suspended or revoked license?

You'll probably be arrested. Usually, driving with a suspended or revoked license is considered a crime that carries a heavy fine and possibly even jail time. At worst, it may be a felony; you'll end up in state prison or with an obligation to perform many hours of community service. The penalties will probably be heaviest if the suspension or revocation was the result of a conviction for driving under the influence of alcohol or drugs (DUI).

Driving for Uber or Lyft

Uber and Lyft provide drivers with a unique employment opportunity: Drivers choose their own hours and can make decent money. Here are some of the basics.

What are some of the legal issues I need to consider before deciding to drive for a service such as Uber or Lyft?

Before signing up, be sure to check out all terms and conditions, including:

- **Driver requirements.** The minimum requirements to be a driver for Lyft and Uber vary by city and state. However, to drive for either company, you must have a valid in-state driver's license, a Social Security number, and be at least 21 years old. Lyft and Uber perform DMV and criminal background checks on all driver applicants.
- **Vehicle requirements.** Your vehicle must meet certain minimum requirements, which again, vary by city and state. But generally, Lyft drivers must have 2004 models or newer, and Uber drivers 2001 models or newer. Both companies require in-state license plates, current registration, and a 19-point vehicle inspection to confirm that the vehicle complies with the minimum requirements.
- **Car insurance.** Lyft and Uber require all drivers to have their own insurance (as required by state law), but both companies provide additional insurance coverage that applies while drivers are on the clock. (For more on insurance, see www.all-about-car-accidents.com/resources/what-uber-and-lyft-drivers-need-to-know-car-insurance.html.)
- **How you get paid.** Lyft drivers get 80% of rider fees. Drivers have two options for getting paid: weekly direct deposits to a checking account or with a debit card through Lyft's Express Pay system. Uber drivers are paid by direct deposit each week.

What are the relevant tax issues?

There's an ongoing legal debate as to whether Lyft and Uber drivers are independent contractors or employees. However, so far, most states have allowed these services to continue classifying drivers as independent contractors. (Read about a California decision that went the other way at www.nolo.com/legal-encyclopedia/california-labor-commissioner-rules-uber driver-employee-not-independent-contractor. html.) Independent contractors are entitled to deduct expenses at tax time. (For a discussion on the types of expenses drivers can deduct, see www.nolo.com/legal-encyclopedia/tips-tax-deductions-uber-lyft-drivers.html.)

ONLINE HELP

To get other questions about driving for Lyft answered and current information, go to http://help.lyft.com/hc/en-us/categories/201234978-Driving-With-Lyft. Uber has a help page at https://help.uber.com.

If You're Stopped by the Police

Most of us know the fear of being pulled over by the police. An officer may stop your car for any number of reasons, including an equipment defect (such as a burned-out headlight), expired registration tags, a moving violation, or your car's resemblance to a crime suspect's car. You may also have to stop at a police roadblock or sobriety checkpoint.

What should I do if a police officer pulls me over?

Remain as calm as possible and pull over to the side of the road as quickly and safely as you can. Roll down your window, but stay in the car—don't get out unless the officer directs you to do so. It's a good idea to turn on the interior light, turn off the engine, put your keys on the dash, and place your hands on top of the steering wheel. In short, make yourself visible and do nothing that can be mistaken for a dangerous move. For example, don't reach for a purse or backpack or open the glove box unless you've asked the officer's permission, even if you are just looking for your license and registration card. The officer may think you're reaching for a weapon.

When speaking with the officer, be as polite as possible. You should generally let the officer do most of the talking, responding to the officer where appropriate.

Can an officer pull me over for a traffic violation and search me or my car?

In most cases, no. Just because an officer has a justifiable reason for making a traffic stop—and even if he or she issues you a valid ticket for a traffic violation—that does not automatically give the officer authority to search you or your car. If the officer has a reasonable suspicion (based on observable facts, and not just a "hunch") that you are armed and dangerous, involved in criminal activity, or the police otherwise consider it an emergency ("exigent circumstances") then the officer can do a "pat-down" search of you, and can search the passenger compartment of your car. The officer can frisk any purses, bags, or other objects within the car that might reasonably contain a weapon. The officer can also search if something illegal (such as drugs) is in plain view—sitting on your passenger seat, for example. The officer does have the authority, however, to ask you and any passengers to exit the car during a traffic stop.

If my car is towed and impounded, can the police search it?

Yes. If your car is impounded, the police are generally allowed to conduct a thorough "inventory" search of it, including its trunk and any closed containers that they find inside. This is true even if your car was towed after you parked it illegally, or if the police recover your car after it is stolen.

The police are required, however, to follow fair and standardized procedures when they search your car. They may not stop you and impound your car simply to perform a search.

I was pulled over at a roadblock and asked to wait and answer an officer's questions. Is this legal?

Yes, as long as the police use a neutral policy when stopping cars (such as stopping all cars or stopping every third car) and minimize any inconvenience to you and the other drivers. The police can't single out your car unless they have good reason to believe that you've broken the law.

Drunk Driving

If you're caught while driving drunk or under the influence of drugs, you'll face serious legal penalties. Many states will put you in jail, even for a first offense, and almost all will impose hefty fines. For a first DUI, some states will suspend your license for 30 days, while others might take away your driving privileges for a year or more.

How drunk or high does someone have to be before he can be convicted of driving under the influence?

In most states, it's illegal to drive a car while "impaired" by the effects of alcohol or drugs (including prescription drugs). Typically, this means that there must be enough alcohol or drugs in the driver's body to prevent him or her from thinking clearly or driving safely. Many people reach this level well before they'd be considered "drunk" or "stoned."

Additionally, if your blood or breath alcohol level is .08% or more, you will likely be charged with a separate drunk driving charge (called "per se" DUI), regardless of whether or not your ability to drive safely was impaired.

How can the police find out whether a driver is under the influence?

Police typically use three methods of determining whether a driver has had too much to be driving:

- **Observation.** A police officer who notices that you are driving erratically —swerving, speeding, failing to stop, or even driving too slowly—can pull you over. Of course, you may have a good explanation for your driving (tiredness, for example), but an officer is unlikely to buy your story if you smell like alcohol, slur your words, or can't seem to think straight.
- **Sobriety tests.** An officer who suspects that you are under the influence will probably ask you to get out of the car and perform a series of balance and speech tests, such as standing on one leg, walking a straight line heel-to-toe, or reciting a line of letters or numbers. The officer will look closely at your eyes, checking for pupil enlargement or constriction, which can be evidence of intoxication.
  If you fail these tests, the officer may arrest you or ask you to take a chemical test.
- **Blood-alcohol level.** All states have implied consent laws requiring drivers who are lawfully arrested for DUI to submit to chemical testing for the purpose of assessing whether and how much the driver has been

drinking. Usually, these tests are of the driver's blood, breath, or urine. Officers typically use chemical tests to determine whether the driver has a blood or breath alcohol concentration of .08% or more—a violation of per se DUI laws. However, depending on the state, alcohol concentrations might also create presumptions about whether the driver was impaired. For example, in some states, an alcohol concentration of .05% or more—though not a per se DUI—creates a presumption that the driver was impaired. In such a situation, the driver could be charged with an impairment DUI based on the presumption, even if the driver's alcohol concentration was less than .08%.

Do I have to take a blood, breath, or urine test if asked to do so by the police?

Drivers who refuse chemical testing in violation of implied consent laws typically face administrative penalties. The driver's license will often be suspended for a period of time and the driver might need to pay a fine or install an ignition interlock device. These administrative penalties for refusing testing are usually in addition to any punishment imposed for a DUI conviction.

Am I entitled to talk to an attorney before I decide which chemical test to take?

The answer depends on where you live. In California, for example, you don't have the right to speak with an attorney first. But some other states allow you to talk to a lawyer before you take a chemical test. If you are unsure of the law in your state, it's a good idea to ask the officer whether you can speak to an attorney before you submit to a chemical test.

When to Get a Lawyer

Defending against a charge of drunk driving is tricky business. To prevail, you'll need someone who understands scientific and medical concepts and can question tough witnesses, including scientists and police officers. If you want to challenge your DUI charge, you're well advised to hire an attorney who specializes in these types of cases.

If I am pulled over, does the officer have to read me my rights before asking how much I had to drink?

No. During a traffic stop, an officer does not have to read you your rights until you are under arrest. (See Chapter 17 for a description of *Miranda* rights.) Determining whether you are "under arrest" can be tricky—you can be under arrest even before a police officer says you are. But if an officer is just asking you questions at the side of the road, or even if you are detained in the officer's car for a few minutes, you are probably not under arrest.

Keep in mind that you don't have to answer an officer's questions, whether you are under arrest or not—and whether or not the officer has read your rights to you.

Reporting to the DMV

In many states, you must report a vehicle accident resulting in physical injury or a certain amount of property damage to the state department of motor vehicles. Check with your insurance agent or your local department of motor vehicles to find out the time limits for filing this report; you might have just a few days. Be sure to ask whether you'll need a particular form for the report.

If you must file a report, and the report asks for a statement about how the accident occurred, make it very brief—and admit no responsibility for the accident. Similarly, if the official form asks what your injuries are, list every injury, not just the most serious or obvious. An insurance company may later gain access to the report, and if you have admitted some fault in it or failed to mention an injury, it might affect your claim.

Traffic Accidents

Anyone who drives or rides in a car long enough is likely to be involved in at least one minor fender-bender. Bicycle or motorcycle riders know the roads are even more dangerous for two-wheelers. And on our crowded streets, pedestrians, too, are often involved in accidents with buses, cars, and bikes. Knowing a few laws of the road, and the best steps to take when an accident occurs, can help ease the pain of any accident—and help make the insurance claims process less painful too.

What should I do if I'm involved in a traffic accident?

The most important thing to do is document the entire situation by taking photos and careful notes soon after the accident. Having documentation (rather than relying on your memory) will help with the claim process—and increase your chances of receiving full compensation for your injuries and vehicle damage. If you have a camera or cellphone, it's a good idea to take lots of photos, or better yet, a video, at the accident scene. Be sure to get shots of any damage to vehicles or property and the roadways surrounding where the accident occurred. If possible, also photograph any injuries resulting from the accident.

Write things down as soon as you can. Begin with what you were doing and where you were going, the people you were with, the time, and the weather. Include every detail of what you saw, heard, and felt. Be sure to include everything that others—those involved in the accident or witnesses—said about the accident.

Finally, take daily notes of the effects of your injuries. Include pain, discomfort, anxiety, loss of sleep, or other problems resulting from your injuries.

Finding Your State's Traffic Rules

The traffic rules are contained in each state's Motor Vehicle Code. You can usually obtain a simplified version of these rules—often called the "Rules of the Road"—from the department of motor vehicles (DMV). Most DMV offices also have the complete Motor Vehicle Code on the Internet.

What determines who is responsible for a traffic accident?

Figuring out who is at fault in a traffic accident is a matter of deciding who was careless. Each state has traffic rules (which apply to automobiles, motorcycles, bicycles, and pedestrians) that tell people how they are supposed to drive and provide guidelines for determining liability.

Sometimes it is obvious that one driver violated a traffic rule that caused the accident —for example, one driver runs a stop sign and crashes into another. In other situations, whether or not there was a violation will be less obvious. Sometimes, neither driver violated a traffic rule, although one driver may still have been careless.

What if the cause of the accident is not clear?

It is sometimes difficult to say that one particular act caused an accident. This is especially true if what you claim the other driver did is vague or seems minor. But if you can show that the other driver made several minor driving errors or committed several minor traffic violations, you can argue that the combination of those actions caused the accident.

Special Rules for No-Fault Policyholders

Several states have some form of no-fault auto insurance, also called personal injury protection. (See "Insuring Your Car," above.)

Under no-fault insurance, the injured person's own insurance company pays medical bills and lost wages (up to certain amounts) in smaller accidents, regardless of who caused the accident. This eliminates injury liability claims and lawsuits. Usually, no-fault does not cover vehicle damage; those claims are still handled by filing a liability claim against the person who is responsible for the accident, or through your own collision insurance.

Who is liable if my car is rear-ended in a crash?

The driver who hit you from behind is almost always at fault, regardless of your reason for stopping. Traffic rules require that a driver travel at a speed at which he or she can stop safely if a vehicle ahead stops suddenly. In rear-end accidents, the vehicle damage provides strong proof of liability. If the other car's front end and your car's rear end are both damaged, there is no doubt that you were struck from behind.

In some situations, both you and the car behind you are stopped when a third car runs into the car behind you, pushing it into the rear of your car. In that case, the driver of the third car is at fault, and you should file a claim against that driver's insurance.

Police Reports: Powerful Evidence

If the police responded to the scene of your accident, they probably made a written accident report (particularly if someone was injured).

Sometimes a police report will plainly state that a driver violated a specific section of the state's motor vehicle laws and that the violation caused the accident. It may even indicate that the officer issued a citation. Other times, the report merely describes or briefly mentions negligent driving.

Any mention in a police report of a legal violation or other evidence of careless driving will provide support for your claim that the other driver was at fault.

Are there any other clear patterns of liability in traffic accidents?

A car making a left turn is almost always liable to a car coming straight in the other direction. According to traffic rules, a car making a left turn must wait until it can safely complete the turn before moving in front of oncoming traffic. There may be exceptions to this rule if:

- the car going straight was going too fast (this is usually difficult to prove)
- the car going straight went through a red light, or
- the left-turning car began its turn when it was safe but something unexpected happened that forced the driver to slow down or stop the turn.

ONLINE HELP

The following sites are good resources for information about cars and driving:

- **www.nolo.com** Nolo offers information about a wide variety of legal topics, including what to do if you're in an accident.
- **www.kbb.com** *Kelley Blue Book* gives you the resale and wholesale values of your vehicle, as well as new car prices.
- **www.edmunds.com** Edmunds offers information about buying a new car, including reviews, comparisons, prices, and strategies.
- **www.bbb.org** The Better Business Bureau offers tips on buying new and used cars, including financing suggestions.
- **www.consumerreports.org** *Consumer Reports* provides articles on how to buy or lease a car and, for a small fee, a price service for both new and used cars.
- **www.drivinglaws.org** Provides state-by-state summaries of motor vehicle laws.
- **www.nhtsa.gov** The National Highway Traffic Safety Administration provides recall notices, service bulletins, defect investigations, consumer complaints, and other data about vehicle problems.

CHAPTER

11

Wills and Estate Planning

It's not that I'm afraid to die. I just don't want to be there when it happens.

—Woody Allen

The first thing that comes to many people's minds when they think of estate planning is property: Who gets what you own when you die? But estate planning encompasses much more—for example, minimizing probate court costs and estate taxes, deciding who will care for your minor children if you can't, appointing people to handle your medical and financial affairs if necessary, and expressing your wishes regarding memorial services and burial. While none of us relish thinking about these things, taking some time to do so now can save your loved ones a great deal of money, pain, and confusion later on.

This chapter answers often-asked questions about estate planning, from basic wills to organ donation. Along the way we consider probate and the many ways to avoid it, taxes, and funeral planning. For information about arranging for someone to make your medical and financial decisions should you become unable to handle them yourself, see Chapter 12.

Wills

Though most Americans are aware that they need a will, the majority—an estimated 70% of us—don't have one. There are lots of reasons we put off making our wills, from fear of lawyers' fees to fear of death. But writing a will doesn't have to be expensive or even terribly complicated. And once it's done, you can rest a little easier, knowing that your wishes are known and will be followed after your death.

What happens if I die without a will?

If you don't make a will or use some other legal method to transfer your property when you die, state law will determine what happens to your property. (This process is called "intestate succession.") Your property will be distributed to your spouse and children or, if you have neither, to other relatives according to state law. If no relatives can be found to inherit your property, it will go into your state's treasury. Also, in the absence of a will, a court will determine who will care for your young children and their property if the other parent is unavailable or unfit.

Do I need a lawyer to make my will?

Probably not. Making a will rarely involves complicated legal rules, and most people can draft their own will with the aid of a good do-it-yourself book, software program, or online form. If you know what you own and whom you care about, and you have a good, clear, plain-English resource to guide you, you should be fine.

But you shouldn't approach the task of will drafting absolutely determined not to consult a lawyer. If you have questions that aren't answered by the resource you're using, a lawyer's services are warranted. Even so, you don't have to turn over the whole project; you can simply ask your questions and then finish making your own will.

For example, you may want to consult a lawyer in these circumstances:

- You have questions about your will or other options for leaving your property.
- You expect to leave a very large amount of assets—over $5 million—that may be subject to estate taxes, or if you live in a state that levies its own estate or inheritance tax.
- You own a small business and have questions as to the rights of surviving owners or your ownership share.
- You want to make arrangements for long-term care of a beneficiary—for example, a child with a disability.
- You fear someone will contest your will on grounds of fraud or claim that you were unduly influenced or weren't of sound mind when you signed it.
- You wish to leave no assets, or very few, to your spouse. It's usually not possible to leave your spouse out of your will unless you live in a community property state, where your spouse already owns half of most assets acquired during marriage. (See "Can I disinherit relatives I don't like?" below.) A lawyer can explain exactly what your spouse is entitled to claim from your estate.

Also, some people simply feel more comfortable having a lawyer review their will, even though their situation has no apparent legal complications.

Making Your Will Legal

Any adult of sound mind is entitled to make a will. (And if you're reading and understanding this book, you're of sound mind.) Beyond that, there are just a few technical requirements:

- The document must expressly state that it's your will.
- You must date and sign the will.
- The will must be signed by at least two witnesses. They must watch you sign the will, though they don't need to read it. Your witnesses should be people who won't inherit anything under the will.

You don't have to have your will notarized. In many states, though, if you and your witnesses sign and notarize an affidavit (sworn statement), you can help simplify the court procedures required to prove the validity of the will after you die.

I don't have much property. Can't I just make a handwritten will?

Handwritten wills that are not signed in front of witnesses are called "holographic" wills. They are legal in about 25 states. To be valid, a holographic will must be written, dated, and signed in the handwriting of the person making the will. Some states allow will writers to use a fill-in-the-blanks form if the rest of the blanks are filled in by hand and the will is properly dated and signed.

If you have very little property, and you want to make just a few specific bequests, a holographic will is better than nothing if it's valid in your state. But because holographic wills are not witnessed, if your will goes before a probate court, the court may be unusually strict when examining it to be sure it's legitimate. It's better to take a little extra time now to get yourself a will that will easily pass muster when the time comes.

Do I need to file my will with a court or in public records somewhere?

No. A will doesn't need to be recorded or filed with any government agency, although it can be in a few states. Just keep your will in a safe, accessible place, and be sure the person in charge of winding up your affairs (your executor) knows where it is.

Can I use my will to name somebody to care for my young children, in case my spouse and I both die suddenly?

Yes. If both parents of a child die while the child is still a minor, another adult—called a "personal guardian"—must step in. You and the child's other parent can use your wills to nominate someone to fill this position. To avert conflicts, you and the other parent should each name the same guardian for a child. (If you have more than one child, however, you do not need to name the same guardian for all of your children.) If a guardian is needed, a judge will appoint your nominee unless the judge concludes that it is not in the best interest of your children.

The personal guardian will be responsible for raising your children until they become legal adults. Of course, you should have complete confidence in the person you nominate, and you should be certain that your nominee is willing to accept the responsibility of raising your children should the need actually arise.

I'm raising a child on my own. Do I have to name the other biological parent as personal guardian, or can I name someone who I think will do a better job?

If one parent dies, the other legal parent usually takes responsibility for raising the child. But if you and the other parent have parted ways, you may feel strongly that the other parent shouldn't have custody if something happens to you. A judge will grant custody to someone else only if the surviving parent:

- has legally abandoned the child by not providing for or visiting the child for an extended period, or
- is clearly unfit as a parent.

How to Leave Property to Young Children

Except for property of little value, the law requires that an adult manage property inherited by children until they turn 18. You can use your will to name someone to manage property inherited by minors, thus avoiding the need for a more complicated court-appointed guardianship. There are many ways to structure a property-management arrangement. Here are four of the simplest and most useful:

1. Name a custodian under the Uniform Transfers to Minors Act

The Uniform Transfers to Minors Act (UTMA) is a law that has been adopted in every state except South Carolina. Under the UTMA, you can choose someone, called a custodian, to manage property you are leaving to a child. If you die when the child is under the age set by your state's law—18 in a few states, 21 in most, 25 in several others—the custodian will step in to manage the property. An UTMA custodianship must end by the age specified by your state's law (18, 21, or up to 25). At that time, your child receives what's left of the trust property outright. If, however, you want to extend property management beyond the age set by your state, you may want to use one of the next three methods.

2. Set up a trust for each child

You can use your will to name someone (called a trustee) who will handle any property the child inherits until the child reaches the age you specify. When the child reaches that age, the trustee ends the trust and gives whatever is left of the trust property to the child.

3. Set up a pot trust for your children

If you have more than one child, you may want to set up just one trust for all of them. This arrangement is usually called a pot or family trust. In your will, you establish the trust and appoint a trustee. The trustee doesn't have to spend the same amount on each child; instead, the trustee decides what each child needs, and spends money accordingly. When the youngest child reaches a certain age, often 18, 21, or 25, the trust ends. At that time, any property left in the trust will be distributed as you direct in the trust document.

4. Name a property guardian

If you wish, you can simply use your will to name a property guardian for your child. Then, if at your death your child needs the guardian, the court will appoint the person you chose. The property guardian will manage whatever property the child inherits, from you or others, if there's no other mechanism (a trust, for example) to handle it. Property management ends when your child becomes a legal adult.

In most cases, it is difficult to prove that a parent is unfit, unless there's evidence of serious problems such as chronic drug or alcohol use, mental illness, or a history of child abuse.

If you honestly believe the other parent is incapable of caring for your child properly or simply won't assume the responsibility, you should write a letter explaining why and attach it to your will. The judge will take it into account, and may appoint the person you choose as guardian instead of the other legal parent.

Can I disinherit relatives I don't like?

It depends on whom you want to disinherit. If it's anyone other than your spouse or child, the rule is very simple: Don't mention that person in your will, and he or she won't receive any of your property. Rules for spouses and children are somewhat more complex.

Spouses. It is not usually possible to disinherit your spouse completely. If you live in a community property state (Arizona, California, Idaho, Louisiana, Nevada, New Mexico, Texas, Washington, or Wisconsin), your spouse automatically owns half of all the property and earnings (with a few exceptions) acquired by either of you during your marriage. You can, however, leave your half of the community property, and your separate property (generally considered to be all property you owned before marriage or received via gift or inheritance during marriage), to anyone you choose.

In all other states, there is no rule that property acquired during marriage is owned by both spouses. To protect spouses from being disinherited, these states give your spouse a legal right to claim a portion of your estate, no matter what your will provides. But keep in mind that these provisions kick in only if your spouse challenges your will. If your will leaves your spouse less than the statutory share and your spouse doesn't object, the document will be honored as written.

These rules also apply to registered domestic partners in states that continue to grant the rights and responsibilities of marriage to domestic partnerships. If you don't plan to leave at least half of your property to your spouse or registered domestic partner, you should consult a lawyer—unless your spouse or partner willingly consents in writing to your plan.

Children. Generally, it's legal to disinherit a child. Some states, however, protect minor children against the loss of a family residence. For example, the Florida Constitution prohibits the head of a family from leaving a residence to anyone other than a spouse if there's a surviving spouse or minor child.

Most states have laws—called "pretermitted heir" statutes—to protect children of any age from being accidentally disinherited. If a child is neither named in your will or specifically disinherited, these laws assume that you accidentally forgot to include that

Make Sure Your Executor Has Access

Your executor's first task is to locate your will, and you can help by keeping the original in a fairly obvious place. Here are some suggestions:

- Store your will in an envelope on which you have written your name and the word "Will."
- Place the envelope in a fireproof metal box, file cabinet, or home safe. An alternative is to place the original in a safe deposit box. But before doing that, learn the bank's policy about access to the box after your death. If, for instance, the safe deposit box is in your name alone, the box can probably be opened only by a person authorized by a court, and then only in the presence of a bank employee. All of this takes time, and in the meantime, your document will be locked away from those who need access to it.
- Wherever you choose to keep your will, make sure your executor (and at least one other person you trust) knows where to find it.

Also consider whether your executor will be able to easily access important documents or accounts that he or she will need to wrap up your estate—for example, prepaid funeral policies, insurance policies, bank records, deeds, or digital assets (like online accounts or digital files). If you think it would be useful, you can leave a separate letter with your will that explains where to find and how to access these documents and accounts.

child. In many states, these laws apply only to children born after you made your will. The overlooked child has a right to the same share of your estate as if you'd left no will. The share usually depends on whether you leave a spouse and on how many other children you have, but it is likely to be a significant percentage of your property. In some states, these laws apply not only to your children but also to any of your grandchildren born to a child who has died.

To avoid any legal battles after your death, if you decide to disinherit a child, or the child of a deceased child, expressly state this in your will. And if you have a new child after you've made your will, remember to make a new will to include, or specifically disinherit, that child.

What happens to my will when I die?

After you die, the person you appointed in your will to be your executor (called a personal representative in some states) is responsible for seeing that your wishes are carried out as directed by your will. The executor may hire an attorney to help wind up your affairs, especially if probate court proceedings are required. Probate and executors are discussed in more detail in the next three sets of questions.

What if someone challenges my will after I die?

Very few wills are ever challenged in court. When they are, it's usually by a close relative who feels somehow cheated out of a rightful share of the deceased person's property.

Generally speaking, only spouses are legally entitled to a share of your property. Your children aren't entitled to anything unless you unintentionally overlooked them in your will. (See "Can I disinherit relatives I don't like?" above.)

To get an entire will thrown out as invalid, someone must go to court and prove that it suffers from a fatal flaw: the signature was forged, you weren't of sound mind when you made the will, or you were unduly influenced by someone.

RESOURCE

For more about wills, see these Nolo products:

- *Quicken WillMaker Plus* (software). Lets you create a valid will and many other important estate planning documents.
- *Nolo's Online Will.* Create your will online easily and quickly, and get lots of help and guidance along the way.
- *Quick & Legal Will Book,* by Denis Clifford. Book that contains forms and instructions for creating a basic will.

Probate

There is only one way you can beat a lawyer in a death case. That is to die with nothing. Then you can't get a lawyer within ten miles of your house.

—Will Rogers

When a person dies, someone must step in to wind up the deceased person's affairs. Bills must be paid, property must be accounted for, and items must be passed on to the people chosen by the deceased person. If state law requires that all this be handled through court proceedings, the process can take many months.

What is probate?

Probate is a legal process that includes:

- if there's a will, proving in court that it is valid (usually a routine matter)
- if there is no will, determining who inherits under state law
- identifying and inventorying the deceased person's property
- having the property appraised
- paying debts and taxes, and
- distributing the remaining property as the will or state law directs.

Typically, probate involves paperwork and court appearances by lawyers, who are paid from estate property that would otherwise go to the people who inherit the deceased person's property. Property left by the will cannot be distributed to beneficiaries until the process is complete.

Probate rarely benefits your beneficiaries, and it certainly costs them money and time. Probate makes sense only if your estate will have complicated problems, such as many debts that can't easily be paid from the property you leave.

Property That Avoids Probate

Not all property has to go through probate. Most states allow a certain amount of assets to pass free of probate, or through a simplified probate procedure. In California, for example, you can pass up to $150,000 of property without probate, and there's a simple transfer procedure for any property left to a surviving spouse.

In addition, property that passes outside of your will—say, through joint tenancy, a transfer on death deed, or a living trust—is not subject to probate. See "Avoiding Probate," below.

Who is responsible for handling probate?

In most circumstances, the executor named in the will takes this job. If there isn't any will, or if the will maker fails to name an executor, the probate court names someone (commonly called an administrator) to handle the process—most often a surviving spouse or domestic partner or the closest capable relative.

If no formal probate proceeding is necessary, the court does not appoint an estate administrator. Instead, a close relative or friend serves as an informal estate representative. Normally, families and friends choose this person, and it is not uncommon for several people to share the responsibilities of paying debts, filing a final income tax return, and distributing property to the people who are supposed to get it.

Executors

An executor is the person you name in your will to handle your property after death. The executor—called a personal representative in many states—must be prepared to carry out a long list of tasks prudently and promptly.

How do I choose an executor?

The most important factor in naming an executor is trust. The person you choose should be honest, with good organizational skills and the ability to keep track of details. If possible, name someone who lives nearby and who is familiar with your financial matters; that will make it easier to do chores like collecting mail and locating important records and papers.

An Executor's Duties

Executors have a number of duties, depending on the complexity of the deceased person's estate. Typically, an executor must do the following:

- **Decide whether or not probate court proceedings are needed.** If the deceased person's property is worth less than a certain amount (it depends on state law), or assets were owned jointly, formal probate may not be required.
- **Figure out who inherits property.** If the deceased person left a will, the executor will read it to determine who gets what. If there's no will, the administrator will have to look at state law (called "intestate succession" statutes) to find out who the deceased person's heirs are.
- **Decide whether or not it's legally permissible to transfer certain items immediately** to the people named to inherit them, even if probate is required for other property.
- **File the will** (if any) and, If probate is required, all required legal papers in the local probate court.
- **Find the deceased person's assets** and manage them during the probate process, which may take up to a year. This may involve deciding whether to sell real estate or securities owned by the deceased person.
- **Handle day-to-day details,** such as terminating leases and credit cards, and notifying banks and government agencies—such as Social Security, the post office, Medicare, and the Department of Veterans Affairs—of the death.
- **Set up an estate bank account** to hold money that belonged to the deceased person or comes in after death—for example, paychecks or stock dividends.
- **Pay continuing expenses**—for example, mortgage payments, utility bills, and homeowners' insurance premiums.
- **Pay debts.** As part of this process, the executor must officially notify creditors of the probate proceeding, following the procedure set out by state law.
- **Pay taxes.** A final income tax return must be filed, covering the period from the beginning of the tax year to the date of death. State and federal estate tax returns may also be required, depending on how much property the deceased person owned at death and to whom the property was left.
- **Supervise the distribution of the deceased person's property** to the people or organizations named in the will.

Many people select someone who will inherit a substantial amount of their property. This makes sense, because a person with an interest in how your property is distributed is likely to do a conscientious job of managing your affairs after your death. This person may also be likely to know where your records are kept and why you want your property left as you have directed.

Whomever you select, make sure the person is willing to do the job. Discuss the position with the person you've chosen before you make your will.

Are there restrictions on whom I may choose as my executor?

Your state may impose some restrictions on who can act as executor. You can't name a minor, a convicted felon, or someone who is not a U.S. citizen. Most states allow you to name someone who lives in another state, but some require that out-of-state executors be a relative or a primary beneficiary under your will. Some states also require that nonresident executors obtain a bond (an insurance policy that protects your beneficiaries in the event of the executor's wrongful use of your estate's property) or name an in-state resident to act as the executor's representative. These complexities underscore the benefits of naming someone who lives nearby. If you feel strongly about naming an executor who lives out of state, be sure to familiarize yourself with your state's rules.

Is it difficult to serve as executor?

Serving as an executor can be a tedious job, but it doesn't require special financial or legal knowledge. Common sense, conscientiousness, and honesty are the main requirements. An executor who needs help can hire lawyers, accountants, or other experts and pay them from the assets of the deceased person's estate.

Essentially, the executor's job is to protect the deceased person's property until all debts and taxes have been paid, and see that what's left is transferred to the people who are entitled to it. The law does not require an executor to display more than reasonable prudence and judgment, but it does require the highest degree of honesty, impartiality, and diligence. This is called a "fiduciary duty"—the duty to act with scrupulous good faith and candor on behalf of someone else.

Does the person named in a will as executor have to serve?

No. When it comes time, an executor can accept or decline this responsibility. And someone who agrees to serve can resign at any time. That's why many wills name an alternate executor, who takes over if necessary. If no one is available, the court will appoint someone to step in.

Does the executor get paid?

The main reason for serving as an executor is to honor the deceased person's request.

But the executor is also entitled to payment. The exact amount is regulated by state law and is affected by factors such as the value of the deceased person's property and what the probate court decides is reasonable under the circumstances. Commonly, close relatives and close friends (especially those who are inheriting a substantial amount anyway) don't charge the estate for their services.

Is a lawyer necessary?

Not always. An executor who is the main beneficiary should definitely consider handling the paperwork without a lawyer if the deceased person's property consists of common kinds of assets (house, bank accounts, insurance), the will seems straightforward, and good resource materials are at hand. Essentially, shepherding a case through probate court requires shuffling a lot of papers. In the vast majority of cases, there are no disputes that require a decision by a judge. So the executor may never see the inside of a courtroom but will probably become familiar with the court clerk's office. The executor may even be able to do everything by mail. Doing a good job requires persistence and attention to tedious detail, but not necessarily a law degree.

If, however, the estate has many types of property, significant tax liability, or potential disputes among inheritors, an executor may want some help.

There are two ways for an executor to get help from a lawyer:

- **Hire a lawyer to answer legal questions as they come up.** The lawyer might also do some research, look over documents before the executor files them, or prepare an estate tax return.
- **Turn the probate over to the lawyer.** If the executor just doesn't want to deal with the probate process, a lawyer can do everything. The lawyer will be paid out of the estate. In most states, lawyers charge by the hour ($200 or more is common) or charge a lump sum. But in a few states, probate law authorizes the lawyer to take a certain percentage of the gross value of the deceased person's estate unless the executor makes a written agreement calling for less. An executor can probably find a competent lawyer who will agree to a lower fee.

Where can an executor get help?

Lawyers aren't the only source of information and assistance. Here are some others:

- **The court.** Probate court clerks will probably answer basic questions about court procedure, but they staunchly avoid saying anything that could possibly be construed as "legal advice." Some courts, however, have lawyers on staff who look over probate documents; they may point out errors in the papers and explain how to fix them.

- **Other professionals.** For certain tasks, an executor may be better off hiring an accountant or appraiser than a lawyer. For example, a CPA may be a big help on some estate tax matters.
- **Legal document preparers.** In many law offices, lawyers delegate probate paperwork to paralegals (nonlawyers who have training or experience in preparing legal documents). Now, in some areas of the country, experienced nonlawyers have set up shop to help people directly with probate paperwork. These businesses don't offer legal advice; they just prepare documents as the executor instructs them, and file them with the court. To find one, an executor can look online or in the yellow pages for "Legal Document Preparer" or "Attorney Services." The executor should only hire someone who has substantial experience in this field and provides references that check out.

RESOURCE

For more information about executors and probate, see these Nolo books:

- *The Executor's Guide*, by Mary Randolph. Explains what executors can expect and how to deal with legal and practical issues such as insurance, benefits, wills, trusts, probate, debts, and taxes.
- *Social Security, Medicare & Government Pensions*, by Joseph Matthews. Explains how to make claims for survivors benefits from the Social Security Administration, Federal Civil Service, and the Department of Veterans Affairs.
- *How to Probate an Estate in California*, by Julia Nissley. Leads you through the California probate process step by step, and it contains all necessary court forms and instructions for filling them out. Although the forms are used only in California, the book contains much information that would be valuable background in any state.

Avoiding Probate

Because probate is time-consuming, expensive, and usually unnecessary, many people plan in advance to avoid it. There are a number of ways to pass property to your inheritors without probate. Some of these probate-avoidance methods are quite simple to set up; others take more time and effort.

Should I plan to avoid probate?

Whether to spend your time and effort planning to avoid probate depends on a number of factors, most notably your age, your health, and your wealth. If you're young and in good health, a simple will may be all you need—adopting a complex probate-avoidance plan now may mean you'll have to redo it as your life situation changes. And if you have very little property, you won't want to spend your time planning to avoid probate. Your property may even fall under your state's probate exemption; most states have laws that allow a certain amount of property to pass free of probate, or through a simplified probate procedure.

But if you're older, in ill health, or own a significant amount of property in your own name, you'll probably want to do some planning to avoid probate.

RESOURCE

For more about avoiding probate, see these Nolo books:

- *8 Ways to Avoid Probate,* by Mary Randolph. Explains simple and inexpensive methods of sparing your family the hassle and expense of probate after your death.
- *Plan Your Estate,* by Denis Clifford. Offers an in-depth discussion of almost all aspects of estate planning, including probate avoidance.

Living Trusts

Whether or not a living trust is right for you depends on exactly what you want to accomplish and how much paperwork you're willing to put up with. Living trusts work wonderfully for many people, but not everyone needs one.

What is a living trust?

A trust is an arrangement under which one person, called the trustee, holds legal title to property on behalf of another. You can be the trustee of your own living trust, keeping full control over all property held in trust.

There are many kinds of trusts. A "living trust" (also called an "inter vivos" trust) is simply a trust you create while you're alive, rather than one that is created at your death under the terms of your will.

All living trusts are designed to avoid probate. Some also help you save on estate taxes, and others let you set up long-term property management.

How does a living trust avoid probate?

Property held in a living trust before your death doesn't go through probate. The successor trustee—the person you appointed to handle the trust after your death—simply transfers ownership to the beneficiaries you named in the trust. In many cases, the whole process takes only a few weeks, and there are no lawyer or court fees to pay. When the property has all been transferred to the beneficiaries, the living trust ceases to exist.

Is it expensive to create a living trust?

The expense of a living trust comes up front. Lawyers charge high fees—much higher than for wills—for living trusts. They commonly charge upwards of $1,000 to draw up a simple trust. If you're going to hire a lawyer to draw up your living trust, you might pay as much now as your heirs would have to pay for probate after your death—which means the trust offers no net savings.

But you don't have to pay a lawyer to create a living trust. With good self-help materials written for nonlawyers, you can create a valid Declaration of Trust (the document that creates a trust) yourself. If you run into questions that a do-it-yourself publication doesn't answer, you may need to consult a lawyer, but you probably won't need to turn the whole job over to an expensive expert.

Isn't it a hassle to own property in a trust?

Making a living trust work for you does require some crucial paperwork. For example, if you want to leave your house through the trust, you must sign and record a new deed showing that you now own the house as trustee of your living trust. This paperwork can be tedious, but the hassles are fewer these days because living trusts are quite commonplace.

Is a trust document ever made public, like a will?

A will becomes a matter of public record when it is submitted to a probate court, as do all the other documents associated with probate—inventories of the deceased person's assets and debts, for example. The terms of a living trust, however, need not be made public.

Don't Forget Your Will!

Even if you make a living trust, you still need a will. Here's why:

A will is an essential backup device for property that you don't transfer to your living trust. For example, if you acquire property shortly before you die, you may not think to transfer ownership of it to your trust—which means that it won't pass under the terms of the trust document. But in your backup will, you can include a clause that names someone to get any property that you don't leave to a particular person or entity.

If you don't have a will, any property that isn't transferred by your living trust or other probate-avoidance device (such as joint tenancy) will go to your closest relatives in an order determined by state law. These laws may not distribute property in the way you would have chosen.

Also, you can use your backup will to name an executor and name guardians for your minor children—you can't do those things with a living trust

Does a trust protect property from creditors?

Holding assets in a revocable trust doesn't shelter them from creditors. A creditor who wins a lawsuit against you can go after the trust property just as if you still owned it in your own name.

How to Avoid Probate

No one probate-avoidance method is right for all people. Which methods, if any, you should use depends on your personal and financial situation. Here are some common techniques to consider:

- **Pay-on-death designations.** Designating a pay-on-death beneficiary is a simple way to avoid probate for bank accounts, government bonds, individual retirement accounts, and in most states, stocks and other securities. In some states, you can even transfer your car or your real estate through such an arrangement. All you need to do is name someone to inherit the property at your death. You retain complete control of your property when you are alive, and you can change the beneficiary if you choose. When you die, the property is transferred to the person you named, free of probate.
- **Joint tenancy.** Joint tenancy is a form of shared ownership where the surviving owner(s) automatically inherits the share of the owner who dies. Joint tenancy is often a good choice for couples who purchase property together and want the survivor to inherit. (Some states also have a similar type of ownership called "tenancy by the entirety" or "community property with right of survivorship" for married couples and domestic partners.)

  Adding another owner to property you already own, however, can create problems. The new co-owner can sell or borrow against his or her share. Also, there are negative tax consequences of giving appreciated property to a joint tenant shortly before death.
- **A living trust.** A revocable living trust is a popular probate-avoidance device. You create the trust by preparing and signing a trust document. Once the trust is created, you can hold property in trust, without giving up any control over the trust property. When you die, the trust property can be distributed directly to the beneficiaries you named in the trust document, without the blessing of the probate court. Living trusts are discussed in more detail in the set of questions below.
- **Insurance.** If you buy life insurance, you designate a beneficiary in your policy. The proceeds of the policy won't go through probate unless you name your own estate as the beneficiary.
- **Gifts.** Anything you give away during your life doesn't have to go through probate.

To learn more about avoiding probate in your state, visit Nolo's Wills, Trusts & Probate section at www.nolo.com.

After your death, however, property in a living trust can be quickly and quietly distributed to the beneficiaries (unlike property that must go through probate). That complicates matters for creditors; by the time they find out about your death, your property may already be dispersed, and the creditors have no way of knowing exactly what you owned (except for real estate, which is always a matter of public record). It may not be worth the creditor's time and effort to try to track down the property and demand that the new owners use it to pay your debts.

On the other hand, probate can offer a kind of protection from creditors. During probate, known creditors must be notified of the death and given a chance to file claims. If they miss the deadline to file, they're out of luck forever.

I'm young and healthy. Do I really need a trust now?

Probably not. At this stage in your life, your main estate planning goals are probably making sure that in the unlikely event of your early death, your property is distributed as you want it to be and, if you have young children, that they are cared for. You don't need a trust to accomplish those ends; writing a will, and perhaps buying some life insurance, would be simpler.

Can a living trust save on estate taxes?

A simple probate-avoidance living trust has no effect on taxes. Some more complicated living trusts, however, can reduce your federal estate tax bill. Federal estate taxes are collected only from very large estates—so few people need to worry about them. (See "Estate and Gift Taxes," below.)

RESOURCE

For more about living trusts, see these Nolo books:

- *Nolo's Online Living Trust.* Lets you make a basic probate-avoidance trust online at www.nolo.com.
- *Make Your Own Living Trust,* by Denis Clifford. Book containing forms and instructions for preparing probate-avoidance living trusts.
- *Plan Your Estate,* by Denis Clifford. A detailed guide to estate planning, including information about living trusts.
- *The Trustee's Legal Companion,* by Liza Hanks and Carol Elias Zolla. Guide to the ins and outs of being the trustee of a living trust.

Estate and Gift Taxes

Many people who consider estate planning wonder about estate and inheritance taxes. The good news is that most people's estates won't have to pay such taxes—federal or state.

Will my estate have to pay taxes after I die?

The federal government imposes estate taxes only if your taxable property is worth well more than $5 million at your death. (The amount is indexed for inflation and goes up each year. For 2016, the exemption amount was $5.45 million.) Married couples can combine their exemption amounts, letting them pass nearly $11 million free of estate tax.

In addition, all assets left to your spouse are not taxable, as long as the spouse is a U.S. citizen. Neither are assets left to a tax-exempt charity.

Don't some states also impose taxes at death?

Some states impose their own inheritance or estate taxes.

Inheritance taxes are paid by your inheritors, not your estate. Typically, how much they pay depends on their relationship to you. For example, Nebraska imposes a 15% tax if you leave $25,000 to a friend, but only 1% if you leave the money to your child. But tax rates vary from state to state. If you live in Maryland, your child wouldn't owe any taxes on a $25,000 inheritance, but your friend could owe 10%.

States That Impose Inheritance Taxes		
Iowa	Maryland	New Jersey
Kentucky	Nebraska	Pennsylvania

Estate taxes collected by states are similar to the estate tax imposed by the federal government. If your estate is large enough, it must pay this tax. Estates may have to pay state tax even if they aren't large enough to owe federal estate tax.

If you're concerned about state taxes, see a tax lawyer in your state (and in any other state where you own real estate).

States That Impose Estate Tax		
Connecticut	Maine	New York
Delaware	Maryland	Oregon
Dist. of Col.	Massachusetts	Rhode Island
Hawaii	Minnesota	Vermont
Illinois	New Jersey	Washington

You can find a listing of your state's estate and inheritance tax laws in *The Executor's Guide*, by Mary Randolph (Nolo).

Are there ways to avoid federal estate taxes?

Yes. One popular method is called an AB trust, sometimes known as a "credit shelter trust," "exemption trust," or "marital bypass trust."

Other common methods include a "QTIP" trust, which enables a surviving spouse to postpone estate taxes that would otherwise be due when the other spouse dies. And there are many different types of charitable trusts, which involve making a sizable gift to a tax-exempt charity. Some of them provide both income tax and estate tax advantages.

Can I avoid paying state taxes?

If your state imposes estate or inheritance taxes, there probably isn't much you can do. But if you live in two states—winter here, summer there—your inheritors may save if you can make your legal residence in the state with lower, or no, taxes.

Can't I just give all my property away before I die and avoid estate taxes?

No. The government long anticipated this one. If you give away more than $14,000 per year (2016 figure) to any one person or noncharitable institution, you are assessed federal gift tax, which applies at the same rate as the estate tax. There are, however, a few exceptions to this rule. You can give an unlimited amount of property to your spouse, unless your spouse is not a U.S. citizen, in which case you can give up to $148,000 per year (2016 figure) free of gift tax. Any property given to a tax-exempt charity avoids federal gift taxes. And money spent directly for someone's medical bills or school tuition is exempt as well.

Gift tax is part of the "unified gift and estate tax." The gift/estate tax will be owed only if the taxable gifts you make during your life, plus the assets you leave at death, add up to more than the exemption amount ($5.45 million per person in 2016). You won't actually pay gift tax until you make more than $5.45 million in taxable gifts (and remember, most ordinary gifts aren't taxable) or until your death, if you leave an estate worth more than the exempt amount. Fewer than 0.5% of all estates owe federal estate tax.

But I've heard that people save on estate taxes by making gifts. How?

You can achieve substantial estate tax savings by making use of the annual gift-tax exclusion for gifts to people and nonexempt organizations. If you give away $14,000 a year for four years, you've removed $64,000 from your taxable estate. And each member of a couple has a separate exclusion. So a couple can give twice the exclusion amount each year to a child free of gift tax. If you have a few children, or other people you want to make gifts to (such as your sons- or daughters-in-law), you can use this method to significantly reduce the size of your taxable estate over a few years.

For example, a couple concerned about estate taxes could give each of their four children $28,000 tax free, for a total of $112,000 per year. In ten years, the couple has given away $1,120,000 and has significantly reduced their federal estate tax liability.

Of course, there are risks with this kind of gift-giving program. The most obvious is that you are legally transferring your wealth. Gift giving to reduce eventual estate taxes must be carefully evaluated to see if you can comfortably afford to give away your property during your lifetime.

RESOURCE

More information about estate and gift taxes is contained in *Plan Your Estate,* by Denis Clifford (Nolo)—a detailed guide to estate planning, including all major methods of reducing or avoiding estate and gift taxes.

Funeral Planning and Other Final Arrangements

Many of us are squeamish when it comes to thinking and talking about death, particularly our own. But there are many good reasons to spend some time considering what you want to have happen to your body after death, including any ceremonies and observances you'd like.

Why should I leave written instructions about my final ceremonies and the disposition of my body?

Letting your survivors know your wishes saves them the difficulties of making these decisions at a painful time. Many family members and friends find that discussing these matters ahead of time is a great relief—especially if a person is elderly or in poor health and death is expected soon.

Planning can also help save money. For many people, death goods and services cost more than anything they bought during their lives except homes and cars. Some wise comparison shopping in advance can help ensure that costs will be controlled or kept to a minimum.

Why not leave these instructions in my will?

A will is not a good place to express your death and burial preferences for one simple reason: Your will may not be located and read until several weeks after you die—long after decisions must be made.

A will should be reserved for directions on how to divide and distribute your property and, if applicable, who should get care and custody of your children if you die while they're still young.

What happens if I don't leave written instructions?

If you die without leaving written instructions about your preferences, state law will determine who has the right to decide how your remains will be handled. In most states, the right—and the responsibility to pay for the reasonable costs of disposing of remains—rests with the following people, in order:

- spouse or registered domestic partner
- child or children
- parent or parents
- the next of kin, or
- a public administrator, who is appointed by a court.

Disputes may arise if two or more people—the deceased person's children, for example—share responsibility for a fundamental decision, such as whether the body of a parent should be buried or cremated. But such disputes can be avoided if you are willing to do some planning and to put your wishes in writing.

What details should I include in a final arrangements document?

What you choose to include is a personal matter, likely to be dictated by custom, religious preference, or simply your own whims. A typical final arrangements document might include:

- the name of the mortuary or other institution that will handle burial or cremation
- whether or not you wish to be embalmed
- the type of casket or container in which your remains will be buried or cremated, including whether you want it present at any after-death ceremony
- who your pallbearers will be, if you wish to have some
- how your remains will be transported to the cemetery and gravesite
- where your remains will be buried, stored, or scattered
- the details of any marker you want to show where your remains are buried or interred, and
- the details of any ceremonies you want before, at the time of, or following your burial, interment, or scattering.

What services can I expect from a mortuary?

Most mortuaries or funeral homes are equipped to handle many of the details related to disposing of a person's remains. These include:

- collecting the body from the place of death
- storing the body until it is buried or cremated
- making burial arrangements with a cemetery
- conducting ceremonies related to the burial
- preparing the body for burial, and
- arranging to have the body transported for burial.

Where can I turn for help in making final arrangements?

From an economic standpoint, choosing the institution to handle your burial is probably the most important final arrangement that you can make. For this reason, many people join nonprofit memorial or funeral societies, which help them find local mortuaries that will deal honestly with their survivors and charge reasonable prices.

Society members are free to choose whatever final arrangements they wish. Most societies, however, emphasize simple arrangements over the costly services often promoted by the funeral industry. The services offered by each society differ, but most societies distribute information on options and explain the legal rules that apply to final arrangements.

If you join a society, you will receive a form that allows you to plan for the goods and services you want—and to get them for a predetermined cost. Many societies also serve as watchdogs, making sure that you get and pay for only the services you choose.

The cost for joining these organizations is low—usually from $20 to $50 for a lifetime membership, although some societies periodically charge a small renewal fee.

To find a funeral or memorial society near you, contact the Funeral Consumers Alliance (information is below).

If you don't want to join a society, you can shop around to find the mortuary or funeral home that best meets your needs in terms of style, proximity, and cost.

Going Green

Burials and cremations can be hard on the environment. Embalming chemicals, metal caskets, concrete burial vaults, and cremation facility emissions take a surprising toll. If you want to make plans that minimize environmental effects, here are some options:

Choose a green cemetery. The Green Burial Council can help you find providers that avoid toxins, use biodegradable materials, and even help to preserve open space. Visit www.greenburialcouncil.org for more information.

Say no to embalming. Embalming fluid contains toxic chemicals—including up to three gallons of formaldehyde—that can seep into soil and groundwater. Embalming rarely serves a legitimate purpose and is almost never required.

Ask for a biodegradable container. You can use a simple wood casket, cardboard box, or shroud for burial. There are also biodegradable urns for ashes that will be buried.

Avoid vaults. Vaults are large containers, usually made from reinforced concrete, that are placed in the ground before a burial. They're not required by law, but many cemeteries demand them because they make it easier to maintain the landscape. The result is that, every year, more than 1.5 million tons of reinforced concrete are buried along with caskets and bodies.

You can look for a cemetery that doesn't require vaults. In a few states, you can even refuse a vault on religious grounds. You may be required to pay an extra fee for grave maintenance.

Cremation conservation. Cremation uses the fewest resources, but it's not entirely clean. It burns fossil fuels and carries the risk of mercury pollution from incinerated fillings. Newer cremation facilities are more efficient, using about half the fuel. If you have amalgam fillings in your teeth, you can ask that they be removed before cremation.

Can my family handle my final arrangements independently, without a mortuary?

There is a slowly growing trend in America for people to care for their own dead, minimizing or even eliminating the involvement of funeral industry personnel. This can mean everything from preparing the body to burying it or transporting it to the cremation facility.

Most states do allow individuals to act completely on their own. But there are rules about how people may proceed—for example, most states have laws that regulate the depth of a site for a body burial. A few states throw up roadblocks to acting independently, requiring that a funeral director handle body disposition.

If you want to ask a family member or friend to handle your disposition independently, the following resources can help you make your plans:

- *Caring for the Dead: Your Final Act of Love,* by Lisa Carlson (Upper Access Press). This book will help you understand how to take care of a body and what laws may apply. It includes a state-by-state guide to funeral and burial practices, as well as directories of cremation facilities and nonprofit funeral consumer groups.
- *Coming to Rest: A Guide to Caring for Our Own Dead*, by Julie Wiskind and Richard Spiegel (Dovetail). This guide covers details from preparing a body to complying with legal requirements and completing paperwork.
- The Funeral Consumers Alliance, www.funerals.org, offers extensive resources to help you make your own plans.

How can I arrange payment for my final arrangements?

Whatever arrangements you make, you have two main options for covering costs. You can:

- pay everything up front (in a lump sum or installments), or
- decide what you want and leave enough money for your survivors to pay the bills.

If you don't do either of these things, and your estate doesn't have enough money to cover the costs, your survivors will have to pay for any final expenses.

Paying in advance. If you want to pay in advance, either all at once or under a payment plan, be sure you're dealing with a reputable provider of goods and services, and document your arrangements clearly.

There are reasons to be cautious about paying up front. Though there are a number of legal controls on how the funeral industry can handle and invest funds earmarked for future services, there have been many reported instances of mismanaged and stolen funds. A great many other abuses go unreported by family members too embarrassed or grief-stricken to complain.

In addition, when mortuaries go out of business, customers who have prepaid may be left without a refund and without recourse. Also, many individuals who move during their lifetimes discover that their prepayment funds are nonrefundable—or that there is a substantial financial penalty for withdrawing or transferring them. In addition, money paid now may not cover inflated costs of the future, meaning that survivors will be left to cover what's left.

Setting aside funds. A safe, simple, and flexible option is to set aside funds that your survivors can use to cover the costs of your final plans.

After making your plans and estimating the cost, you can tuck away that sum (perhaps adding a bit to cover inflation or unexpected expenses) in an easily accessible account. Tell the bank or financial institution that you want to set up a payable-on-death account. You can designate a beneficiary—a good choice might be the executor of your will or successor trustee of your living trust—who can claim the money immediately upon your death. One warning: The beneficiary will have no legal obligation to use these funds for your final arrangements, so be sure that person understands what the funds are for and that you trust the person to do as you ask.

RESOURCE

More about final arrangements is available from The Funeral Consumers Alliance, a nonprofit organization that can help you locate a funeral or memorial society near you. Call 800-765-0107 or go to www.funerals.org.

Quicken WillMaker Plus (Nolo) (software), lets you create a final arrangements document, in addition to a valid will, and other documents. In states that allow it, you can also use WillMaker's power of attorney for health care to name an agent to make final arrangements on your behalf.

Get It Together, by Melanie Cullen and Shae Irving (Nolo), helps you organize and store all of your important records, including your final wishes and arrangements.

Body and Organ Donations

In addition to making other arrangements for your funeral and burial or cremation, you may want to arrange to donate some or all of your organs.

How can I arrange to donate my body for education or scientific research after my death?

Arrangements for whole body donations must usually be made while you are alive, although some medical schools will accept a cadaver through arrangements made after death.

The best place to contact to arrange a whole body donation is the nearest medical school.

How can I arrange to donate my body organs for others to use after my death?

The principal method for donating organs is by indicating your intent to do so on a donor card or in a health care directive (see the next chapter).

In most states, you can obtain an organ donation card from the department of motor vehicles. Depending on where you live, you can check a box, affix a stamp or seal, or attach a separate card to your license, indicating your wish to donate one or more organs. Some states also have online registries where you can state your wish to become an organ donor.

Even if you have not signed a card or other document indicating your intent to donate your organs, your next of kin can approve a donation after you die. If you do put your intent in writing, make sure you tell family members you have done so. Even if you have indicated in writing that you want to donate your organs, an objection by your next of kin will often defeat your wishes; medical personnel usually do not proceed in the face of an objection from relatives. The best safeguard is to discuss your wishes with close friends and relatives, emphasizing your strong feelings about donating your organs.

ONLINE HELP

Get extensive information about wills and estate planning on Nolo.com. The Wills, Trust & Probate section of Nolo's website provides hundreds of articles, from pets and estate planning to state overviews of probate. In addition to the estate planning books and software mentioned throughout this chapter, Nolo's store offers online forms for a will and a living trust.

CHAPTER

12

Health Care Directives and Powers of Attorney

There is no mortal whom sorrow and disease do not touch.

—**Euripides**

Many of us fear that we may someday become seriously ill and unable to handle our own affairs. Who would act on our behalf to pay bills, make bank deposits, watch over investments, and deal with the paperwork required to collect insurance and government benefits? Who would make arrangements for our medical care and see that our wishes for treatment are carried out?

Preparing a few simple documents—health care directives and a durable power of attorney for finances—can ease these worries by ensuring that your affairs will stay in the hands of the trusted people you choose. This chapter answers your questions about these documents and how they work, as well as what happens if a court appoints a conservator—that is, a person who will manage your affairs if you haven't drafted legally valid instructions naming someone to take over.

Health Care Directives

If you're like most people, you aren't eager to spend time thinking about what would happen if you became unable to direct your own medical care because of illness, an accident, or advanced age. But if you don't do at least a little bit of planning—writing down your wishes about the kinds of treatment you do or don't want to receive and naming someone you trust to oversee your care—these important matters could wind up in the hands of estranged family members, doctors, or sometimes even judges, who may know very little about what you would prefer.

There are two basic documents that allow you to set out your wishes for medical care: a living will and a durable power of attorney for health care. It's wise to prepare both. In some states, the living will and the power of attorney are combined into a single form—often called an advance directive. In fact, all of these documents are types of health care directives—that is, documents that let you specify your wishes for health care in the event that you become unable to speak for yourself.

What is a living will?

A living will—sometimes called a health care declaration or something similar—is a written statement that details the type of medical care you want (or don't want) if you become incapacitated. A living will bears no relation to the conventional will or living trust used to leave property at death; it's strictly a place to spell out your health care preferences.

You can use your living will to say as much or as little as you wish about the kind of health care you want to receive.

Your Medical Care in an Emergency

In addition to living wills and health care powers of attorney, some people may make a Do Not Resuscitate (DNR) order or a Physician's Orders for Life Sustaining Treatment (POLST) form. Both types of forms allow you to leave instructions about what kind of treatments you want to receive in emergency situations when health care providers may not have time to determine whether you have a valid living will that describes your wishes.

DNR orders. A DNR order tells emergency medical personnel that you do not wish to be administered cardiopulmonary resuscitation (CPR). DNR orders are used both in hospitals and in situations where a person might require emergency care outside of the hospital. In most states, a doctor's signature is required to make the DNR valid.

POLST Forms. Most states are starting to use a form that is similar to a DNR order, but differs in a few important ways. The form is most often called Physician's Orders for Life Sustaining Treatment (POLST), though some states use other terms. A POLST form may be used in addition to—or instead of—a DNR order. Unlike a DNR order, a POLST form includes directions about life-sustaining measures—such as intubation, antibiotic use, and feeding tubes—in addition to CPR. The POLST form helps to ensure that medical providers will understand your wishes at a glance. To be valid, the form must be signed by a doctor or other approved health care professional.

What is a durable power of attorney for health care?

A durable power of attorney for health care gives another person authority to make medical decisions for you if you are unable to make them for yourself. This person is usually called your agent but, depending on your state, may also be called your proxy, patient advocate, surrogate, or something similar.

If you make a living will, part of your health care agent's job will be making sure that your wishes are carried out as you intend. Your agent can also make any necessary health care decisions for you that your living will does not cover.

If you don't know anyone you trust enough to name as your health care agent, it is still important to complete and finalize a living will recording your wishes for health care. That way, your doctors will still know what kind of medical care you do or do not want.

What happens if I don't have any health care documents?

If you do not make a living will or durable power of attorney for health care, the doctors who attend you will decide what kind of medical care you will receive. For consent, they will turn to a close relative—usually your spouse, registered domestic partner, parent, or adult child.

Problems may arise if those closest to you disagree about what treatment is proper.

In the most extreme circumstances, these battles end up in court, where a judge—who usually has little medical knowledge and no familiarity with you—is called upon to decide the course of your treatment. Legal battles can be avoided if you take the time to make a document expressing your wishes.

What should I cover in my living will?

You don't need to become a medical expert to complete your living will, but it's a good idea to become familiar with the kinds of medical procedures that are commonly administered to patients who are seriously ill.

Life-prolonging medical care. In most states, living wills state whether or not you want to receive life-prolonging treatments at the end of life. Such procedures typically include:

- transfusions of blood and blood products
- cardiopulmonary resuscitation (CPR)
- diagnostic tests
- dialysis
- administration of drugs
- use of a respirator, and
- surgery.

If you want more information, you can discuss these treatments with your doctor or a patient representative at a hospital or health insurance plan office, or you can turn to self-help resources for more detailed information.

Food and water. If you are permanently comatose or close to death from a serious illness, you may not be able to survive without the administration of food and water. Unless you indicate that treatment should be withheld, doctors will use intravenous (IV) feeding or tubes to provide you with a mix of nutrients and fluids. IV feeding, where fluids are introduced through a vein in an arm or a leg, is a short-term procedure. Tube feeding, however, can be carried on indefinitely.

Permanently unconscious patients can sometimes live for years with artificial feeding and hydration without regaining consciousness. If food and water are removed, death will occur in a relatively short time due to dehydration, rather than starvation. Such a course of action generally includes a plan of medication to keep the patient comfortable.

When you make your health care documents, you can choose whether you want artificially administered food and water withheld or provided. This decision is difficult for many people. Keep in mind that as long as you are able to communicate your wishes, by whatever means, you will not be denied food and water if you want them.

Palliative care—or pain relief. If you want death to occur naturally—without life-prolonging intervention—it does not mean you must forgo treatment to alleviate pain or keep you comfortable. This type of care is often called "palliative care."

Rather than focusing on a cure or prolonging life, palliative care emphasizes quality of life and dignity by helping a patient remain comfortable and free from pain until life ends naturally. Palliative care may be administered at home, in a hospice facility, or at a hospital.

You may wish to spend some time educating yourself about palliative care. You can include your feelings and preferences about such care in your living will.

How Pregnancy May Affect Your Health Care Directives

There is one situation in which your specific health care directions might be challenged or ignored completely: when you are pregnant. If you may become pregnant, it's a good idea to explicitly state what you want if your health care documents go into effect while you are carrying a child.

Whether or not doctors will honor your wishes depends on several factors, including how far along you are in your pregnancy, the risks to you and the unborn child, and the policies of individual doctors and health care facilities. If you are in your second or third trimester, doctors are likely to administer all medical care they deem necessary to keep you and the fetus alive.

Do doctors have to follow my wishes?

Health care providers are generally required to comply with the wishes you set out in your health care documents—and to honor your health care agent's authority as long as the agent's directions are a reasonable interpretation of your wishes.

In some situations, however, a health care provider is permitted to reject a medical decision made by you or your agent. This may be true if:

- the decision goes against the conscience of the individual health care provider
- the decision goes against a policy of a health care institution that is based on reasons of conscience, or
- the decision would lead to medically ineffective health care or health care that violates generally accepted health care standards applied by the health care provider or institution.

But this doesn't mean that your health care instructions can be ignored. A health care provider who refuses to comply with your wishes or the directions of your health care agent must promptly inform you or your agent. And if you or your agent wishes, the provider must immediately take steps to transfer you to another provider or institution that will honor your directive. In some states, a health care provider who intentionally violates these rules may be legally liable for damages.

When will my health care documents take effect?

Your health care documents take effect if your doctor determines that you lack the ability—often called the "capacity"—to make your own health care decisions. Lacking capacity usually means that:

- you can't understand the nature and consequences of the health care choices that are available to you, and
- you are unable to communicate your own wishes for care, either orally, in writing, or through gestures.

Practically speaking, this means that if you are so ill or injured that you cannot express your health care wishes, your documents will spring immediately into effect. If there is any question about your ability to understand and communicate your treatment choices, your doctor (with the input of your health care agent or close relatives) will decide whether it is time for your health care documents to become operative.

In some states, it is possible to give your health care agent the authority to manage your medical care immediately. If your state allows this option, you may prefer to make an immediately effective document so that your agent can step in to act for you at any time, without the need to involve a doctor in the question of whether or not your health care document should take effect.

Making your document effective immediately will not give your agent the authority to override what you want in terms of treatment; you will always be able to dictate your own medical care if you have the ability to do so. And even when you are no longer capable of making your own decisions, your health care agent must always act in your best interests and diligently try to follow any health care wishes you've expressed in your health care directive or otherwise.

How do I choose a health care agent?

The person you name as your health care agent should be someone you trust—and someone with whom you feel confident discussing your wishes. Though your agent need not agree with your wishes for your medical care, you should believe that the person you choose respects your right to get the kind of medical care you want.

The person you appoint to oversee your health care wishes could be a spouse or partner, relative, or close friend. Keep in mind that your agent may have to fight to assert your wishes in the face of a stubborn medical establishment—and against the wishes of family members who may be driven by their own beliefs and interests, rather than yours. If you foresee the possibility of a conflict in enforcing your wishes, be sure to choose an agent who is strong-willed and assertive.

While you need not name someone who lives in the same state as you do, proximity may be an important factor. The reality is that the person you name may be called upon to spend weeks or months near your bedside, making sure medical personnel abide by your health care wishes. If you name someone who lives far away, make sure that person is willing to travel and stay with you a while. The agent's job may demand it.

You should not choose your doctor or an employee of a hospital or nursing home where you receive treatment to be your agent. In fact, the laws in many states prevent you from naming such a person. In a few instances, this legal constraint may frustrate your wishes. For example, you may wish to name your spouse or partner as your representative, but that person may be ruled out if he or she works as a hospital employee. Many states have created exceptions to allow close family members who work in medical facilities to serve as agents. However, if the law in your state bans your first choice, you will have to name another person to serve.

Organ Donation and Body Disposition

Most of your agent's authority under a durable power of attorney for health care will end upon your death. In many states, however, you can give your agent permission to oversee the disposition of your body, including authorizing an autopsy or carrying out your wishes for organ donation. If you want your agent to have these powers, you should say so in your power of attorney document.

If you have specific wishes about these matters, your living will is a good place to write them down. Your agent is legally required to follow your instructions whenever possible.

How much power will my health care agent have?

In most states, your agent will have the authority to make all health care decisions for you unless you specifically limit your agent's authority in your power of attorney document. This means that your agent will normally be permitted to:

- consent or refuse consent to any medical treatment that affects your physical or mental health (there are usually exceptions to this rule for situations such as extreme psychiatric treatments and termination of pregnancy, and your agent is not permitted to authorize any act that violates the wishes you've stated in your living will)
- hire or fire medical personnel
- make decisions about the best medical facilities for you
- visit you in the hospital or other facility even when other visitors are restricted
- gain access to medical records and other personal information, and
- get court authorization, if required to obtain or withhold medical treatment, if for any reason a hospital or doctor does not honor your living will or the authority of your health care agent.

Keep in mind that as long as you are able to understand and communicate your own wishes, your agent cannot override what you want. Your agent steps in only if you can no longer manage on your own.

Make Your Documents Legal

There are a few requirements you must meet to make valid health care directives. In most states, you must be 18 years old, though a few states allow parents to make health care directives for their minor children. All states require that the person making a health care directive be able to understand what the document means, what it contains, and how it works.

Also, every state requires that you sign your documents. If you are physically unable to sign them yourself, you can direct another person to sign them for you.

You must sign your documents, or have them signed for you, in the presence of witnesses or a notary public—sometimes both, depending on your state's law. The purpose of this additional formality is to make sure that at least one other person can confirm that you were of sound mind and of legal age when you made the documents.

Where can I get health care directive forms?

There are a number of ways to find the proper health care documents for your state; you don't need to consult a lawyer to obtain or prepare them.

Here are some likely sources for forms and instructions:

- local senior centers
- local hospitals (ask to speak with the patient representative; by law, any hospital that receives federal funds must provide patients with appropriate forms for directing health care)
- your regular physician
- your state's medical association
- Caring Connections. This site lets you download free health care directives for your state at www.caringinfo.org. You can also call the organization's HelpLine at 800-658-8898.
- *Quicken WillMaker Plus.* This software from Nolo walks you step by step through the process of writing your own health care directives. In addition, you can use the program to prepare a valid will, durable power of attorney for finances, and other important legal documents.

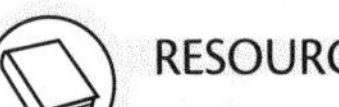

RESOURCE

Get more information about health care directives and more on Nolo.com. The Living Wills & Medical Powers of Attorney section of Nolo.com provides lots of free legal and practical information about health care directives—including state-specific information about living wills, powers of attorney for health care, and POLST forms.

Durable Powers of Attorney for Finances

A durable power of attorney for finances is a simple, inexpensive, and reliable way to arrange for someone to make your financial decisions should you become unable to do so yourself. It's also a wonderful thing to do for your family members. If you do become incapacitated, the durable power of attorney will likely appear as a minor miracle to those close to you.

How does a durable power of attorney work?

When you create and sign a power of attorney, you give another person legal authority to act on your behalf. This person is called your attorney-in-fact or, in some states, your agent. The word "attorney" here means anyone authorized to act on another's behalf; it's most definitely not restricted to lawyers.

A "durable" power of attorney stays valid even if you become unable to handle your own affairs (incapacitated). If you don't specify that you want your power of attorney to be durable, it will automatically end if you later become incapacitated.

When does a durable power of attorney take effect?

There are two kinds of durable powers of attorney for finances: those that take effect immediately and those that don't take effect unless and until someone (usually a doctor or two) certifies that you can no longer manage your financial affairs. Which kind you should make depends, in part, on when you want your attorney-in-fact to start handling tasks for you.

If you want someone to take over some or all of your affairs now, you should make your document effective as soon as you sign it. Then, your attorney-in-fact can begin helping you with your financial tasks right away—and can continue to do so if you later become incapacitated.

On the other hand, you may feel strongly that your attorney-in-fact should not take over unless you are incapacitated. In this case, you have two options. If you trust your attorney-in-fact to act only when it's absolutely necessary, you can go ahead and make an immediately effective document. Legally, your attorney-in-fact will then have the authority to act on your behalf—but won't do so before deciding that you can't handle your affairs yourself.

If you're uncomfortable giving your attorney-in-fact authority now, you can add language to your durable power of attorney to make what's known as a "springing" document. It won't take effect until at least one person (usually a doctor) certifies, in writing, that you can't manage your finances.

There are some real inconveniences involved in creating a springing power of attorney, however. First, the process of obtaining the certification of your incapacity can be time-consuming and complicated for your attorney-in-fact, and may delay the handling of your affairs. (You may even be required to prepare special release forms under a law called HIPAA, authorizing doctors to release information to your attorney-in-fact.) Second, some people may be reluctant to accept a springing power of attorney, even though your attorney-in-fact has obtained the required doctors' statements and your document is perfectly legal. A bank, for example, might question whether you have, in fact, become incapacitated. These hassles could further disrupt the handling of your finances. For these reasons, many experts recommend against making a springing document. If you truly trust your attorney-in-fact, it makes more sense to create a document that takes effect immediately, and then tell your attorney-in-fact when to actually step in.

How do I create a durable power of attorney for finances?

To create a legally valid durable power of attorney, all you need to do is properly complete and sign a fill-in-the-blanks form that's a few pages long. Some states have their own forms.

After you fill out the form, you must sign it in front of a notary public. In some states, witnesses must also watch you sign the document. If your attorney-in-fact will have authority to deal with your real estate, you must put a copy on file at the local land records office. (In just two states, North and South Carolina, you must record your power of attorney for it to be durable.)

RESOURCE

Create a personalized state-specific durable power of attorney using WillMaker Plus (Nolo). WillMaker Plus helps you create a durable power of attorney that conforms to your state's laws and fits your unique needs. And importantly, as you create your document, the program provides plain-English guidance and support every step of the way.

Some banks, title companies, insurance companies, brokerage companies, and other financial institutions have their own durable power of attorney forms. If you want your attorney-in-fact to have an easy time with these institutions, you may need to prepare two (or more) durable powers of attorney: your own form and forms provided by the institutions with which you do business.

What happens if I don't have a durable power of attorney for finances?

If you become incapacitated and you haven't prepared a durable power of attorney for finances, a court proceeding is probably inescapable. Your spouse, closest relatives, or companion will have to ask a court for authority over at least some of your financial affairs.

If you are married, your spouse does have some authority over property you own

The Attorney-in-Fact's Duties

Commonly, people give an attorney-in-fact broad power over their finances. But you can give your attorney-in-fact as much or as little power as you wish. You may want to give your attorney-in-fact authority to do some or all of the following:

- use your assets to pay your everyday expenses and those of your family
- buy, sell, maintain, pay taxes on, and mortgage real estate and other property
- collect benefits from Social Security, Medicare, or other government programs or civil or military service
- invest your money in stocks, bonds, and mutual funds
- handle transactions with banks and other financial institutions
- buy and sell insurance policies and annuities for you
- file and pay your taxes
- operate your small business
- claim property you inherit or are otherwise entitled to
- transfer property into your living trust
- manage your online accounts
- represent you in court or hire someone to represent you, and
- manage your retirement accounts.

Whatever powers you give the attorney-in-fact, the attorney-in-fact must act in your best interests, keep accurate records, keep your property separate, and avoid conflicts of interest.

together—to pay bills from a joint bank account, for example. There are limits, however, on your spouse's right to handle property owned by both of you. And, of course, your spouse has no authority over property you own alone.

If your relatives go to court to get someone appointed to manage your financial affairs, they must ask a judge to rule that you cannot take care of your own affairs—a public airing of a very private matter. And like any court proceeding, it can be expensive if your relatives must hire a lawyer. Depending on where you live, the person appointed may be called a conservator of the estate, guardian of the estate, committee, or curator. When this person is appointed, you lose the right to control your own money and property.

The appointment of a conservator is usually just the beginning of your family's days in court. Often the conservator must:

- post a bond—a kind of insurance policy that pays if the conservator steals or misuses property
- prepare (or hire a lawyer or accountant to prepare) detailed financial reports and periodically file them with the court, and
- get court approval for certain transactions, such as selling real estate or making slightly risky investments.

A conservatorship isn't necessarily permanent, but it may be ended only by the court. Conservatorships are discussed in more detail in the next set of questions.

I have a living trust. Do I still need a durable power of attorney for finances?

A revocable living trust can be useful if you become incapable of taking care of your financial affairs. That's because the person who will distribute trust property after your death (the successor trustee) can also, in most cases, take over management of the trust property if you become incapacitated.

Few people, however, transfer all their property to a living trust, and the successor trustee has no authority over property that the trust doesn't own. So a living trust isn't a complete substitute for a durable power of attorney for finances.

Can my attorney-in-fact make medical decisions on my behalf?

A durable power of attorney for finances does not give your attorney-in-fact legal authority to make medical decisions for you.

You can, however, prepare a durable power of attorney for health care, a document that lets you choose someone to make medical decisions on your behalf if you can't. In most states, you'll also want to write out your wishes in a living will, which tells your doctors your preferences about certain kinds of medical treatments if you can't communicate your wishes.

Health care documents are discussed in the previous section of this chapter.

When does the durable power of attorney end?

It ends at your death. That means that you can't give your attorney-in-fact authority to handle things after your death, such as paying your debts, making funeral or burial arrangements, or transferring your property to the people who inherit it. If you want your attorney-in-fact to have authority to wind up your affairs after your death, use a will to name that person as your executor.

Your durable power of attorney also ends if:

- **You revoke it.** As long as you are mentally competent, you can revoke a durable power of attorney at any time.
- **A court invalidates your document.** This happens rarely, but a court may declare your document invalid if the judge concludes that you were not mentally competent when you signed it, or that you were the victim of fraud or undue influence.
- **You get a divorce.** In a handful of states, if your spouse is your attorney-in-fact and you divorce, your ex-spouse's authority is automatically terminated. In any state, however, it is wise to revoke your durable power of attorney after a divorce and make a new one.

- **No attorney-in-fact is available.** A durable power of attorney must end if there's no one to serve as attorney-in-fact. To avoid this problem, you can name an alternate attorney-in-fact in your document.

RESOURCE

For more information about durable powers of attorney for finances, see *WillMaker Plus* (software from Nolo). It walks you step by step through the process of writing your own durable power of attorney for finances. You can also use the program to prepare a valid will, health care directives, and other useful legal documents.

Conservatorships

A conservatorship is a legal arrangement that gives an adult the court-ordered authority and responsibility to manage another adult's financial affairs. Many states use the terms "conservator" and "guardian" interchangeably, or use other terms such as "custodian" or "curator." In this book, we use the term "guardian" for a person who makes personal decisions for a child or an incapacitated adult, and "conservator" for someone who takes care of financial matters for an incapacitated adult. The adult who needs help is called the "conservatee."

If you need information about guardianships for children, see Chapter 15.

When is a conservatorship necessary?

Conservatorships are permitted only for those who are so incapacitated that they cannot manage their own financial affairs. Generally, conservatorships are established for people who are in comas, suffer from advanced stages of Alzheimer's disease, or have other serious illnesses or injuries.

Conservatorships are rarely needed for people who have made—or can knowingly sign—financial documents, such as a durable power of attorney for finances. (See the previous set of questions.)

Adults May Need Guardians, Too

In addition to help with finances, an incapacitated adult may also need assistance with personal matters, such as medical decisions (if the adult has not prepared a health care directive) and decisions about where the adult will live and what daily activities will look like. If a court appoints someone to take care of these things, that person is usually called a "guardian" or "conservator of the person." The incapacitated adult is often called the "ward." An incapacitated adult may need a guardian, a conservator, or both. The same person can be appointed to take both jobs. As with conservators, guardians are supervised by, and held accountable to, a court.

What are the advantages of a conservatorship?

Conservatorships are subject to court supervision, which provides a powerful safeguard for an incapacitated adult's (the conservatee) property. To prevent a conservator from mismanaging the person's property, most courts require the conservator to provide periodic reports and accountings that give details about the conservatee's assets and how the conservatee's money was spent. Many courts also require the conservator to seek permission before making major decisions about the conservatee's property, such as whether to sell real estate.

What are the downsides to a conservatorship?

Conservatorships are time-consuming and expensive; they often require court hearings and the ongoing assistance of a lawyer. The paperwork can also be a hassle because, as mentioned above, the conservator must keep detailed records and file court papers on a regular basis.

In addition, a conservator must usually post a bond (a kind of insurance policy that protects the conservatee's estate from mishandling). The bond premiums are paid by the conservatee's estate—and are an unnecessary expense if the conservator is competent and trustworthy.

Occasionally, however, a conservator will mismanage a conservatee's assets. Common abuses range from reckless handling of the conservatee's assets to outright theft. Although each state has rules and procedures designed to prevent mishandling of assets, few have the resources to keep an eye on conservators and follow through if they spot trouble. Many cases of incompetence or abuse go unnoticed.

Finally, a conservatorship can be emotionally trying for the conservatee. All court proceedings and documents are public records, which can be embarrassing for someone who values independence and privacy.

How are conservators compensated for their services?

The conservatee's estate must reimburse the conservator for necessary expenses and must usually pay for the conservator's services—if these payments are "reasonable" in the eyes of a court. Generally, payments are made to professional or public conservators, but a family member who has been appointed conservator may also seek compensation by making a request to the court.

Are there ways to block a conservatorship?

Before a court approves a conservatorship, notice must be given to the proposed conservatee and the conservatee's close family members. Anyone—including the proposed conservatee, family members, and friends—may object to the conservatorship in general, or to the specific choice of conservator. The person who wants to block the conservatorship must file papers with the court, inform all interested parties (the proposed conservatee, family members, and possibly close friends), and attend a legal hearing. The final decision is up to a judge.

The best way to avoid a conservatorship is to prepare a durable power of attorney for finances before a health crisis occurs. That way, someone you've handpicked will be able to step in and make decisions for you if necessary. (For information about preparing a durable power of attorney, see the previous set of questions.)

How does a judge choose a conservator?

When a conservatorship petition is filed in court, a judge must decide whom to appoint. Often, just one person is interested in taking on the role of conservator—but sometimes several family members or friends vie for the position. If no one suitable is available to serve as conservator, the judge may appoint a public or other professional conservator.

When appointing a conservator, a judge follows certain preferences established by state law. Most states give preference to the conservatee's spouse, adult children, adult siblings, or other blood relatives—and some states now give priority to a registered domestic partner. But a judge has the discretion to pick the person he or she thinks is best for the job. Without strong evidence of what the conservatee would have wanted, however, it is unlikely that a nonrelative would be appointed over a relative. Because of this, conservatorship proceedings may cause great heartache if an estranged relative is chosen as conservator over the conservatee's partner or close friend.

Who financially supports the conservatee?

If the conservatee has the means, money for support will come from the person's own assets. But a conservator should seek all financial benefits and coverage for which the conservatee may qualify. These benefits may include Social Security, medical insurance, Veterans Administration benefits, pension and retirement benefits, disability benefits, public assistance, and Supplemental Security Income. When needed, close family members (including the conservator) often contribute their own money to help support a conservatee.

When does a conservatorship end?

A conservator must care for the conservatee's finances until the court issues an order ending the arrangement. This ordinarily happens when:

- the conservatee dies
- the conservatorship estate is used up
- the conservatee regains the ability to handle financial matters, or

- the conservator becomes unable or unwilling to handle the responsibilities. In this situation, the conservatorship itself does not end, but someone else takes over the conservator's duties.

ONLINE HELP

The following sites are good resources for information regarding health care directives and powers of attorney:

- **www.nolo.com** Nolo offers information on a wide variety of legal topics, including health care directives, powers of attorney, and conservatorships.
- **www.nhpco.org** The National Hospice and Palliative Care Organization provides extensive information on end-of-life health care options and choices. They also provide access to free health care directive forms.
- **http://billmoyers.com/series/on-our-own-terms-moyers-on-dying** "On Our Own Terms" is a Bill Moyers public television documentary on end-of-life medical treatment. The site features interviews with professionals, patients, and loved ones—all of whom share insights and perspectives on making difficult health care choices.
- **www.hankdunn.com** This website offers a free downloadable book titled *Hard Choices for Loving People: CPR, Palliatic Care Feeding Tubes, Comfort and the Patient With a Serious Illness*, by Hank Dunn (Quality of Life Publishing Company). The book is a well-written resource that features a particularly good discussion of the issues surrounding artificial nutrition and hydration.
- **www.growthhouse.org** Growth House is a gateway to helpful resources and information on life-threatening illnesses and end-of-life care.

CHAPTER

13

Older Americans

To be seventy years young is sometimes far more cheerful and hopeful than to be forty years old.

—Oliver Wendell Holmes, Jr.

For many older Americans, the final years are no longer the Golden Years. Worries over limited incomes—and the real threat of being financially ruined by any extended bout with the medical system—crowd out thoughts of leisure and fulfillment.

There is help available for supplementing limited incomes and covering medical care in your later years, but you have to take some initiative to find it. The sooner you start planning, the better.

Retirement Plans

In the world of retirement planning, there are two broad categories of plans that are potentially available to you: individual plans and employer plans. There are only two types of individual plans: traditional individual retirement accounts (IRAs) and Roth individual retirement accounts (Roth IRAs). There are many types of employer plans, the most common of which are profit-sharing plans, including 401(k)s,SEPs, SIMPLEs, and defined benefit plans. You can read more about each of these types of plans below.

Congress created these plans to provide an incentive for individuals to save for their own retirement—and to encourage employers to chip in as well. To make the pot as sweet as possible, both categories offer tax breaks to those who participate.

Of course, too much sugar can be bad for you, and Congress, ever mindful of our well-being, put some penalties in the mix as well. It wanted to make sure that people actually used the money for retirement (and not for, say, a trip to Maui). As a result, the rules can be strict about how much you can take out of the plans and when you can do it. These rules vary depending on the type of plan at issue, but one thing is always true: You should educate yourself about the dos and don'ts before taking money out of your plan. Otherwise, you could face stiff penalties and back taxes.

What is an individual retirement plan?

Individual retirement plans are accounts that you can set up for yourself, without any connection to your employer, using income you have earned. Regardless of where you work or whether you change jobs, the individual plan always belongs to you. And you can establish an individual plan even if your employer also provides a separate employer retirement plan for you. Think of it as your own personal retirement savings account, separate from anything your employer funds or makes available.

There are two types of individual plans: traditional IRAs and Roth IRAs. Traditional IRAs are available to everyone. In a traditional IRA, you can contribute a maximum of $5,500 for 2016, or $6,500 if you reach age 50 by the end of the year. In future years, these figures are subject to increase with inflation. To make a contribution, you must have earned at least that much in taxable compensation during the year. The exact amount you are allowed to contribute will depend on whether you also contribute to a Roth IRA. (See below.)

That money can then grow, sheltered in the account, temporarily free of taxes. If you meet certain income requirements, you can get a tax break on the money you contribute. You don't have to worry about taxes again until you take the money out.

Roth IRAs are available only to people who meet certain income requirements. The contribution limits for Roth IRAs are the same as those described above for traditional IRAs. The money will grow tax free. The exact amount you can contribute will depend on whether you also contribute to a traditional IRA. (See below.) Although you will pay taxes on the money you contribute, you won't pay taxes on any of the growth, nor will you pay taxes on the money when you take it out of the account.

How can I establish an IRA for myself?

Opening an IRA—be it a traditional IRA or a Roth IRA—is no more complicated than opening an ordinary bank account. The first step is to find a financial institution (such as a bank or a brokerage firm) to hold the assets for you. Then contact the institution to request the necessary paperwork. Many institutions even allow you to download or submit the paperwork online. The paperwork is very simple—usually one or two pages requesting basic information. Send the paperwork and a check for your contribution amount back to the institution. That's it. Depending on the institution you choose, you may have to take the additional step of selecting mutual funds in which to invest your money.

What is an employer retirement plan?

An employer retirement plan is just what it sounds like: a plan set up by your employer to fund your retirement. Beyond that general similarity, however, employer plans can vary greatly. In some employer plans, the employer contributes all of the money and guarantees you a set amount of income during your retirement. On the other end of the spectrum, other types of plans don't require the employer to contribute anything—or even guarantee that there will be money in the plan when you need it.

There are many types of employer plans; two of the most common are defined benefit plans and defined contribution plans.

Defined benefit plans promise a specific dollar amount to each participant beginning at retirement. The promised payment is usually based on a combination of factors, such as the employee's earnings and years of service to the company. Generally speaking, the employer is the one who contributes money to the plan. When people speak of "pensions," they are usually thinking of defined benefit plans. These types of plans are becoming very rare indeed.

In a defined contribution plan, there is no guarantee of money at retirement, and the employer does not bear the full burden of contributing to the plan. Rather, the employer establishes the framework of the plan so that you, the employee, can contribute some of your income to the plan. Sometimes, but not always, the employer contributes money to your account as well. Both you and the employer get tax breaks on whatever money you contribute, and the money grows in the plan tax deferred. That means you pay taxes on the money only when you withdraw it from the plan. The risk of defined contribution plans is that they don't guarantee that there will be money in the account when you retire. If you manage the account well, and if luck is with you, your assets will grow in the account and be there when you retire. If you manage the account poorly, however, or if you have bad luck, you could end up with far less than you need—or nothing at all.

What is a 401(k) plan?

A 401(k) is the most common type of employer defined contribution plan. The employer establishes the program in which employees can contribute a portion of their salary to the account. The employer can contribute money to the account as well, but it doesn't have to. The employees then direct the investment of the account funds into various investment vehicles (such as stock mutual funds, money market accounts, and bond funds) chosen by the employer. As with all defined contribution plans, there is no guarantee that a participant will receive a particular amount of money at retirement. It all depends on how the investments do.

What is a Roth 401(k) plan?

A Roth 401(k) plan is an option that can be added to a traditional 401(k) plan; it cannot exist on its own. If your employer wants to establish a Roth 401(k) plan, it must establish a regular 401(k) plan and then add a provision to the plan documents that would establish a separate Roth 401(k) account. You could then contribute part of your salary to either the regular 401(k) plan or the Roth 401(k) plan—or perhaps split the contribution between the two accounts.

You may only deposit after-tax salary deferral contributions to the Roth 401(k) account. No employer contributions and no pretax employee contributions are permitted. Therefore, the entire account will contain only after-tax contributions from your salary plus pretax earnings on those contributions.

Because the Roth 401(k) is part of a regular 401(k) plan, most of the rules that apply to a regular 401(k) plan also apply to a Roth

401(k) plan. For example, the contribution limits are the same. But there are significant differences in how the contributions will be taxed when they come out of the plan. Typically, you won't pay taxes on the Roth 401(k) money when you take it out of the account in retirement, but penalties apply to early withdrawal of your contributions or earnings.

What are SEP and SIMPLE IRAs?

SEP and SIMPLE IRAs have misleading names. Even though they have "IRA" as part of their moniker, they really are employer plans, not individual plans. In other words, these plans can only be established by business entities, not individuals.

If I am self-employed, what kinds of retirement plans are available to me?

Self-employed people—like everyone else—can participate in individual plans (Roth and traditional IRAs) as well as in special types of employer plans commonly called Keoghs.

Keoghs include most of the usual types of employer plans—such as 401(k) plans—but with rules designed specifically for businesses owned by self-employed individuals.

What does it mean to be vested in my retirement plan?

If you are vested in your company's retirement plan, you can take it with you when you leave your job. For example, if you are 50% vested, then you can take 50% of the account with you when you go.

In the case of a defined contribution plan (such as a 401(k) plan), you are always 100% vested in the money that you have contributed to the plan. How vested you are in the money your employer has contributed, however, depends on the plan's terms. For example, the plan may allow you to vest over time—perhaps 50% for your first year of employment and 50% for your second.

Is my retirement plan protected from creditors?

Most employer plans are safe from creditors thanks to a federal law called the Employee Retirement Income Security Act (ERISA). This law requires all plans under its control to include provisions that prohibit the assignment of plan assets to a creditor. The U.S. Supreme Court has ruled that ERISA protects plans from creditors even when the plan participant is in bankruptcy.

Unfortunately, Keogh plans that cover only self-employed business owners (that is, plans that do not also cover employees) are not protected from creditors by ERISA. Neither are IRAs, whether traditional, Roth, SEP, or SIMPLE.

Even though IRAs are not protected by ERISA, many states have laws in place that protect them from creditors.

When can I start taking money out of my retirement plan?

When Congress created the various types of retirement plans, it intended for you to keep the money in the plan until you retired. And it also intended you to actually use the money during retirement, not to sock it away it to pass down to your children or grandchildren.

As a result, there are two broad sets of rules that govern taking money out of a retirement plan: One set requires you to start taking money out beginning at age 70½. The other set penalizes you if you try to take money out before you reach age 59½—unless your withdrawal meets one of the exceptions to the rule against early withdrawals (for example, to buy a new house).

If you take money out too early, or if you fail to take money out when the rules require you to, then you will have to pay a penalty and, depending on the circumstances, back taxes.

It's important to note that early withdrawal penalties and back taxes don't apply to contributions you make to a Roth IRA. You can withdraw your contributions (not the accumulated earnings on your contributions) at any time without paying penalties or taxes.

The details of the rules depend on what type of plan is at issue (for example, a 401(k), a SEP, or a traditional IRA) and the rules of your particular plan (for example, your company can make its own 401(k) more restrictive than the law requires).

If you have questions about taking money out of your retirement plan, ask your plan administrator.

RESOURCE

For more information about retirement plans, see these Nolo books:

- *IRAs, 401(k)s & Other Retirement Plans: Taking Your Money Out,* by Twila Slesnick and John Suttle. Explains the different types of retirement plans and the rules that apply when you want to withdraw funds.
- *The Essential Guide to Federal Employment Laws,* by Lisa Guerin and Sachi Barreiro. Contains an entire chapter devoted to ERISA.

ONLINE HELP

The following sites are good resources for information about retirement plans:

- **www.irs.gov** The IRS's website offers a number of helpful fact sheets and publications on retirement accounts, including Publication 590, *Individual Retirement Arrangements (IRAs).*
- **www.morningstar.com** This investment site offers lots of information on planning for retirement and setting up and managing retirement accounts.

Social Security

Social Security is the general term for a number of related programs—retirement, disability, dependents, and survivors benefits. Together, these programs provide workers and their families with money when their normal flow of income shrinks because of retirement, disability, or death.

Social Security Benefits: A Guide to the Basics

Four basic categories of Social Security benefits are paid based upon the record of your earnings: retirement, disability, dependents, and survivors benefits.

Retirement benefits. You may choose to begin receiving retirement benefits at any time after you reach age 62; the amount of benefits will increase for each year you wait until age 70. The increase in delayed benefits varies from 4% to 8%, depending on the year in which you were born. But no matter how long you wait to begin collecting benefits, the amount you receive will probably be only a small percentage of what you were earning.

Because so many variables are thrown into the mix in computing benefit amounts—some of them based on your individual work record and retirement plans, some of them based on changes and convolutions in Social Security rules—it is impossible to give you what you want most: a solid estimate of the amount that will appear on your retirement benefit check.

Disability benefits. If you are under 65 but have met the work requirements and are considered disabled under the program's medical guidelines, you can receive benefits roughly equal to what your retirement benefits would be.

Dependents benefits. If you are the spouse of a retired or disabled worker who qualifies for retirement or disability benefits, you and your minor or disabled children may be entitled to benefits based on the worker's earning record. This is true whether or not you actually depend on your spouse for your support.

Survivors benefits. If you are the surviving spouse of a worker who qualified for retirement or disability benefits, you and your minor or disabled children may be entitled to benefits based on your deceased spouse's earnings record.

Unfortunately, the amount of money these programs provide rarely fills the gap. The combination of rising living costs, stagnating benefit amounts, and penalties for older people who continue to work make the amount of support offered by Social Security less adequate with each passing year. This shrinking of the Social Security safety net makes it that much more important for you to learn how to get the maximum benefits to which you are entitled.

How much can I expect to get in Social Security benefits?

There is no easy answer to this question. The amount of benefits to which you are entitled under any Social Security program is based not on need but on how much income you earned during your years of working. In most jobs, both you and your employer must pay Social Security taxes on the amounts you earned. Workers also have to pay Social Security taxes on reported self-employment income. Social Security keeps a record of your earnings over your working lifetime and pays benefits based upon the average amount earned.

To give you an idea, the average monthly payment for Social Security disability benefits in 2016 was $1,166, and the average retirement payment was $1,341. The maximum payment for both disability benefits and retirement benefits at full retirement age was $2,639. These amounts increase most years.

Who is eligible to collect benefits?

The specific requirements vary depending on the type of benefits, the age of the person filing the claim, and if you are claiming as a dependent or survivor, the age of the worker. However, there is one general requirement that everyone must meet: The worker on whose earnings record the benefit is to be paid must have worked in "covered employment" for a sufficient number of years—that is, earned what Social Security calls "work credits"—by the time the worker claims retirement benefits, becomes disabled, or dies. To find out about your eligibility, call the Social Security Administration (SSA), 800-772-1213, or visit its website at www.ssa.gov to request a Social Security Statement. (Click "my Social Security.")

Special Social Security eligibility rules apply to some specific types of workers, including federal, state, and local government workers; workers for nonprofit organizations; members of the military; household workers; and farmworkers. If you have been employed for some time in one of these jobs, check with the SSA for more information.

Seniors who aren't eligible for Social Security retirement or disability benefits may be eligible for SSI, which stands for Supplemental Security Income. The SSI program provides a small monthly payment to those who are over 65 or disabled and have very low income and assets. For an individual, the asset limit is $2,000 (not counting your house or car), and for couples, the limit is $3,000. Income limits vary by state.

How are my benefit amounts calculated?

The amount of any benefit is determined by a formula based on the average of your yearly reported earnings in covered employment since you began working. But yearly limits are placed on earnings credits, no matter how much you actually earned in those years.

How can I find out what I've earned so far?

The SSA keeps a running computer tally of your earnings record and work credits, tracking both through your Social Security number. The SSA keeps this information on what is called a Social Security

If You Find an Error

Some government watchers estimate that the SSA makes mistakes on at least 4% of the total official earnings records it keeps. So make sure that the Social Security Number noted on your earnings statement is your own and that earned income amounts listed on the agency's records mesh with the earnings listed on your income tax forms or pay stubs.

If you have evidence that the SSA has made an error, call its helpline at 800-772-1213, Monday through Friday from 7 a.m. to 7 p.m. This line takes all kinds of Social Security questions and is often swamped, so be patient. It is best to call early in the morning or late in the afternoon, late in the week, or late in the month. Have all your documents on hand when you call.

If you would rather speak with someone in person, call your local Social Security office and make an appointment, or drop in during regular business hours. Bring two copies of your benefits statement and the evidence that supports your claim of higher income. That way, you can leave one copy with the Social Security worker. Write down the name of the person with whom you speak so that you can reach the same person when you follow up.

It may take several months to have the corrections made in your record. And once the SSA confirms that it has corrected your record, request another benefits statement to make sure the correct information is in your file.

Statement. The statement is no longer mailed to you every year; you can obtain the statement online at www.ssa.gov (see "my Social Security").

Can I collect more than one type of benefit at a time?

No. Even if you technically qualify for more than one type of Social Security benefit, you can collect just one. For example, you might meet the requirements for both retirement and disability, or you might be eligible for benefits based on both your own retirement and that of your retired spouse. But you may only collect one benefit.

If your own earnings record is low and your spouse's earnings record is high, you may be entitled to higher benefits as a dependent than you would be by collecting your own retirement or disability benefits. A Social Security field representative can estimate what your monthly benefits would be under the various scenarios. Contact your local Social Security office for details. Find yours at the Social Security website www.ssa.gov, or by calling 800-772-1213.

Can I choose which benefit to claim, my spousal benefit or my retirement benefit?

People who turned 62 before 2016 can file for Social Security and choose whether to collect dependents (spousal) retirement benefits or their own retirement benefit. (Some choose to delay taking their own retirement benefit since their benefit increases the longer they wait to claim it.)

Those who turned 62 in 2016 or later cannot choose which benefit to claim; when they file for Social Security, Social Security will pay them the highest benefit they qualify for, which can be their own retirement benefit or their spousal benefit.

Can I claim spousal benefits if I'm divorced?

You are eligible for dependents benefits if both you and your former spouse have reached age 62, your marriage lasted at least ten years, and you have been divorced for at least two years. This two-year waiting period does not apply if your former spouse was already collecting retirement benefits before the divorce.

If you are collecting dependents benefits on your former spouse's work record and then you marry someone else, you lose your right to those benefits. You may, however, be eligible to collect dependents benefits based on your new spouse's work record. If you divorce again, you can return to collecting benefits on your first spouse's record, or on your second spouse's record if you were married for at least ten years the second time around.

Can I keep a job even after I start collecting retirement benefits?

Yes—and many people do just that. But if you plan to work after retirement, be aware that the money you earn may cause a reduction in the amount of your Social Security benefits until you reach full retirement age. The amount of income you're allowed to earn without losing a portion of your benefits depends on your age and yearly changes in the amounts allowed.

If you are under full retirement age and you earn income over the year's limit, your Social Security retirement benefits are reduced by one dollar for every two dollars over the limit. In 2016, the limit on earned income is $15,720 per year.

Sign Up Three Months Before Your Birthday

If you need to receive benefit payments at the youngest eligibility age, file your claim three months before the birthday on which you will become eligible. This will give the SSA time to process your claim so that you will receive the benefits on time. If you file a claim later, you cannot get benefits retroactively for months during which you were eligible but before you applied.

Anyone who is eligible for Social Security benefits is also eligible for Medicare coverage at age 65. (For more information about Medicare, see the next series of questions.) Even if you are not going to claim Social Security benefits at age 65—because your benefit amount will be higher if you wait—you can sign up for Medicare coverage three months before your 65th birthday.

How do I claim my Social Security benefits?

You can apply for benefits at your local Social Security office, by phone, or on the Internet at www.ssa.gov.

A Social Security worker in your local office can answer your questions. Find the office closest to you in your telephone directory under the listing for U.S. Government, Social Security Administration, or under U.S. Government, Department of Health and Human Services, Social Security Administration. Alternately, call the SSA at 800-772-1213, or go to www.ssa.gov.

If illness or disability prevents you from visiting your local office, call for accommodations. The most important thing is to act promptly and apply for the benefits to which you are entitled.

What should I do if I feel I've been wrongly denied my benefits?

If your application for benefits is denied, don't despair. Many decisions are changed on appeal. For example, almost half of all disability appeals, which are by far the most common, are favorably changed during the appeal process.

In most states, there are four possible levels of appeal following any Social Security decision. The first is called reconsideration; it is an informal review that takes place in the local Social Security office where your claim was filed. The second level is a hearing before an administrative law judge; this is an independent review of what the local Social Security office decided, made by someone outside the local office. The third level is an appeal to the Social Security Appeals Council in Washington, DC. And the final level is filing a lawsuit in federal court.

Appealing a Social Security claim need not be terribly difficult, as long as you properly organized and prepared your original claim. In many situations, the appeal is simply another opportunity to explain why you qualify for a benefit. In other cases, you'll need to present a few more pieces of information that better explain your situation. The key is to figure out why there was a misunderstanding or error, and put forth your most compelling evidence and arguments to overcome it.

Begin your appeal by completing a simple, one-page form you can get from the Social Security office or download at www.ssa.gov. It is called a *Request for Reconsideration* (SSA 561-U2). You'll be asked for basic information such as your name and Social Security number. Then you will need to state, very briefly, the reasons why you think you were unfairly denied benefits or were allotted lower benefits than you believe you earned.

When you submit your form, attach any other material you want the administrators to consider, such as recent medical records or a letter from a doctor or employer about your ability to work. You must send in the completed *Request for Reconsideration* within 60 days after you receive written notice that you were denied benefits.

RESOURCE

For more information about Social Security, see these Nolo books:

- *Social Security, Medicare & Government Pensions*, by Joseph Matthews. Explains Social Security rules and offers strategies for dealing with the Social Security system.
- *Nolo's Guide to Social Security Disability*, by David Morton, M.D. Explains the Social Security disability process and the criteria for getting disability for over 200 illnesses and injuries.

ONLINE HELP

The following sites are excellent resources on Social Security:

- **www.ssa.gov** The Social Security website provides extensive information on everything related to Social Security, whether you receive benefits now or want to get an estimate of future benefits. You can also contact the Social Security Administration by phone at 800-772-1213 for general questions about eligibility and applications or to find the location of the nearest office.
- **www.disabilitysecrets.com** You can find helpful information about filing for Social Security disability and appealing a denial at this website.
- **www.nasuad.org** The National Association of States United for Aging and Disabilities includes a state-by-state list of departments or commissions on aging (search "state agency website links" on the site); these agencies give information and provide advice about problems with Social Security claims. You can also find your state agency by checking the phone book under Aging or Elderly for the agency in your state.

Medicare

Give me health and a day and I will make the pomp of emperors ridiculous.

—Ralph Waldo Emerson

Over the last several decades, Medicare has been carving an inroad into the mountain of consumer health care costs. At present, the Medicare system provides some coverage for over 50 million people, most of them seniors. Medicare pays for most of the cost of hospitalization and much other medical care for older Americans—about half of all medical costs for people over 65.

Despite its broad coverage, Medicare does not pay for many types of medical services, and it pays only a portion of the costs of other services. To take maximum advantage of the benefits Medicare does provide, to protect yourself against the gaps in Medicare coverage, and to understand the current political debate about the program's future, you must become well informed about how the Medicare system works.

Medicare, Medicaid: What's the Difference?

People are sometimes confused about the differences between Medicare and Medicaid. Medicare was created to address the fact that older citizens have medical bills significantly higher than the rest of the population, while they have less opportunity to earn enough money to cover those bills. Eligibility for Medicare is not tied to individual need. Rather, it is an entitlement program; you are entitled to it because you or your spouse paid for it through Social Security taxes.

Medicaid, on the other hand, is a federal program for low-income people, set up by the federal government and administered differently in each state.

Although you may qualify and receive coverage from both Medicare and Medicaid, there are separate eligibility requirements for each program; being eligible for one program does not necessarily mean you are eligible for the other. If you qualify for both, Medicaid will pay for most Medicare Part A and B premiums, deductibles, and co-payments.

What is Medicare?

Medicare is a federal government program that helps older and some disabled people pay their medical bills. The program is divided into four parts: Part A, Part B, Part C, and Part D. Part A is called hospital insurance and covers most of the costs of a stay in the hospital, as well as some follow-up costs after time in the hospital. Part B, medical insurance, pays some of the cost of doctors and outpatient medical care. Part C is an alternative to Parts A or B called "Medicare Advantage," a type of managed care. And Part D, prescription drug coverage, covers some of the cost of prescription medications taken at home.

Who is eligible for Medicare Part A coverage?

Most people age 65 and over receive free Medicare hospital coverage, based on their work records or on their spouse's work records. However, people over 65 who are not eligible for free Medicare Part A coverage can enroll in it and pay a monthly fee for the same coverage—at least $226 per month according to current rules.

If you pay for Part A hospital insurance, you must also enroll in Part B medical insurance, for which you pay an additional monthly premium.

How much of my bill will Medicare Part A pay?

All rules about how much Medicare Part A pays depend on how many days of inpatient care you have during what is called

Inpatient Care Covered by Medicare Part A

The following list gives you an idea of what Medicare Part A does, and does not, cover during your stay in a participating hospital or skilled-nursing facility. However, even when Part A pays for something, there are significant financial limitations on its coverage.

Medicare Part A hospital insurance covers:

- a semiprivate room (two to four beds per room); a private room if medically necessary
- all meals, including medically required diets
- regular nursing services
- special-care units, such as intensive care and coronary care
- blood transfusions; you pay for the first three pints of blood, unless you arrange to have them replaced by an outside donation of blood to the hospital
- drugs, medical supplies, and appliances furnished by the facility, such as casts, splints, or a wheelchair; also, outpatient drugs and medical supplies if they let you leave the hospital or facility sooner, hospital lab tests, X-rays, and radiation treatment billed by the hospital
- operating and recovery room costs, and
- rehabilitation services, such as physical therapy, occupational therapy, and speech pathology provided while you are in the hospital or nursing facility.

Medicare Part A hospital insurance does not cover:

- personal convenience items such as television, radio, or telephone
- private-duty nurses, or
- a private room, unless medically necessary.

a "benefit period" or "spell of illness." The benefit period begins the day you enter the hospital or skilled-nursing facility as an inpatient and continues until you have been out for 60 consecutive days. If you are in and out of the hospital or nursing facility several times but have not stayed out completely for 60 consecutive days, all your inpatient bills for that time will be figured as part of the same benefit period.

Medicare Part A pays only certain amounts of a hospital bill for any one benefit period—and the rules are slightly different depending on whether you receive care in a hospital, psychiatric hospital, skilled-nursing facility, or at home or through a hospice. You must also pay an initial deductible—currently $1,288 per benefit period (2016)—before Medicare will pay anything.

Services Covered by Medicare Part B

Part B medical insurance is intended to cover basic medical services provided by doctors, clinics, and laboratories. The lists of services specifically covered and not covered are long, and do not always make a lot of sense.

Part B insurance pays for:

- doctors' services (including surgery) provided at a hospital, doctor's office, or your home
- some screening tests, such as colorectal cancer screening, bone-density tests, mammograms, and Pap smears
- medical services provided by nurses, surgical assistants, or laboratory or X-ray technicians
- an annual flu shot
- a onetime physical (called a "wellness exam") done within six months after you enroll in Medicare Part B
- medical equipment and supplies, such as splints, casts, prosthetic devices, body braces, heart pacemakers, corrective lenses after a cataract operation, oxygen equipment, glucose-monitoring equipment and therapeutic shoes for diabetics, wheelchairs, and hospital beds
- services provided by pathologists or radiologists while you're an inpatient at a hospital
- outpatient hospital treatment, such as emergency room or clinic charges, X-rays, tests, and injections
- an ambulance, if medically required for a trip to or from a hospital or skilled-nursing facility
- medicine administered to you at a hospital or doctor's office
- some kinds of oral surgery
- some of the cost of outpatient physical and speech therapy
- manual manipulation of out-of-place vertebrae by a chiropractor
- part-time skilled nursing care, physical therapy, and speech therapy provided in your home
- Alzheimer's-related treatments
- limited counseling by a clinical psychologist or social worker or mental health day treatment
- limited services by podiatrists and optometrists, and
- scientifically proven obesity therapies and treatments.

What kinds of costs does Medicare Part B cover?

Part B is medical insurance. It is intended to help pay doctor bills for treatment in or out of the hospital. It also covers many other medical expenses when you are not in the hospital, such as medical equipment and tests.

The rules of eligibility for Part B medical insurance are much simpler than for Part A: If you are age 65 or over and are either a U.S. citizen or a U.S. lawful permanent resident who has been here for five consecutive years, you are eligible to enroll in Medicare Part B medical insurance. This is true whether or not you are eligible for Part A hospital insurance. You will have to pay a monthly premium—$104.90 in 2016 (But if you first enroll in Part B in 2016 or you're not collecting Social Security benefits, you'll pay $121.80). And a surcharge is added for people with high incomes. The amount of the surcharge depends on your adjusted gross income.

How much of my bill will Medicare Part B pay?

When all of your medical bills are added up, you will see that Medicare pays, on average, only about half the total. There are three major reasons why Part B medical insurance pays for so little.

First, Medicare does not cover a number of major medical expenses, such as routine physical examinations, medications, glasses, hearing aids, and dentures. And note that you'll have to pay a yearly deductible of $166 (in 2016).

Second, Medicare pays only a portion of what it decides is the proper amount—called the approved charges—for medical services. When Medicare decides that a particular service is covered and determines the approved charges for it, Part B medical insurance usually pays only 80% of those approved charges; you are responsible for the remaining 20%.

However, there are now several types of treatments and medical providers for which Medicare Part B pays 100% of the approved charges rather than the usual 80%. These categories of care include: home health care (for skilled care only), clinical laboratory services, and flu and pneumonia vaccines.

Finally, the approved amount may seem reasonable to Medicare, but it is often considerably less than what doctors actually charge. If your doctor or other medical provider does not accept assignment of the Medicare charges, you are personally responsible for paying the difference (this is called balance billing).

What do I need to know about Medicare Part D?

Medicare covers some of the costs of prescription medications taken at home. Medicare Part D is administered through private insurance companies that offer Medicare-approved prescription drug plans. The

Part D prescription drug program replaces drug coverage that was previously available through Medigap plans, most Medicaid coverage, and most managed care plans.

States With Limits on Billing

Several states, including Connecticut, Massachusetts, Minnesota, New York, Ohio, Pennsylvania, Rhode Island, and Vermont, have passed balance billing or charge-limit laws. These laws forbid a doctor from billing patients for the balance of the bill above the amount Medicare approves. The patient is still responsible for the 20% of the approved charge not paid by Medicare Part B.

The specifics of these patient-protection laws vary from state to state: Some forbid balance billing to any Medicare patient, others apply the restriction only to patients with limited incomes or assets. To find out the rules in your state, contact your state department or commission on aging. Find yours at www.nasuad.org, the website of National Association of States United for Aging and Disabilities (NASUAD). Search "State agency website links" to find your state. You can also call the NASUAD at 202-898-2578.

If you are entitled to Medicare Part A or enrolled in Medicare Part B, or Part C, you may join a Part D prescription drug plan. Participation is voluntary, but if you delay signing up for a Part D plan, you will pay a penalty in the form of a larger premium for each month you were eligible to enroll but didn't.

How much will my prescriptions cost under a Medicare Part D plan?

Your cost for prescription drugs under a Part D plan can vary widely depending on a number of factors. The following figures are for 2016:

Premium. Monthly premiums vary depending on the plans available in your area and the particular plan you choose—premiums range from $0 to $50 per month.

Deductible. You pay the first $360 per year of the cost of your prescription medications. A few high-premium plans waive this deductible.

Co-payment. Once your total annual drug expense reaches $360 (and before it reaches $3,310), you pay 25% of your drug costs as a co-payment. Your co-payment may be higher for brand-name drugs or less for generics, depending on your plan.

Coverage gap. Once your total drug expense reaches $3,310 (and before it reaches $4,850), you must pay the entire amount of your drug costs. Your plan generally pays no part of your prescription drug costs within this coverage gap, although a few high-premium plans may pay some portion of your costs. However, in 2016, brand-name prescription drugs must be sold at a 55% discount to anyone who reaches the coverage gap, and generic drugs must be sold at a 42% discount.

Catastrophic coverage. If your total annual prescription drug cost exceeds $4,850, the plan will pay 95% of all further costs; you'll pay the remaining 5%, up to $2.95 for a generic drug and up to $7.40 for all other drugs.

Low-income subsidies. There are several categories of low-income subsidies available to help pay some or all of your Part D coverage, called "Extra Help." To find out if you qualify for a low-income subsidy, visit www.ssa.gov and go to the Medicare section.

How do I choose the right plan?

Not all plans are alike, and choosing the best plan for you involves several steps. Look carefully at the plans you are considering and choose a plan that covers most, if not all, of your regular medications. Consider your overall costs under each plan you're considering, including the amount you'll pay for premiums, deductibles, and co-payments. And find out whether any plan you're considering offers coverage within the coverage gap.

Finding a Part D Plan

You may enroll only in a plan that operates in the state where you live. To find out about plans in your area, contact one of these agencies:

- The Centers for Medicare and Medicaid Services at 800-MEDICARE (800-633-4227) or at www.medicare.gov.
- The State Health Insurance Assistance Program (SHIP) in your state—sometimes called the Health Insurance Counseling and Advocacy Program (HICAP). For the nearest SHIP or HICAP office, check www.shiptacenter.org.
- Your state department of insurance (find yours at the National Association of Insurance Commissioners website: www.naic.org/state_web_map.htm).

RESOURCE

For more Information about Medicare, see:

- *Social Security, Medicare & Government Pensions,* by Joseph Matthews (Nolo). Explains Medicare rules and offers strategies for dealing with the Medicare system.
- The Social Security Administration website, at www.ssa.gov. Provides a variety of informative publications. Also check out www.medicare.gov, for extensive information of Medicare eligibility, costs, coverage, claims, and more. You can also call 800-MEDICARE for questions regarding billing and claims.

Finding a Caregiver or Residential Care Facility

As Americans live increasingly longer lives, many require ongoing, long-term care. Elders may need help with daily activities—grooming, bathing, preparing meals, or just getting around. Or, they may need full-time care in a residential treatment facility. Whether you are thinking about your own future or seeking care for a relative who needs help, you have many options to consider.

How do I choose between in-home care and a residential facility?

It may depend on the type of care that you or your loved one requires. Much of the care seniors need is not medical or nursing care, but help with day-to-day activities. These may include bathing, using the toilet, getting dressed, eating, getting in and out of bed or a chair, and walking around. For people with Alzheimer's disease or other cognitive impairment, home care may consist primarily of making sure that the person does not become lost, disoriented, or injured.

For this type of help, home care is often better than residential care. Home care is provided one-to-one, whereas residential facilities have staff-to-resident ratios of one-to-ten or more. And by choosing and monitoring a home care agency or individual home care providers, you may be better able to control the quality of care. On the other hand, tracking the effectiveness of home care is primarily up to the family, whereas residential facilities have professional staff members who are supposed to check regularly on the quality of nonmedical care provided.

Cost is another consideration in the type of care you choose. There is a significant range in nursing home costs, depending on location, size, and facilities. It is an expensive level of care: For a private room, you can expect to pay an average of more than $90,000 annually for nursing home care. Assisted living facilities range widely in cost, from $2,000 to $5,000 or more per month, depending on what level of care is needed. And nonmedical home care averages $21 per hour. However, costs vary widely by region. To see the averages in your area, go to www.genworth.com/costofcare.

What types of in-home care are available?

Home care providers can help with a variety of medical and personal needs, including:

- **Health care**—nursing, physical and other rehabilitative therapy, medicating, monitoring, and medical equipment
- **Personal care**—assistance with personal hygiene, dressing, getting in and out of a bed or chair, bathing, and exercise
- **Nutrition**—meal planning, cooking, meal delivery, or driving the senior to meals away from home
- **Homemaking**—housekeeping, shopping, home repair, and household paperwork
- **Social and safety needs**—escort and transportation services, companions, overall planning, and program coordination service.

If you're not sure whether a particular type of care can be safely and adequately delivered at home, consult a doctor that you trust.

How do I find a good in-home caregiver?

The best way to find a good caregiver is by referral. Ask your family physician about getting in-home help, or consult a public health nurse. These professionals should be able to put you in touch with reputable home-care services. And don't forget to ask family, friends, and neighbors for referrals.

Caregivers who provide medical care must be licensed or certified by your state's home care licensing agency. So when you need medical or nursing care—not just assistance with daily activities—you should seek help from certified agencies rather than independent caregivers.

If you need nonmedical care, you can hire an independent caregiver or an agency—your caregiver does not need to be licensed or certified to provide care. Because of this, it is very important to check references carefully and to find out what credentials a potential caregiver has. For example, ask whether the caregiver has had CPR and first aid training or any other health care training. Also, be sure to define the tasks that you need the caregiver to perform and make sure that he or she is willing and able to do them.

Finally, after you've hired a caregiver, be sure to have a backup plan in place just in case your caregiver gets sick or needs to take time off.

Special Considerations for People with Alzheimer's

People with Alzheimer's disease have special needs when it comes to residential care:

- **Space.** Look for a facility that allows active residents to move about freely, while keeping the space safe.
- **Other residents.** Alzheimer's-only facilities often have educational programs, family counseling, and support groups that might not be available elsewhere. And the staff can organize meals, activities, and care solely with Alzheimer's residents in mind.
- **Staff.** Try visiting at different times of day, including meal times, to see how well the staff interacts with the residents. Is the staff calm and soothing, treating the residents with respect and acknowledging their comments and requests? Do the residents seem comfortable with the staff?
- **Special programs.** People with Alzheimer's can benefit from programs to help residents stay mentally alert, such as arts and crafts work, reading, word games, and outings. Find out what special programs are offered.
- **Medication and medical care.** Find out whether the facility is licensed to administer drugs by injection and deliver other types of medical care that a patient cannot self-administer. People with Alzheimer's may need regular medical attention so having a facility that can assist with medical care is important.

What types of care are available from residential care facilities?

If you need full-time assistance, a residential care facility may be the right choice. There are many levels of care available in long-term residential facilities. Care ranges from intensive 24-hour care for the seriously ill (called skilled nursing care) to long-term personal assistance and health monitoring with very little active nursing (often called custodial care). Some facilities provide only one level of care, while others provide several levels at the same location.

Skilled nursing facilities provide short-term, intensive medical care and monitoring for people recovering from acute illness or injury. Other facilities—called nursing homes, board and care homes, sheltered care homes, or something similar—provide custodial care, long-term room and board, and 24-hour assistance with personal care and other health care monitoring, but not intensive medical treatment or daily nursing.

For someone with severe physical or mental limitations, it is crucial to find a facility that provides the kind of attention and care that meets the individual's specific needs. For people who need little or no actual nursing care, the task is to find a facility that provides physical, mental, and social stimulation rather than merely bed and board.

How do I find a good residential care facility?

We've all heard about poor facilities that provide substandard living conditions or even a dangerous lack of care. But there are also excellent long-term care facilities that provide high-quality care while assisting residents to maintain active lives with a full measure of dignity. Because there are many levels and types of nursing and personal care, your task is to find a good, affordable facility that provides the services you need.

As with finding an in-home caregiver, your best bet is to ask for referrals. Here are some good places to start:

- **Relatives, friends, and neighbors.** They may have had experience with a long-term care facility or know someone who has, and are often your best sources of information.
- **Hospital discharge planner.** The discharge planner may help if you or your loved one is going straight from a hospital to a long-term care facility.
- **Your doctor.** Ask your doctor about personal experience with any facilities in your area.
- **Organizations focusing on specific illness.** Check with organizations that focus on the illness or disability at issue, such as the American Heart Association, the American Cancer Society, the American Diabetes Association, or the Alzheimer's Disease Foundation.
- **National long-term care organizations.** A number of private organizations, such as Leading Age (formerly the American Association of Homes for the Aging; see www.leadingage.org),

specialize in long-term care and give referrals to local facilities.

- **Government agencies.** You can often get targeted referrals from the federal Area Agencies on Aging (see www.n4a.org), or from state and local agencies found through Senior Referral and Information numbers in the white pages of the phone book or your local county social services or family services agency. You can find local help in your area (whether it's long-term housing options or in-home services) from Eldercare Locator, a program of the U.S. Administration on Aging. Check their website at www.eldercare.gov, or call 800-677-1116.
- **Church, ethnic, or fraternal organizations.** Ask about long-term care facilities that members have used successfully or that are operated by or affiliated with the church or organization.

Is financial assistance available to help pay for a caregiver or nursing home?

Under certain conditions, you may be able to get financial assistance to help pay for care.

Medicare. Medicare will pay some nursing home costs for Medicare beneficiaries who require skilled nursing or rehabilitation services. To be covered, you must receive the services from a Medicare-certified skilled nursing home after a qualifying hospital stay (generally a stay of at least three days is required). To learn more about Medicare payment for skilled nursing home costs, visit www.medicare.gov or call 800-MEDICARE (800-633-4227).

Alternately, if a doctor prescribes medically necessary home health care for a homebound senior, Medicare will cover some of the costs if you use a Medicare-approved home health agency. Medicare will not, however, pay for a caregiver who provides nonmedical assistance.

Medicaid. Medicaid is a state and federal program that will pay most nursing home costs for people with very low income and few assets. Eligibility varies by state—check your state's requirements to find out whether you are eligible. Medicaid will pay only for nursing home care provided in a facility certified by the government to provide service to Medicaid recipients. For more information about Medicaid payments, call your state's Medicaid office.

Other financial assistance. Here are some additional options for financial assistance:

- **Long-term care insurance.** The benefits and costs of these private insurance plans vary widely. Those who have this type of insurance may have coverage for some costs of custodial care.
- **Medicare Supplemental Insurance.** This private insurance is often called Medigap because it helps pay for gaps in Medicare coverage such as deductibles and co-payments. Most

Medigap plans will help pay for skilled nursing care, but only when that care is covered by Medicare.

- **Managed care plans.** A managed care plan will not help pay for care unless the nursing home has a contract with the plan. If the home is approved by your plan, find out whether the plan also monitors the home for quality of nursing care.
- **Counseling and assistance.** The State Health Insurance Assistance Program (SHIP) in your state, sometimes called the Health Insurance Counseling and Advocacy Program (HICAP), provides counselors who can review your existing coverage and find any government programs that may help with your expenses. For the nearest SHIP or HICAP office, check www.shiptacenter.org.
- **Help for veterans.** Some veterans may find coverage for custodial care through the Veterans Health Administration. Priority is given to veterans with service-connected disabilities.

RESOURCE

For more information about elder care, see *Long-Term Care: How to Plan & Pay for It*, by Joseph Matthews (Nolo). It explains the alternatives to nursing facilities and shows you how to find the best care you can afford.

ONLINE HELP

The following sites are good resources for information about elder care:

- **www.nolo.com** Nolo offers information about a wide variety of legal topics, including issues affecting older Americans.
- **www.eldercare.gov** The Eldercare Locator, a program of the Administration on Aging, provides a guide to local resources for a wide variety of issues, including elder abuse prevention, health insurance, legal assistance, long-term care, transportation, and more. In addition to checking their website, you can reach the Eldercare Locator at 800-677-1116.
- **www.aarp.org** The American Association of Retired Persons offers helpful information on a range of issues for older people—including family, health, money matters, work, housing, and Social Security.
- **www.aoa.gov** The Administration on Aging's website provides directories of resources that can help with aging issues—along with a host of articles covering topics such as retirement planning, housing alterations, and Medicare fraud.
- **www.pbgc.gov** The Pension Benefit Guaranty Corporation (PBGC) was established to protect pension benefits, primarily by giving financial assistance to some types of plans that have become insolvent. Its site provides information on pension rights and benefits, including what to expect if your pension plan changes hands and how to appeal an adverse pension decision.

CHAPTER

14

Spouses and Partners

Love is love's reward.

—John Dryden

We all know how the story goes: Boy meets girl, boy and girl fall in love, get married, and live happily ever after. Or, sometimes boy meets boy, or girl meets girl—with the same fairy tale hopes and dreams.

What we often don't see are the details: Where do boy and girl get a marriage license, and do they need blood tests first? What should girl and girl do if they choose not to marry, but want to buy a house together? And what if the fairy tale turns sour, and one partner wants to end it?

Our intimate relationships aren't usually the stuff of childhood tales. There are a lot of real-world concerns—emotional and practical—that need attention every day. The questions and answers in this chapter will help you with some of the legal questions, tasks, and troubles that may surface during the course of your relationship. Keep in mind that laws in this area vary, sometimes dramatically, from state to state. We've put together an overview to get you started, but be certain to confirm your state's law before you act on any of the information given here.

Living Together—Gay or Straight

Many laws are designed to govern and protect the property ownership rights of married couples. In most states, no such laws exist for unmarried couples. If you and your partner are unmarried, you must take steps to protect your relationship and define your property rights. You will also face special concerns if you are raising children together.

When we refer to "unmarried" couples, we mean opposite-sex and same-sex couples who aren't legally married or in a registered domestic partnership or civil union. For those couples who are in a registered marriage-like relationship in one of the states that still offer them, special rules apply. These are covered separately in "Domestic Partnership and Civil Unions," below. The following questions apply to unmarried and unregistered couples.

My partner and I don't own much property. Do we really need a written contract covering who owns what?

If you haven't been together long and don't own much, it's probably not necessary. But the longer you live together, the more important it is to prepare a written contract making it clear who owns what—especially if you begin to accumulate a lot of property.

Otherwise, you might face a serious (and potentially expensive) battle if you split up and can't agree on how to divide what you've acquired. And when things are good, taking the time to draft a well-thought-out contract helps you clarify your intentions.

My partner makes a lot more money than I do. Should our property agreements cover who is entitled to her income and the items we purchase with it?

Absolutely. Although each person starts out owning all of his or her job-related income, many states allow couples to change this arrangement by a written contract or even a contract implied from the circumstances of how you live. These implied contracts often lead to misunderstandings during a breakup. For example, if you don't have a written agreement stating whether income will be shared or kept separate, one partner might falsely claim the other promised to split his income 50-50. Although this can be tough to prove in court, the very fact that the partner can bring a lawsuit creates a huge problem. For obvious reasons, it's an especially good idea to make a written agreement if a person with a big income is living with and supporting someone with little or no income.

What is palimony?

"Palimony" is not a legal concept, but a word coined by journalists to describe alimony-like support paid by one unmarried partner to the other after a breakup. Unmarried partners are not legally entitled to such support payments or a share of each others property unless they have an agreement saying they are. In the famous case of *Marvin v. Marvin,* the California Supreme Court ruled that a person who cohabitated and later sued for support could argue that an *implied* contract existed between the partners. To avoid a cry for palimony, it's best to have a written agreement about whether one person will make payments to the other if the relationship ends.

My partner and I have a young son, and I'm thinking of giving up my job to become a full-time parent. How might I be compensated for my loss of income?

This is mostly a personal—not a legal—question. If you and your partner decide that compensation is fair, there are many ways to arrange it. For example, you could make an agreement stating that if you break up while you're still providing child care, your partner will pay an agreed-upon amount to help you make the transition to a new situation. Or, you might agree in writing that your partner will pay you a salary during the time you stay at home, including Social Security and other legally required benefits.

Am I liable for the debts of my partner?

Not unless you have specifically taken on the responsibility to pay a particular debt—for example, you are a cosigner or the debt is charged to a joint account. By contrast, husbands and wives, and, in some cases, domestic partners, are generally liable for all debts incurred during marriage, even those incurred by the other person. The one exception for unmarried couples applies if you have registered as domestic partners in a location where the domestic partner law states that you agree to pay for each other's "basic living expenses" (food, shelter, and clothing). See "Domestic Partnership and Civil Unions," below.

If one of us dies, how much property will the survivor inherit?

It depends on whether the deceased partner made a will or used another estate planning device such as a living trust or joint tenancy agreement to leave property to the surviving partner. In some states registered domestic or civil union partners may automatically inherit a portion of a deceased partner's property, but some of these laws carry restrictions and are by no means the safest or easiest way to plan for inheritances. The bottom line is simple: To protect a person you live with, you must specifically leave property to that person using a will, living trust, or other legal document.

Parenting Concerns of Unmarried Couples

Unmarried couples face unique concerns when they raise children together.

- Straight couples who have children together should take steps to ensure that both are recognized as the legal parents. Both parents should be listed on the birth certificate, and the father should sign a statement of paternity. Even better, both parents should sign a statement of parentage acknowledging the father's paternity.
- All unmarried couples face potential obstacles when adopting together because all states favor married couples as adoptive parents. For more information about adoption by unmarried couples, see Chapter 15.
- Parents who have children from former marriages face potential prejudice in some places if they are battling an ex-spouse for custody while living with a partner. In some states, this is a greater concern for lesbian and gay parents than for straight ones, as judges (with the exception of a few states that come down hard on all unmarried couples) tend to be more tolerant of opposite-sex cohabitation than same-sex cohabitation.

Buying a House? Make an Agreement

It's particularly important to make a written property agreement if you buy a house together; the large financial and emotional commitments involved are good reasons to take extra care with your plans. Your contract should cover at least four major areas:

How is title (ownership) listed on the deed? One choice is as "joint tenants with rights of survivorship," meaning that when one of you dies, the other automatically inherits the whole house. Another option is as "tenants in common," meaning that when one of you dies, that person's share of the house goes to whomever the deceased partner named in a will or trust, or goes to blood relatives if the deceased partner left no estate plan.

How much of the house does each of you own? If it's not 50-50, can the person who owns less than half increase his or her share—for example, by working on the house or paying a larger share of the mortgage?

What happens to the house if you break up? Will one of you have the first right to stay in the house (perhaps to care for a young child) and buy the other out, or will the house be sold and the proceeds divided?

If one of you has a buyout right, how will the house be appraised, and how long will the buyout take? Often, couples agree to use the real estate broker they used to buy the house to appraise it, and then give the buying partner one to five years to pay off the other.

If I am injured or incapacitated, can my partner make medical or financial decisions on my behalf?

Not unless you have executed a document called a "durable power of attorney" (sometimes included in a "Health Care Directive"), giving your partner the specific authority to make those decisions. Without a durable power of attorney, huge emotional and practical problems can result. For example, the fate of a severely ill or injured person could be in the hands of a biological relative who disapproves of the relationship and won't honor the wishes of the ill or injured person. It is far better to prepare the necessary paperwork so the loving and knowing partner will be the primary decision maker. For more information about durable powers of attorney, see Chapter 12.

If my partner and I live together long enough, won't we have a common law marriage?

Probably not. In a handful of states (listed below), couples can become legally married without a license or ceremony. This type of marriage is called a common law marriage. Contrary to popular belief, a common law marriage is not created when two people simply live together for a certain number of years. In order to have a valid common law marriage, the couple must do all of the following:

- live together for a significant period of time (not defined in any state)

- hold themselves out as a "married couple"—typically this means using the same last name, referring to the other as "my husband" or "my wife," and filing a joint tax return, and
- intend to be married.

When a common law marriage exists, the spouses receive the same legal treatment given to formally married couples, including the requirement that they go through a legal divorce to end the marriage.

States That Recognize Common Law Marriage

Alabama	New Hampshire*
Colorado	Ohio (if created before 10/10/91)
District of Columbia	Oklahoma
Georgia (if created before 1/1/97)	Pennsylvania (if created before 1/1/05)
Idaho (if created before 1/1/96)	Rhode Island
Iowa	South Carolina
Kansas	Texas
Montana	Utah

* For inheritance purposes only.

RESOURCE

For more information about living together, see these Nolo books:

- *Living Together: A Legal Guide for Unmarried Couples,* by Ralph Warner, Toni Ihara, and Frederick Hertz. Explains the legal rules that apply to unmarried couples and includes sample contracts about jointly owned property.
- *A Legal Guide for Lesbian & Gay Couples,* by Frederick Hertz and Emily Doskow. Sets out the law and contains sample agreements for same-sex couples.

Domestic Partnership and Civil Unions

Even though same-sex marriage is now legal all across the U.S., a small number of states still allow marriage-like relationships for unmarried same-sex and heterosexual couples. Each of these states has different rules (if one partner is over 62 years old), and we can't set them all out in detail here, but this section will explain domestic partnership and civil union relationships in general. You'll need to check with a lawyer in your state to learn more about how these laws might affect you.

What makes us domestic partners?

Many unmarried couples call themselves "domestic partners" because they live together in a committed relationship. It's a perfectly reasonable phrase to use, but if you live in a state where a legal form of domestic partnership is available, just considering yourself domestic partners and referring to yourselves that way isn't enough to make you eligible for the benefits your state offers—you must register formally with the state for that.

Many employers offer domestic partnership benefits to their employees, meaning that the employees' domestic partners, whether registered or not, are treated like spouses for purposes of benefits such as health insurance and paid family leave. The employer can decide what the criteria are for being domestic partners. And, again, if you live in a state with domestic partner benefits, filling out a form with your employer to get health coverage for your partner doesn't mean you are registered with the state.

If your employer doesn't offer domestic partner coverage and you want to get involved in trying to establish a program at your workplace, check out the Unmarried Equality website at www.unmarried.org.

In California, District of Columbia, Nevada, Oregon, and Washington State, the term "domestic partnership" has a very specific legal meaning: Only couples who have registered with the state are domestic partners, and as a result they have a slew of rights and responsibilities that are almost identical to those that come with marriage. Colorado, Hawaii, Illinois, and New Jersey still offer civil unions that confer the rights and responsibilities of marriage. Most of these states restrict who can register—only same-sex couples and heterosexual couples in which at least one partner is 62 or older are allowed to register as domestic partners.

Are domestic partnerships and civil unions the same as marriage?

These marriage-like relationships are very similar to marriage in some states, but with one very big difference. Although states might treat couples who register or enter into civil unions like married people for purposes of the laws of those states (see "State Benefits for Unmarried Same-Sex Couples," below) the federal government won't recognize unmarried same-sex relationships. This means unmarried couples (even if they are in a "civil union" or "domestic partnership") can't file joint federal tax returns, apply for Social Security survivors benefits if one partner dies, or rely on any of the many other federal laws that affect married couples.

However, because the U.S. Supreme Court has overturned the federal Defense of Marriage Act or DOMA and ruled that same-sex couples have a right to marriage in all 50 states and D.C., same-sex couples who are legally married are now entitled to the same federal benefits opposite-sex married couples receive. See the "Marriage" section, below for details.

If you are a same-sex couple living in one of the states where a marriage-like relationship is still available, it's a good idea to do some research, consider the issue carefully, and even think about talking to a lawyer before you take the plunge into domestic partnership or a civil union. Now that marriage is available to all same-sex couples, you should carefully consider the pros and cons of each type of relationship before making a decision.

If my boyfriend and I become domestic partners, am I responsible for his debts?

In most states, domestic partners aren't responsible for each other's debts (and aren't entitled to share in each other's income, either). But in states such as California and New Jersey where domestic partnerships or civil unions bring most of the same rights and responsibilities of marriage, it's a different story. Partners are responsible for all debts incurred during the partnership, even those that one person incurred without the other person's knowledge.

RESOURCE

For more information about same-sex marriages, domestic partnerships, and civil unions, see *Making It Legal*, by Frederick Hertz and Emily Doskow (Nolo). This book provides a comprehensive review of same-sex relationship laws and issues such as special needs of same-sex couples with children.

Premarital Agreements

Love reasons without reason.

—William Shakespeare

A premarital agreement is a written contract created by two people planning to be married—and now, that includes same-sex couples planning to marry or enter into marriage-like relationships in states that still offer marriage-equivalent registered domestic partnerships or civil unions.

A prenuptial or preregistration agreement typically lists all of the property each person owns, as well as their debts, and specifies what each person's property rights will be after they tie the knot. Premarital agreements often specify how property will be divided—and whether spousal support (alimony) will be paid—in the event of a divorce or breakup. In addition, an agreement may set out the couple's intentions about distributing property after one of them dies. (This is especially useful for second marriages, when one or both spouses want to preserve property for children or grandchildren from a former union.) In some states, a premarital agreement is known as an "antenuptial agreement," or in slightly more modern terms, as a "prenuptial agreement" or "prenup."

Are premarital agreements legal?

As divorce and remarriage have become more prevalent, and with growing equality between the sexes, courts and legislatures are increasingly willing to uphold premarital agreements. Today, every state permits them, although a prenup that is judged unfair, that seems to encourage divorce, or that otherwise fails to meet state requirements can be set aside. And courts won't uphold agreements of a nonmonetary nature. For example, you can agree on how you will divide your property if you divorce, but you can't sue your spouse for refusing to take out the garbage, even if your premarital agreement says that he or she must do so every Tuesday night.

Same-sex couples who are planning to marry can make a prenup just like opposite sex couples do. And couples planning to enter into a registered domestic partnership or civil union can also make agreements that are the equivalent of prenups—sometimes called prepartnership or preregistration agreements. These agreements ordinarily must comply with all the same rules that apply to prenuptial agreements.

Should my fiancé and I make a premarital agreement?

Whether you should make a premarital agreement depends on your circumstances and on the two of you as individuals. Most premarital agreements are made by couples who want to circumvent the mandates of state law in the event of a divorce or at death. Often this happens when one partner wishes to keep certain items of property if the marriage ends—for example, a considerable income or a family business. Perhaps most frequently, premarital agreements are made by individuals who have children or grandchildren from prior marriages. The premarital agreement allows the partner to ensure that most or all property passes to the children or grandchildren rather than to the current spouse.

States That Have Adopted the Uniform Premarital Agreement Act*

Arizona	Maine
Arkansas	Montana
California	Nebraska
Connecticut	Nevada
Delaware	New Mexico
District of Columbia	North Carolina
Florida	North Dakota
Hawaii	Oregon
Idaho	Rhode Island
Illinois	South Dakota
Indiana	Texas
Iowa	Utah
Kansas	Virginia

* Although Wisconsin is typically included in the list of states that have adopted the law, its law bears little resemblance to the Act.

Are there rules about what can or cannot be included in a premarital agreement?

A law called the Uniform Premarital Agreement Act provides legal guidelines for people who wish to make agreements before they marry regarding the following: ownership, management, and control of property; property disposition on separation, divorce, and death; alimony; wills; and life insurance beneficiaries.

States that haven't adopted the Act (or that have adopted it with changes) have other laws, which often differ from the

Act in minor ways. For example, a few states do not allow premarital agreements to modify or eliminate a spouse's right to receive court-ordered alimony at divorce.

In every state, whether covered by the Act or not, couples are prohibited from making binding provisions about child-support payments or custody.

Can my fiancé and I make our premarital agreement without a lawyer?

You and your fiancé can go a long way toward making your own agreement by evaluating your circumstances, agreeing on what you want your agreement to cover, and even writing a draft of the contract. But if you want to end up with a clear and binding premarital agreement, you'll eventually have to enlist a good lawyer to help you. In fact, you will need two lawyers—one for each of you. That may sound like surprising advice from advocates of self-help law, but it's true.

The laws governing marriage contracts vary widely from state to state. Unless you want to invest your time learning the ins and outs of your state's matrimonial laws, you'll want to find a lawyer who can help you put together an agreement that meets state requirements and says what you want it to say.

This explains the desirability of having one lawyer, but why two? Some courts closely scrutinize premarital agreements for fairness. If you want your agreement to pass muster, having an independent lawyer advise each of you will go a long way toward convincing a court that the agreement was negotiated fairly. While most courts don't require that each party to a premarital agreement have a lawyer, the absence of separate independent advice for each party is a red flag to judges.

Finally, on a practical note, having separate legal advisers can help you and your fiancé prepare a balanced agreement that you both understand and that doesn't leave either of you feeling that you've been taken advantage of.

To start considering the issues, check out *Prenuptial Agreements: How to Write a Fair & Lasting Contract,* by Katherine E. Stoner and Shae Irving (Nolo). For domestic partners in California, there's also *Prenups for Partners: Essential Agreements for California Domestic Partners,* a Nolo eGuide by Katherine E. Stoner. These resources will help you figure out whether you need an agreement, take you through the steps of deciding what you might want in it, and help you figure out how to find and work with lawyers.

I've been living with someone for several years, and we've decided to get married. Will our existing property agreement be enforceable after we are married?

Probably not. Your property agreement may apply to the period of time when you were unmarried, but not to your postmarriage rights and responsibilities. To be enforceable, premarital contracts must be made in contemplation of marriage. This means that unless your living-together contract is made shortly before your marriage, when you both plan to be married, a divorce court will disregard it. In your situation, it's best to review your contract and rewrite it as a premarital agreement.

Marriage

There is more of good nature than of good sense at the bottom of most marriages.

—Henry David Thoreau

Marriage is the legal union of two people. When you are married, your responsibilities and rights toward your spouse concerning property and support are defined by the laws of the state in which you live. The two of you may be able to modify the rules set up by your state, however, if you want to. See "Premarital Agreements," above.

Your marriage can only be terminated by a court granting a divorce or an annulment.

What are the legal rights and benefits conferred by marriage?

Marriage brings with it many rights and benefits, including the rights to:

- file joint income tax returns with the IRS and state taxing authorities
- create a "family partnership" under federal tax laws, allowing you to divide business income among family members (this will often lower the total tax on the income)
- create a marital life estate trust
- receive spouse's and dependents Social Security, disability, unemployment, veterans, pension, and public assistance benefits
- receive a share of your deceased spouse's estate under intestate succession laws
- claim an estate tax marital deduction
- sue a third person for wrongful death and loss of consortium
- sue a third person for offenses that interfere with the success of your marriage, such as alienation of affection and criminal conversation (these lawsuits are available in only a few states)
- receive family rates for insurance
- avoid the deportation of a noncitizen spouse
- enter hospital intensive care units, jails, and other places where visitors are restricted to immediate family
- make medical decisions about your spouse in the event of disability, and
- claim the marital communications privilege, which means a court can't force you to disclose what you and your spouse said to each other confidentially during your marriage.

Requirements for Marriage

You must meet certain requirements in order to marry. These vary slightly from state to state, but essentially require that you:

- are at least the age of consent (usually 18, though sometimes you may marry younger with your parents' consent)
- are not too closely related to your intended spouse
- have the mental capacity—that is, you understand what you are doing and the consequences your actions may have
- are sober at the time of the marriage
- are not married to anyone else
- get a blood test (in just a few states), and
- obtain a marriage license.

What's the difference between a "marriage license" and a "marriage certificate"?

The difference is as simple as "before" and "after." A marriage license is the piece of paper that authorizes you to get married. A marriage certificate is the document that proves you are married.

Typically, couples obtain a marriage license, have the wedding ceremony, and then have the person who performed the ceremony file a marriage certificate with the appropriate county office. (This may be the office of the county clerk, recorder, or registrar, depending on where you live.) The county will then send the married couple a certified copy of the marriage certificate within a few weeks after the ceremony.

Most states require both spouses, the person who officiated, and one or two witnesses to sign the marriage certificate; often this is done just after the ceremony.

Where can we get a marriage license?

You may apply for a marriage license from a city or county official—usually the county clerk or recorder, a district or probate court clerk, or a municipal or town clerk—in the state where you want to be married. (In some circumstances, you must apply in the county or town where you intend to be married—this depends on state law.) You'll have to pay a fee for your license (anywhere from $10 to $80), and you may also have to wait a few days before it is issued.

In some states, you'll have to wait a short period of time after you get your license—one to three days—before you tie the knot. In special circumstances, this waiting period can be waived. Licenses are good for 30 days to one year, depending on the state. If your license expires before you get married, you can apply for a new one.

For more specific information about marriage license laws in your state, check your state's website for vital statistics, your city or county website, or www.statelocalgov.net.

Do all states require blood tests? And why are they required?

A handful of states still require blood tests for couples planning to marry, but most do not.

Premarital blood tests check both partners for venereal disease and women for rubella (measles). The tests may also disclose that someone carries a genetic disorder such as sickle cell anemia or Tay-Sachs disease. You will not be tested for HIV, but in some states the person who tests you will provide you with information about HIV and AIDS. In most states, the blood test may be waived for people over 50 and for other reasons, including pregnancy or sterility.

If either partner tests positive for a venereal disease, what happens depends on the state where you are marrying. Some states may refuse to issue you a marriage license. Other states may allow you to marry as long as you both know that the disease is present.

Who can perform a marriage ceremony?

Nonreligious ceremonies—called civil ceremonies—must be performed by a judge, justice of the peace, or court clerk who has legal authority to perform marriages, or by a person given temporary authority by a judge or court clerk to conduct a marriage ceremony. Religious ceremonies must be conducted by a clergy member—for example, a priest, minister, or rabbi. Native American weddings may be performed by a tribal chief or by another official, as designated by the tribe.

Are there requirements about what the ceremony must include?

Usually, no special words are required as long as the spouses acknowledge their intention to marry each other. Keeping that in mind, you can design whatever type of ceremony you desire.

It is customary to have witnesses to the marriage, although they are not required in all states.

What is a common law marriage?

In 15 states and the District of Columbia, couples can become legally married if they:

- live together for a long period of time
- hold themselves out to others as husband and wife, and
- intend to be married.

These marriages are called common law marriages. Contrary to popular belief, two people who live together for a certain number of years do not have a common law marriage unless they intend to be married and act as if they are.

When a common law marriage exists, the spouses receive the same legal treatment given to formally married couples, including the requirement that they go through a legal divorce to end the marriage.

To find out whether your state recognizes common law marriages, see the list earlier in this chapter.

State Benefits for Unmarried Same-Sex Couples

Although same-sex marriage is now legal in the U.S., same-sex couples may choose to remain unmarried for any number of personal or financial reasons. For some, a domestic partnership or civil union may be a better option. If you're a member of a same-sex couple living in one of the following states, you can take advantage of laws that allow you to register your partnership and receive many of the benefits granted to married couples. (See "Domestic Partnership and Civil Unions," above.)

California. California will continue to process domestic partnerships. To register a domestic partnership in California, visit the California Secretary of State website at www.sos.ca.gov/dpregistry. Or call 916-653-3984 for more information.

Colorado. For more information on civil unions including how to apply for one in Colorado, go to www.one-colorado.org/your-rights/civil-unions.

D.C. For information on domestic partnerships in the District of Columbia, see the DC.gov Department of Health website at http://doh.dc.gov/service/domestic-partnership.

Hawaii. To learn about registering your partnership in Hawaii, visit the website of Hawaii's Vital Records office at http://health.hawaii.gov/vitalrecords.

Illinois. For more information about the benefits of civil unions in Illinois go to the Equality Illinois website at www.equalityillinois.us/issue/marriage.

Nevada. For information on domestic partnerships and how to register in Nevada, visit the Nevada Secretary of State's website at www.nvsos.gov and find the drop-down menu called "Licensing Center" and click on the link for domestic partnerships.

New Jersey. For more information on civil unions and domestic partnerships in New Jersey, see the New Jersey Department of Health website at www.state.nj.us/health (click on the link "Vital Records") or 609-292-4087.

Oregon. Check the Vital Records section of the Oregon Health Authority website at http://public.health.oregon.gov/BirthDeathCertificates/RegisterVitalRecords/Pages/dp.aspx.

Washington. To learn more about Washington's domestic partnership law, go to the Secretary of State's website at www.secstate.wa.gov/corps/domesticpartnerships.

ONLINE HELP

Make sure to keep up to date on same-sex marriage by checking the websites of Lambda Legal (www.lambdalegal.org) and the National Center for Lesbian Rights at www.nclrights.org.

Divorce

There is no disparity in marriage like unsuitablility of mind and purpose.

—Charles Dickens

Divorce is the legal termination of a marriage. In some states, divorce is called dissolution or dissolution of marriage. A divorce usually includes division of marital property and, if necessary, arrangements for child custody, alimony, and child support. It leaves both people free to marry again.

How does an annulment differ from a divorce?

Like a divorce, an annulment is a court procedure that dissolves a marriage. But an annulment treats the marriage as though it never happened. For some people, divorce carries a stigma, and they would prefer their marriage be annulled. Others prefer an annulment because it may be easier to remarry in their church if their marriage ends by annulment rather than divorce.

Grounds for annulment vary slightly from state to state. Generally, an annulment may be obtained for one of the following reasons:

- **misrepresentation or fraud**—for example, a spouse lied about the capacity to have children, lied about being of the age of consent, or failed to mention still being married to someone else
- **concealment**—for example, concealing an addiction to alcohol or drugs, conviction of a felony, children from a prior relationship, a sexually transmitted disease, or impotence
- **refusal or inability to consummate the marriage**—that is, refusal or inability to have sexual intercourse with one's spouse, or
- **misunderstanding**—for example, one person wanted children and the other did not.

These are the grounds for civil annulments. Within the Roman Catholic church, a couple may obtain a religious annulment after obtaining a civil divorce, in order for one or both spouses to remarry through a religious ceremony in the church.

Most annulments take place after a marriage of a very short duration—a few weeks or months—so there are usually no assets or debts to divide or children for whom custody, visitation, and child support are a concern. When a long-term marriage is annulled, however, most states have provisions for dividing property and debts, as well as determining custody, visitation, child support, and alimony. Children of an annulled marriage are *not* considered illegitimate.

When are married people considered separated?

Many people are confused about what it means to be "separated"—and it's no wonder, given that there are four different kinds of separations:

Trial separation. When a couple lives apart for a test period, to decide whether or not to separate permanently, it's called a trial separation. Even if they don't get back together, the assets they accumulate and debts they incur during the trial period are usually considered jointly owned. A trial separation is a personal choice, not a legal status.

Living apart. Spouses who no longer reside in the same dwelling are said to be living apart. In some states, living apart without intending to reunite changes the spouses' property rights. For example, some states consider property accumulated and debts incurred from the time when a couple starts living apart until they divorce to be the separate property or debt of the person who accumulated or incurred it.

Permanent separation. When a couple decides to split up, it's often called a permanent separation. It may follow a trial separation, or may begin immediately when the couple starts living apart. In most states, all assets received and most debts incurred after permanent separation are the separate property or responsibility of the spouse incurring them. In some states, assets and debts are joint until divorce papers are filed, regardless of when you separate.

Legal separation. A legal separation results when parties live separately and a court rules on the division of property, alimony, child support, custody, and visitation—but does not grant a divorce. The money awarded for support of the spouse and children under these circumstances is often called separate maintenance (as opposed to alimony and child support).

What is a "no-fault" divorce?

"No-fault" divorce describes any divorce where the spouse suing for divorce does not have to prove that the other spouse did something wrong. All states allow divorces regardless of who is at "fault," but some states also allow parties to try to prove fault if they want to.

To get a no-fault divorce, one spouse must simply state a reason recognized by the state. In most states, it's enough to declare that the couple cannot get along (this goes by such names as "incompatibility," "irreconcilable differences," or "irremediable breakdown of the marriage"). In nearly a dozen states, however, the couple must live apart for a period of months or even years in order to obtain a no-fault divorce.

Is a no-fault divorce the only option even when there has been substantial wrongdoing?

In 15 states, yes. The majority of states allow a spouse to select either a no-fault divorce or a fault divorce. Why choose a fault divorce? Some people don't want to wait out the period of separation required by their state's law for a no-fault divorce. And in some states, a spouse who proves the other's fault may receive a greater share of the marital property, more alimony, or get custody of the children.

The traditional fault grounds are:

- cruelty (inflicting unnecessary emotional or physical pain)—this is the most frequently used ground
- adultery
- desertion for a specified length of time
- confinement in prison for a set number of years, and
- physical inability to engage in sexual intercourse, if it was not disclosed before marriage.

What happens in a fault divorce if both spouses are at fault?

Under a doctrine called "comparative rectitude," a court will grant the spouse who is least at fault a divorce when both parties have shown grounds for divorce. Years ago, when both parties were at fault, neither was entitled to a divorce. The absurdity of this result gave rise to the concept of comparative rectitude.

Can a spouse successfully prevent a court from granting a divorce?

One spouse cannot stop a no-fault divorce. Objecting to the other spouse's request for divorce is itself an irreconcilable difference that would justify the divorce.

A spouse can prevent a fault divorce, however, by convincing the court of the absence of fault. In addition, several other defenses to a divorce may be possible:

- **Collusion.** If the only no-fault divorce available in a state requires that the couple separate for a long time and the couple doesn't want to wait, they might pretend that one of them was at fault in order to manufacture a ground for divorce. This is collusion because they are cooperating in order to mislead the judge. If, before the divorce, one spouse no longer wants a divorce, that spouse could raise the collusion as a defense.
- **Condonation.** Condonation is someone's approval of another's activities. For example, a wife who does not object to her husband's adultery may be said to condone it. If the wife sues her husband for divorce, claiming he has committed adultery, the husband may argue as a defense that she condoned his behavior.
- **Connivance.** Connivance is the setting up of a situation so that the other person commits a wrongdoing. For example, a wife who invites her

husband's lover to the house and then leaves for the weekend may be said to have connived his adultery. If the wife sues her husband for divorce, claiming he has committed adultery, the husband may argue as a defense that she connived—that is, set up—his actions.

- **Provocation.** Provocation is the inciting of another to do a certain act. If a spouse suing for divorce claims that the other spouse abandoned her, her spouse might defend the suit on the ground that she provoked the abandonment.

Keep in mind that although these defenses exist, most courts will eventually grant the divorce. This is because of the strong public policy against forcing people to stay married against their will.

Do you have to live in a state to get a divorce there?

All states require a spouse to be a resident of the state for a certain length of time (six weeks to one year, depending on the state) before filing for a divorce there. Someone who files for divorce must offer proof of having lived in the state for the required length of time.

Can one spouse move to a different state or country to get a divorce?

If one spouse meets the residency requirement of a state or country, a divorce obtained there is valid even if the other spouse lives somewhere else. The courts of all states will recognize the divorce.

Any decisions the court makes regarding property division, alimony, custody, and child support, however, may not be valid unless the nonresident spouse consented to the jurisdiction of the court or later acts as if the foreign divorce was valid—for example, by paying court-ordered child support.

I'm a great housekeeper. I get divorced. I keep the house.

—Zsa Zsa Gabor

How is property divided at divorce?

It is common for a divorcing couple to decide how to divide their property and debts themselves, rather than leave it to the judge. But if a couple cannot agree, they can submit their property dispute to the court, which will use state law to decide generally how to divide the property.

Division of property does not necessarily mean a physical division. Rather, the court awards each spouse a percentage of the total value of the property. Each spouse gets items whose value adds up to the percentage awarded.

Courts divide property under one of two schemes: equitable distribution or community property.

- **Equitable distribution.** Assets and earnings accumulated during marriage are divided equitably (fairly). A judge must consider a number of factors in order to determine what would be fair. Sometimes this means the assets are divided equally (50-50), but just as often it does not. Equitable distribution principles are followed everywhere except the community property states listed just below.
- **Community property.** In Arizona, California, Idaho, Louisiana, Nevada, New Mexico, Texas, Washington, and Wisconsin, all property of a married person is classified as either community property (owned equally by both spouses) or as the separate property of one spouse (property that is accumulated prior to the divorce or acquired by gift or inheritance). At divorce, community property is generally divided equally between the spouses, while each spouse keeps his or her separate property. In Alaska, couples can agree in writing to have their property treated as if they lived in a community property state.

Very generally, here are the rules for determining what's community property and what isn't:

Community property includes all earnings during marriage and everything acquired with those earnings. All debts incurred during marriage, unless the creditor was specifically looking to the separate property of one spouse for payment, are community property debts.

Separate property of one spouse includes gifts and inheritances given just to that spouse, personal injury awards received by that spouse, and the proceeds of a pension that vested (that is, the pensioner became legally entitled to receive it) before marriage. Property purchased with the separate funds of a spouse remain that spouse's separate property, though states differ on whether income from separate property (such as rent or dividends) is separate or community property.

A business owned by one spouse before the marriage remains that spouse's separate property during the marriage, although a portion of it may be considered community property if the business increased in value during the marriage or both spouses contributed to its worth.

Property purchased with a combination of separate and community funds is part community and part separate property, as long as a spouse is able to show that some separate funds were used. Separate property mixed together with community property generally becomes community property.

My spouse and I are thinking of using a divorce mediator. Is there anything we should know before we begin the process?

More and more couples are turning to mediation in order to negotiate divorce agreements. In a divorce mediation, the parties jointly hire a trained, neutral mediator—often a lawyer—to help them negotiate and reach a settlement. Mediation almost always takes less time, is less expensive, and results in a more solid agreement than using a lawyer to take the case to court. Of course, every divorcing spouse should know and understand his or her legal rights before agreeing to a settlement, even one reached through mediation. You might want to consult a lawyer or do some independent legal research early in the process and then have a lawyer review the agreement before signing. (See Chapter 16 for general information on mediation and Chapter 15 for more information on mediating disputes about child custody and visitation. And see *Divorce Without Court: A Guide to Mediation & Collaborative Divorce,* by Katherine E. Stoner (Nolo).)

I've heard some divorces take months or even years to become final. Is there a way I can get child support and access to the family's more reliable car during this time?

If you've already decided to divorce, and you have financial or child-rearing concerns, you may benefit from a *pendente lite* action, which literally means "pending the litigation." In a *pendente lite* procedure, a court may sign orders providing for temporary alimony, child support, and asset distribution if appropriate. A lawyer is usually involved because the paperwork can be complicated. A *pendente lite* order lasts until it is modified by the final divorce judgment. It can even set the tone for the final divorce order, if custody and money arrangements are functioning satisfactorily during the time the divorce is being settled.

RESOURCE

For more information about divorce, see:

- *Nolo's Essential Guide to Divorce,* by Emily Doskow (Nolo). A thorough 50-state guide to the ins and outs of divorce, including state rules as to residency requirements for divorce, length of separation required, and grounds for divorce.
- *Divorce After 50: Your Guide to the Unique Legal & Financial Challenges,* by Janice Green (Nolo). Thoroughly explains the special issues faced by the over-50 crowd.
- *Divorce Without Court: A Guide to Mediation & Collaborative Divorce,* by Katherine E. Stoner (Nolo). Provides divorcing couples with all the information they need to work with a neutral third party to resolve differences and find solutions.
- *Divorce & Money: How to Make the Best Financial Decisions During Divorce,* by Violet Woodhouse and Matthew J. Perry (Nolo). Explains the financial aspects of divorce and property division.
- *Annulment: Your Chance to Remarry Within the Catholic Church,* by Joseph P. Zwack (Harper One), explains how to get a religious annulment.

Domestic Violence

Domestic violence occurs more often than most of us realize. People who are abused range in age from children to the elderly, and come from all backgrounds and income levels. The majority of those subjected to domestic violence are women abused by men, but women also abuse other women, men abuse men, and women abuse men. If you're being hurt at home, the first thing to do is to get away from the abuser and go to a safe place where you're unlikely to be found. Then, find out about your options for getting help.

What kind of behavior is considered domestic violence?

Domestic violence can take a number of forms, including:

- physical behavior (slapping, punching, pulling hair, or shoving)
- forced or coerced sexual acts or behavior (unwanted fondling or intercourse, or sexual jokes and insults)
- threats of abuse (threatening to hit, harm, or use a weapon)
- psychological abuse (attacks on self-esteem, controlling or limiting another's behavior, repeated insults, or interrogation)
- stalking (following a person, appearing at a person's home or workplace, making repeated phone calls, or leaving written messages), or
- cyberstalking (repeated online action or email that causes substantial emotional distress).

Typically, many kinds of abuse go on at the same time in a household.

If I leave, how can I make sure the abuser won't come near me again?

The most powerful legal tool for stopping domestic violence is the temporary restraining order (TRO). A TRO is a decree issued by a court that requires the violent partner to leave you alone. The order may require, for example, that the perpetrator stay away from the family home, your workplace or school, your children's school, and other places you frequent (such as a gym, friend's house, or church). The order will also prohibit further acts of violence.

Many states make it relatively easy for you to apply for a TRO. In New York, California, and some other states, for example, the court clerk will hand you a package of forms and will even assist you in filling them out. In other areas, nonlawyers may be available to help you complete the forms. When you've completed your forms, you'll go before a judge to show evidence of the abuse, such as hospital or police records or photographs. You can also bring in a witness, such as a friend or relative, to testify to the abuse. Judges are often available to issue emergency protective orders (EPOs) after normal business hours because violence can occur any time—not just during business hours. These typically stay in place for a short time until you can appear at a hearing and request a TRO.

Programs for Abusive Men

A number of programs have been established to help abusive men change their behavior. You can get more information from the following organizations:

- Abusive Men Exploring New Directions (AMEND)
  2727 Bryant Street, Suite 350
  Denver, CO 80211
  303-832-6363
- EMERGE: A Men's Counseling Service
  2464 Massachusetts Ave., Suite 101
  Cambridge, MA 02140
  617-547-9879
  www.emergedv.org

In my community, judges don't issue TROs after 5 p.m. How can I get protection?

Contact your local police department. In many communities, the police can issue something called an emergency protective order when court is not in session. An emergency protective order usually lasts only for a brief period of time, such as a weekend or a holiday, but otherwise it is the same as a temporary restraining order. On the next business day, you will need to go to court to obtain a TRO.

Finding a Safe Place

Many communities have temporary homes called battered women's shelters where women and their children who are victims of domestic violence may stay until the crisis passes or until they are able to find a permanent place to relocate. The best way to find these shelters is to consult the local police, welfare department, neighborhood resource center, or women's center. You can also look in your phone book or search online for Crisis Intervention Services, Human Service Organizations, Social Service Organizations, Family Services, Shelters, or Women's Organizations. In some states, the police are required to provide a battering victim with a list of referrals for emergency housing, legal services, and counseling services.

If you're having trouble finding resources in your area, you can contact the National Coalition Against Domestic Violence (NCADV), 303-839-1852, www.ncadv.org. NCADV provides information and referrals for abused women and their children, and they may know of assistance programs near you. Or you can contact the National Domestic Violence Hotline, 800-799-SAFE (7233), www.thehotline.org. You can also check out the website of the Women's Law Initiative, which provides state-by-state information and resources on domestic violence, at www.womenslaw.org.

Are TROs and emergency protective orders only available when the abuser is a spouse?

No, in most states, the victim of an abusive live-in lover, including one of the same sex, can obtain a TRO or emergency protective order. In a few states, the victim of any adult relative, an abusive lover (non–live-in), or even a roommate can obtain such an order. In some states, if victims and abusers do not live in the same household and are not lovers, the domestic violence laws do not apply. However, in this situation, other criminal laws—such as antistalking laws—may come into play. To learn about your state's rule, contact a local crisis intervention center, social service organization, or battered women's shelter.

What should I do once I have a TRO?

Register it with the police in the communities where the abuser has been ordered to stay away from you—where you live, work, attend school or church, and where your children go to school. Call the appropriate police stations for information about how to register your order.

What if the abuse continues after I have a TRO?

Although TROs are often effective, a piece of paper obviously cannot stop an enraged spouse or lover from trying to harm or intimidate you.

If the violence continues, contact the police. They can take immediate action and are far more willing to intervene when you have a TRO than when you don't. Of course, if you don't have a TRO or if it has expired, you should also call the police—in all states, domestic violence is a crime whether or not you already have a TRO.

Help for Abused Gay Men and Lesbians

The following organizations provide information and support for battered gay men and lesbians:

- The National Domestic Violence Hotline, at 800-799-SAFE, is a national toll-free number that provides information to callers (gay and straight) about shelters and assistance programs in their area. You can also check out the hotline's website at www.thehotline.org.
- The New York City Gay & Lesbian Anti-Violence Project maintains a website at www.avp.org, and their 24-hour hotline number is 212-714-1141.
- San Francisco's Community United Against Violence has a hotline at 415-333-HELP, and their website address is www.cuav.org.
- Massachusetts residents can contact the GLBTQ Domestic Violence Project at 800-832-1901. Their website is located at www.glbtqdvp.org.

Getting Legal Help

If you want to take legal action against your abuser or you need other legal help related to domestic abuse, the following organizations can refer you to assistance programs in your area:

- The National Coalition Against Domestic Violence (NCADV), 303-839-1852, www.ncadv.org.
- The National Domestic Violence Hotline, 800-799-SAFE (7233), 800-787-3224 (TTY), www.thehotline.org.

The police should respond to your call by sending out officers. In the past, police officers were reluctant to arrest abusers, but this has changed in many communities where victims' support groups have worked with police departments to increase the number of arrests. You can press criminal charges at the police department, and ask for criminal prosecution. Documentation is crucial if you want to go this route. Be sure to insist that the officer responding to your call makes an official report and takes photographs of your injuries, no matter how slight. Also, get the report's prospective number before the officer leaves the premises.

If you do press charges, keep in mind that only the district attorney decides whether or not to prosecute. If you don't press charges, however, the chance is extremely low that the district attorney will pursue the matter. In some states, if the injury is severe, the prosecutor may decide to pursue the case and urge your cooperation.

Changing Your Name

You may be thinking of changing your name for any number of reasons—perhaps you're getting married or divorced, or maybe you just want a name that suits you better. Whatever the reason, you'll be glad to know that name changes are common—and usually fairly easy to accomplish.

I'm a woman who is planning to be married soon. Do I have to take my husband's name?

No. When you marry, you are free to keep your own name, take your husband's name, or adopt a completely different name. Your husband can even adopt your name, if that's what you both prefer. Give some careful thought to what name feels best for you. You can save yourself considerable time and trouble by making sure you are happy with your name choice before you change any records.

Can my husband and I both change our names—to a hyphenated version of our two names or to a brand-new name?

Yes. Some couples want to be known by a hyphenated combination of their last

Changing Identification and Records

To complete your name change, you'll need to tell others about it. Contact the people and institutions you deal with and ask what type of documentation they require to make your name change official in their records. Different institutions have different rules. Most private institutions (such as banks and insurance companies) will simply require you to complete a form. Public agencies (like the department of motor vehicles) may require a copy of a court order.

It's best to start by getting a Social Security card, and then driver's license, in your new name. Once you have those pieces of identification, it's usually fairly simple to acquire others or have records changed to reflect your new name.

Here are the people and institutions to notify of your name change:

- Social Security Administration
- department of motor vehicles
- department of records or vital statistics (issuers of birth certificates)
- banks, brokers, and other financial institutions
- creditors and debtors
- landlords or tenants
- telephone and utility companies
- state taxing authority
- insurance agencies
- friends and family
- employers
- schools
- post office
- registrar of voters
- real estate recorders' offices
- passport office
- public assistance (welfare) office, and
- Veterans Administration.

Many government agencies provide instructions on how to register a name change with the agency via their websites. (For information on how to find government websites, see the "Legal Research" appendix.) For example, you can download the form for changing your name on your Social Security card at www.ssa.gov/online/ss-5.pdf.

names, and some make up new names that combine elements of each. For example, Ellen Berman and Jack Gendler might become Ellen and Jack Berman-Gendler or, perhaps, Ellen and Jack Bergen. You can also pick a name that's entirely different from the names you have now, just because you like it better. But if you adopt an entirely new name, you'll have to follow the rules discussed below.

What if I do want to take my husband's name? How do I make the change?

If you want to take your husband's name, simply start using the name as soon as you are married. Use your new name consistently, and be sure to change your name on all of your identification, accounts, and important documents (because this type of name change is so embedded in our culture, you generally won't need a court order). To change some of your identification papers—your Social Security card, for example—you'll simply need a certified copy of your marriage certificate, which you should receive within a few weeks after the marriage ceremony.

In many states, a wife may automatically take her new husband's name after marriage, but a husband must go to court for an official name change. And if you both want to change your names to an entirely new, shared last name, you'll have to go to court for that in most states, too.

For a list of people and institutions to contact about your name change, see "Changing Identification and Records," above.

I took my husband's name when I married but now we're getting divorced, and I'd like to return to my former name. How do I do that?

In most states, you can request that the judge handling your divorce make a formal order restoring your former or birth name. If your divorce decree contains such an order, that's all the paperwork you'll need. In some states, you can even have a completed divorce case reopened to provide for a name change. You'll want to get certified copies of the order as proof of the name change—check with the court clerk for details. Once you have the necessary documentation, you can use it to have your name changed on your identification and personal records.

If your divorce papers don't show your name change, you can usually still resume your former name without much fuss, especially if it's your birth name and you have a birth certificate to prove it. In many states, you can simply begin using your former name consistently and have it changed on all your personal records (see "Changing Identification and Records," above).

After my husband and I are divorced and I return to my former name, can I change the last name of my children as well?

Traditionally, courts ruled that a father had an automatic right to have his child keep his last name if he continued to actively perform his parental role. But this is no longer true. Now a child's name may be changed by court petition when it is in the best interest of the child to do so. However, it's not your decision alone, and if your ex-husband doesn't agree to the change, you'll have to ask a judge. When deciding to grant a name change, courts consider many factors, such as the length of time the father's name has been used, the strength of the mother-child relationship, and the child's need to identify with a new family unit (if the change involves remarriage). The courts must balance these factors against the strength and importance of the father–child relationship. What this all boils down to is that it's up to the judge to decide which name is in the child's best interest (and most judges won't change a child's name without a very good reason).

Keep in mind that even if you do change your children's last name, you won't be changing paternity—that is, the court's recognition of who is the children's father, and the rights and obligations that come with that recognition. Nor will a name change affect the rights or duties of either parent regarding visitation, child support, or rights of inheritance. Changes such as these occur only if the parental roles are altered by court order—for example, a new custody decree or a legal adoption.

That's "Mr. Three" to You

Minnesota's Supreme Court once ruled that a man who wanted to change his name to the number "1069" could not legally do so, but suggested that "Ten Sixty-Nine" might be acceptable.

I just don't like my birth name, and I want to change it. Can I choose any name I want?

There are some restrictions on what you may choose as your new name. Generally, the limits are as follows:

- You cannot choose a name with fraudulent intent—meaning you intend to do something illegal. For example, you cannot legally change your name to avoid paying debts, keep from getting sued, or get away with a crime.
- You cannot interfere with the rights of others, which generally means adopting a famous person's name in circumstances likely to create confusion.
- You cannot use a name that would be intentionally confusing. This might be a number or punctuation—for example, "10," "III," or "?".
- You cannot choose a name that is a racial slur.
- You cannot choose a name that could be considered a "fighting word," which includes threatening or obscene words, or words likely to incite violence.

Do I have to file forms in court to change my birth name?

Traditionally, most states allowed people to change their names by usage, without court proceedings. A name change by usage is accomplished by consistently using a new name in all aspects of your personal, social, and business life for a significant period of time. No court action is necessary, and it is free. (Minors and prison inmates generally aren't allowed to take advantage of this rule.)

Practically speaking, however, you will probably want to get an official court document changing your name. Especially in this day and age, with concerns about identity theft and national security, having a court order will make it much easier to get everyone to accept your new name. You won't be able to get certain types of identification—such as a new passport, birth certificate attachment, or (in most states) a driver's license—unless you have a court document, so, as a practical matter, a court-ordered name change is much more effective.

You can find out what your state requires by contacting your local court clerk. Many state courts have name change forms on their websites. Go to the "Courts" or "Judiciary" section of your state's home page and look for "Forms." You can look at your state's statutes in a local law library—start in the index under "Name" or "Change of Name."

How do I implement my name change?

The most important part of accomplishing your name change is to let others know you've taken a new name. Although it may take a little time to contact government agencies and businesses, don't be intimidated by the task—it's a common procedure.

The practical steps of implementing a name change are:

- **Advise officials and businesses.** Contact the various government and business agencies with which you deal and have your name changed on their records. See "Changing Identification and Records," above.
- **Enlist help of family and friends.** Tell your friends and family that you've changed your name and you now want them to use only your new one. It may take those close to you a while to get used it. Some of them might even object to using the new name, perhaps fearing the person they know so well is becoming someone else. Be patient and persistent.
- **Use only your new name.** If you are employed or in school, go by your new name there. Introduce yourself to new acquaintances and business contacts with your new name.

If you've made a will or other estate planning document (such as a living trust), it's best to replace it with a new document using your new name. Your beneficiaries won't lose their inheritances if you don't, but changing the document now will avoid confusion later.

Finally, remember to change your name on other important legal papers. For example, if you've made a durable power of attorney for finances and health care directives in your old name, you should replace them. However, it is usually not necessary to rewrite a contract that you made in your former name—for instance, an agreement to provide or receive services from someone—because both sides are still bound by the agreement's terms. Simply inform the other party to the contract that, going forward, you'd like to conduct all dealings in your new name.

RESOURCE

For more information about changing your name, see:

- *How to Change Your Name in California,* by Lisa Sedano and Emily Doskow (Nolo). Provides complete information on changing your name in California.
- Many state court websites provide name change forms. A good resource for links to state courts is the National Center for State Courts, at www.ncsc.org.
- Local law libraries are good sources of information for name changes. Look under "Name" or "Change of Name" in the index of your state's statutes, or ask the reference librarian for help. You can also research state laws on the Internet. See the appendix for more about doing your own legal research.
- The Transgender Law Center (www.transgenderlawcenter.org) and Lambda Legal (www.lambdalegal.org) provide information and resources on name changes and identity documents for transgender people.

ONLINE HELP

The following sites are good resources for spouses and partners:

- **www.nolo.com** The Divorce & Family Law section of the Nolo website offers information about a wide variety of legal topics, including marriage and relationships, divorce, and domestic violence. The Immigration section of Nolo.com includes articles on marriage-based visas or green cards and fiancé visas.
- **www.divorcenet.com** Divorcenet.com provides FAQs, articles, and information on a wide range of divorce issues.
- **www.unmarried.org** Unmarried Equality provides information and support for unmarried couples of all stripes.
- **www.lambdalegal.org** and **www.nclrights.org** The websites of Lambda and the National Center for Lesbian Rights provide the latest news and laws affecting LGBT people, including same-sex marriage and transgender rights.
- **www.ncadv.org** The National Coalition Against Domestic Violence offers help, information, and links for those affected by domestic violence.
- **www.womenslaw.org** The Women's Law Initiative provides extensive state-by-state information and resources on domestic violence and sexual assault, and relevant federal immigration and military laws.

CHAPTER

15

Parents and Children

A child of five could understand this. Fetch me a child of five.

—Groucho Marx

Raising children is a big job, and an emotional subject even when family relationships are well established and running smoothly. An adoption, divorce, or guardianship proceeding adds extra stress, requiring us to juggle law, finance, and our highly charged feelings. Be reassured, however, that there are many people who can help you find your way through family law proceedings, including knowledgeable lawyers, mediators, counselors, and therapists. In this chapter, we get you started by answering common questions about the laws that affect parents and their children.

Adopting a Child

Adoption is a court procedure by which an adult legally becomes the parent of someone who is not the adult's biological child. Adoption creates a parent-child relationship that is recognized for all purposes—including child support obligations, inheritance rights, and custody. The birth parents' legal relationship to the child is terminated, unless a legal contract allows them to retain or share some rights or the adoption is a stepparent or domestic partner adoption, in which case only the parent without custody, if there is one, loses parental rights.

This section discusses the general legal procedures and issues involved in adopting a child, including the advantages and disadvantages of various types of adoption and some of the special concerns of single people or unmarried couples (gay and straight) who want to adopt a child. Stepparent adoptions and the rights of relatives are discussed later in this chapter.

Who can adopt a child?

As a general rule, any adult who is found to be a "fit parent" may adopt a child. Married or unmarried couples may adopt jointly, and unmarried people may adopt through a procedure known as a single-parent adoption.

Some states have special requirements for adoptive parents, like requiring an adoptive parent to be a certain number of years older than the child. And some states require the adoptive parent to live in the state or the county for a certain length of time before they are allowed to adopt. You will need to check the laws of your state to see whether any special requirements apply to you. And keep in mind that if you're adopting through an agency, you may have to meet strict agency requirements in addition to requirements under state law.

Even if you find no state or agency barriers to adopting a child, remember that some people or couples are likely to have a harder time adopting than others. A single man or a lesbian couple may not legally be prohibited from adopting—although in a few places these prohibitions do exist—but may have a harder time finding a placement than would a married couple.

I'm single, but I'd like to adopt a child. What special concerns will I face?

As a single person, you may have to wait longer to adopt a child, or be flexible about the characteristics of the child you adopt. Agencies often "reserve" healthy infants and younger children for two-parent families, putting single people at the bottom of their waiting lists. And birth parents themselves often want their children to be placed in a two-parent home.

If you're a single person wishing to adopt, you should be prepared to make a good case for your fitness as a parent. You can expect questions from case workers about why you haven't married, how you plan to support and care for the child on your own, what will happen if you do marry, and other questions that will put you in the position of defending your status as a single person. To many single adoptive parents, such rigorous screening doesn't seem fair, but it is common.

Agencies serving children with special needs may be a good option for single people, as such agencies often cast a wider net when considering adoptive parents. Of course, you shouldn't adopt a special-needs child unless you feel truly comfortable with the idea of meeting that child's needs—but being flexible will make the obstacles to single-parent adoptions easier to overcome.

My long-term partner and I prefer not to get married, but we'd like to adopt a child together. Will we run into trouble?

There is no specific prohibition against unmarried opposite-sex couples adopting children—sometimes called two-parent adoptions. However, you may find that agencies are biased toward married couples. You may have a longer wait for a child, or you may want to consider adopting a child that is more difficult to place—an older or special-needs child, for example.

Is it still very difficult for lesbians and gay men to adopt children?

The level of difficulty for gay and lesbian adoption depends—in large part—on your marital status and where you live. Now that same-sex marriage is legal everywhere in the United States, gay and lesbian married couples have the same adoption rights as opposite-sex married couples. For example, all states allow same-sex married couples to pursue a joint adoption, where two people petition to adopt a child together at the same time.

A stepparent adoption is where one spouse adopts the other spouse's child—who is either the other spouse's biological child or legal child by a previous adoption. Same-sex married couples can use the same stepparent adoption procedures available to all married couples. Same-sex couples that are registered in domestic partnerships or civil unions can use similar adoption procedures in states that recognize their relationships.

In 16 jurisdictions—California, Colorado, Connecticut, D.C., Idaho, Illinois, Indiana, Maine, Massachusetts, Montana, New Jersey, New York, Oklahoma, Oregon, Pennsylvania, and Vermont—unmarried and unregistered gay and lesbian couples can petition for a second-parent adoption, which allows one partner to adopt the other partner's child, without the first parent losing any parental rights.

Even if a state adoption statute does not specifically mention sexual orientation, a judge might find that a prospective adoptive parent is unfit just because of the person's sexual orientation. And before a case even gets to court, adoptive parents have to pass muster with a social services agency, which also might be biased against same-sex parents.

On the other hand, many gay men and lesbians have been able to adopt children. If you have questions, you should speak with an adoption attorney in your area to determine what the best options are for you and your family.

RESOURCE

For more about same-sex relationships and parenting, check out *A Legal Guide for Lesbian & Gay Couples,* by Frederick Hertz and Emily Doskow (Nolo). And to learn the ins and outs of legal partnership, see *Making It Legal: A Guide to Same-Sex Marriage, Domestic Partnerships & Civil Unions,* by Frederick Hertz with Emily Doskow (Nolo).

ONLINE HELP

The following sites are good resources on same-sex couples and adoption:

- **www.hrc.org** The Parenting section of the Human Rights Campaign website includes information on state adoption laws affecting LGBT individuals and same-sex couples.
- **www.nclrights.org** and **www.lambdalegal.org** The websites of the National Center for Lesbian Rights and Lambda Legal offer information and resources on adoption by same-sex couples.
- **www.familyequity.org/get_informed/equality-maps.** The Family Equality Council website provides a Foster and Adoption Laws map that contains up-to-date summaries on adoption laws across the U.S.

Can I adopt a child whose race or ethnic background is different from mine?

Usually, yes. You do not need to be of the same race as the child you want to adopt, although some states do give preference to prospective adoptive parents of the same race or ethnic background as the child. Adoptions of Native American children are governed by a federal law—the Indian Child Welfare Act—that outlines specific rules and procedures that must be followed when adopting a Native American child.

Whose consent is needed for an adoption to take place?

For any adoption to be legal, the birth parents must consent to the adoption, unless their parental rights have been legally terminated for some other reason, such as a finding that they are unfit parents. All states prohibit birth parents from giving their consent to an adoption until after the child's birth, and some states require even more time to pass—typically three to four days after the birth—before the parents are allowed to consent. Some states also allow the birth parents a period of time within which they can revoke their consent—in some cases, up to 30 days. This means that birth parents can legally change their minds about putting their child up for adoption at any point before (or shortly after) the child is born.

What are some of the advantages and disadvantages of an agency adoption?

Using an agency to manage your adoption can be helpful for a number of reasons. Agencies are experienced in finding children, matching them with parents, and satisfying the necessary legal requirements of the adoption. Agencies will do most of the legwork of an adoption, from finding a birth parent to finalizing the papers, and they'll walk adoptive parents through many of the crucial steps in between, such as conducting the home study, obtaining the necessary consents, and advising parents on the state's specific legal requirements.

One key advantage of an agency adoption is the extensive counseling that agencies provide throughout the process. Typically, counseling is available for adoptive parents, birth parents, and the children (if they are older). Careful counseling can help everyone involved weather the emotional, practical, and legal complexities that are likely to arise during the adoption.

Preadoption counseling for a birth mother can also help ensure that she is really committed to giving up her child for adoption and reduce the likelihood that she might change her mind at the last minute, leading to heartbreak for the potential adoptive parents.

Finally, many agencies specialize in certain kinds of children; this may be helpful if you want, for example, to adopt an infant, a child of a different race than yours, or a child with special medical needs. Some agencies also offer international adoption services.

On the downside, private agencies are often extremely selective when choosing adoptive parents. This is because they have a surplus of people who want to adopt and a limited number of available children. Most agencies have long waiting lists of prospective parents, especially for healthy, white infants. Agencies weed out parents using criteria such as age, marital status, income, health, religion, family size, personal history (including criminal records), and residency requirements.

Additionally, agencies often wait to place the child in the adoptive home until all necessary consents have been given and become final. Because of this, a child may be placed in foster care for a few days or weeks, depending on the situation and the state's law. This delay concerns many adoptive parents who want the child to have a secure, stable home as soon as possible. Some agencies get around this by placing infants immediately through a type of adoption known as a "legal risk placement": If the birth mother decides she wants her child back before her rights have been legally terminated, the adoptive parents must let the child go.

Public agencies usually have many children ready to be adopted, but they often specialize in older or special-needs children. If you want a newborn, a public agency might not be able to help you. Also, public agencies may not provide many other services such as the much-needed counseling that private agencies offer.

How do I find an adoption agency?

There are an estimated 3,000 adoption agencies in the United States, public and private. If you live in a state like California or New York, you'll have more options than if you live in a less populated state. But wherever you live, you'll probably have to do some searching to find an agency that meets your needs and is able to work with you. You can call or look online for a national adoption organization for referrals to get you started. The websites of several organizations are listed at the end of this section.

Be persistent with the agencies you contact. If they tell you that there are no children, ask whether there is a waiting list. Then ask other questions, such as: Is the waiting list for child placement or a home study? How do you determine who may file an application? Can I fill out an application now? If not, when can I? Do you hold orientation meetings? If so, when will the next one be held? Ask whether you can speak with other parents in circumstances similar to yours who have adopted through the agency. These parents may provide valuable information about the service they received from the agency, how long the process took, and whether they were ultimately happy with the outcome. Screen the agencies as much as they screen you.

How can I check on the reputation of an adoption agency?

As discussed above, you can and should speak with other parents who have adopted through the agency. In addition, you should check out the agency's accreditation. Start with the licensing department of your state. It can tell you whether the agency has been cited for licensing violations, or whether the licensing office has received any complaints about the agency. You can also request a copy of the state's rules governing agencies so that you understand the standards to which your agency is held.

Types of Adoption

Agency Adoptions. In an agency adoption, a child is placed with adoptive parents by a public agency, or by a private agency licensed and/or regulated by the state. Public agencies generally place children who have become wards of the state because they were orphaned, abandoned, or abused. Private agencies are often run by charities or social service organizations. Children placed through private agencies are usually brought to an agency by parents who have or are expecting a child that they want to give up for adoption.

Independent Adoptions. In an independent or private adoption, a child is placed with adoptive parents without the assistance of an agency. Some independent adoptions are arranged directly between the birth parents and the adoptive parents, while others are arranged through an intermediary such as a lawyer, adoption facilitator, doctor, or clergyperson. Whether or not an intermediary is used, a lawyer is essential because of the legal complexities involved. Most states allow independent adoptions, though many regulate them quite carefully. A few states will not allow adoptions arranged through an intermediary; others do not permit advertising in connection with independent adoptions; and many limit how much adoptive parents may pay a birth mother for maternity expenses.

Identified Adoptions. An identified, or designated, adoption is one in which the adopting parents locate a birth mother (or the other way around) and then ask an adoption agency to handle the rest of the adoption process. In this way, an identified adoption is a hybrid of an independent and an agency adoption. Prospective parents are spared the waiting lists of agencies by finding the birth parents themselves, but reap the other benefits of agencies, such as the agency's experience with legal issues and its counseling services. Identified adoptions provide an alternative to parents in states that ban independent adoptions.

International Adoptions. In an international adoption, the adoptive parents take responsibility for a child who is a citizen of a foreign country. In addition to satisfying the adoption requirements of both the foreign country and the parents' home state in the United States, the parents must obtain an immigrant visa for the child through U.S. Citizenship and Immigration Services (USCIS) and the State Department. The USCIS has its own rules for international adoptions, such as the requirement that the adoptive parents of orphans be either married or, if single, at least 25 years old. The USCIS also requires adoptive parents to complete several forms and submit a favorable home study report. You'll find more about international adoption below.

Second-Parent Adoptions. A second-parent adoption (sometimes called a coparent adoption) allows a lesbian or gay man to adopt a partner's biological or adopted child.

Types of Adoption (continued)

Many lesbian couples do second-parent adoptions, where one partner has a child through donor insemination and the other partner adopts the child as a second parent. This type of adoption has been recognized in many states. However, some states—including Mississippi, Nebraska, North Carolina, Ohio, Utah, and Wisconsin—have expressly disapproved of this type of adoption.

Relative Adoptions. When a child is related to the adoptive parent by blood or marriage, the adoption is a relative adoption—also sometimes called a "kinship adoption." The most common example of this type of adoption is a stepparent adoption, in which a parent's new spouse adopts a child from a previous partner. Grandparents often adopt their grandchildren if the parents die while the children are minors. These adoptions are usually simpler than nonrelative adoptions.

Stepparent Adoptions. See "Stepparent Adoptions," below.

The staff at your state's department of social services may also be able to give you information about the agency. Finally, you can check your state or local department of consumer affairs to see if it handles complaints about adoption agencies. And while it's always wise to take online reviews with a grain of salt, put the agency's name into a search engine like Google or Yahoo and see whether others have weighed in.

Are agency adoptions very expensive?

They can be. Agencies charge fees to cover the birth mother's expenses as allowed by state law; these expenses may include medical costs, living expenses during the pregnancy, and costs of counseling. Add to this the agency's staff salaries and overhead, and charges can mount up quickly.

Many agencies charge a flat fee for adoptions, while others add the birth mother's expenses to a fixed rate for the agency's services. Some agencies use a sliding scale that varies with adoptive parents' income levels, usually with a set minimum and maximum fee. Most agencies charge a lower rate for handling special-needs adoptions.

Public agencies generally do not charge fees for placing children in adoptive homes.

What are the costs involved in an independent adoption?

Because each situation is unique, fees for independent adoptions vary widely. Prospective parents must generally cover the costs of finding a birth mother, all costs related to the pregnancy and birth, and the legal costs involved in the adoption process.

Some states also include the birth mother's living expenses during the pregnancy. Expenses such as hospital bills, travel costs, phone bills, home study fees, attorneys' fees, and court costs can easily exceed $20,000.

You Can't Buy a Baby

It is illegal in all states to buy or sell a baby. All states, however, allow adoptive parents to pay certain "reasonable" costs that are specifically related to the adoption process. Each state has its own laws defining the expenses that may be paid by adoptive parents in any kind of adoption proceeding—agency or independent. If you pursue an independent adoption, you must adhere to these laws when you give any money to the birth mother. And agencies are regulated to make sure that they charge adoptive parents only for the costs that the state allows.

Most states allow the adoptive parents to pay the birth mother's medical expenses, counseling costs, and attorneys' fees. Some states allow payments to cover the birth mother's living expenses such as food, housing, and transportation during pregnancy. Most states require all payments to be itemized and approved by a court before the adoption is finalized. Be sure you know and understand your state's laws, because providing or accepting prohibited financial support may subject you to criminal charges. Furthermore, the adoption itself may be jeopardized if you make improper payments.

What should I keep in mind when deciding whether to pursue an independent adoption?

Birth and adoptive parents are sometimes attracted to independent adoptions because they allow control over the entire adoption process. Rather than relying on an agency as a go-between, the birth parent and adoptive parents can meet, get to know each other, and decide for themselves whether the adoption should take place. Independent adoptions also avoid the long waiting lists and restrictive qualifying criteria that are often involved in agency adoptions. Plus, independent adoptions usually happen much faster than agency adoptions, often within a year of beginning the search for a child.

One major drawback to independent adoptions is that they are heavily regulated in many states and illegal in a few. Some states that allow independent adoptions prohibit adoptive parents from advertising for birth mothers or intermediaries from advertising their adoption services. Be sure to check your state's laws before you proceed. Your state's website (find yours at www.usa.gov) will have information on adoption laws and policies. Look for links to the state health and human services agency.

Another concern is that birth parents might not receive adequate counseling during the adoption process. This may leave your agreement more vulnerable to unraveling. Furthermore, some states extend the period in which birth parents may revoke their consent for independent adoptions; this places your agreement at additional risk.

Finally, independent adoptions are a lot of work. Adoptive parents often spend enormous amounts of time—and money—just finding a birth mother, not to mention the efforts required to follow through and bring the adoption to a close. Some parents decide afterwards that pursuing an independent adoption ate up too much time and money, and they hire an agency to do the work for their next adoption.

What's a home study?

All states require adoptive parents to undergo an investigation to make sure that they are fit to raise a child. Typically, the study is conducted by a state agency or a licensed social worker who examines the adoptive parents' home life and prepares a report that the court will review before approving the adoption. Some states do not require the agency to submit a report to the court. These states allow the agency or social worker to decide whether the prospective parents are fit to adopt. Common areas of inquiry include:

- financial stability
- marital stability
- lifestyles
- other children
- career obligations
- physical and mental health, and
- criminal history.

In recent years, the home-study process has become more than just a method of investigating prospective parents; it serves to educate and inform them as well. The social worker helps to prepare the adoptive parents by discussing issues such as how and when to talk with the child about being adopted, and how to deal with the reaction that friends and family might have to the adoption.

Can I adopt a child from another country?

If you're a U.S. citizen (or, in some cases, a green card holder), you can adopt a foreign child through an American agency that specializes in intercountry adoptions—or you can adopt directly (although this is much less common). If you prefer a direct adoption, you will have to adhere not only to the adoption laws of your state but also to U.S. immigration laws and the laws of the country where the child is born. It will be a complex process, so be prepared for some tangles. Do as much research as you can before you fly off to find a child; the more you know about the chosen country's adoption system ahead of time, the better off you'll be when you get there.

For practical reasons, most prospective parents focus on adopting an orphan. If you adopt a child who is not an orphan, the child must be under the age of 16. If you adopt from a country that is not party to the Hague Convention (discussed below), the child (nonorphan) must also live in

Open Adoptions

An open adoption is one in which there is some degree of contact between the birth parents and the adoptive parents both before and after the adoption. Often this includes contact between the birth parents and the child as well. There is no one standard for open adoptions; each family works out the arrangement that works best for them. Some adoptive parents consider meeting the birth parents just once before the birth of the child, while others form ongoing relationships that may include written correspondence or visits.

Open adoptions often help reduce stress and worry by eliminating the power of the unknown. Rather than fearing the day that a stranger will come knocking on their door to ask for the child back, adoptive parents are reassured by knowing the birth parents personally and dealing with them directly. This openness can be beneficial to the child as well, who will grow up with fewer questions—and misconceptions—than might a child of a "closed" adoption.

If you want your adoption to be open and decide to use an agency, be sure to find out their policies on open placements. Some agencies offer only closed or "semi-open" adoptions and will not provide identifying information about birth or adoptive parents even if both families want the adoption to be open. On the other hand, independent adoptions—where allowed—permit birth and adoptive families to determine what degree of contact is agreeable to all.

your legal custody for two years before you begin the child's immigration process. This means that you'd have to either live overseas for those two years or find a temporary visa that would allow the child to stay in the United States for two years—and there are no visas designated for this purpose.

An orphan is a child whose parents have died, disappeared, or abandoned the child, or whose one remaining parent is not able to care for the child and consents irrevocably to the child's adoption and immigration to the United States. If there are two known parents, the child will not qualify as an orphan under any circumstances.

U.S. immigration laws require that prospective adoptive parents be U.S. citizens and married or, if single, at least 25 years old. And the country from which you're adopting probably has its own requirements as well. In 2008, the United States became part of the Hague Adoption Convention, an international agreement to safeguard international adoptions. Hague requirements include the use of accredited adoption agencies, transparency and accountability regarding costs, and procedures that ensure children have not been abducted or trafficked. You can still adopt from a non-Convention country, but the requirements and procedures will be different, and the protections offered by the Convention are significant.

The agencies you'll need to interact with include with the U.S. Citizenship and Immigration Services (USCIS). Along with the various government forms, you will need to submit a number of documents, including a favorable home study report.

Because of the procedural complexities you'll want to use an experienced international adoption agency. Much of the paperwork for an intercountry adoption can be completed even if you haven't yet identified a specific child to adopt. Advance preparation is a valuable option because the USCIS paperwork often takes a long time to process and may hold up the child's arrival in the United States even after all foreign requirements have been met.

Finally, be sure to check your own state laws for any preadoption requirements. Some states, for instance, require you to submit the written consent of the birth mother before they approve the entry of the child into the state. Some experts recommend that parents who adopt overseas readopt the child in their own state in order to make sure that the adoption fully conforms to state law; some foreign countries require that a readoption be completed before the adoption is considered finalized.

For more information about intercountry adoptions, see the resource list at the end of this section.

What should my adoption petition say?

A standard adoption petition will generally include five pieces of information:

- the names, ages, and address of the adoptive parents
- the relationship between the adoptive parents and the child to be adopted
- the legal reason that the birth parents' rights are being terminated (usually that they consented to the termination)
- a statement that the adoptive parents are appropriate people to adopt the child, and
- a statement that the adoption is in the child's best interests.

Sometimes, the written consent of the birth parents or a court order terminating their parental rights is filed along with the petition. Other times, the termination occurs a bit later in the process. Adoptive parents also often include a request for an official name change for the child.

Do I need an attorney to handle the adoption of my child?

If you do not use an agency, yes. And even if you do use an agency, you will probably need to hire a lawyer to draft the adoption petition and to represent you at the hearing. Although there is no legal requirement that a lawyer be involved in an adoption, the process can be quite complex and should be handled by someone with experience and expertise. The exception is a stepparent adoption, which in most places is quite simple and which you might be able to handle yourself. See "Stepparent Adoptions," below. When seeking a lawyer, find out how many adoptions the lawyer has handled, and whether any of them were contested or developed other complications.

When is an adoption considered final?

All adoptions—agency or independent—must be approved by a court. The adoptive parents must file a petition to finalize the adoption proceeding; there will also be an adoption hearing.

Before the hearing, anyone who is required to consent to the adoption must receive notice. Usually this includes the biological parents, the adoption agency, the child's legal representative if a court has appointed one, and a child who is old enough (12 to 14 years in most states).

At the hearing, if the court determines that the adoption is in the child's best interest, the judge will issue an order approving and finalizing the adoption. This order, often called a final decree of adoption, legalizes the new parent–child relationship and usually changes the child's name to the name the adoptive parents have chosen.

Stepparent Adoptions

The majority of adoptions in the United States are stepparent adoptions, in which the biological child of one parent is formally adopted by that parent's new spouse. This type of adoption may occur when one biological parent has died or has left the family after a divorce, and the remaining parent remarries. While most stepparents do not formally adopt their stepchildren, those who do obtain the same parental rights as biological parents. This section discusses some of the issues that arise when a stepparent adopts a stepchild.

My new spouse wants to adopt my son from a previous marriage. Are there special adoption rules for stepparents?

Generally speaking, a stepparent adoption is much easier to complete than a nonrelative adoption. The procedure is generally the same as for any adoption, but specific steps are sometimes waived or streamlined. For instance, waiting periods, home studies, and even the adoption hearing are sometimes dispensed with in a stepparent adoption.

In all stepparent adoptions, however, the child's other parent, if there is one, will need to consent to the adoption. If the other parent refuses to consent, the adoption will not be allowed unless that parent's parental rights are terminated for some other reason—abandonment or unfitness, for example.

My new husband has a great relationship with my ten-year-old son and wants to adopt him. My son communicates about once or twice a year with his birth father, who will consent to the adoption. Is adoption the right thing to do?

Stepparent adoptions can be complicated when the noncustodial biological parent is still alive and in contact with the child. There may be no legal reason why the adoption cannot take place, but the emotional impact of the adoption also should be considered.

If an adoption will bring stability to your new family and help your son feel more secure, it may be the right choice. But no matter how well your son gets along with your new husband, he may feel conflicting loyalties between his adoptive father and his birth father, and this may be hard for him to handle. Generally speaking, the less contact your son has with his birth father, the more sense it makes to go through with the adoption.

Besides the impact on the child (which should be of primary importance), also make sure your ex-husband understands that giving consent to the adoption means giving up all parental rights to his son, including any right to visit him or make decisions for him regarding issues such as medical treatment or education. In addition, he would no longer be responsible for child support once his parental rights were terminated.

Your new husband should be aware that if he adopts your son, and you and he divorce, he will be responsible for paying child support. Of course, he will also be entitled to visitation or custody.

I had my daughter when I was unmarried, and we haven't heard from her father for several years. I'm now married to another man, and he wants to adopt my daughter. Do I have to find her biological father and get his consent to the adoption before it can take place?

The adoption cannot take place until the absent parent either gives consent or has his parental rights terminated for some other reason. That being said, there are a few specific ways to proceed with an adoption when one biological parent is out of the picture.

First, it is possible to go forward without a biological parent's consent if you can prove that the absent parent has not exercised any parental rights and convince the court that it's appropriate to legally terminate that parent–child relationship. Most states' laws allow parental rights to be terminated when a parent has willfully failed to support the child or has abandoned the child for a period of time, usually a year. Generally, abandonment means that the absent parent hasn't communicated with the child or supported the child financially.

If the absent parent is a father, another common way to terminate his parental rights is to show that he is not, legally speaking, the presumed father of the child. Most states have laws establishing who the presumed father of a child is in certain situations. In this case, you won't have to prove that the father has abandoned the child. You simply must show that he does not meet the legal definition of presumed father. For instance, in all states, a man who is married to a woman at the time she gives birth is legally presumed to be the child's father. Another way of establishing presumed fatherhood in many states is by marrying the mother after the child has been born and being named as the father on the child's birth certificate.

If you can show that the father doesn't meet any of the tests in your state for presumed fatherhood, the court may terminate his rights and allow you to proceed without his consent. If, however, the father meets one of the state's tests for presumed fatherhood, you'll need either to obtain the father's consent to the adoption or have his rights terminated by proving abandonment, willful failure to support the child, or parental unfitness—or by giving him notice of the adoption proceeding and hoping he doesn't interfere or object. If he doesn't, you'll be able to complete the adoption.

Adoption Rights: Birth Parents, Grandparents, and Children

The rights of parents to raise and care for their children have traditionally received strong legal protection. Courts have long recognized that the bond between parents and children is a profound one, and the law will not interfere with that bond except in the most carefully defined circumstances. Adoption generally involves creating a parent–child relationship where there previously was none—and sometimes negating someone's parental rights in the process. Balancing the legal rights of the parties involved can sometimes be difficult. This section discusses how the legal rights of birth parents, grandparents, and children can be affected by the adoption process.

Are birth parents allowed to change their minds and take children back even after they've been placed in the adoptive parents' home?

Even after the birth parents have consented to an adoption and the child is living in the adoptive home, many states allow birth parents to change their minds for a set period of time. Depending on the state, the birth parents have the right to withdraw consent weeks or even months after the placement. Though it can be nerve-wracking—and sometimes devastating—for the adoptive parents who have begun to care for the child, it's important that they understand that birth parents have this right. Adoptive parents should find out how long their state allows for birth parents to legally withdraw consent.

The birth mother of the baby we were going to adopt just decided she wants to keep her child. She's eight months pregnant, and we've paid all of her medical bills during her pregnancy. Can we get our money back?

Unless the mother agrees to pay you back, you're probably out of luck. Especially with independent adoptions, paying a birth mother's allowable costs is a risk for adoptive parents. Birth parents often change their minds, and courts will not force them to pay back the expenses paid by the adoptive parents.

My girlfriend is pregnant and I'm the father. I want to keep the baby, but she wants to place the baby with an adoptive family. Can she do that?

No. If you acknowledge that you're the father of the child, your consent is needed before the baby can be adopted. The rights of fathers have gotten much more attention in recent years and are now more strongly protected by the law. However, fathers' rights vary greatly from state to state, and the law in this area is far from settled. If you don't want to see your baby adopted, you should be sure to acknowledge paternity and make it clear to the mother that you won't allow your parental rights to be terminated. You should file a paternity action to establish your parental rights.

My husband and I found an expectant mother who wants us to adopt her baby. But her mother is trying to talk her out of giving up the child. Can a grandparent legally object to an adoption?

No. The parents of a birth mother don't have any legal right to stop her from giving up the baby. Also, grandparents won't necessarily be favored as adoptive parents over nonrelative parents. (One big exception to this rule is the adoption of Native American children, where a special federal law applies.)

That said, however, grandparents often hold a lot of sway over birth parents, and in many cases have convinced them at the last minute not to give up their babies. If you know that the grandparents are actively trying to talk the birth mother out of the adoption, you should consider that there's an increased risk that the adoption might fall through. In this situation, it's especially important to keep in close touch with the birth mother and make extra efforts to encourage open communication. You'll have to judge for yourself how confident you feel about proceeding with a birth mother whose family is opposed to the adoption.

I was adopted as a baby. Now I'm 25 and I want to find my birth parents. Do I have a legal right to obtain my birth records?

In most adoptions, the original birth records and other case documents are "sealed" by the court that finalizes the adoption, which means that no one can see them without the court's permission. But as attitudes toward adoption have become more open, states have come up with a variety of ways for adopted children to find their birth parents, some of which do not require the unsealing of records.

Only a few states offer adult adopted children open access to original birth certificates. More popular is a system called "search and consent," in which an adopted child has an agency contact the birth parent, who then either agrees to be identified or says no. If the birth parent consents, then the agency provides the information to the child. The most common system is a mutual consent registry, used in about 25 states, in which birth parents and adopted children provide identifying information about themselves to the registry. If a birth parent and that parent's adopted child both appear within a registry, the agency in charge of the registry will share the information with each of them, enabling them to contact each other.

If one of these options isn't available or doesn't work for you, it may be possible to obtain your birth records. Generally, a court will unseal a record for "good cause," such as a need for medical or genetic information.

The best way to start your search is to contact a local adoption agency that knows your state's laws and procedures for contacting birth parents. The National Adoption Information Clearinghouse and the North American Council on Adoptable Children are good sources for referrals to local agencies (see below for contact information).

Another useful tool in searching for birth parents is the Internet. Dozens of organizations and services designed to help adopted children find their birth families have cropped up on the Web, as well as individuals posting their own searches.

ONLINE HELP

The websites of the following organizations provide good resources on adopting a child:

- **www.childwelfare.gov/adoption** The Child Welfare Information Gateway provides a wide range of information about adoption as well as referrals to local agencies and support groups.
- **www.adoption.com** This comprehensive website provides information about adoption agencies, international adoption, and many other adoption issues. The site includes links to state adoption laws, such as access to adoption records.

- **www.nclrights.org** The National Center for Lesbian Rights provides help to gay men and lesbians who want to adopt.
- **www.adoptionhelp.org** The Independent Adoption Center is a national nonprofit organization that specializes in open adoptions.
- **www.nacac.org** The North American Council on Adoptable Children (NACAC) provides extensive adoption resources and links to related organizations, from adoption agencies to postadoption support groups.
- **https://travel.state.gov/content/adoptionsabroad/en.html** The United States Department of State, and the United States Citizenship and Immigration Services, at www.uscis.gov (click on "Adoption") have all the information and forms you will need for an international adoption, including an explanation of The Hague Convention. Also, the book *How to Get a Green Card,* by Ilona Bray (Nolo), includes a discussion of international adoptions.

Child Custody and Visitation

You can't shake hands with a clenched fist.

—**Indira Gandhi**

When parents separate or divorce, the term "custody" serves as shorthand for "who lives with and cares for the children" under the divorce decree or judgment. In most states, custody is split into two types: physical custody and legal custody. Physical custody refers to the responsibility of actually taking care of the children day to day, while legal custody involves making decisions that affect their interests (such as medical, educational, and religious decisions). In states that don't distinguish between physical and legal custody, the term "custody" implies both types of responsibilities.

For information on how to find your state's custody law, see the "Legal Research" appendix. Also, the Legal Information Institute, at www.law.cornell.edu/wex/child_custody, has an excellent summary of child custody laws, cases, and resources.

Does custody always go to just one parent?

No. Courts frequently award at least some aspects of custody to both parents. This is called joint custody, and it usually takes one of three forms:

- joint physical custody (children spend a relatively equal amount of time with each parent)
- joint legal custody (medical, educational, religious, and other decisions about the children are shared), or
- both joint legal and joint physical custody.

In every state, courts are willing to order joint legal custody, but about half the states are reluctant to order joint physical custody unless both parents agree to it and they appear to be sufficiently able to communicate and cooperate with each other to make it work. In some states, courts automatically award joint legal custody unless the children's best interests—or a parent's health or safety—would be compromised. If parents don't share joint physical custody, one will have primary physical custody and the other visitation.

Can someone other than the parents have physical or legal custody?

Sometimes neither parent can suitably assume custody of the children, perhaps because of substance abuse or a mental health problem. In these situations, others may be granted custody of the children or be given a temporary guardianship or foster care arrangement by a court.

What factors do courts take into account when deciding who gets custody of the children?

A court gives the "best interests of the child" the highest priority when deciding custody issues. What the best interests of a child are in a given situation depends upon many factors, including:

- the child's age, sex, and mental and physical health
- the mental and physical health of the parents
- the lifestyle and habits of the parents, including whether the child is exposed to secondhand smoke or drug use in the home and whether there is any history of child abuse
- the love and emotional ties between the parent and the child, as well as the parent's ability to give the child guidance
- the parent's ability to provide the child with food, shelter, clothing, and medical care
- the child's established living pattern (school, home, community, religious institution)
- the quality of the available schools
- the child's preference, if the child is old enough to weigh the alternatives and provide a mature opinion or preference (children are usually consulted once they reach the age of 12 or so), and
- the ability and willingness of each parent to foster healthy communication and contact between the child and the other parent.

Assuming that none of these factors clearly favors one parent over the other, most courts tend to focus on which parent is likely to provide the children a more stable environment. With younger children, this may mean awarding custody to the parent who has been the child's primary caregiver. With older children, this may mean giving custody to the parent who is best able to foster continuity in education, neighborhood life, religious institutions, and peer relationships.

Are mothers more likely to be awarded custody than fathers?

In the past, most states provided that custody of children of "tender years" (age five and under) had to be awarded to the mother when parents divorced. This rule is now rejected in most states, or relegated to the role of tiebreaker if two fit parents request custody of their preschool children. Most states require their courts to determine custody based only on the children's best interests, without regard to the sex of the parent.

As it turns out, many divorcing parents agree that the mother will have primary custody (especially of very young children) after a separation or divorce, and that the father will exercise reasonable visitation.

Are there special issues if a gay or lesbian parent is seeking custody or visitation rights?

The courts are all over the map when it comes to gay parents and custody or visitation. In many states, there are now laws that prohibit using sexual orientation alone as a basis for denying custody or visitation. Other states say that if the parent's sexual orientation would cause harm to the child, it's okay to deny custody or visitation. And there are also still places where homophobic judges make decisions about parents' rights to spend time with their children based solely on the parent being LGBT. Unless you live in a fairly progressive community, if your spouse or partner is trying to use your sexual orientation as a factor in a custody fight, hire a lawyer.

My partner and I broke up after eight years. During that time I was artificially inseminated, and we raised the child together. Now she wants visitation. Is that possible even if she isn't related by blood to my child and hasn't adopted the child?

Again, courts are all over the map on this question. In some states, courts have held that a nonbiological parent who has established a psychological parent–child relationship with a partner's biological child is entitled to visitation and, in some cases, to legal status as a parent. In other places, courts have shut out nonbiological parents entirely based on the absence of a genetic or legal relationship between the nonbiological parent and child. The law is certainly not settled, and the best course of action is usually to try to mediate an agreement rather than going to court and fighting over kids you have raised together. There's more about mediation in Chapter 16.

Is race ever an issue in custody or visitation decisions?

The U.S. Supreme Court has ruled it unconstitutional for a court to consider race when a noncustodial parent petitions for a change of custody. In that case, a white couple had divorced, and the mother had been awarded custody of their son. She remarried an African American man and moved to a predominantly African American neighborhood. The father filed a request for modification of custody based on the changed circumstances. A Florida court granted the modification, but the U.S. Supreme Court reversed, ruling that societal stigma, especially one based on race, cannot be the basis for a custody decision. (*Palmore v. Sidoti,* 466 U.S. 429 (1984)).

When a court awards physical custody to one parent and "visitation at reasonable times and places" to the other, who determines what's reasonable?

The parent with physical custody is generally in the driver's seat regarding what is reasonable. This need not be bad if the parents cooperate to see that the kids spend a maximum amount of time with each parent. Unfortunately, it all too often translates into very little visitation time with the noncustodial parent, and lots of bitter disputes over missed visits and inconvenience. To avoid such problems, many courts now prefer for the parties to work out a fairly detailed parenting agreement that sets the visitation schedule and outlines who has responsibility for decisions affecting the children.

The judge in my divorce case has mentioned a parenting agreement. What is that?

A parenting agreement is a detailed, written agreement between divorcing parents that describes how they will deal with visitation, holiday schedules, vacation, religion, education, and other issues related to their child. More and more, courts are encouraging, and even requiring, the use of parenting agreements during divorce proceedings. If couples discuss and agree upon how to deal with issues affecting their children—rather than having the judge make an independent ruling on those issues—they are more likely to stick to the terms of the agreement.

I have sole custody of my children. My ex-spouse, who lives in another state, has threatened to go to court in his state and get the custody order changed. Can he do that?

All states and the District of Columbia have enacted the Uniform Child Custody Jurisdiction Act (UCCJA), or the Uniform Child Custody Jurisdiction and Enforcement Act (UCCJEA). These laws determine which court may make a custody determination and which court must defer to an existing determination from another state. Having similar laws in all states helps standardize how custody decrees are treated. It also helps solve many problems created by parental kidnapping or disagreements over custody between parents living in different states.

In general, a state may make a custody decision about a child only if it meets one of these tests (in order of preference):

- The state is the child's home state. This means the child has lived in the state for the six previous months, or was living in the state but is absent because a parent took the child to another state. (A parent who wrongfully removed or retained a child in order to create a "home state" will be denied custody.)

- The child has significant connections in the state with people such as teachers, doctors, and grandparents. (A parent who wrongfully removed or retained a child in order to create "significant connections" will be denied custody.)
- The child is in the state and either has been abandoned or is in danger of being abused or neglected if sent back to the other state.
- No other state can meet one of the above three tests, or a state that can meet at least one test has declined to make a custody decision.

If a state cannot meet one of these tests, the courts of that state cannot make a custody award, even if the child is present in the state. If more than one state meets the above standards, the law specifies that only one state may make custody decisions. This means that once a state makes a custody award, other states must stay out of the dispute.

Can custody and visitation orders be changed?

After a final decree of divorce or other order establishing custody and visitation is filed with a court, parents may agree to modify the custody or visitation terms. This modified agreement (also called a "stipulated modification") may be made without court approval. If one parent later reneges on the agreement, however, the other person may not be able to enforce it unless the court has approved the modification. Thus, it is generally advisable to obtain a court's blessing before relying on such agreements. Courts usually approve modification agreements unless it appears that they are not in the best interests of the child.

If a parent wants to change an existing court order and the other parent won't agree to the change, the parent who wants the change must file a motion (a written request) asking the court that issued the order to modify it. Usually, courts will modify an existing order only if the parent asking for the change can show a "substantial change in circumstances." This requirement encourages stability and helps prevent the court from becoming overburdened with frequent modification requests. Here are some examples of a substantial change in circumstances:

- **Geographic move.** If a custodial parent makes a move that will seriously disrupt the stability of the child's life, the move may constitute a changed circumstance that justifies the court's modification of a custody or visitation order. Some courts switch custody from one parent to the other, although the increasingly common approach is to ask the parents to work out a plan under which both parents may continue to have significant contact with their children. If the parents can't reach an agreement, what the court will do depends on where you live. Courts in some states will permit the move unless the other parent can show that the child will be adversely affected. In other states, the court will carefully examine the best interests of the child—looking at factors such as switching schools and distance from relatives—and make a decision about which parent should have custody.

- **Change in lifestyle.** If substantial changes in a parent's lifestyle threaten or harm the child, the other parent can often succeed in changing custody or visitation rights. If, for example, a custodial parent begins working at night and leaving a nine-year-old child alone, the other parent may request a change in custody. Similarly, if a noncustodial parent begins drinking heavily or taking drugs, the custodial parent may file a request for modification of the visitation order (asking, for example, that visits occur only when the parent is sober, or in the presence of another adult). What constitutes a lifestyle sufficiently detrimental to warrant a change in custody or visitation rights varies tremendously depending on the state and the particular judge deciding the case.

I've heard that media… approach to solving disa… child custody and visitatio…

Yes, in most cases. Mediation … adversarial process where a neut… (a mediator) meets with disputing p…ons to help them settle a dispute. The mediator does not have power to impose a solution on the parties but assists them in creating an agreement of their own. (In a few states, however, the court may ask the mediator to make a recommendation if the parties cannot reach an agreement.)

There are several important reasons why mediation is superior to litigation for resolving custody and visitation disputes:

- Mediation usually does not involve lawyers or expert witnesses (or their astronomical fees).
- Mediation usually produces a settlement after five to ten hours of mediation over a week or two. (Child custody litigation can drag on for months or even years.)
- Mediation enhances communication between the spouses and makes it much more likely that they will be able to cooperate on child-raising issues after the divorce or separation. Experts who have studied the effects of divorce on children universally conclude that children suffer far less when divorcing or separating parents can cooperate.

How to Find a Family Law Mediator

Many states require mediation in custody and visitation disputes, and a number of others allow courts to order mediation. In these situations, the court will direct the parents to a mediator and will pay for the services. Parents can also find and pay the mediator themselves. With increasing frequency, family law attorneys are offering mediation services for child custody and other divorce-related disputes, as are a number of nonlawyer community mediators. Two good resources for finding a family law mediator in your area are a website at www.mediate.com, or a national mediation organization called The Association for Conflict Resolution (www.acrnet.org).

Things are so bitter between my ex and me that it's hard to see us sitting down together to work things out. How can mediation possibly work?

Mediators are very skilled at getting parents who are bitter enemies to cooperate for the sake of their children. The more parents can agree on the details of separate parenting, the better it will be for them and their children. And mediators are skilled at getting the parents to recognize this fact and move forward toward negotiating a sensible parenting agreement. If the parents initially cannot stand to be in the same room with each other, the mediator can meet with each parent separately and ferry messages back and forth until agreement on at least some issues is reached. At this point, the parties may be willing to meet face-to-face.

Custodial Interference

In most states, it's a crime to take a child from a parent with the intent to interfere with that parent's physical custody of the child (even if the taker also has custody rights). This crime is commonly referred to as "custodial interference." In most states, the parent deprived of custody may sue the taker for damages and get help from the police to have the child returned.

If a parent without physical custody (who may or may not have visitation rights) removes a child from—or refuses to return a child to—the parent with physical custody, it is considered kidnapping or child concealment in addition to custodial interference. Federal and state laws have been passed to prosecute and punish parents guilty of this type of kidnapping, which is a felony in over 40 states.

In many states, interfering with a parent's custody is a felony if the child is taken out of state. Many states, however, recognize good-cause defenses, including that the taker acted to prevent imminent bodily harm to the child or to the adult who took the child. In addition, some states let a parent take a child out of state if the parent is requesting custody in court and has notified the court or police of the child's location.

RESOURCE

For more information about child custody, see these Nolo books:

- *Nolo's Essential Guide to Child Custody & Support,* by Emily Doskow. Provides step-by-step guidance on child custody, from choosing a plan to enforcing (or changing) child support, and includes 50-state resources on custody and child support laws.
- *Building a Parenting Agreement That Works: Child Custody Agreements Step by Step,* by Mimi Lyster Zemmelman. Shows separating or divorcing parents how to create a win-win custody agreement.

ONLINE HELP

For legal information, referrals, and assistance on custody for lesbian and gay parents, see the website of the National Center for Lesbian Rights at www.nclrights.org.

Child Support

Children have more need of models than of critics.

—Joseph Joubert

Child support is an emotional subject. Parents who are supposed to receive it on behalf of their children often do not. Parents who are supposed to pay it often cannot, or choose not to for a variety of reasons that are not legally recognized. It is the children who suffer the most when child support levels are inadequate or obligations are not met. Therefore, the trend in all states is to increase child support levels and the ways child support obligations can be enforced.

How long must parents support their children?

Biological parents and adoptive parents must support a child until:

- the child reaches the age of majority (and sometimes longer if the child has special needs or is in college)
- the child is on active military duty
- the parents' rights and responsibilities are terminated (for example, when a child is adopted), or
- the child has been declared emancipated by a court. (Emancipation can occur when a minor has demonstrated freedom from parental control or support and an ability to be self-supporting.)

How are child support obligations affected by a divorce or separation?

When one parent is awarded sole or primary custody of a child (custodial parent), the other parent (noncustodial parent) typically is required to fulfill the child support obligation by making payments to the custodial parent. The custodial parent meets his or her support obligation through the custody itself. When parents are awarded joint physical custody in a divorce, the support obligation of each is often based on the ratio of each parent's income to their combined incomes, and the percentage of time the child spends with each parent.

Are fathers who never married the mother still required to pay child support?

The short answer to this question is yes. When a mother is not married, however, it's not always clear who the father is. An "acknowledged father" is any biological father of a child born to unmarried parents whose paternity has been established by either his own admission or the agreement of the parents. Acknowledged fathers are required to pay child support.

Additionally, a man may be presumed to be the father of a child if he welcomes the child into his home and openly holds the child out as his own. In some states, the presumption of paternity is considered conclusive, which means it cannot be disproved, even with contradictory blood tests.

The obligation to pay child support does not depend on whether a court ordered it. Most unmarried fathers encounter this principle when the mother seeks public assistance. Sooner or later the welfare department will ask the court to order the father to reimburse it, based on his support obligation and income during the period in question. Sometimes the government catches up with the father many years later, and the father is required to pay thousands of dollars in back support that he never knew he owed.

Calculating Child Support

Each state has guidelines for calculating child support, based primarily on the parents' incomes and the amount of time each parent spends with the children. These guidelines vary considerably from state to state. In addition, judges in some states have considerable leeway in setting the actual amount, as long as the general state guidelines are followed. But an increasing number of states impose very strict guidelines that leave the judges very little latitude.

In most states, the guidelines specify factors that a court must consider in determining who pays child support, and how much. These factors usually include:

- the needs of the child—including health insurance, education, day care, and special needs
- the income and needs of the custodial parent
- the paying parent's ability to pay, and
- the child's standard of living before divorce or separation.

To find your state's guidelines, check with your state child support enforcement agency; you can find yours on the website of the National Child Support Enforcement Association (www.ncsea.org). Most states also have child-support calculators, on their websites. You can also access child support calculators for each state on the AllLaw.com site at www.alllaw.com/calculators/Childsupport.

Do fathers have the same right to child support as mothers?

Yes. If you're a father with custody, you have the right to ask for child support. Both parents have a duty to support their children, and that duty doesn't discriminate between genders.

Is a stepparent obligated to support the children of the person to whom he or she is married?

No, unless the stepparent legally adopts the children.

How does the court determine how much child support I can afford to pay?

When evaluating your ability to pay child support, the court looks at your net income. This is your gross income from all sources—such as wages, investment income, rents from real property, or public benefits—minus any mandatory deductions. Mandatory deductions include income taxes, Social Security payments, and health care costs. In most states, courts don't consider other types of automatic deductions from your paycheck (such as wage attachments or credit union payments) or debt obligations (such as loan or credit card payments) when figuring net income. The law places a high priority on child support. Courts would rather see other debts go unpaid than have a child suffer from inadequate support. One exception is other child-support obligations. In some states, courts allow you to deduct the amount of child support you pay for other children from your gross income.

Some courts consider reasonable expenses you incur for the necessities of life—for example, rent, mortgage, food, clothing, and health care. But this usually does not include the cost of tuition, eating in restaurants, or entertainment. Again, the theory is that support of your children should come before these types of personal expenses. In a growing number of states, courts will not consider any personal expenses when determining your ability to pay support.

Can the court base its child-support order on what I am able to earn as opposed to what I'm actually earning?

In most states, the judge is authorized to examine a parent's ability to earn as well as what the parent is actually earning, and order higher child support if there is a discrepancy. Actual earnings are an important factor in determining a person's ability to earn but are not conclusive where there is evidence that a person could earn more.

For example, assume a parent with an obligation to pay child support leaves his current job and enrolls in medical or law school, takes a job with lower pay but good potential for higher pay in the future, or takes a lower-paying job that provides better job satisfaction. In each of these situations, a court may base the child-support award on the income from the original job (ability to earn) rather than on the new income level (ability to pay). The basis for this decision would be that the children's current needs take priority over the parent's career plans and desires.

What happens if a parent falls behind on child-support payments?

Each installment of court-ordered child support is due on the date set out in the order. When a person does not comply with the order, the overdue payments are called arrearages or arrears. Judges have become very strict about enforcing child-support orders and collecting arrearages. While the person with arrears can ask a judge to order lower future payments, the judge will usually insist that the arrearage be paid in full, either immediately or in installments. In fact, judges in most states are prohibited by law from retroactively modifying a child-support obligation.

> EXAMPLE: Joe has a child support obligation of $300 per month. Joe is laid off of his job, and six months pass before he finds another one with comparable pay. Although Joe could seek a temporary decrease on the grounds of diminished income, he lets the matter slide and fails to pay any support during the six-month period. Joe's ex-wife later brings Joe into court to collect the $1,800 arrearage. Joe cannot obtain a retroactive ruling excusing him from making the earlier payments.

In addition, back child support cannot be cancelled in a bankruptcy proceeding. This means that once it is owed, it will always be owed until the parent pays.

My ex-spouse is refusing to pay court-ordered child support. How can I see to it that the order is enforced?

Under the Uniform Interstate Family Support Act (UIFSA), your state's child support enforcement agency (or official) must help you collect the child support your ex-spouse owes, even if your ex has moved out of state. The U.S. Office of Child Support Enforcement has a helpful locator tool to help you find your local child support agency. Go to: www.acf.hhs.gov/programs/css and click on "Child Support Professionals."

These efforts might range from meeting with your ex and arranging a payment schedule to attaching his salary. If you live in a different state from your ex-spouse, the agency will help you get your state court to issue a support order (sometimes called a petition), which will be forwarded to an agency or court in the state where your ex lives for enforcement. Most of these services are free or low cost.

In recent years, the federal government has taken an aggressive approach to enforcing child support orders. The Child Support Recovery Act of 1992 makes it a federal crime for a parent to willfully refuse to make support payments to a parent living in another state. The support owed must be more than $5,000 and must have gone unpaid for more than a year for criminal sanctions to apply.

The federal government has also made it much easier to track a delinquent parent's assets with resources such as the Federal Parent Locator Services and provisions in the Personal Responsibility and Work Opportunity Reconciliation Act of 1996 (PRWORA). PRWORA requires employers to report all new hires to their state's child support enforcement agency. The agency then forwards this data to the National Directory of New Hires, a centralized registry that matches new employees with parents who owe child support, then quickly sets up wage-withholding orders for these delinquent parents. PRWORA also requires all states to enter into agreements with financial institutions—such as banks, savings and loan institutions, credit unions, insurance companies, and money market funds—to match the account records of parents who owe child support. Under this Financial Institution Data Match Program (FIDM), when a match is identified, the information is sent to the state within 48 hours, so the accounts can be seized. Other methods of child-support enforcement include withholding federal income tax refunds, denying a passport, and suspending or restricting a business, occupational, or driver's license. Many states have also enacted laws that revoke a delinquent parent's hunting, fishing, or boating license.

As a last resort, the court that has issued the child-support order can hold a delinquent ex-spouse in contempt and, in the absence of a reasonable explanation for the delinquency, impose a jail term. This contempt power is exercised sparingly in most states, primarily because most judges would rather keep the payer out of jail and in the workforce—earning money to pay child support.

I think our existing child support order is unfair. How can I change it?

You and your child's other parent may agree to modify the child support terms, but even an agreed-upon modification for child support must be approved by a judge to be legally enforceable.

If you and your ex can't agree on a change, you must ask the court to hold a hearing in which each of you can argue your own side of the proposed modification. As a general rule, the court will not modify an existing order unless the parent proposing the modification can show changed circumstances. This rule encourages stability and helps prevent the court from becoming overburdened with frequent modification requests.

Depending on the circumstances, a modification may be temporary or permanent. Examples of the types of changes that frequently support temporary modification orders are:

- a child's medical emergency
- the payer's temporary inability to pay (for instance, because of illness or an additional financial burden such as a medical emergency or involuntary job loss), or
- temporary economic or medical hardship on the part of the parent receiving support.

A permanent modification may be awarded under one of the following circumstances:

- either parent receives additional income from remarriage
- changes in the child-support laws
- job change of either parent
- cost of living increase
- disability of either parent, or
- changes in the needs of the child.

A permanent modification of a child support order will remain in effect until support is no longer required or the order is modified at a later time—again, because of changed circumstances.

Do I have to pay child support if my ex keeps me away from my kids?

Yes. Child support should not be confused with custody and visitation. Every parent has an obligation to support his or her children. With one narrow exception, no state allows a parent to withhold support because of disputes over visitation. The exception? If the custodial parent disappears for a lengthy period so that no visitation is possible, a few courts have ruled that the noncustodial parent's duty to pay child support may be considered temporarily suspended.

No matter what the circumstances, if you believe that your ex is interfering with your visitation rights, the appropriate remedy is to go back to court to have your rights enforced or modified, rather than to stop making support payments.

RESOURCE

For more information about child support, see *Nolo's Essential Guide to Child Custody & Support,* by Emily Doskow (Nolo). This book provides detailed advice on child support, including how to estimate support obligations and tax issues. The book includes 50-state resources on child support.

ONLINE HELP

The following sites are good resources regarding child support:

- **www.acf.hhs.gov/programs/css**
  Federal Office of Child Support Enforcement
  202-401-9383
- **www.ncsea.org**
  National Child Support Enforcement Association
  703-506-2880

Guardianship of Children

A guardianship is a legal arrangement in which an adult has the court-ordered authority and responsibility to care for a child (someone under 18 in most states) or an incapacitated adult. This section focuses on guardianships of children. Chapter 12 discusses conservatorships for adults.

A guardianship may be necessary if a child's parents die or if the child has been abandoned, is not receiving adequate care, or is being abused in some way.

What does a guardian do?

Typically, a guardian takes care of a child's personal needs, including shelter, education, and medical care. A guardian may also provide financial management for a child, though sometimes a second person (often called a "conservator" or "guardian of the estate") is appointed for this purpose.

What is the difference between a guardianship and an adoption?

An adoption permanently changes the relationship between the adults and child involved. The adopting adults legally become the child's parents. The biological parent (if living) gives up all parental rights and obligations to the child, including the responsibility to pay child support. If a biological parent dies without a will, the child who was adopted by someone else has no right to inherit.

If You Want to Avoid a Formal Guardianship

An adult who is taking care of a child may have strong reasons to avoid becoming a legal guardian—for example:

- The caretaker expects that the child's parents will not consent to a legal guardianship.
- Dynamics between family members are such that filing for a guardianship might set off a battle for legal custody. (This would be especially likely where a stepparent and one biological or legal parent care for a child.)
- The caretaker doesn't want his or her personal life scrutinized in court or by a court-appointed investigator.

Some adults try to slide by and raise children (often grandchildren or other relatives) without any legal court authorization. If you go this route, you could run into problems with institutions that want authority from a parent or court-appointed legal guardian. Some communities and institutions are, however, very accommodating of people who are bringing up someone else's children. California, for example, has created a form called a Caregiver's Authorization Affidavit, which gives a nonparent permission to enroll a child in school and make medical decisions on the child's behalf without going to court. Research the laws for your state, or talk to a knowledgeable family law attorney, to find out whether there are ways for you to care for a child short of becoming a legal guardian.

Are You Prepared to Be a Guardian?

An obvious but important question to ask yourself before you take any steps to establish a guardianship is whether you're truly prepared for the job.

- Do you want the ongoing responsibilities of a legal guardianship—including potential liability for the child's actions?
- If you're managing the child's finances, are you willing to keep careful records, provide a court with periodic accountings, and go to court when you need permission to handle certain financial matters?
- What kind of personal relationship do you have with the child? Do you want to act as the legal parent of this child for the duration of the guardianship?
- Will the guardianship adversely affect you or your family because of your own children, health situation, job, age, or other factors?
- Do you have the time and energy to raise a child?
- What is the financial situation? If the child will receive income from Social Security, public assistance programs, welfare, a parent, or the estate of a deceased parent, will this be enough to provide a decent level of support? If not, are you able and willing to spend your own money to raise the child?
- Do you anticipate problems with the child's relatives—including parents—who may suddenly reappear and contest the guardianship? (This is rare, but it can happen.)
- What kind of relationship do you have with the child's parents? Will they support the guardianship, or will they more likely be hostile, antagonistic, or interfering?

It's smart to consider your options carefully before initiating a guardianship proceeding. Honestly answering the questions above may help you with your decision.

Although a guardianship establishes a legal relationship between a child and adult, it does not sever the legal relationship between the biological parents and the child. For example, the biological parents are legally required to provide financial support for the child. And if a biological parent dies without a will, the child has certain automatic inheritance rights.

May I be appointed guardian if the child's parents object?

It depends on how a judge sees the situation. You'll need to start by filing guardianship papers in court. A court investigator will likely interview you, the child, and the child's parents and make a recommendation to the judge. The judge will then review the case and decide whether to appoint you. As a general rule, guardianships are not granted unless:

- the parents voluntarily consent
- the parents have abandoned the child, or
- a judge finds that it would be detrimental to the child for the parents to have custody.

If a child lives with me, do I need a guardianship?

You won't need a guardianship if the child is only staying with you for a few weeks or months. But anyone who anticipates caring for a child for a period of years will probably need a legal guardianship. Without this legal arrangement, you may have trouble registering the child in school, arranging for medical care, and obtaining benefits on the child's behalf. In addition, you'll have no right to keep the child if the parents want to end the arrangement—even if you think they're not capable of caring for the child properly.

When does a guardianship end?

A guardianship ordinarily lasts until the earliest of these events:

- the child reaches the age of majority (often 18)
- the child dies
- the child's assets are used up—if the guardianship was set up solely for the purpose of handling the child's finances, or
- a judge determines that a guardianship is no longer necessary.

Even if a guardianship remains in force, a guardian may step down from the role with permission from the court. In that case, a judge will appoint a replacement guardian.

Who financially supports a child under a guardianship?

Unless a court terminates the biological parents' rights (uncommon in most guardianship situations), the parents remain responsible for supporting their child. In practice, however, financial support often becomes the guardian's responsibility. The guardian may choose to pursue financial benefits, such as public assistance and Social Security, on the child's behalf.

Any funds the guardian receives for the child must be used for that child's benefit. Depending on the amount of money involved, the guardian may be required to file periodic reports with a court showing how much money was received for the child and how it was spent.

Is it true that parents may need a guardianship of their own child?

It's strange but true: Sometimes parents need to establish a particular type of guardianship—called a "guardianship of the estate"—to handle their own child's finances, even if the child lives with them. This situation usually arises when significant amounts of property (at least $5,000 in most states) are given directly to a child.

Understandably, institutions and lawyers are reluctant to turn assets over to parents when they were intended for a child. A guardianship of the estate relieves the institution from liability, and the parents are directly accountable to a court to show how funds are spent and invested.

> EXAMPLE: The Thompsons lived next door to an elderly widow, who was extremely fond of their small daughter. When the widow died, she left her house to little Suzy Thompson. The lawyer handling the widow's estate suggests that Suzy's parents go to court to establish a guardianship of their child's estate. The house is then transferred into the name of Suzy's guardianship estate, which her parents manage until she reaches adulthood.

While this system is effective in protecting children's assets from unscrupulous parents, setting up a formal guardianship of the estate involves time and money that well-meaning parents sometimes find burdensome. For this reason, all states have passed laws to make it easier to give money or property to children. These laws provide simple, inexpensive procedures by which gifts to minors (typically up to $10,000) can be managed by their parents without setting up a formal guardianship of the estate. The gift-giver must simply name, in a will or a trust document, someone to manage the gift until the child reaches adulthood. No court involvement is required. (For more information about leaving property to children, see Chapter 11.)

I have young children, and I'm worried about who will care for them if something happens to me. How can I name a guardian?

You can use your will to name a guardian for your children. The specifics are discussed in Chapter 11.

ONLINE HELP

The following sites are good resources for information regarding parenthood:

- **www.nolo.com** Nolo offers information about a wide variety of legal topics, including laws that affect parents and their children.
- **www.adoption.com** This site provides information about adoption agencies, international adoption, and many other adoption issues.
- **www.divorcenet.com** Divorcenet provides general information, including articles about mediation and child custody and links to state resources. The site also gives answers to frequently asked family law questions.
- **www.law.cornell.edu/wex/child_custody** The Legal Information Institute at Cornell Law School provides links to many of the family laws available on the Web, including laws governing adoption, child custody, and children's rights.

CHAPTER

16

Courts and Mediation

Ninety percent of our lawyers serve ten percent of our people. We are over-lawyered and under-represented.

—Jimmy Carter

The average citizen's ability to gain access to the American justice system is significantly determined by economic status. The wealthy can afford experienced lawyers—the legal system's gatekeepers—while many others are frozen out. Fortunately, there are some alternatives to all-out legal war, which can help to level the legal playing field. Mediation, expanded small claims courts, and family courts that make nonlawyers welcome are all part of the changing landscape. So, too, are public and private websites, many of which provide legal information as well as low-cost forms and the instructions necessary to complete routine legal tasks. Together, these changes give hope that all Americans will have improved access to our legal system in the years ahead.

Representing Yourself in Court

A man was arrested in New York for impersonating a lawyer over a lengthy period of time. Assistant Manhattan District Attorney Brian Rosner said one judge told him: *"I should have suspected he wasn't a lawyer. He was always so punctual and polite."*

With lawyers' fees often running in excess of $250 an hour, it may make sense to represent yourself in a small civil (noncriminal) lawsuit. The task may seem daunting, but if you have a good do-it-yourself resource to guide you and, if possible, someone who knows the ropes to coach you when you need help, you really can act as your own lawyer—safely and efficiently.

Before you decide to represent yourself, you may want to explore the possibility of getting free legal assistance. Below are several instances in which you may be able to get an attorney to represent you for free. If none of these matches your situation, or if you simply wish to represent yourself, you'll also want to explore whether your court offers help to the self-represented either in person or on the Internet.

Is it ever truly sensible to appear in court without a lawyer?

When it comes to small claims court, which is designed to be accessible to nonlawyers, the answer is yes. But sometimes, it also makes sense to represent yourself in a more formal court proceeding. Hiring a lawyer is rarely feasible, economically, for disputes about amounts less than $50,000 and often costs more than it's worth even for disputes in the $50,000 to $100,000 range. If you're fighting over these types of amounts, representing yourself may be your only reasonable option.

Free Legal Help

Here are some situations when you may qualify for free legal help from an attorney.

If you face criminal charges. If you've been charged with a crime and cannot afford to hire your own lawyer, you have a constitutional right to an attorney at the government's expense. At your request, an attorney, often from a public defender's office, can be appointed to represent you when you are formally charged in court with a criminal offense. See Chapter 17 for more on the subject.

If you've been injured. If you have been significantly injured and it appears that someone else is at least partially at fault, many lawyers will agree to represent you on a "contingency fee" basis. This means that you pay attorneys' fees only if the attorney recovers money for you, in which case the attorney takes an agreed-upon percentage of that total as fees. Even if a lawyer takes your case on a contingency-fee basis, however, you still have to pay costs, which can add up to thousands of dollars. Costs include court filing fees, court reporters' fees, expert witness fees, jury fees, and administrative fees, such as for maintaining files, making copies, and mail and delivery service charges. The good news is that if you win your case, the judge will usually order your adversary to pay you back for these costs. And many lawyers agree to pay your costs up front, then get reimbursed when the case settles or ends—so if you win, you won't have to pay these costs out of pocket.

If you qualify for legal aid. If you can't afford an attorney, you may qualify for free legal assistance. Legal aid lawyers are government-funded lawyers who represent people with low incomes in a variety of legal situations, including eviction defense, denial of unemployment compensation or other benefits, and consumer credit problems. If you think you might qualify, look online or in your telephone directory, or ask a local attorney, lawyer referral service, or elected representative for the nearest legal aid or legal services office.

If your claim involves an issue of social justice. If your dispute involves a civil rights or social justice issue, an attorney or nonprofit organization with an interest in that issue may represent you on a free or "pro bono" (for the public good) basis. For example, if your claim involves sexual harassment by an employer, abuse by a spouse or partner, discrimination in housing or employment, freedom of speech or religion, or environmental pollution, you may find an attorney or nonprofit organization willing to represent you pro bono. Help is much more likely to be forthcoming if your claim raises new and important issues of law. Contact a local bar association or a private organization that deals with the kind of problem you face, such as the ACLU, the NAACP Legal Defense Fund, the Natural Resources Defense Council, the National Women's Law Center, or the Lambda Legal Defense and Education Fund (gay and lesbian rights).

Are you saying that for small cases, the cost of hiring a lawyer is too high, given the amount at stake?

Because most lawyers charge hefty hourly fees, and any contested court case can rack up at least dozens of hours of attorney time, it is obvious that attorneys' fees can quickly dwarf what is at stake in many disputes. But the problem is really more fundamental: No matter how important the case, many people just don't have the money to pay a lawyer's hourly rate in the first place. Unless the case is for a personal injury or another type of dispute that lawyers will handle for a contingency fee (a percentage of the total recovery)—or the lawyer quotes a reasonable fixed fee to deal with the dispute from start to finish—the person will either have to go it alone or give up the lawsuit altogether.

If I decide to represent myself, how can I handle the technical rules and complex legal language?

Essentially, you have two choices. Get the dispute diverted to mediation (see "Mediation," below), where things are done in plain English and procedural rules are kept to a minimum, or take the time to learn how to navigate a formal court proceeding. Getting up to speed on court procedures will take some effort, but it is far from impossible. Fortunately, Nolo publishes an excellent primer, *Represent Yourself in Court,* by Paul Bergman and Sara J. Berman, which covers all the basics.

Court Information Online and at the Courthouse

Courts in all 50 states post legal information and useful forms and instructions on the Internet. Generally, small claims and family (divorce) courts provide the most helpful information, but many courts are striving to become more accessible to the general public and those representing themselves. Here's how to find court websites:

- Nolo's website, at www.nolo.com, provides links to federal, state, and local courts around the country. It also provides access to information about small claims court in many states.
- The National Center for State Courts, at www.ncsc.org, has a comprehensive directory of links to state, local, federal, and international courts.
- The federal Judiciary's website (www.uscourts.gov) lists federal court websites.

Increasingly, family courts are providing plain-English information and simplified forms to self-represented litigants for claims involving divorces, child custody or support, domestic violence, or other family law problem. Many courts have established comprehensive family law centers right at the courthouse, where trained staff help nonlawyers successfully achieve their goals.

Will I really be able to learn everything I need to know to represent myself competently?

Again, the basics of how to bring or defend a case aren't difficult. But trying to get on top of every nuance of procedure and strategy is tricky. That's why we suggest a two-pronged approach: Learn how to handle routine representation tasks yourself, while hiring a lawyer as a self-help law coach to provide advice on strategy and tactics as needed. In many situations, hiring a lawyer to coach your self-help efforts will cost only about 10% to 20% of what it would cost to hire the lawyer to do the entire job.

How do I decide whether to sue someone?

You need to answer three fundamental questions in order to decide whether it's worthwhile to go forward:

- Do I have a good legal case?
- Can I prove my case?
- Can I collect when I win?

If the answer to any of these questions is no, you probably won't want to sue.

How hard is it to collect a court judgment?

That depends on your opponent. Most reputable businesses and individuals will pay what they owe. But if your opponent tries to stiff you, collecting can be a costly, time-consuming struggle. Unfortunately, the court won't collect your money for you or even provide much help; it will be up to you to identify the assets you are legally entitled to take, and then collect what you're owed.

How to Find a Lawyer Coach

Ten years ago, trying to find a lawyer who would help guide you through the legal system was next to impossible. Today, given the surplus of personal service lawyers and a gradual change for the better in the profession's attitude toward self-helpers, it's much easier. Because law is an increasingly specialized field, however, you'll want to find someone who is knowledgeable about your type of problem. Try to get a referral from someone else who has recently worked with lawyers on a similar issue. For example, if you're opening a small business and want to find an appropriate lawyer to provide occasional guidance, you might talk to the owners of excellent local businesses to find out which lawyers they use. Once you have a few names, make and pay for a first appointment (lawyers will respect you far more if you don't beg for a free consultation). Come right out and ask whether the lawyer is prepared to help you help yourself. If you're persistent, you're likely to find a lawyer who meets your needs. For more, see "Finding and Working With a Lawyer," below.

If an individual is working or owns valuable property—such as land or investments—collection is less difficult; you can instruct your local law enforcement agency (usually the sheriff, marshal, or constable) to garnish the debtor's wages or attach nonexempt property. The same is true of a successful business, especially one that receives cash directly from customers; you can authorize your local sheriff or marshal to collect your judgment right out of the cash register. And in many states, if you are suing a contractor or other businessperson whose work requires a state license, you can apply to have the license suspended until the judgment is paid.

But if you can't identify a ready source of funds—for example, you're dealing with an unlicensed contractor of highly doubtful solvency—think twice before suing. A judgment will be of no value to you if the business or individual is insolvent, goes bankrupt, or disappears before you get your money.

How can I tell whether I have a good case?

Lawyers break each type of legal claim ("cause of action," in attorney-speak) into a short list of required elements: the facts you'll have to prove in order to win. As long as you know what the elements are for your type of lawsuit, it's usually fairly easy to determine whether your case is legally sound. For example, a lawsuit against a contractor for doing substandard construction would be for breach of contract (the contractor agreed either orally or in writing to do the job properly). The legal elements for this type of lawsuit are:

Contract formation. You must show that you have a legally binding contract with the contractor. If you have a written agreement, this element is easy to prove. Without a written contract, you will have to show that you had an enforceable oral (spoken) contract, or that an enforceable contract can be implied from the circumstances of your situation.

Performance. You must prove that you did what was required of you under the terms of the contract. Assuming you have made agreed-upon payments and otherwise met the terms of the agreement, you'll have no problems with this element.

Breach. You must show that the contractor failed to meet contractual obligations. This is usually the heart of the case—you'll need to prove, for example, that the contractor failed to do agreed-upon work or did work of poor quality.

Damages. You must show that you suffered an economic loss as a result of the contractor's breach of contract. Assuming the work must be redone or finished, this element is also easy to prove. You also must show evidence of the amount you lost.

The legal elements for other types of lawsuits are different. You can find outlines for the most common in *Represent Yourself in Court,* by Paul Bergman and Sara J. Berman (Nolo).

Is it difficult to prepare the paperwork to file a lawsuit?

Actually, it's often fairly easy and inexpensive—especially if you learn how to do basic legal research and prepare drafts of the papers, restricting your lawyer's role to that of checking your work. Initiating a lawsuit is straightforward in many states, where court clerks provide preprinted fill-in-the-blanks forms for many types of lawsuits. And many state and local courts make free forms available on their own websites.

Even in states where lawsuits are filed the old-fashioned way, using paragraphs of appropriate legal jargon on numbered legal paper, the actual wording you'll need to use is almost always available from lawyer "forms books" or online—see, for example, the forms available on the California Courts website at www.courts.ca.gov/forms.htm. These information sources, which are routinely used by lawyers, are available at most larger law libraries and are usually fairly easy for the nonlawyer to understand.

I've filed my lawsuit. What do I need to do next?

Before your case is scheduled for trial, you'll need to do a number of things, including meeting with your opponent and filing and responding to paperwork designed to reduce or narrow the issues to be tried. Court rules cover many of these tasks—for example, whether and when a settlement conference must take place, when papers must be filed, and how to place a case on the court's trial calendar. You can get these rules from the court clerk and often on the Web as well. Unfortunately, many clerks are not willing to provide help beyond handing out a copy of often confusing written rules.

In addition to procedural maneuverings, you'll probably have to deal with "discovery"—formally asking people and organizations to give you documents and information relating to your case, and responding to your opponent's requests for documents and information from you. This process is left largely up to you and the other parties to the lawsuit. For example, you might want to take the deposition (an oral statement given under oath) of the other party and one or more witnesses to find out what they are likely to say at trial. Additional types of discovery include interrogatories (written questions to the other party), a request to hand over documents, or a request that the other party admit certain facts (stipulations).

What are the advantages of taking a deposition?

Depositions—questioning the other party or a witness before trial—have several big advantages as compared to the other types of discovery mentioned above:

- You can learn a great deal about your adversary's case, so as to avoid surprise in the courtroom.
- You can offer a deposition transcript into evidence at trial if the deponent (the person you questioned) is unavailable to give live testimony. This rule explains why you might consider deposing a helpful witness who is seriously ill or planning to move out of the area.

- If a witness says something different at trial than at the deposition, you can read the inconsistent deposition testimony into the trial record to impeach (attack) the deponent's credibility.

EXAMPLE: You have sued your former employer for firing you because you missed work to serve on a jury in a lengthy trial. Before trial you take the deposition of your former supervisor, Paul Chepick. At the deposition, Chepick testified that your work performance had been satisfactory before you took off for jury duty. At trial, Chepick testifies that you were fired not because of your jury service but because of a number of work-related problems. Because Chepick's deposition testimony contradicts his trial testimony, you could read the deposition testimony into the record at trial to show that he changed his story—and call his honesty into question.

- As compared to conducting discovery by asking written questions (interrogatories), depositions allow more flexibility in questioning because you hear a deponent's answer before you ask the next question. For example, assume that a deponent unexpectedly refers to an important business meeting that you didn't know about. In a deposition, you can immediately follow up with questions about what took place during this meeting.
- You can take anyone's deposition. You can depose your adversary, an employee who works for your adversary, a bystander who witnessed a key event, an expert witness hired by your opponent—or even your opponent's attorney (but only on a very limited basis)! By contrast, you can send written questions (interrogatories) only to your opponent, not to witnesses.
- You hear testimony directly from an individual deponent. While your adversary's lawyer will probably attend the deposition and can consult with the deponent during recesses (breaks in the testimony), the deponent has to answer the questions. By contrast, attorneys often play a major role in preparing the answers to written interrogatories and usually help clients answer them in a way that provides you with as little information as possible.
- You can use a deposition to get and ask about documents (or other tangible items) using a notice of deposition (to depose your opponent) or a subpoena duces tecum (to depose a nonparty witness). In either case, you can list items you want the deponent to bring to the deposition.

Are there any downsides to taking a deposition?

Unfortunately, deposing an adversary or a witness who supports your adversary also has some disadvantages. Weigh these considerations very carefully before you decide to take a deposition:

- Depositions are the most expensive discovery tool. Even if you are representing yourself (and therefore not paying an attorney to take or attend a deposition), you must pay a court reporter to transcribe the testimony and prepare a written transcript. While costs vary somewhat by locality, it's not unusual for a court reporter to charge $5 or more per page of transcript. A day of deposition testimony can fill up more than 150 pages, meaning that a daylong deposition may cost you upwards of $750. If you win your case, however, the judge may order your adversary to pay your deposition costs.
- If you are involved in a lawsuit against a good-sized business or governmental entity and don't know which witnesses are most likely to have important information, you may end up paying dearly to depose a witness whose favorite phrase is, "I don't know." By contrast, written interrogatories give you access to "corporate knowledge." This means that when you send interrogatories to a business adversary, you are entitled to answers from any employee who knows them.
- Effective deposition questioning is a difficult skill, even for many attorneys. You have to pose questions carefully in order to be sure that you know how adverse witnesses will testify at trial. If your questions are vague or you forget to cover a topic, you won't be prepared for your opponent's evidence at trial or be able to show that a witness's story has changed (and therefore should not be believed).
- Your adversary's lawyer can be present at a deposition. The attorney may throw you off track by objecting to your questions. Also, an adversary's attorney can help witnesses "refresh their recollections" during recesses. Finally, seeing you in action will allow the attorney to estimate your own credibility and ability to represent your case in court. And by listening to your questions, the opposing attorney may learn as much about your case as you learn about your adversary's.
- If you depose an adverse witness who becomes unavailable for trial, your adversary will be able to offer the deposition transcript into evidence at trial.

When my case finally makes it to the courtroom, I'm afraid I won't know what to say, when to say it, or even where to stand. How can I learn what to do?

It's not as hard as you might think to learn how to conduct yourself in court. This is especially true if your trial is before a judge without a jury, because many judges make an effort to simplify jargon and procedure for self-represented parties. And there are several practical steps you can take to learn the ropes:

- Attend a few trials involving similar issues. You'll see that it won't be that difficult to present your story and evidence to a judge.
- Carefully read a self-help book such as Nolo's *Represent Yourself in Court,* by Paul Bergman and Sara J. Berman, which explains in great detail what you'll need to do. For example, you'll want to prepare and practice a brief but thorough opening statement to tell the judge what your case is about.
- Prepare a trial notebook that outlines each major aspect of your case and what you need to do and say at each point. For example, once you've taken the other side's deposition or asked written questions (interrogatories), you'll probably have a pretty good idea what the person will say at trial. You can use your trial notebook to prepare a carefully crafted outline of what you plan to ask in court. Similarly, because you will know before trial who else will testify for the other side, your trial notebook should contain a well-organized list of points you want to cover when you have a chance to question (cross-examine) the witnesses.

A Typical Trial

Most trials begin with each side making an opening statement—each party presents an overview of the case, including what that party expects to prove. The next stage is direct examination, during which the plaintiff (the person who filed the suit) gives testimony about what happened and supports it with witnesses' statements and other relevant evidence. After each of the plaintiff's witnesses testifies, the defendant gets a chance to cross-examine. In doing so, the defendant attempts to produce testimony favorable to the defense version of events and to cast doubt on the reliability or credibility of the plaintiff's witnesses. Finally, both sides get to make a closing argument explaining to the judge or jury why they should win.

What types of evidence win trials?

As mentioned above, in addition to having a legally sound case, you need to be able to prove it before a judge or jury. Technically, (for most types of cases) this means you have to prove each required legal element of your cause of action by a preponderance (more than 50%) of the evidence. Practically, it usually means focusing on one or two disputed elements of a case (for example, whether your remodeling contractor breached the contract by using substandard materials, doing poor work, or installing equipment not called for in the contract). Unfortunately, too many self-represented litigants try to rely primarily on their own oral rendition of events and overlook the need to back up their story with tangible evidence. Depending on the key issues that must be proved, you will want to present things like photos, contracts, cost estimates to redo the work, or government records. In addition, you'll want to question witnesses who either saw or heard what happened (overheard a boss demanding sex with a subordinate, for example) or are qualified to render an expert opinion on a key aspect of the case (such as a master tile layer's testimony that the installation of the tile floor in your kitchen was botched).

What about actually examining (presenting) witnesses? I'm more than a little intimidated by having to act like one of the lawyers on *The Good Wife* TV show.

And well you should be. It's not easy being an actor. But fortunately, appearing in a routine court proceeding isn't that difficult, as long as you know the basic rules. For instance, when you present the testimony of eyewitnesses or expert witnesses, you do so by asking a series of questions. First you need to show that your eyewitness has personal knowledge of the event in question, or that an expert witness is qualified to render an opinion on the issues in dispute. This means you must show that your eyewitness personally observed, heard, smelled, touched, or tasted whatever the witness is testifying to—for example, that your witness was on the spot and overheard the contractor you are suing talking to someone about the details of your garage job. Or, in the case of expert witnesses, that their opinion is based on a careful and accurate review of the facts of the case. Second, you must ask questions that allow witnesses to explain whatever they know without putting words in their mouth (called "leading the witness"). You can learn the basic techniques of how to question a witness and how to object to any improper questions your opponent asks by reading a good self-help book and watching a trial or two.

Do I have a right to have my case heard by a jury?

For some types of civil cases, such as those involving child support or custody, or a request for an injunction (to stop the city from cutting down a tree, for example), you are not entitled to a jury trial. And in some courts, the parties in all small civil cases must first try to resolve the case between themselves via mediation before initiating any type of trial. But in most civil cases, including those involving personal injury, breach of contract, professional malpractice, libel, or slander, you are entitled to a jury trial if you want one.

You may, however, want to think twice before you request a jury trial; it will be more complicated and harder to handle a case on your own before a jury than it would be to represent yourself before a judge. Not only can it be tricky to participate in the jury selection process, but formal procedural and evidentiary rules will almost surely be more rigorously enforced when a jury is involved. In short, most who go it alone are better off trying their case to a judge and avoiding this added level of complexity. But the other party has a say, too. If that person demands a jury, you will have to try your case before a panel of your peers.

RESOURCE

For more information about representing yourself in court, see these Nolo books:

- *Represent Yourself in Court: How to Prepare & Try a Winning Case,* by Paul Bergman and Sara J. Berman. We have mentioned this Nolo book a number of times because it is quite simply the only publication that competently explains all aspects of a civil court trial, including how to determine whether you have a good case, line up persuasive witnesses, present effective testimony in court, cross-examine opponents, and even pick a jury.
- *Nolo's Deposition Handbook,* by Paul Bergman and Albert Moore. Thoroughly covers the deposition process. Whether you are represented by a lawyer or representing yourself, this book explains how to prepare for your deposition, how to respond to questions, and how to cope with the tricks lawyers may use to influence your testimony. It also contains an excellent chapter on deposing expert witnesses.
- *Win Your Lawsuit: Sue in California Superior Court Without a Lawyer,* by Judge Roderic Duncan. Gives California readers all the necessary information, strategic advice, and forms to bring or defend a civil lawsuit worth up to $25,000.
- *The Lawsuit Survival Guide,* by Joseph Matthews. Designed to help people who are represented by lawyers understand what's going on in their case and work effectively with their lawyers. Available as an eBook at www.nolo.com.

Small Claims Court

Small claims court judges resolve disputes involving relatively modest amounts of money. The people or businesses involved present their cases to a judge or court commissioner under rules that encourage a minimum of legal and procedural formality. The judge then makes a decision (a judgment) reasonably promptly. Although procedural rules about filing and serving papers differ from state to state, the basic approach to preparing and presenting a small claims case is remarkably similar everywhere.

Small Claims Court Limits for the 50 States	
Alabama	$6,000
Alaska	$10,000
Arizona	$3,500
Arkansas	$5,000
California	$10,000 for individuals, except that a plaintiff may not file a claim over $2,500 more than twice a year. Other limits apply.
Colorado	$7,500
Connecticut	$5,000 (no limit for landlord-tenant cases involving security deposit claims)
Delaware	$15,000
District of Columbia	$5,000
Florida	$5,000
Georgia	$15,000 (no limit in eviction cases.)
Hawaii	$5,000 (no limit for landlord-tenant cases involving security deposit claims)
Idaho	$5,000
Illinois	$10,000
Indiana	$6,000 ($8,000 in Marion County)
Iowa	$5,000
Kansas	$4,000
Kentucky	$2,500
Louisiana	$5,000
Maine	$6,000
Maryland	$5,000
Massachusetts	$7,000 (no limit for property damage caused by a motor vehicle)
Michigan	$5,000
Minnesota	$10,000 ($4,000 for claims involving consumer credit transactions, $15,000 for claims involving money or personal property subject to criminal forfeiture)
Mississippi	$3,500

Small Claims Court Limits for the 50 States (continued)	
Missouri	$5,000
Montana	$7,000
Nebraska	$3,600
Nevada	$10,000
New Hampshire	$7,500
New Jersey	$3,000 ($5,000 for claims relating to security deposits)
New Mexico	$10,000
New York	$5,000; $3,000 (town and village justice courts)
North Carolina	$10,000
North Dakota	$15,000
Ohio	$3,000
Oklahoma	$7,500
Oregon	$10,000
Pennsylvania	$12,000
Rhode Island	$2,500
South Carolina	$7,500
South Dakota	$12,000
Tennessee	$25,000 (no limit in eviction suits or suits to recover personal property)
Texas	$10,000
Utah	$10,000
Vermont	$5,000
Virginia	$5,000
Washington	$5,000
West Virginia	$5,000
Wisconsin	$10,000 (no limit in eviction suits)
Wyoming	$6,000

How much can I sue for in small claims court?

The limit is usually between $3,000 and $15,000, depending on your state. For instance, the maximum is $15,000 in Delaware, and $5,000 in Michigan and Vermont. (See the chart above for your state's limit.)

Can every kind of case be resolved in small claims court?

No. Small claims courts primarily resolve small monetary disputes. In a few states, however, small claims courts may also rule on a limited range of other types of legal disputes, such as evictions or requests for the return of an item of property (restitution). You cannot use small claims court to file a divorce, guardianship, name change, or bankruptcy, or to ask for emergency relief (such as an injunction to stop someone from doing an illegal act).

When it comes to disputes involving money, you can usually file in small claims court based on any legal theory that would be allowed in any other court—for example, breach of contract, personal injury, intentional harm, or breach of warranty. A few states do, however, limit or prohibit small claims suits based on libel, slander, false arrest, and a few other legal theories.

Finally, suits against the federal government or a federal agency, or even against a federal employee for actions relating to the person's employment, cannot be brought in small claims court. Suits against the federal government normally must be filed in a federal district court or another federal court, such as tax court or the court of claims. Unfortunately, there are no federal small claims procedures available except in federal tax court.

Are there time limits for filing a small claims court case?

Yes. State-established rules, called statutes of limitations, dictate how long you may wait to file a lawsuit after the key event giving rise to the lawsuit occurs or, in some instances, is discovered. Statutes of limitations rules apply to all courts, including small claims.

You'll almost always have at least one year to sue (measured from the event or, sometimes, from its discovery). Often, you'll have much longer. But if you're planning to sue a state or local government agency, you'll usually need to file a formal claim with that agency within three to six months of the incident. Only after your initial complaint is denied are you eligible to file in small claims court. If some time has passed since the incident giving rise to your lawsuit—for example, after the breach of a written contract or a personal injury—you may need to do a little research to determine whether you can still file your claim. Check your state's legal code under the index heading "statute of limitations." (See the "Legal Research" appendix for information on how to do this in the library or online.)

Where should I file my small claims lawsuit?

Assuming the other party lives or does business in your state, you probably have to sue in the small claims court district closest to that person's residence or headquarters. In some instances, you also may be able to sue in the court district where a contract was signed or a personal injury (such as an auto accident) occurred. Check with your small claims clerk for detailed rules.

If a defendant has no contact with your state, you'll generally have to sue in the state where the defendant lives or does business. Because most major corporations operate in all states, it's easy to sue most of them almost anywhere. But small businesses typically only conduct business in one or a few states, which means you may have to bring the lawsuit where the defendant is located.

Will I get paid if I win the lawsuit?

Not necessarily. The court may decide in your favor, but it won't collect your money for you. So before you sue, always ask, "Can I collect if I win?" If not, think twice before suing.

Some people and businesses are judgment proof—that is, they have little money or assets and aren't likely to acquire more in the foreseeable future. In short, if they don't pay voluntarily, you may be out of luck. If the person you're suing has a steady job, it should be reasonably easy to collect by garnishing wages if you win. If not, try to identify another collection source, such as a bank account or real property, before going forward. For people who seem to have no job or assets, ask yourself whether they are likely to be more solvent in the future. Court judgments are good for ten to 20 years in many states and can usually be renewed for longer periods. Consider whether the person might inherit money, graduate from college, get a good job, or otherwise have an economic turnaround not too far down the road.

If I'm sued in small claims court but the other party is really at fault, can I countersue?

In some states, you can and must countersue if your claim is based on the same event or transaction that led to the lawsuit. If you don't, you risk losing the right to bring that claim. In other states, these counterclaims are not mandatory, and you can sue separately later. No matter what the technical rules, you'll want to countersue promptly.

If the amount you sue for is less than the small claims limit, your case will probably remain in that court. If, however, you want to sue for more, check with your small claims clerk for applicable rules. Often, you'll need to have the case transferred to a different court that has the power to decide cases involving larger amounts of money.

If You Want to Avoid Going to Court

If you are eager to recover what's owed to you but you want to avoid the trouble of bringing a lawsuit, you have a couple of options to consider. First, even if you've been rudely turned down in the past, ask for your money at least once more. This time, make your demand in the form of a straightforward letter that briefly reviews the key facts of the dispute and concludes with the statement that you'll file in small claims court in ten days unless payment is promptly received. Unlike an angry conversation, where the other party may assume you'll never follow up, a polite but direct demand letter is like tossing a cup of cold water in your opponent's face. It really gets the message across that you're serious about getting paid. Because many individuals and small business people have a strong aversion to appearing at a public trial (including the time and inconvenience it will take), making it clear you are prepared to file a lawsuit can be a surprisingly effective way to get the other party to talk settlement. If your letter does get your adversary to the bargaining table, be ready to agree to a reasonable compromise.

There are three good reasons to do so. First, studies show that those who win in small claims court rarely get everything they asked for. Second, by compromising, you save yourself the time and anxiety of preparing and presenting your case in court. And finally, if your case settles, you're more likely to get paid right away, which means that you avoid potential collection problems.

Many states offer, and a few require, community- or court-based mediation designed to help parties settle their small claims disputes. Mediation often works best where the parties have an interest in staying on good terms, as is generally the case with neighbors, family members, or small business people who have done business together for many years. In addition, many defendants are willing to reach a mediated settlement to avoid having an official court judgment appear on their record. For these and other reasons, resolving small disputes through mediation can be remarkably successful. For more information about mediation, see "Mediation," below.

What should I do to prepare my small claims case?

Whether you are a plaintiff (the person suing) or a defendant (the person being sued), the key to victory is not what you say but the evidence you bring with you to court to back up your story. After all, the judge has no idea who you are and whether your oral (spoken) testimony is reliable. And your opponent is likely to claim that your version is wrong.

It follows that your chances of winning will greatly increase if you carefully collect and present convincing evidence. Depending on the facts of your case, a few of the evidentiary tools you can use to convince the judge you are right include eyewitnesses, photographs, letters from experts, or written contracts.

What's the best way to present my case to a judge?

First, understand that the judge is busy and has heard dozens of stories like yours. To keep the judge's attention, get to the point fast by describing the event that gave rise to your claim. Immediately follow up by stating how much money you are requesting. To be able to do this efficiently, it's best to practice in advance. Here is an example of a good start: "Your Honor, my car was damaged on January 10, 2017, when the defendant ran a red light at Rose and Hyacinth Streets in the town of Saginaw and hit my front fender. I have a canceled check to show it cost me $1,927 to fix the fender."

After you have clearly stated the key event and the amount of your loss, double back and tell the judge what led up to the problem. For example, you might next explain that you were driving below the speed limit and had entered the intersection when the light was green, and when the defendant came barreling through the red light, you did your best to avoid her car. Then it would be time to present any eyewitnesses, police reports, or other evidence that backs up your version of events.

Will witnesses need to testify in person?

If possible, it's best to have key witnesses speak their piece in court. But if this isn't convenient, the rules of most small claims courts allow you to present a clearly written memo or letter. (Be sure to check your state's rules.) Have the witness start the statement by establishing who he or she is. ("My name is John Lomax. I've owned and managed Reo's Toyota Repair Service for the last 17 years.") In clear, unemotional language, the witness should explain what he or she observed or heard. ("I carefully checked Mary Wilson's engine and found that it has been rebuilt improperly, using worn-out parts.") Finally, the witness should try to anticipate any questions a reasonable person might ask and provide the answers. ("Although it can take a few days to get new parts for older engines, such as the one Mary Wilson owned, it is easy and common practice to do so.")

A Court Without Lawyers?

In a handful of states you must appear in small claims court on your own. In most states, however, you can be represented by a lawyer if you like. But even where it's allowed, hiring a lawyer is rarely cost-efficient. Most lawyers charge too much given the relatively modest amounts of money involved in small claims disputes. Happily, several studies show that people who represent themselves in small claims cases usually do just as well as those who have a lawyer.

If I lose my case in small claims court, can I appeal?

The answer depends on where you live. In some states, either party may appeal within a certain period of time, usually between ten and 30 days, and have a new trial in which a new judge hears the case from scratch. In other states, appeals are granted only if the small claims judge made a legal mistake. And some states have their own unique rules. In California, for example, a defendant who loses may appeal to the Superior Court within 30 days. A plaintiff who loses may not appeal at all but can make a motion to correct clerical errors or to correct a decision based on a legal mistake.

To find the appeals rules for your state, call your local small claims court clerk or refer to the appendix for information on how to get them in the library or online.

RESOURCE

For more information about small claims court, see: *Everybody's Guide to Small Claims Court,* by Ralph Warner (Nolo) (National and California versions). It explains how to evaluate your case, prepare for court, and convince a judge you're right. The book includes small claims court rules for all 50 states, including citations for relevant statutes, dollar limits, rules on service of process, jury trials, and more. (Much of this state-specific information is also available in the Small Claims Court section of www.nolo.com.) Nolo's small claims book also contains a useful section on trying to negotiate or mediate a compromise with the other party without going to court, and it explains the most useful courtroom techniques and tactics to convincingly present evidence, witnesses, and your own testimony.

Mediation

I'd rather jaw, jaw, jaw, than war, war, war.

—Winston Churchill

If you're involved in a legal dispute, you may be able to settle it without going to court. One way to do this is to work out a solution with the help of a mediator—a neutral third person. Unlike a judge or an arbitrator, a mediator will not take sides or make a decision but will help each party evaluate goals and options in order to come up with a solution that works for everyone. One exception to this rule is made for child-custody mediations in a few states (such as California), where a mediator has the power to recommend a solution to a judge if the parties cannot agree.

When you reach an agreement with an opposing party through mediation, you can make it legally binding by writing down your decisions in the form of an enforceable contract.

What kinds of cases can be mediated?

Most civil (noncriminal) disputes can be mediated, including those involving contracts, leases, small business ownership, employment, and divorce. For example, a divorcing couple might engage in mediation to work out a parenting agreement. Similarly, estranged business partners might choose mediation to work out an agreement to divide their business. Nonviolent criminal matters, such as claims of verbal or other personal harassment, can also be successfully mediated.

Finally, you may want to consider mediation if you get into a scrape with a neighbor, roommate, spouse, partner, or coworker. Mediation can be particularly useful when the participants have some kind of personal relationship, because it is designed to identify and resolve not just the immediate problem but also any tensions and unresolved issues that led up to it. For example, if one neighbor sues another for making outrageous amounts of noise, the court will usually deal with only that issue—and by declaring neighbor A the winner and neighbor B the loser, may worsen long-term tensions. In mediation, however, each neighbor will be invited to present all issues in dispute. It may turn out that overly loud neighbor B was being obnoxious in part because neighbor A's dog constantly tore up his lawn or A's son's pickup truck often blocked a shared driveway. In short, because mediation is designed to surface and solve all problems, it's a far better way to restore long-term peace to the neighborhood, home, or workplace.

How long does mediation take?

People who mediate through programs offered by small claims court are often able to settle their disputes in an hour or less. Slightly more complicated cases (such as consumer claims, small business disputes, or auto accident claims) are usually resolved after a half day or, at most, a full day of mediation. Cases with multiple parties often last longer: Add at least an hour of mediation time for each additional party. Major business disputes—those involving lots of money, complex contracts, or business dissolution—may last several days or more.

Private divorce mediation, where a couple aims to settle all the issues in their divorce —property division and alimony, as well

The Six Stages of Mediation

While mediation is a less formal process than going to court, it is more structured than many people imagine. A full-scale mediation typically involves at least six distinct stages, as discussed below. However, in some small claims, child custody, and other publicly funded mediation procedures, time constraints mean that some of these stages are combined.

1. Mediator's Opening Statement

After the disputants are seated at a table, the mediator introduces everyone, explains the goals and rules of the mediation, and encourages each side to work cooperatively toward a settlement.

2. Disputants' Opening Statements

Each party is invited to tell, in his or her own words, what the dispute is about, how he or she has been affected by it, and how it might be resolved. While one person is speaking, the other is asked not to interrupt.

3. Joint Discussion

The mediator may try to get the parties talking directly about what was said in the opening statements. This is the time to determine what issues need to be addressed.

4. Private Caucuses

Often considered the guts of mediation, the private caucus gives each party a chance to meet privately with the mediator (usually in a nearby room) to discuss the strengths and weaknesses of that party's position, and to propose new ideas for settlement. The mediator may caucus with each side as many times as seems necessary. In mediation procedures sponsored by small claims courts and other public agencies, where time is short, this step may be shortened or skipped, and the parties move on to joint negotiation. And some mediators don't use private caucuses at all, but keep the parties together for the entire negotiation.

5. Joint Negotiation

After caucuses, the mediator may bring the parties back together to negotiate face-to-face.

6. Closure

This is the end of the mediation. If an agreement has been reached, the mediator may put its main provisions in writing as the parties listen. The mediator may ask each side to sign the written summary of agreement or suggest they take it to lawyers for review. If the parties want to, they can write up and sign a legally binding contract. If no agreement was reached, the mediator will review whatever progress has been made and advise everyone of their options, such as meeting again later, going to arbitration, or going to court.

as child custody, visitation, and support—may require half a dozen or more mediation sessions spread over several weeks or months.

How is mediation different from arbitration?

A mediator normally has no authority to render a decision; it's up to the parties themselves—with the mediator's help—to work informally toward their own agreement. An arbitrator, on the other hand, conducts a contested hearing between the parties and then, acting like a judge, makes a legally binding decision. The arbitrator's decision-making power may, however, be limited based on a written agreement between the parties. For example, the parties may agree in advance that the arbitrator is limited to making an award of monetary damages of between $200,000 and $500,000. Arbitration has long been used to resolve commercial and labor disputes. An arbitration proceeding typically resembles a court hearing, with witnesses, evidence, and arguments.

Why should I consider having my case mediated?

If you've given up on negotiating a settlement of your dispute directly with the other party, mediation may be the most painless and efficient way to solve it. Compared to a lawsuit, mediation is swift, confidential, fair, and low cost. And because you must agree to any mediated resolution of your case, you won't be blindsided by an outrageously unfair judgment.

Mediation sessions are usually scheduled quickly, and most sessions last only a few hours or a day, depending on the type of case. In contrast, lawsuits often take many months, or even years, to resolve. Another advantage of mediation is confidentiality. With very few exceptions (for example, where a criminal act or child abuse is involved), what you say during mediation cannot legally be revealed outside the mediation proceedings or used later in a court of law.

Mediating instead of litigating will nearly always save you money. In many parts of the country, nonprofit community mediation centers or mediators employed by a small claims or other court handle relatively minor consumer, neighborhood, workplace, and similar disputes free or for a nominal charge. Private dispute resolution companies tackle more complex cases for a fraction of the cost of bringing a lawsuit. A half-day mediation of a personal injury claim, for example, may cost each side about $500 to $1,000. By comparison, a full-scale court battle could cost $50,000 or more, sometimes much more.

Finally, agreements reached through mediation are more likely to be carried out than those imposed by a judge. After a lawsuit, the losing party is almost always angry and often prone to look for ways to violate the letter or spirit of any judgment.

In contrast, a number of studies show that people who have freely arrived at their own solutions through mediation are significantly more likely to follow through.

How can I be sure mediation will produce a fair result?

In mediation, you and the opposing party will work to craft a solution to your own dispute. Unless you freely agree, there will be no final resolution. This means that you can bring your own sense of fairness into the process—you don't have to rely on a judge or arbitrator to make a decision that may not take all of your concerns into account. It also means that it's possible for both parties to feel that the outcome was fair, as opposed to a court process, which will always result in a winner and a loser.

Mediation also allows you to agree to things that would never be ordered in court, where a judge has only the power to order one person to pay money to the other. In mediation, by contrast, you and the other party can agree to nonmonetary solutions like a written apology, a timeline for doing something (for example, building a new fence), or a conditional solution like payment of money only if one party fails to take certain agreed-upon steps.

For all these reasons, and particularly because you won't have a solution forced on you, it's likely that a successful mediation will result in a solution you think is fair.

A piece of paper, blown by the wind into a law court, may in the end only be drawn out by two oxen.

—Chinese Proverb

How can I find a good mediator?

It depends on the type of dispute you're involved in. Many cities have community mediation centers that do an excellent job of handling most types of routine disputes (consumer problems, neighbor disputes, landlord–tenant fights). For more complicated disputes (business termination, personal injury, breach of contract) it is often better to turn to a private mediator or mediation center. Two good online sources of information are the American Arbitration Association, www.adr.org, and www.mediate.com. Private divorce mediations are usually handled by sole practitioners or small, local mediation groups. Get a list from the phone book or the Internet and check references carefully.

Are there some cases that should not be mediated?

All parties to a dispute must agree to mediate, so if one party refuses or isn't competent to participate, a dispute cannot be mediated. In addition, mediation may also not be the best choice in certain other types of cases, such as:

- One of the parties is attempting to set a legal precedent that interprets or defines the law—for example, to establish a new civil right. Legal precedents cannot be set in mediation because mediation agreements do not decide who is "right" or "wrong," and are usually not made public.
- A person believes the case will result in a huge verdict against a big company (or even a small company with a big bank account or plenty of insurance). Because of the tendency toward compromise in mediation, hitting a legal "jackpot" is more likely in a jury trial.
- One person feels intimidated or intellectually overwhelmed by the other, in which case it's hard to arrive at a true meeting of the minds. It's often possible, however, to remedy a power imbalance by arranging for the more vulnerable person to participate with an advisor—perhaps a lawyer.
- There is a history of domestic abuse between the parties. It may be impossible to reach a fair agreement when one party feels threatened or fearful.

If I choose mediation, will I still need a lawyer?

In most mediations, it's not necessary to have a lawyer participate directly. This is because the parties are trying to work together to solve their problem—not trying to convince a judge or arbitrator of their point of view—and because mediation rules are few and straightforward. If your case involves substantial property or legal rights, however, you may want to consult with a lawyer before the mediation to discuss the legal consequences of possible settlement terms. You may also want to condition any agreement you make on a lawyer's approval.

RESOURCE

For more information about mediation, see:

- *Mediate, Don't Litigate,* by Peter Lovenheim and Lisa Guerin (Nolo). Thoroughly explains the mediation process and shows you how to choose a mediator, prepare a case, and conduct yourself during a mediation. Available as an eBook only, at www.nolo.com.
- *Divorce Without Court: A Guide to Mediation & Collaborative Divorce,* by Katherine E. Stoner (Nolo). Provides divorcing couples with all the information they need to work with a neutral third party to resolve differences and find solutions, helping couples avoid court battles, save money, get through a divorce quickly, and minimize negative effects on children.
- *Building a Parenting Agreement That Works: Child Custody Agreements Step by Step,* by Mimi Lyster Zemmelman (Nolo). Provides a step-by-step method for overcoming obstacles and putting together a practical parenting agreement that everyone—especially the children—can live with.

- *When Push Comes to Shove: A Practical Guide to Mediating Disputes*, by Karl Slaikeu (Jossey-Bass). A how-to mediation guide for lawyers, managers, and human resource professionals.
- *Getting to Yes: Negotiating Agreement Without Giving In*, by Roger Fisher and William Ury (Penguin). A classic book on negotiating strategy.

Finding and Working With a Lawyer

Although it sometimes makes good economic sense to represent yourself in a lawsuit, there are circumstances in which you might want to hire a lawyer. If you don't have the time or inclination to learn all of the legal rules and procedures that you'll have to follow in court, your case has the potential to win you (or cost you) lots of money, or you simply feel like you're in over your head, hiring a lawyer can be a wise investment. The trick is to find a lawyer who is knowledgeable, professional, and fair—and to do your part to make sure your professional collaboration is productive. This section answers some questions about finding and working with a lawyer. And in case your legal relationship goes south, we also offer some information on handling problems with your lawyer.

While the focus here is on hiring and working with a lawyer in cases involving disputes with another party and going to court, the advice is useful to anyone hiring a lawyer—for example, to draft a complicated estate plan or handle paperwork involved with a real estate investment. Also, if your case involves criminal law, see Chapter 17 which discusses working with a lawyer in criminal cases.

How can I find a good lawyer?

Perhaps the best way to find a good lawyer is through referrals—recommendations from friends, family members, business associates, or local trade or bar associations. The goal is to find a lawyer who can provide the right kind of representation for you in a particular dispute. This means you might need to speak with several lawyers before finding one who is right for the job.

Many lawyers charge nothing for an initial meeting to discuss the possibility of representing a client. However, some lawyers require potential clients to pay a consultation fee—a fee for meeting with the lawyer to discuss the facts and law relating to the lawsuit and the possibility of working together. Generally, this fee should cover any time the lawyer spends reviewing documents, researching the law, and meeting with you. If you are unwilling or unable to pay a consultation fee, ask the lawyer to waive the fee. Even lawyers who usually charge a consultation fee will probably meet with you for free if they believe you have a strong case.

Where can I get referrals to an appropriate lawyer?

Lawyer referrals can come from many sources.

Other lawyers. Lawyers frequently refer cases to one another. Any lawyer probably knows, or knows some other lawyer who knows, a lawyer who specializes in the area of law that covers your case.

Business associates and trade organizations. If a lawsuit arises out of a business dispute, people in the same or other businesses might have been involved in litigation of their own. If so, they may be able to refer you to lawyers they used and liked, or warn about lawyers with whom they had bad experiences. Trade organizations or local groups that represent the interests of business owners, such as your state or local chamber of commerce, may also have lawyers to recommend.

Friends and acquaintances. As an initial referral device, it can be very useful to canvass friends and acquaintances to get referrals to lawyers whom they found helpful. However, a personal recommendation is never enough. A lawyer who does well for one client, or has the time and energy to devote to one case, won't necessarily do as well on another case.

Lawyer directories. There are many online lawyer directories that can help you find an attorney, including Nolo's Lawyer Directory at www.nolo.com/lawyers, which provides detailed information on the lawyers who participate, organized by location and area of expertise, such as landlord-tenant. Two other useful online resources are Lawyers.com and Martindale.com. You can search on these sites by practice area and location, and find detailed information, including ratings, on individual lawyers.

Bar association referral service. Many county and city bar associations offer lawyer referral services for the public. You can contact these services by calling the local bar association and asking for the lawyer referral line, or, increasingly, through the Internet. Once you describe the type of case for which you're seeking a lawyer, the service provides the names of local lawyers who specialize in that area of the law. However, most bar associations do not screen lawyers for competency or experience, so a referral is *not* the same as a recommendation.

Government agencies. Certain state and federal government agencies are responsible for enforcing laws that protect the public. For example, the Equal Employment Opportunity Commission (EEOC) enforces the laws prohibiting discrimination in the workplace, and the Securities and Exchange Commission (SEC) acts to prevent investors from being defrauded. In some cases, these agencies will get directly involved in a lawsuit, particularly if the lawsuit addresses important and new legal issues in the field. Even if they don't take the case, a few government agencies will refer you to local lawyers who handle similar lawsuits. As with referrals from bar associations, however, these referrals may not be screened.

Once I have some referrals, what should I do next?

The first step when you're shopping for a lawyer is to call the lawyers who have been referred by others. Often, a member of the lawyer's staff will ask you questions about the case and ask who referred you. If the lawyer is available and interested in the case, you can arrange a meeting at the lawyer's office.

During this meeting, you can ask about the lawyer's litigation experience, find out the lawyer's initial view of the case, discuss fee arrangements and legal strategy, and check out the lawyer's communication skills. All of these factors will help you decide whether to hire this lawyer. Of course, the lawyer will also use this meeting to decide whether to take your case. The lawyer will be thinking about the case's strengths and weaknesses, how lucrative the case might be, how much work the case would require, and whether the two of you are likely to get along during the litigation.

Do lawyers specialize in particular areas of law?

Yes. Like doctors, most lawyers specialize. Some handle divorces, some give tax advice, some work on corporate mergers, some write wills and contracts, some do criminal defense. Some do a little of this and a little of that. But unless a lawyer has at least some experience in the legal area involved in your case, you'll probably want to keep looking.

The facts in every lawsuit are different. At the same time, every lawsuit has many procedural similarities. This means that it is neither practical nor necessary to look for a lawyer who has experience handling lawsuits that are "exactly" like your case. But the lawyer should have experience in that area of law. For example, if a lawsuit involves the breakup of a partnership that ran a florist business, you don't need to find a lawyer who has previously handled cases dealing with florists or flowers—but you will definitely want a lawyer with experience litigating business partnership disputes.

How You Can Make a First Meeting Successful

Before your first meeting with a lawyer, gather your thoughts and your paperwork. Think about all the important incidents that led to the dispute. It is a good idea to write down these events, either in timeline form or simply as a description—as if you were telling the story in a letter. If you do make a written summary, bring it with you to the meeting with the lawyer. Also bring the names and addresses of witnesses—anyone who might have information about the dispute. And bring any documents—contracts, letters, business records, plans, or photographs, for example—that relate to the case.

The lawyer I want to hire works in a law firm. Will other people in the firm also work on my case?

Probably. The individual lawyer who is responsible for all major decisions in the lawsuit—and who actually handles major legal maneuvers and trial if the case gets that far—is known as the lead attorney. But in law offices large and small, a certain amount of work on any lawsuit is done by people other than this primary lawyer. Other lawyers in the office (often called associates), paralegals (trained legal assistants similar to nurses in a doctor's office), and legal secretaries all will perform tasks during the course of litigation.

This division of labor is due in part to erratic demands on lawyers' time. Also, much legal work is routine and therefore can be done equally well by legal workers with less training (and lower salaries). It is a division of labor that can help or hurt a client. You benefit if work gets done more quickly, efficiently, and at a lower cost by others in the office. This might be the case if the lead attorney would not be able to get to the work right away. If you are paying by the hour, it can be to your financial advantage to have routine work done by people with a lower hourly rate. On the other hand, your case might be harmed if important work is left to members of the office with less training or experience.

You should ask who will work on which parts of the lawsuit. Of course, a lawyer does not know in advance exactly who will do every piece of work. But the lawyer can at least describe how busy he or she is likely to be over the next six months to a year, and therefore how much attention the lawyer can devote to the case. For example, if the lawyer is to begin a big trial within the next few months, the lawyer will have very little time or energy for any other cases during that time.

Also, you should discuss which parts of the litigation the lawyer intends to handle personally, such as the trial, depositions of the opposing parties and key witnesses, and preparing you for your own deposition.

What should I ask potential lawyers about fees and costs?

When choosing a lawyer, one of the most important considerations is the amount of the lawyer's fee and how it will be calculated. You should discuss fee arrangements at the outset, before deciding whether to hire a lawyer. If the lawyer will charge by the hour, you should have an open and honest discussion about how much you can or are willing to pay for the entire litigation. A lawsuit can be conducted in quite different ways—the more aggressively it is waged, the more you'll pay in fees.

You should also ask the lawyer for some general idea—though it might be quite speculative this early in the process—of how much you might receive from, or have to pay to, the other side at the conclusion of the lawsuit. Once you've discussed these figures, the lawyer can conduct the lawsuit so that attorneys' fees remain in balance with your potential gains or losses. If fees get too high, you will both know that it's time to consider a settlement rather than to continue headlong with the lawsuit.

How much do lawyers charge per hour?

Lawyers charge in several different ways, some of which are covered in the questions that follow. The most common form of lawyer compensation is the hourly rate. Rates range from $100 to $400 per hour—or more. As with most other services, rates tend to be higher in major urban areas. The hourly rate charged for work by less-experienced lawyers in the same office is usually substantially lower than rates charged by more senior attorneys or partners. If the lawyer's office uses paralegals and charges separately for their time, their hourly rate will probably be in the $50 to $150 per hour range. Most lawyers keep painfully close track of, and charge for, every minute they spend on a case. Lawyers usually mark their work time in tenth-of-an-hour increments (six-minute chunks). So, if they spend even one minute on a case—a quick phone call, reviewing and signing a letter—they bill you for a tenth of an hour.

What is a retainer?

A lawyer who will be paid an hourly fee may ask you to pay a lump-sum deposit at the beginning of the case to guarantee payment for the lawyer's initial work. Once this "down payment," known as a retainer, is received, the lawyer deposits it in a bank trust account. The lawyer withdraws fees from the retainer as the lawyer works on the case and bills the client for the time. Lawsuit costs—such as copying or messenger fees—may also be charged against the retainer.

What can I do initially to control hourly fees?

Because paying by the hour can become so expensive so quickly, you might want to discuss money-saving measures with the lawyer at the very beginning of the case. Such measures might include:

- **Discounted rate.** Some lawyers will agree to reduce the hourly rate they charge if they work more than a certain number of hours on a case in any one month. For example, a lawyer might charge $150 per hour for the first 20 hours of work on the case in a month, but then only $100 for every additional hour in that month.
- **Cap on total fee.** By the time most disputes get to the lawsuit stage, both sides have a pretty good idea of how much money is at stake. Based on how much you stand to gain or lose, you and your lawyer might be able to gauge how much (in lawyers' fees) it is worth spending to win, or to protect against losing. For example, if you are suing to recover $50,000 in damages, you might want the lawyer to agree to try to settle the lawsuit once legal fees reach

$20,000 or so. Otherwise, legal fees might eat up most of your potential winnings. You should discuss this kind of balancing—legal fees versus the total amount at stake in the lawsuit—at the start of the case. If possible, you and your lawyer should agree on a maximum fee amount. When legal fees near that figure, the lawyer can push to settle the case—even if the settlement is not as good as you might have hoped.

- **Prior approval of legal maneuvers.** You might be able to control some hourly legal fees by making sure the lawyer discusses major legal procedures with you before beginning work on them. A conscientious, client-friendly lawyer will do this anyway—but it doesn't hurt to raise the issue at the outset.
- **Careful billing review.** If you are paying a lawyer by the hour, you must keep abreast of the lawyer's work. Most lawyers' offices send an itemized bill every month. The bill includes, by date, a brief description of the work a lawyer or paralegal has done that month on the case and how long (in tenths of hours) the work took. Make sure there have been no major, time-consuming legal maneuvers that you did not previously hear about from your lawyer. Also, if certain aspects of the case are running up a lot of attorneys' fees, you might want to raise the possibility of cutting down in that area of the litigation. Finally, if the total lawyers' fees will soon become unaffordable or will exceed what you stand to win in the case, you must discuss the possibility of settling the case quickly, rather than continuing with expensive litigation.

What is a contingency fee?

In certain kinds of cases, lawyers charge what is called a contingency fee. Instead of billing by the hour, the lawyer waits until the case is over, then takes a certain percentage of the amount won. If you win nothing, the lawyer gets no fee. In this way, the lawyer shares your risk of losing or of winning less than expected. A contingency fee also rewards the lawyer for helping to win a higher amount—the more the lawyer wins for you, the more the lawyer gets. This method of payment was developed to permit lawyers to aggressively represent those people who want to sue for damages but don't have the money to pay a lawyer as the case goes along.

Contingency fees are most often used in personal injury and medical malpractice cases. The person who is suing (the plaintiff) arranges to pay based on the amount of money recovered, while the person being sued (the defendant) pays a lawyer by the hour. You may also be able to use a contingency fee if you are suing a business or organization for potentially high compensation—in cases involving employment discrimination, harassment or wrongful termination, patent or trademark infringement, personal or business fraud, or unfair competition.

A Lawyer's Time Is Your Money

If your lawyer charges by the hour, the meter is running whenever you have a conversation. Before you pick up the phone or make an appointment, think about whether you really need to talk to your lawyer. A secretary might be able to handle scheduling issues, make sure you get copies of important documents, and take care of other basic requests.

If you have questions for your attorney, write them down before you call or visit. This way, you can be sure to get all your questions answered at once and avoid getting charged for a second or third conversation. If you have information you need to share with your lawyer—thoughts about potential witnesses, answers to discovery requests, or comments on a pleading, for example—consider writing them down in a letter. Finally, don't use your lawyer—especially not a lawyer you are paying by the hour—as a shoulder to cry on or an emotional sounding board. Lawyers aren't trained as therapists or counselors—and will charge you for their time if you ask them to act like one.

How much do lawyers charge as a contingency fee?

The standard contingency fee in personal injury cases is 33% of the amount of compensation the plaintiff obtains in a settlement. Sometimes, the fee rises to 40% at a point around 60 to 90 days before the trial date. Fees rise whether or not the trial actually takes place. The reason for this increase is that a lawyer's work increases tremendously once the case nears trial. Contingency-fee rates in other cases are similar, though they can range from 25% to 50% depending on the amount of work a lawyer must do, the potential for a large fee, and the risk of getting no fee at all.

Although one-third is the standard contingency fee, some lawyers will consider either a lower rate or a mixture of rates, depending on the case. You might successfully negotiate with a lawyer for a lower rate, perhaps 20% to 25% of any settlement before the case is set for trial, if:

- it seems virtually certain that you will recover damages—the only question is how much the award will be
- you are likely to receive a large award, and
- the attorney will not have to do a lot of complicated or time-consuming legal work.

In cases involving a large potential recovery, you might try to negotiate a sliding scale fee schedule. In these arrangements, the lawyer's rate goes down as the compensation goes up. For example, a lawyer might agree to a sliding fee scale of 33% for recovery of up to $100,000 and 25% for all amounts over $100,000. Or a lawyer might agree to a more graduated scale, with 33% up to $100,000, 25% for $100,000 to $250,000, and 15% for all amounts above $250,000. The better your case, the more willing a lawyer will be to negotiate this type of arrangement.

Should I tell my lawyer things that might hurt my case?

Yes. Under a rule called the attorney-client privilege, a lawyer is under the strictest legal instructions never to reveal anything a client tells the lawyer. The protection provided by this privilege extends to your statements to any member of the lawyer's staff, or to anyone hired by the lawyer to work on the case.

Because the attorney-client privilege is so broad, you should tell your lawyer all negative and potentially damaging information as well as those facts that might help your case. A lawyer who knows about potential problems can develop legal tactics to counter or explain them—that is part of a lawyer's job. It is the things you *don't* tell your lawyer that often cause the most trouble. If the lawyer is caught by surprise by a damaging piece of information, it might be too late for damage control.

How can I help my lawyer do a good job?

There are many things a good lawyer should do to keep your relationship on the right track, such as informing you of important developments in the case, including you in the decision-making process, and preparing you for important lawsuit events, like testifying in court or answering questions in a deposition.

There are also some things you can do to help your lawyer advocate more effectively on your behalf. Following these tips will save you time and money—and may lead to a more successful result in your lawsuit.

- **Keep your lawyer informed.** As soon as you hire a lawyer, tell the lawyer everything that might pertain to the dispute. Hand over any documents or other items that might be relevant. If you aren't sure whether a particular fact or document is important, err on the side of full disclosure. Lawyers are trained to sift through information and determine what is useful and what is not. Your lawyer might be able to use a fact or document you thought was insignificant as the basis for a creative legal argument. And if the information might harm your case, the lawyer will have plenty of time to prepare defensive maneuvers.
- **Carefully prepare summaries, timelines, and other materials.** At the beginning of a lawsuit, your lawyer may ask you to write down important facts or a summary of events leading up to the lawsuit. Lawyers request this information in different forms—some will ask for a timeline, others

for a detailed written summary, and others might simply request a few notes or ask you to tell them all the facts in person. No matter what your lawyer requests, make sure that what you write or say is accurate. Your lawyer will base your claims and defenses on this information.

- **Search thoroughly for documents and information.** During the course of a lawsuit, your lawyer may ask you for a particular document or certain facts relating to an important incident. Remember, you have much easier access to information about your lawsuit than the lawyer does. Try to answer these requests promptly.
- **Promptly respond to your lawyer's requests.** During a lawsuit, lawyers often have to work under very tight deadlines. The more time you give your lawyer to digest the material you provide, the better job your lawyer can do using that material to prepare important legal papers. If you aren't able to respond quickly, let your lawyer know as soon as possible. Your lawyer might be able to get an extension of time from your opponent or the court, or rearrange other matters to accommodate the delay.
- **Keep your lawyer apprised of your schedule.** There are certain events in a lawsuit in which you must participate. Often, these events are scheduled weeks or months in advance. Most of these events can be postponed or moved up to accommodate your schedule, if the lawyer has enough advance warning that you won't be available. But be prepared to change your plans if you must—a judge might insist on holding important events (including your trial) on a particular date, regardless of your availability.

May your life be filled with lawyers.

—Mexican Curse

I've lost confidence in my lawyer. Can I fire him?

You have the right to end a relationship with a lawyer at any time. But if the lawyer you don't like is representing you on a contingency-fee basis (for a percentage of any recovery), it is often better not to part ways unless the lawyer's services really are substandard and you have a better lawyer lined up or feel you can handle the case yourself. That's because unless lots of money is involved, it can often be hard to find a second lawyer who will agree to pick up your case in the middle. Changing lawyers under a contingency-fee arrangement usually means any fee from the recovery you eventually get will have to be split between the two lawyers—something the second lawyer may not want to agree to, especially if that lawyer will have to clean up after the first.

I fired my lawyer, but I need my file. How do I get it?

Ask for it, or sign an authorization allowing your new attorney to get it. Even if you have a fee dispute with your former lawyer or you simply have not paid your bill, you are entitled to your file. If you have decided to represent yourself, demand that the lawyer turn your file over to you. If the lawyer refuses, contact your state's bar association for help.

I'm pretty sure my lawyer screwed up my case. Can I sue for malpractice?

Yes. But unfortunately, it is very hard to win a malpractice case. Malpractice means that the lawyer failed to use the ordinary skill and care that would be used by other lawyers in handling a similar problem or case under similar circumstances.

To win a malpractice case against an attorney, you must prove four basic things:

- duty—that the attorney owed you a duty to act properly
- breach—that the attorney breached the duty, was negligent, made a mistake, or did not act as promised
- causation—that this conduct caused you harm, and
- damages—that you suffered financial losses as a result.

Causation may be your biggest hurdle. To win a malpractice case, you usually must prove not only that your lawyer made a mistake but that you would have won the underlying case if the lawyer hadn't mishandled it. Then, you will have to show that if you had won the underlying case, you would have been able to collect from the defendant. For example, let's say you were hit by a car when you were walking across the street, and you hired a lawyer who didn't file the lawsuit on time, with the result that your claim was legally dead. You sue for malpractice and can easily prove the lawyer's negligence and the driver's liability. But to win the malpractice case against your lawyer, you'd also have to show that the driver had the ability to pay your claim. If you can't show that the driver had the assets to pay the judgment, you won't win your malpractice case, even though the lawyer clearly blew it and the driver was clearly at fault.

It can be tough to find a lawyer to represent you in a legal malpractice case, especially if you want to pay on a contingency-fee basis (that is, the lawyer would get a share of whatever you win). Because these cases can be difficult and time-consuming, lawyers are generally reluctant to accept any but the strongest cases, unless quite a bit of money is involved.

My lawyer seems to have stopped working on my case. Is this malpractice?

The longer your attorney ignores you and your case, the more likely it is to amount to malpractice. You should act quickly to see that your case is properly handled, and get another lawyer if necessary. Writing or faxing a letter expressing your concerns and asking for a meeting is a good first step.

Big Bills

If you receive an unexpectedly large bill, your lawyer may have overcharged you. In this situation, you have six options:

- You can pay the entire bill and vow not to go near that attorney again.
- You can pay the part of the bill you think is reasonable, with a letter explaining why you are refusing to pay the rest.
- You can refuse to pay anything until the lawyer agrees to accept less as full payment.
- In most states and situations, you can request fee arbitration from a state or local bar association, usually before a panel made up of local lawyers and perhaps one or two nonlawyers. Arbitration is a process where a supposedly neutral decision maker resolves your fee dispute. But when it comes to disputes over legal fees, you will normally want to follow this approach only if it is "nonbinding," meaning that you are free to reject the arbitrator's decision. That's because whenever an arbitration is conducted by a panel dominated by lawyers, you risk getting a biased result.
- You can pay the bill and file a complaint with your state attorney disciplinary agency.
- You can pay the bill and sue your attorney for a refund.

While weighing these options, keep in mind that a lawyer who has not been paid has far more motive to settle for a reasonable amount than does a lawyer who has already received half of your fee. So, even if you believe your attorney is entitled to part of the big bill, it often makes sense to try to arrive at a mutually acceptable compromise before you pull out your checkbook.

My lawyer originally said my case was worth six figures but now suggests that I settle for peanuts. Can I sue the lawyer for the difference?

No. It's possible that newly discovered facts made your case worth less than first thought. Or, your lawyer may have initially given you an optimistic estimate of the value of your case to get your business. In either case, this does not amount to malpractice. To find out, get your file from your lawyer and get a second opinion as to the value of your case. If another reputable lawyer believes you are being advised to settle for too little, consider changing lawyers.

Can I sue my lawyer for settling my case without my authorization?

Yes, but you would have to prove that your lawyer settled the case for less than it was worth.

I'm worried that my lawyer may have misused money I paid as a retainer. What should I do?

If you seriously suspect your lawyer has misused or misappropriated money held for you in trust, complain to your state's attorney regulatory agency right away. Although regulation of lawyers is lax in most states, complaints about stealing clients' money are almost always taken seriously, so you should get a prompt response.

RESOURCE

For more information about finding and working with a lawyer, see *The Lawsuit Survival Guide: A Client's Companion to Litigation,* by Joseph Matthews (Nolo). It is a step-by-step guide for people who are involved in a lawsuit and can help you find a good lawyer, work successfully with your lawyer, and avoid problems right from the start. Available as a downloadable eBook only at www.nolo.com.

ONLINE HELP

The following sites are good resources for courts and mediation:

- **www.nolo.com** Nolo's website offers self-help information about a wide variety of legal topics, including representing yourself in court, small claims court, mediation, and how to handle problems with your lawyer. It also provides links to federal, state, local, and small claims courts around the country, and includes a lawyer directory.
- **www.ncsc.org** The National Center for State Courts' website provides links to state and local court websites. These sites often contain helpful legal information, court forms, and instructions.
- **www.uscourts.gov** The federal judiciary's website provides links to federal court websites.

My Lawyer Won't Call Me Back!

It isn't malpractice if your lawyer fails to return phone calls, but it may be a sign of trouble. Try to find out why your lawyer isn't calling you back. (The lawyer may be busy, rude, sick, or procrastinating.) As you do this, examine the possibility that your lawyer may be avoiding you for a good reason—you may be too demanding. A good way to deal with this situation is to write or fax the lawyer a polite but straightforward letter explaining your difficulty in communicating and asking for a phone call or meeting to reestablish or restore your relationship. If your lawyer really has abandoned you, contact your state's bar association to find out what you can do.

CHAPTER

17

Criminal Law and Procedure

It is a less evil that some criminals should escape than that the government should play an ignoble part.

—Oliver Wendell Holmes

The word "criminal" reflects our society's belief that certain acts are unacceptable and that people who commit these acts should be punished. Because going to jail is such a serious consequence, however, our state and federal constitutions put strict limits on how far a prosecutor can go to obtain a conviction. As a result—and perhaps as a price—the court system sometimes appears to protect the criminal rather than the victim. On the other hand, if the system doesn't place a heavy burden on government prosecutors, we risk sending innocent people to jail and making it easier for our government to slide into totalitarian practices. One thing is certain: No matter what type of system we have for prosecuting and punishing people who commit crimes, it will always be a matter of great controversy.

Criminal Law and Procedure: An Overview

A crime is any behavior that is punishable by imprisonment or fine (or both). State legislatures have an almost unlimited ability to decide which behaviors are considered crimes, and often their decisions do more than simply define socially unacceptable behaviors—they also reflect the values and judgments of the legislators. For example, most state legislatures define welfare fraud as a crime, and welfare recipients who cheat can end up in jail.

The federal government also has broad power to decide what constitutes a crime, Congress can define behavior as a crime only if the U.S. Constitution authorizes Congress to regulate that type of behavior in the first place. But the federal constitution gives Congress jurisdiction over lots of activity. For example, the Constitution gives Congress the power to "regulate commerce ... among the several States." Congress, therefore, can make many activities—such as racketeering—illegal if the actions cross state lines or affect commerce that involves more than one state.

Who decides how the criminal justice system works?

Though legislators have a lot of power to decide whether certain behavior should be a crime, many rules limit the ways in which the state or federal government can prosecute someone for a crime. These restrictions start with the U.S. Constitution's Bill of Rights, which provides basic protections like the right to refuse to incriminate oneself, the right to confront one's accusers, and the right to a trial by jury. State constitutions may offer more protections than federal law, but they cannot take away federal rights. Federal and state legislatures can pass laws governing how criminal procedures work in their jurisdictions, but these laws cannot reduce the protections offered by the federal and state constitutions.

The interplay between constitutional provisions and legislative enactments is regulated by our courts. Courts decide whether a particular legislative rule, court practice, or police action is permissible under federal and state constitutional law. What may seem like a slight variation from one case to another can be, in the eyes of a court, the determining factor that leads to a vastly different result. For example, suppose a police officer detains a burglary suspect on the street. The officer has reason to think the suspect is armed and dangerous, so he frisks the suspect. The officer feels a hard object in the suspect's pocket. Suspecting that the object is a weapon, the officer reaches into the pocket and finds both a cardboard cigarette box and a packet of heroin. This action by the police officer—reaching into the pocket to protect the officer's safety—would be a permissible search under the rulings of most courts, and the heroin could be admitted in court as evidence. However, if the officer had initially felt a soft object that obviously was not a weapon, then reaching into the suspect's pocket might have been an illegal search, in which case the heroin couldn't be used as evidence.

Caution!

The material in this chapter is designed to give you a general overview of several important criminal law topics. As you read, keep in mind that the criminal justice system differs in many small but important ways from state to state, county to county, and even court to court. This means that some of the material in this chapter may not be applicable in your area.

Because we cannot precisely describe the law in your state and what is likely to happen in any particular case, consider this chapter a place to get started. To get more specific and reliable information, do some research, and consult a knowledgeable criminal defense attorney.

What's the difference between a felony and a misdemeanor?

Most states break their crimes into two major groups—felonies and misdemeanors. Whether a crime falls into one category or the other depends on the potential punishment. If a law provides for imprisonment for longer than a year (or for time in prison), the crime is usually considered a felony. If the potential punishment is for a year or less, then the crime is usually considered a misdemeanor. In some states, certain crimes, called "wobblers," may be either a misdemeanor or a felony, because under some conditions the potential punishment may be imprisonment for less than a year, and in other situations, more than a year in prison.

Behaviors punishable only by fine (such as traffic violations) are usually considered infractions. But a legislature may on occasion punish behavior only by fine and still provide that it is a misdemeanor—possession of small amounts of marijuana might fall into this category.

How can I tell from reading a criminal statute whether I'm guilty of the crime it defines?

All criminal statutes define crimes in terms of acts and a required state of mind, usually described as the actor's "intent." These requirements are known as the "elements" of the offense. A prosecutor must convince a judge or jury that the person charged with the crime (the defendant) did the acts and had the intent described in the statute. For example, commercial burglary might be defined as entering a structure (such as a store) belonging to another person, with the intent to commit petty or grand theft (that is, to steal) or any felony. To convict a person of this offense, the prosecutor would have to prove each of three elements:

1. The defendant entered the structure.
2. The structure belonged to another person.
3. The defendant entered the structure intending to commit petty or grand theft or any felony.

What is the presumption of innocence?

All people accused of crime are legally presumed to be innocent until they are convicted, either in a trial or as a result of pleading guilty (or "no contest"). This presumption means not only that the prosecutor must convince the jury of the defendant's guilt, but also that the defendant need not say or do anything in his or her own defense. If the prosecutor can't convince the jury that the defendant is guilty, the defendant goes free.

What does it mean to prove guilt "beyond a reasonable doubt"?

To convict a defendant of a crime, the prosecution must prove the defendant's guilt beyond a reasonable doubt. This does not mean that the prosecution must prove guilt beyond *all* doubt, nor does it mean proof beyond *some* doubt. Rather, it means something in between. Exactly what that something is can be hard to define (indeed, courts and lawyers have struggled with this throughout history), but everyone agrees that a jury must have a high degree of certainty of the defendant's guilt before it can convict.

If I'm accused of a crime, am I guaranteed a trial by a jury?

Yes, in most cases. The U.S. Constitution guarantees the right to a jury trial to anyone accused of any crime where the maximum punishment is more than six months in jail and to anyone accused of an otherwise "serious" crime. Some states guarantee a jury trial for any misdemeanor or felony charge, even where the maximum possible sentence is six months or less. The right to a jury trial has usually been interpreted to require a six-to-12-person jury that must arrive at a unanimous decision to convict or acquit. (In most states, a lack of unanimity is called a "hung jury," and the defendant will go free unless the prosecutor decides to retry the case.)

If I do not have any witnesses who will testify on my behalf, can I still win at trial?

Yes. Defendants sometimes go to trial without having anyone testify for them. In such a situation, the defendant's lawyer will focus on cross-examining the prosecution witnesses in order to poke holes in the prosecutor's case, trying to prove that reasonable doubt exists. Defense attorneys rely on a variety of arguments to discredit the prosecutor's witnesses. Some common arguments include:

- Prosecution witnesses are biased against the defendant and therefore are lying or grossly exaggerating.
- Prosecution witnesses are mistaken in their observations for some reason—for example, because the lighting was bad, they were under the influence of drugs or alcohol, or they were too far away.
- Evidence from police laboratories is unreliable because the machines were not properly maintained or the technicians were not properly trained.
- Prosecution witnesses are lying to get a good deal on the criminal charges they are facing. (Prosecution witnesses are often alleged criminals who have been offered a deal to testify against the defendant.)

What these arguments have in common is that they do not depend on defense evidence. Rather, they rely on the presumption of innocence and the prosecutor's failure to overcome it by proving guilt beyond a reasonable doubt.

Why would an innocent defendant choose not to testify?

A criminal defendant has a right not to testify, and jurors will be told that they cannot assume anything negative if the defendant decides to keep quiet. Of course, some jurors nevertheless presume that a defendant who doesn't testify is guilty. But there are some excellent reasons why an innocent defendant might remain silent in court:

- If the defendant has previously been convicted of a crime, the prosecutor may be able to ask questions about it—but only if the defendant testifies. Evidence of a previous crime may cause some jurors to think that the defendant is guilty of the current crime, too.
- If the defendant testifies, the prosecutor may be able to bring out other

information that discredits the defendant's reputation and testimony.
- Some defendants have a poor demeanor when speaking in public. A judge or jury may not believe a defendant who, though telling the truth, is a nervous witness and makes a bad impression.
- The defendant may have a perfectly good story that would nevertheless sound fishy to the average jury in that particular locale.

What is self-defense—and how can a defendant prove it?

Self-defense is a common defense asserted by someone charged with a crime of violence, such as battery (striking someone), assault with a deadly weapon, or murder. The defendant admits committing the act but claims that it was justified by the other person's threatening actions. The core issues in most self-defense cases are:

- Who was the aggressor?
- Did the defendant reasonably believe that self-defense was necessary?
- If so, was the force used by the defendant reasonable?

Self-defense is rooted in the belief that people should be allowed to protect themselves from physical harm. This means that a person does not have to wait to actually be struck before acting in self-defense. Someone who reasonably believes that a physical attack is imminent typically has the right to strike first and prevent the attack. But someone who uses more force than is reasonable may be guilty of a crime, even though some level of force was justifiable.

When can a defendant win an acquittal on grounds of insanity?

The insanity defense is based on the principle that punishment is justified only if the defendant is capable of controlling the behavior and understanding that the acts committed were wrong. Because some people suffering from mental disorders are not capable of knowing or choosing right from wrong, the insanity defense prevents them from being criminally punished.

Despite its ancient origins (it seems to have begun in England in 1505), the insanity defense remains controversial. Victim-oriented critics point out that a person killed by an insane person is just as dead as a person killed by someone who is sane; they argue that people should be punished for the harm they cause regardless of their mental state. Critics also question the ability of psychiatrists, judges, and jurors to determine whether a person suffers from a mental disorder and to link mental disorders to the commission of crimes.

The insanity defense is an extremely complex topic; many scholarly works are devoted to explaining its nuances. Here are some major points of interest:

- Despite popular perceptions to the contrary, defendants rarely enter pleas of "not guilty by reason of insanity." On the few occasions that the defendant does make such a plea, judges and jurors rarely support it.

- Because neither the legal system nor psychiatrists can agree on a single meaning of insanity in the criminal law context, various definitions are employed. The most popular definition is the "M'Naghten rule," which essentially defines insanity as "the inability to distinguish right from wrong." Another common test is known as "irresistible impulse": People who act out of an irresistible impulse know that an act is wrong, but because of mental illness, cannot control their actions.
- Defendants found not guilty by reason of insanity are not automatically set free. They are usually confined to a mental institution and not released until their sanity is established. These defendants can spend more time in a mental institution than they would have spent in prison had they been convicted.
- An insanity defense normally rests on the testimony of at least one psychiatrist, who testifies after examining the defendant and the facts of the case. Courts appoint psychiatrists at government expense to assist poor defendants who cannot afford to hire their own. The prosecution will normally hire another psychiatrist, whose opinion may differ from the defense psychiatrist's.

Competency to Stand Trial

Aside from insanity as a defense to criminal charges, the question may arise as to whether a defendant is mentally capable of facing a trial. Defendants cannot be prosecuted if they suffer from a mental disorder that prevents them from understanding the proceedings and assisting in the preparation of their defense. Based on a defendant's unusual behavior, a judge, prosecutor, or defense attorney may ask that trial be delayed until the defendant has been examined and found able to understand the proceedings. If a judge finds that a defendant doesn't understand what's going on, the defendant may be placed in a mental institution until competence is reestablished. At that time, the trial will be held.

Can a defendant use drinking or drug use as a defense?

Defendants who commit crimes under the influence of drugs or alcohol sometimes argue that their mental functioning was so impaired that they cannot be held accountable for their actions. Generally, however, voluntary intoxication does not excuse criminal conduct. The law assumes that people know (or should know) that alcohol and drugs affect mental functioning—they are therefore legally responsible if they commit crimes as a result of their voluntary use of these substances.

Some states allow an exception to this general rule. If the defendant is accused of committing a crime that requires what's known as "specific intent" (intending to commit an act *and* intending to cause a specific result by that act), the defendant can argue that he or she was too drunk or high to have that intent. This is only a partial defense, however, because it doesn't entirely excuse the defendant's actions. In this situation, the defendant will usually be convicted of another crime that doesn't require proof of a specific intent—for example, assault with a deadly weapon instead of assault with the intent to commit murder.

If You Are Questioned by the Police

> *There is plenty of law at the end of a nightstick.*
>
> **—Grover A. Whalen**

If a police officer wants to stop and question you, whether you must comply—at least by stopping—depends on the circumstances and the officer's reasons. This section explores some of the common questions people have about their rights and responsibilities when approached by a law enforcement officer.

If an officer wants to stop me while I'm walking on the street and I know I've done nothing wrong, should I comply?

Police officers may interfere with your freedom of movement only if they have observed unusual activity or received information suggesting that criminal activity is afoot and that you are or were involved. Even if the officers are mistaken, however, you do not have the right to keep walking. As long as the officers have a good faith belief in your connection to criminal activity, they are allowed to detain you. But, this doesn't mean that you must answer all of an officer's questions. (See below.)

If I am legally stopped by a police officer on the street, can I be searched?

Yes and no. A police officer is permitted to briefly frisk your outer clothing for weapons if the officer reasonably suspects you are armed and dangerous.

A frisk is different from a search, however. A search may be conducted for evidence of a crime or contraband (an illegal item) and may be much more intrusive than a frisk. An officer may not search you without more of a reason to believe that you committed a crime or that you're hiding an illegal item. (See "Searches and Seizures," below.)

How a Frisk Becomes a Search—And Possibly an Arrest

When frisking a person for weapons, the police are attuned not only to the feel of possible weapons under clothing, but also to the feel of packaged drugs. Although a frisk may not turn up a weapon, it may turn up a suspicious package that the officer knows is commonly used to carry illegal drugs or some other illegal substance. A discovery of such an item may give the officer the right to conduct a more intensive search of the person's clothing. The lesson here is that a frisk often leads to a search. And if either produces an illegal substance, it may result in an arrest.

If I am questioned by a police officer after being stopped on the street, do I have to respond?

The general rule is that you don't have to answer any questions that the police ask you. This rule comes from the Fifth Amendment to the U.S. Constitution, which protects you from self-incrimination. As with all rules, however, there are exceptions. For example, many states have "stop and identify" laws. Under these laws, if a police officer reasonably suspects that someone has engaged in criminal activity, the officer can detain that person and ask for identification. A person who refuses to provide identification commits the crime of resisting an officer's lawful order. (*Hiibel v. Nevada*, U.S. Sup. Ct. 2004.)

If You Run Away

It is not unusual for people who are approached by the police to run away. Some courts have recognized that people of color, in particular, have a well-founded fear of unfair treatment at the hands of the police, and that many people will avoid contact with the police not because they are guilty of a crime, but because they reasonably believe that they may be mistreated or unjustly accused. Other courts view evasive behavior as evidence of guilt, however, and allow the police to rely on the attempt to run away as a key factor justifying a detention.

Defense lawyers often advise people not to talk to the police about a crime unless they clearly weren't involved and want to help the police solve it. And even then, they say, it's not a bad idea to politely demur until you have your own attorney (potentially a public defender) by your side. In fact, saying that you invoke your right to silence is crucial: The U.S. Supreme Court has held that, in many situations, if you don't, the prosecution can later argue at trial that your silence indicated guilt.

Searches and Seizures

Most people instinctively understand the concept of privacy. At the same time, most of us acknowledge that society is served when the police, in appropriate circumstances, are allowed to look for and seize contraband, stolen goods, and evidence of a crime.

In an attempt to balance our desires for privacy against the legitimate needs of the police, the Fourth Amendment of the U.S. Constitution prohibits only unreasonable searches and seizures by officers. Generally, this means that the police may conduct a search of your home, barn, car, boat, office, personal or business documents, or any other property if:

- the police can show that it is more likely than not that a crime has occurred and that they will probably find evidence or contraband if they are allowed to search (this requirement is called "probable cause"), and
- a judge agrees there is probable cause and issues a search warrant, or the police are permitted to search without a warrant because of the particular circumstances involved.

So, for a search to be legal under the Constitution, the police must have both probable cause to conduct the search and a search warrant (although the warrant requirement has many exceptions, some of which we discuss below). If the search is illegal, whatever it turns up is generally inadmissible in court.

How Private Is Your Property?

Generally, if the police are able to view contraband or evidence on your property without actually entering that property, they have not conducted a search. In other words, you cannot have a reasonable expectation of privacy in an area that can legitimately be seen from outside your property. This means that the police can use what they have seen as the basis for getting a warrant to come in and take a closer look. Or, if the situation calls for prompt action (the need to stop a drug deal, for instance), they may enter without a warrant.

Law enforcement officers are allowed to take aerial photographs or come close enough to overhear your conversations—these actions are not considered searches. On the other hand, without a warrant or an exception to the rule requiring a warrant, officers are not allowed to use sophisticated equipment, such as thermal-imaging devices, to discover what is on your property or to eavesdrop on your conversations. In general, if the investigation method is highly artificial and high-tech, it's likely to be considered a search. Where the line is drawn, however, is not necessarily clear or consistent from state to state.

When is a police investigation considered a search?

A police investigation is not a search unless it intrudes on a person's privacy. In other words, if a person did not have a legitimate expectation of privacy in the place or thing searched, no search has occurred, at least not for the purpose of determining whether the Fourth Amendment has been violated.

Courts ask two questions to determine whether a person had a legitimate expectation of privacy in the place or things searched:

- Did the person expect some degree of privacy?
- Is the person's expectation reasonable —that is, one that society is willing to recognize?

For example, a person expects not to have an audience in the house, and most people—including judges and juries—would consider that expectation to be reasonable. Therefore, if the police install a hidden video camera in someone's home, the action is considered a search and must meet the Fourth Amendment's requirement of reasonableness. (The police would need a warrant.)

On the other hand, if the police glance into a car and see a weapon on the front seat, they have not conducted a "search" because it is unlikely that a person would think that the front seat of a car is private—after all, anyone can look through the car windows and see what's on the seat.

What is a search warrant?

A search warrant is a kind of permission slip, signed by a judge, that allows the police to enter private property to look for particular items. It is addressed to the owner of the property, and it tells the owner that a judge has decided that it is reasonably likely that certain contraband or evidence of criminal activities will be found in specified locations on the property.

As a general rule, the police are supposed to apply for a warrant before conducting a search of private property.

What does it take to get a search warrant?

A judge will issue a search warrant if the police can show that:

- it is more likely than not that a crime has taken place, and
- items connected to the crime are likely be found in a specified location on the property to be searched.

To convince the judge of these facts, the police tell the judge what they know about the situation. Usually, the information given to the judge is based either on the officers' own observations or on the secondhand observations of an informant.

The police are limited in their ability to use secondhand information. As a general rule, the information must be reliable given the circumstances. A judge will normally deem information to be reliable if it is corroborated by police observation. For example, a citizen's tip that a suspect regularly delivers drugs to a certain location would be corroborated if an officer observes that suspect's routine. But corroboration is not necessary in every case. Sometimes a judge will issue a warrant if the source of the information is known to the police and has provided trustworthy information in the past, and sometimes the judge won't insist upon even that.

What are the police allowed to do after they obtain a search warrant?

Once the police have a search warrant, they are entitled to enter the designated property to search for the items listed on the warrant. Legally, the search is supposed to be confined to the specific areas described in the warrant. For example, if the search warrant includes only the living room, the search should not extend into the kitchen, bathroom, or bedroom. But there are exceptions to this limitation that allow broader searches. For example, the police may search beyond the terms of the warrant in order to ensure their safety and the safety of others (officers are generally allowed to conduct "protective sweeps" when entering homes) or discover more about possible evidence or contraband that is in plain view elsewhere on the property.

For instance, although a warrant might be issued for the search of a house's ground floor, the search might legitimately expand upstairs if the police see a stack of drugs at the top of the stairs.

Do the police always need a warrant to conduct a search?

No. In many situations, police may legally conduct a search without first obtaining a warrant. Here are a few.

- **Consent searches.** If the police ask your permission to search your home, purse, briefcase, or other property, and you agree, the search is considered consensual, and they don't need a warrant.
- **Searches that accompany an arrest.** When a person is placed under arrest, the police may search the person and the immediate surroundings.
- **Searches necessary to protect the safety of the public.** The police don't need a warrant if they have a reasonable fear that their safety, or that of the public, is in imminent danger. For example, an officer who came across a suspected bomb-making operation while walking his beat might be justified in entering the building immediately and seizing the dangerous materials inside. And in the famous O.J. Simpson case, the police justified their entry onto O.J. Simpson's property on the grounds that they feared for the safety of other family members.
- **"Hot pursuit" searches.** Police may enter private dwellings to search for criminals who are fleeing the scene of a crime.

Can the police track a suspect's car using a GPS device?

The Supreme Court has ruled (*United States v. Jones*, 2012) that unless police have a warrant, they cannot install a GPS tracking device on a suspect's car. Any evidence uncovered as a result of such a warrantless intrusion cannot be used in court. Although nine justices agreed that such a search was illegal, the justices did not agree as to why the search violated the Fourth Amendment (prohibiting illegal searches). Five of the nine justices based their decision on the physical planting (or trespass) of the GPS device on the vehicle. The other four justices believed that it was the warrantless GPS tracking, itself, not the physical installation that violated the Fourth Amendment. As a result, the Supreme Court did not answer the bigger question: Whether—in the absence of a physical intrusion onto a defendant's car—the government can remotely track an individual's whereabouts by monitoring cell phone records or other technology.

Can my roommate—or my landlord—give the police permission to search my apartment?

The police may search your apartment if someone in charge of the premises gives permission. If you and your roommate share common areas (such as the kitchen and living room), your roommate can authorize a search of those areas. But your roommate cannot give permission to search your separate bedroom.

Similarly, your landlord cannot give permission to search your apartment. Although the landlord owns the property, your monthly check guarantees your privacy at home. This is true even if you are behind in your rent or your landlord has sued to evict you. Until there's a court order that permits your landlord to enter and retake the premises, the landlord cannot come in without your permission, except in case of emergency, such as a fire. (But keep in mind that many states allow a landlord to enter to make repairs or for inspections, which usually require reasonable notice, typically 24 hours.) If the police can point to circumstances that would justify immediate entry, however—such as the sound of a ferocious fight—they may enter without permission from anyone.

Arrests and Interrogations

I haven't committed a crime. What I did was fail to comply with the law.

—David Dinkins

Indeed, the law continues to evolve. (Some courts think officers shouldn't have to get warrants to access records that track a cell phone's location.) An arrest occurs when a police officer armed with an arrest warrant utters the words "you're under arrest," or when a police officer's actions cause you to reasonably believe that you are not free to leave. The restraint must be more than a mere detention on the street (discussed above). Although in most situations the police will take you to the police station for booking (photographs and finger-printing), it is also possible for an officer to arrest and book you at the crime scene, then release you when you give a written promise to appear in court at a later time.

After the police arrest you, they will often question you in order to find out more about the crime, your role in it, and whether there may be other suspects. There are several constitutional protections that you may invoke during police interrogations.

When do the police need a warrant to make an arrest?

As long as the police have good reason (called "probable cause") to believe that a crime has been committed and that the person they want to arrest committed the crime, they can, with limited exception, make an arrest without asking a judge for a warrant.

There are few situations in which the adage "a man's home is his castle" still applies, but an arrest at home is one of them. The police must usually have a warrant to arrest a person at home. Also, the police usually cannot make warrantless arrests for misdemeanors that don't occur in their presence.

How do the police obtain an arrest warrant?

An officer must present sworn evidence to a judge that a crime has occurred and that the police have probable cause to believe that the crime was committed by the person they want to arrest. If the judge agrees, a warrant will be issued. The police are then entitled to seize the person.

If the police make an illegal arrest but find evidence of guilt, is the arrested person set free?

Not necessarily. But if a search is conducted during the arrest and turns up incriminating evidence, the evidence may be kept out of the person's trial on the grounds that it is "fruit of the poisonous tree"—that is, the evidence was found as the result of an improper arrest. Also, if the illegally arrested person makes any statements to the police after being arrested, the statements generally may not be used as evidence. This is true whether or not the arrested person was "read his rights." (See below.)

Can a person who is charged with a crime be forced to give bodily samples?

Yes, usually. You might think that being forced to give bodily samples—such as blood, hair, fingernail clippings, or DNA—is a violation of constitutional rights. But despite the Fourth Amendment prohibition against unreasonable searches and the Fifth Amendment protection against self-incrimination, law enforcement is frequently allowed to take bodily samples from people who have been arrested.

If I'm arrested, do the police have to "read me my rights"?

No. They don't need to read your rights unless they want to question you. However, if they don't read you your rights, the prosecutor generally can't use anything you say in response to custodial questioning as evidence against you at trial. What are these rights? Popularly known as the *Miranda* warning (ordered by the U.S. Supreme Court in *Miranda v. Arizona*), your rights consist of the familiar litany invoked by T.V. police immediately upon arresting a suspect:

- You have the right to remain silent.
- If you do say anything, what you say can be used against you in a court of law.
- You have the right to have a lawyer present during any questioning.
- If you cannot afford a lawyer, one will be appointed for you if you so desire.

It doesn't matter whether an interrogation occurs in a jail or at the scene of a crime, on a busy downtown street or in the middle of an open field: If you are in custody (deprived of your freedom of action in any significant way), the police must give a *Miranda* warning if they want to question you and use your answers as evidence at trial. If you are not in police custody, however, no *Miranda* warning is required. This exception comes up when the police informally stop someone on the street to ask questions about a recent crime and the person blurts out a confession.

Will a judge dismiss my case if I was questioned without a *Miranda* warning?

No. Many people mistakenly believe that a case will be thrown out of court if the police fail to give *Miranda* warnings to the arrested person. What *Miranda* actually says is that a warning is necessary if the police interrogate an in-custody suspect and want to use any of the suspect's answers as evidence. If the police fail to give you a *Miranda* warning, in most situations nothing you say in response to the questioning can be used as evidence to convict you. In addition, under the "fruit of the poisonous tree" rule, if the police obtain evidence as a result of an interrogation that violates the *Miranda* rule, that evidence may also be inadmissible at trial. If there is sufficient other evidence to convict you beyond any statements you made to the police, you can still be convicted even when the police don't give *Miranda* warnings.

What's the best way to assert my right to remain silent if I am being questioned by the police?

If you're under arrest and you wisely choose to remain silent at least until you have a chance to consult a lawyer, you should tell that to your interrogator. If you just keep your mouth shut and say nothing, the police can legally continue to question you, and if they do, you might eventually say something you later regret. (Somewhat ironically, the general rule is that you have to say something to claim your right to remain silent.) However, you don't have to use a precise set of words to invoke your *Miranda* rights. After an officer gives you a *Miranda* warning, you can stop the questioning by saying something like:

- "I don't want to talk to you; I want to talk to an attorney."
- "I refuse to speak with you."
- "I invoke my privilege against self-incrimination."
- "I claim my *Miranda* rights."

In general, if the police continue to question you after you have clearly asserted your right to remain silent or your right to counsel, they have violated *Miranda*. (There are subtle differences between invoking the right to silence and the right to counsel.) As a result, for the most part, anything you say after invoking your right(s) will not be admissible as evidence of guilt at your trial.

How heavy-handed can the police get when asking questions?

Information that you voluntarily disclose to a police officer is generally admissible at trial. The key word is "voluntary." Police officers are not allowed to use physical force or psychological coercion to get you to talk to them. (They are, however, often allowed to deceive you to some extent.) If police officers obtain information through any of these illegal means, the information probably cannot be used by the prosecutor at trial regardless of whether you invoked your *Miranda* rights.

Reality Check: Cops Usually Win a Swearing Contest

Defendants often claim that police officers coerced them into talking. And it's just as common for police officers to say that the defendants spoke voluntarily. If the police physically coerce a defendant into talking, the defendant can try to prove it with photos of marks and bruises. But it may be difficult to provide clear evidence of police brutality, and a defendant often cannot offer independent evidence to support claims of psychological coercion. Judges, believing that defendants have a greater motivation to lie than do police officers, usually side with the police and conclude that no coercion took place. (Interviews are, however, often at least on audio.)

Can the police question me after I ask for a lawyer?

If you tell the police that you want to talk to a lawyer—whether it's a lawyer you hire to represent you or a lawyer to be appointed by the court—they must immediately stop the interview. What's more, the police aren't allowed to start questioning you again until you've had the chance to speak to an attorney. You can invoke this right at any time during the interview, even if you've already answered some questions.

If you invoke only the right to remain silent, the police may reinitiate questioning at a later time, provided that they honor the right to remain silent. What it means to "honor" the right to remain silent after a suspect invokes it isn't always entirely clear. Courts consider the circumstances of renewed questioning, including the passage of time, whether the police gave fresh *Miranda* warnings, and whether they asked questions about a different crime.

Bail

Those who expect to reap the blessings of freedom must ... undergo the fatigue of supporting it.

—Thomas Paine

Many people, especially those arrested for minor misdemeanors, are given citations at the scene of an arrest telling them when to appear in court, and then are immediately released. Others, however, are put in jail. Often, a person's first thought upon landing in jail is how to get out—and fast. The usual way to do this is to post bail. This section answers common questions about the bail system, including its version of Monopoly's "Get Out of Jail Free" card—called release O.R.

What does it mean to "post bail"?

Bail is cash or a cash equivalent that an arrested person gives to a court to ensure that the person will appear in court when ordered to do so. If the defendant appears in court at the proper time, the court refunds the bail. But if the defendant doesn't show up, the court keeps the bail and issues a warrant for the defendant's arrest.

Bail can take any of the following forms:

- cash or check for the full amount of the bail
- property worth the full amount of the bail
- a bond—that is, a guaranteed payment of the full bail amount, or
- a waiver of payment on the condition that the defendant appear in court at the required time, commonly called release on one's "own recognizance" or simply "O.R."

Who decides how much bail I have to pay?

Judges are responsible for setting bail. Because many people want to get out of jail immediately and, depending on the day of arrest, it can take days to see a judge, most jails have standard bail schedules that specify bail amounts for common crimes. You can get out of jail quickly by paying the amount set forth in the bail schedule.

Are there restrictions on how high my bail can be?

The Eighth Amendment to the U.S. Constitution requires that bail not be excessive.

This means that bail should not be used primarily to raise money for the government; it's also not to be used to punish a person for being suspected of committing a crime. Remember: The primary purpose of bail is to allow the arrested person to remain free until convicted of a crime and at the same time ensure his or her return to court.

So much for theory. In fact, many judges set an impossibly high bail in particular types of cases, knowing that the high bail will effectively keep the suspect in jail until the case is over. (The U.S. Supreme Court has indicated that pretrial detention on the basis of dangerousness is not per se unconstitutional. (*United States v. Salerno,* U.S. Sup. Ct. 1987.))

What can I do if I can't afford to pay the bail listed on the bail schedule?

If you can't afford the amount of bail on the bail schedule, you can ask a judge to lower it. Depending on the state, your request must be made either in a special bail-setting hearing or when you appear in court for the first time, usually called your arraignment.

How do I pay for bail?

You may provide for the full bail amount yourself; you may alternatively buy a bail bond. A bail bond is like a check held in reserve: It represents your promise to the provider of the bond that you will appear in court when you are supposed to. You pay a bond seller to post a bond (a certain sum of money) with the court, and the court keeps the bond in case you don't show up. You can usually buy a bail bond for about 10% of the amount of your bail; this premium is the bond seller's fee for taking the risk that you won't appear in court.

A bond that costs 10% of the bail amount may sound like a good deal compared to posting cash bail, but buying a bond may cost more in the long run. If the full amount of the bail is paid, it will be refunded (less a small administrative fee) when the case is over and all required appearances have been made. In contrast, a bond seller's fee is nonrefundable. In addition, the bond seller may require "collateral." This means that the person who pays for the bail bond must also give the bond seller a financial interest in some of the person's valuable property. The bond seller can cash in on this interest if the suspect fails to appear in court.

Nevertheless, if you can't afford your bail and you don't have a friend or relative who can help out, a bond seller may be your only option.

Is it true that a defendant can sometimes get out of jail without posting bail?

Yes. This is generally known as releasing someone on their "own recognizance," or "O.R." A defendant released O.R. must simply sign a promise to show up in court. The defendant doesn't have to post bail. A defendant commonly requests release O.R. at the first scheduled court appearance. If the judge denies the request, the defendant then asks for low bail.

In general, defendants who are released on O.R. have strong ties to the community, making them unlikely to flee. Factors that may convince a judge to grant an O.R. release include:

- having family members (most likely parents, a spouse, or children) living in the community
- having resided in the community for many years
- being employed
- having little or no past criminal record, or only criminal problems that were minor and occurred many years earlier, and
- having been charged with previous crimes and having always appeared as required.

These kinds of factors may be relevant not only to O.R., but also to bail.

Getting a Lawyer

Justice oft leans to the side where your purse hangs.

—**Danish proverb**

If you are accused of a crime, you might face the possibility of going to jail. This fact alone will most likely drive you to look for a good lawyer. Unfortunately, private criminal defense lawyers don't come cheap, and you may not be able to afford one. This doesn't mean you'll be completely at the mercy of the government, however. For the most part, you have the right to be represented by an attorney if the state is trying to deprive you of your liberty. This means that a court may be required to appoint a lawyer to represent you for free—or for a fee you can afford. This section discusses the role of private and court-appointed attorneys in the criminal process and offers suggestions for finding a private attorney if you can afford one.

How can I get a court to appoint a lawyer for me?

Normally, if you want a court to appoint a lawyer for you at government expense, you must:

- ask the court to appoint a lawyer, and
- provide details about your financial situation.

Your first opportunity to ask the court to appoint a lawyer is usually your first court appearance, often called your arraignment or bail hearing. The judge will probably ask you whether you are represented by a lawyer. If you're not, the judge will then ask whether you want to apply for court-appointed counsel. If you say yes, some courts will appoint a lawyer right on the spot and finish your arraignment. Other courts will delay your case and appoint a lawyer only after reviewing and approving your economic circumstances and deciding you qualify for court-appointed counsel.

Each state (or even county) makes its own rules about who qualifies for a free lawyer. Also, the seriousness of the charge may affect a judge's decision about whether you are eligible for free legal assistance. For example, a judge may recognize that a wage-earner can afford the cost of representation for a minor crime but not for a crime involving the prospect of a complicated and lengthy trial.

If you don't qualify for free help but can't afford the full cost of a private lawyer, you may still obtain the services of a court-appointed attorney. Most states provide for "partial indigency," which means that at the conclusion of the case, the judge will require you to reimburse the state or county for a portion of the costs of representation.

Do I need a lawyer at my arraignment?

In most criminal courts the arraignment is where you first appear before a judge and enter a plea of guilty or not guilty to the offense charged. Assuming you enter a plea of not guilty, which almost every defendant does at this early stage, the following might happen:

- the judge sets a date for the next procedural event in your case
- the judge considers any bail requests that you or the prosecutor make
- the judge appoints a lawyer for you, if appropriate, and
- the judge asks you to "waive time"—that is, give up your right to have the trial or other statutory proceedings occur within specified periods of time.

Most people can, if necessary, handle this proceeding without an attorney. However, it's almost always better to have a lawyer, whether court-appointed or privately retained.

If I'm poor, will a judge appoint a public defender to represent me?

Because most criminal defendants are unable to afford their own attorneys, many states have public defender's offices. Typically, each local office has a chief public defender and a number of assistant public defenders (P.D.s). P.D.s are fully licensed lawyers whose sole job is to represent poor defendants in criminal cases. Because they appear daily in the same courts, P.D.s can gain a lot of experience in a short period of time. And because they work daily with the same cast of characters, they learn the personalities (and prejudices) of the judges, prosecutors, and local law enforcement officers—important information to know when assessing a case and conducting a trial.

My county doesn't have a public defender's office. How will the court provide an attorney for me?

In areas that don't have a public defender's office, the courts often maintain a list of attorneys and appoint them on a rotating basis to represent people who can't afford to hire their own lawyers.

Do public defenders provide the same quality of representation as regular lawyers?

Despite the severe financial constraints on their offices, public defenders often provide representation that is at least as competent as that provided by private defense attorneys. In some public defenders' offices, the representation is the best a defendant could hope for. Many offices are staffed by experienced and dedicated attorneys. Despite good intentions and training, however, public defenders are often asked to perform too much work for not enough money, which can cut into their abilities to be effective.

How can I get a second opinion on my public defender's advice?

Like all attorneys, public defenders are ethically obligated to vigorously defend their clients' interests. Undoubtedly, most lawyers live up to their ethical duties. But defendants who think that their court-appointed attorneys are not representing them adequately can buy advice from a private defense attorney. Even a low-income person may be able to pay for a short "second opinion" consultation.

How can I find a private defense lawyer?

People who have been recently arrested often need to talk to a lawyer as soon as possible. The most urgent priority is often getting a lawyer to help arrange release and provide some information about what's to come in the days ahead.

You can look to the following sources for a referral depending on your circumstances (such as being in or out of custody). Be sure to check out the credentials and experience of any lawyer you're considereing:

- **Civil practitioners.** Defendants who know an attorney in civil practice can ask that attorney to recommend a criminal defense lawyer. (Some civil practitioners are also competent to represent clients in criminal matters, at least for the limited purpose of arranging for release from jail following an arrest.)
- **Family members or friends,** who may either know of a criminal defense lawyer or at least have the time to pursue additional reference sources, such as family clergy, doctors, or other professionals. (If you're able, you can consult people you trust for referrals on your own.)
- **Bail bond sellers,** who are usually in regular contact with defense lawyers.
- **Courthouse visits.** Defendants can visit a local courthouse and sit through a few criminal hearings. If a particular lawyer impresses a defendant, the defendant can ask for that lawyer's card (after the hearing has concluded) and then call for an appointment.
- **Lawyer directories.** Free or low-cost resources like lawyer directories and bar association referral panels

can help you find consultation or representation. Here are some free sites with directories:

- **Nolo's Lawyer Directory.** Nolo has an easy-to-use online directory of lawyers, organized by location and area of expertise. You can find the directory and its comprehensive profiles at www.nolo.com/lawyers.
- **Lawyers.com.** At Lawyers.com you'll find a user-friendly search tool that allows you to tailor results by area of law and geography. You can also search for attorneys by name. Attorney profiles prominently display contact information, list topics of expertise, and show ratings —by both clients and other legal professionals.
- **Martindale.com.** Martindale.com offers an advanced search option that allows you to sort not only by practice area and location, but also by criteria like law school. Whether you look for lawyers by name or expertise, you'll find listings with detailed background information, peer and client ratings, and even profile visibility.

Should I expect a lawyer to guarantee a good result?

No. Toasters come with guarantees; attorneys don't. Defendants should be wary of lawyers who guarantee satisfactory outcomes. Too much of what may happen is beyond a defense lawyer's contol for a guarantee to make sense. A lawyer who guarantees a good result may simply be trying a hard-sell tactic to get your business—and promising to win is against the legal code of ethics. That said, a lawyer should be able to assess the strength of the evidence against you and may have valuable insight into local prosecutors' and judges' handling of cases similar to yours.

What is a private lawyer likely to cost?

It's impossible to give a definitive answer. Attorneys set their own fees, which vary according to such factors as:

- **The probable complexity of the case.** Most attorneys charge more for felonies than for misdemeanors, because felonies carry greater penalties, often require more court appearances, and so on.
- **The attorney's experience.** Generally, less-experienced attorneys set lower fees than their more-experienced colleagues.
- **Geography.** Just as gasoline and butter cost more in some parts of the country than others, so do lawyers.

A defendant charged with a misdemeanor should not be surprised by a legal fee in the low thousands of dollars. The fee may vary depending on whether you end up going to trial—trials typically involve much more work than negotiated dispositions. And most attorneys want all or a substantial portion of the fee paid up front.

Can I arrange for a contingency fee in a criminal case?

No. A contingency fee is an arrangement where the lawyer gets paid only if the case is successful. These arrangements are not allowed in criminal cases.

Can I change lawyers if I'm unhappy with the one I hired?

Generally, defendants who hire their own attorneys have the right to fire them at any time, without court approval. A defendant doesn't have to show "good cause" or even justify the firing. Of course, changing lawyers will probably be costly. In addition to paying the new lawyer, the defendant will have to pay the original lawyer whatever portion of the fee the original lawyer has earned.

Limits on Your Right to Change Lawyers

Your right to change lawyers is limited by the prosecutor's and court's right to keep cases moving on schedule. If you want to change attorneys on the eve of trial, for example, your new attorney is likely to agree to represent you only if the trial is delayed so the lawyer can prepare. The prosecutor may oppose delay, possibly because witnesses won't be available to testify later on. In these circumstances, the judge might deny your request to change lawyers.

What if I'm not happy with my court-appointed lawyer? Can I get a new one?

Probably not. Defendants with court-appointed lawyers often ask for new ones. Sometimes the problems are the same as those that could be encountered with any retained lawyer: inability to communicate, personality conflicts, or dissatisfaction with strategy. In addition, clients who are represented by court-appointed lawyers often assume that the representation is substandard.

Requests for a new court-appointed lawyer are rarely granted. However, if a defendant is able to offer concrete proof of inadequate representation—for example, because communications with a court-appointed lawyer have completely broken down—the defendant may be able to successfully pursue a motion for substitution of attorney. And, in some situations, a court-appointed attorney might agree to a substitution.

Why do some defendants choose to represent themselves?

Defendants choose to represent themselves for a variety of reasons:

- Some defendants can afford to hire a lawyer but don't do so because they think the likely punishment is not severe enough to justify the expense.
- Some defendants believe (often mistakenly) that an attorney who

represented them previously was ineffective, and figure they can do just as well on their own.

- Some defendants believe that lawyers are part of an overall oppressive system and seek to make a political statement by representing themselves.
- Some defendants want to take responsibility for their own destiny.
- Some defendants who are in jail can gain privileges through self-representation, such as access to the jail's law library. Also, not bound by lawyers' ethical codes, self-represented defendants may try to delay proceedings by overloading the court with paperwork.

How can I tell whether I should represent myself?

The most obvious rule is that the more severe the charged crime, the less sensible it is to represent yourself. (But remember: Even convictions for seemingly small offenses can have lasting consequences—for example, on employment opportunities.) Defendants charged with minor traffic offenses should rarely hire an attorney. Otherwise, it's almost always advisable for anyone charged with a crime to be represented by a lawyer. Even if a lawyer cannot avoid a conviction together, a good attorney can often achieve a much better negotiated result than a layperson could.

How to Find Out What Your Punishment Is Likely to Be

It can be hard for a defendant to find out what sentence a judge is likely to hand out in a given case. This information can't be found in statutes or court rules. Rather, information about a likely sentencing is part of the hidden law that lawyers learn from being in the trenches. Defendants who want to know what the punishment is likely to be upon conviction might take the following steps:

- Pay a private defense attorney for consultation. An experienced defense attorney can often make well-informed predictions as to likely punishment. An attorney might not even charge you to provide this kind of limited insight.
- Call your local public defender's office. Public defenders often have an "attorney of the day" or "duty attorney" assigned to answer questions. While you may not get advice specific to your case, the attorney will probably tell you what the standard sentence is for the crime you're charged with.
- Find an attorney through someone you trust. Someone like a family member or friend might know an experienced lawyer who can give you information.

RESOURCE

For more information about crimes and criminal procedure, see *The Criminal Law Handbook,* by Paul Bergman and Sara J. Berman (Nolo). It answers common questions on just about every aspect of the criminal justice system, including searches, lineups, arraignments, plea bargains, sentencing, and more.

ONLINE HELP

The following sites are good resources for criminal law:

- **www.nolo.com** Nolo's website offers information about a wide variety of legal topics, including criminal law and procedure.
- **www.criminaldefenselawyer.com** This Nolo site provides extensive legal information on many different crimes, their penalties, and possible defenses.
- **www.drivinglaws.org** This Nolo site has all kinds of information on DUI/DWI and traffic violations.

Glossary

401(k) plan A deferred-compensation savings program in which employees invest part of their pretax wages, sometimes with added employer contributions. Income taxes on the amounts invested and earned are not due until the employee withdraws money from the fund, usually at retirement.

A

AB trust A trust that allows couples to reduce or avoid estate taxes at the death of the second spouse. Also called a bypass trust.

acquittal A decision by a judge or jury that a defendant in a criminal case is not guilty of a crime.

adjustable rate mortgage (ARM) A mortgage loan with an interest rate that fluctuates in accordance with a designated market indicator—such as the weekly average of one-year U.S. Treasury Bills—over the life of the loan.

administration (of an estate) The court-supervised process of paying debts and transferring assets after someone has died.

adoption A court procedure by which an adult becomes the legal parent of someone who is not the adult's biological child.

annuity A purchased policy that pays a fixed amount of benefits every year for the life of the person entitled to those benefits under the policy.

annulment A court procedure that dissolves a marriage and treats it as if it never happened—except that children of an annulled marriage are still considered "legitimate."

appeal A written request to a higher court to modify or reverse the judgment (or criminal sentence) of a trial court or intermediate-level appellate court. Review is limited to the record at trial.

appellate court A higher court that reviews the decision of a lower court when a losing party files an appeal.

arbitration A procedure for resolving disputes out of court in which one or more neutral third parties—called the arbitrator or arbitration panel—hears evidence and renders a decision, like a judge.

arraignment A court appearance in which criminal charges are formally presented to a defendant. The court typically asks the defendant to respond by entering a plea, which is usually "not guilty," at this stage.

arrest A situation in which the police take someone suspected of a crime into custody.

arrest warrant A document issued by a judge or magistrate that authorizes the police to arrest someone.

articles of incorporation A document filed with state authorities to form a corporation.

assault (1) A civil "tort" that can be the basis of a lawsuit or (2) Crime. To "assault" someone is typically to cause the victim to fear immediate physical harm. Actual physical contact is not necessary. In some states, an assault is also a completed attempt to harm.

attorney-in-fact A person, also called an "agent," named in a written power of attorney document and given authority to act on behalf of the person who signs the document, called the principal.

audit An examination of the financial records of a person, business, or organization, typically undertaken to clean up careless or improper bookkeeping, or to verify that proper records are being kept. Audits are also conducted by the IRS in order to determine whether a person or business owes taxes.

B

bail Something of value—often money—posted with the court to ensure that an arrested person who is released from jail will show up at all required court appearances.

balloon payment A large final payment due at the end of a loan, typically a home or car loan, to pay off the amount remaining on the loan.

bankruptcy trustee A person appointed by a bankruptcy court to oversee the case of a person or business that has filed for bankruptcy.

battery The civil "tort" or crime of intentionally touching someone in a harmful way or offensive way. Unintentional contact is not battery.

beneficiary A person or organization that is legally entitled to receive benefits through a legal device, such as a will, trust, or life insurance policy, or from a government agency.

bylaws The rules that govern the internal affairs or actions of a corporation.

C

C corporation A corporation whose profits are taxed separately from its owners under Subchapter C of the Internal Revenue Code.

capital gains The profit on the sale of a capital asset, such as stock or real estate.

capitalized interest Accrued interest that is added to the principal balance of a loan while the borrower is not making payments or when payments are insufficient to cover both the principal and interest due.

case A term that most often refers to a lawsuit—for example, "I filed my small claims case." "Case" also refers to a written decision by a court.

certification mark A name, symbol, or other device used by an organization to vouch for the quality or geographic origin of products and services provided by others.

child support Money paid by parents to support their children until the children reach the age of majority or become emancipated—usually by getting married, entering the armed forces, or living independently.

circuit court In many states, the name used for the principal trial court. In the federal system, the name for the appellate courts, which are organized into 13 circuits.

civil case A noncriminal lawsuit in which an individual, business, or government entity sues another to protect, enforce, or redress private rights. There are hundreds of varieties of civil cases, including suits for breach of contract, probate, divorce, negligence, and copyright violations.

collateral Property that guarantees payment of a secured debt.

collection agency A company hired by a creditor to collect a debt.

collective mark A name, symbol, or other device used by members of a group or organization to identify the goods or services it provides.

collision damage waiver *See* "loss damage waiver."

collision insurance coverage A type of car insurance that pays for damages to the insured vehicle that result from a collision with another vehicle or object.

common law Rules that are established by court decisions and not by statutes, regulations, or ordinances.

common law marriage In some states, a type of marriage in which couples can become legally married (without a license or ceremony) by living together for a long period of time, representing themselves as a married couple, and intending to be married.

community property A method used in some states to define the ownership of property acquired—and the responsibility for debts—incurred during marriage. In states with community property laws, all earnings during marriage and all property acquired with those earnings are considered community property that belongs equally to each spouse. Likewise, all debts incurred during marriage are community property debts.

conservator Someone appointed by a judge to oversee the affairs of an incapacitated person. A conservator may also be called a guardian, committee, or curator.

constitution The system of fundamental laws and principles that lay down the nature, functions, and limitations of a government body. The United States Constitution is the supreme law of the United States. States also have constitutions. State constitutions can give people *more* rights than does the U.S. Constitution but cannot take away rights provided in the U.S. Constitution.

contingency fee A method of paying a lawyer for legal representation by which, instead of an hourly or per-job fee, the lawyer receives a percentage of the money the client obtains after settling or winning the case.

cooling-off rule A rule that allows a consumer to cancel certain contracts within a specified time period (typically three days) after signing.

copyright The right granted under federal law for the owner of a creative work (such as a book, motion picture, musical composition, software, or artwork), to prohibit unauthorized use of the work.

corporation A legal structure authorized by state law that allows a business to organize as a separate legal entity from its owners, thereby shielding them from personal liability from business debts and obligations, and allowing the business to take advantage of corporate tax rules.

counterclaim A defendant's court papers that claim that the plaintiff—not the defendant—committed legal wrongs, and the defendant is entitled to money damages or other relief. In some states, a counterclaim is called a cross-complaint.

covenants, conditions, & restrictions (CC&Rs) Restrictions governing the use of real estate, usually enforced by a homeowners' association and passed on to the new owners of property.

credit insurance Insurance that pays off a loan if the person who owes the money dies or becomes disabled.

credit report A report of your credit history, prepared by a credit reporting agency.

credit reporting agency A private, for-profit company that collects and sells information about a person's credit history.

creditor A person or entity (such as a bank) to whom a debt is owed.

crime A type of behavior that has been defined by the state or federal government as deserving of punishment. The punishment for a crime may include imprisonment, a fine, or both.

custody (of a child) The legal authority to make decisions affecting a child's interests (legal custody) and the responsibility to take care of the child (physical custody).

D

death taxes A term sometimes used to describe estate or inheritance taxes, which may be levied at death. Estate tax, collected by the IRS and some states, is based on the value of property left behind. A few states also levy inheritance tax, which is based on who inherits property.

debtor A person or business that owes money.

deductible Something that is taken away or subtracted. Under an insurance policy, for example, the deductible is the maximum amount that an insured person must pay toward the losses before beginning to collect money from the insurer.

deed A document that transfers ownership of real estate.

deed in lieu of foreclosure A method of avoiding foreclosure by which the lender accepts ownership of the property in place of the money owed on the mortgage.

default The failure to perform a legal duty. For example, a borrower defaults on a mortgage or car loan by failing to make the loan payments on time, failing to maintain adequate insurance, or violating some other provision of the agreement.

defendant The person against whom a lawsuit is filed. In certain states, and in certain types of lawsuits, the defendant is called the respondent.

defined benefit plan A type of pension plan that pays a definite, predetermined amount of money when the worker retires or becomes disabled. The amount received is based on length of service with a particular employer.

defined contribution plan A type of pension plan that does not guarantee any particular pension amount upon retirement. Instead, the employer and/or employee pays a certain amount into the pension fund every month, or every year, for each employee.

dependents benefits A type of Social Security benefit available to the spouse and minor or disabled children of a retired or disabled worker who qualifies for either retirement or disability benefits under the program's guidelines.

deposition A tool used by one party in pretrial case investigation (called "discovery") to question the other party or a witness in the case. All questions are answered under oath and recorded by a court reporter, who creates a deposition transcript.

design patent A patent issued on a new and original design that does not affect the functioning of the underlying device.

disability benefits Money paid from Social Security to those who qualify because of their work and earnings record and who meet the program's medical guidelines defining disability.

dischargeable debts Debts that can be erased in bankruptcy.

discovery A formal investigation—governed by court rules—that is conducted before a trial. Discovery allows one party to question other parties (and sometimes witnesses) and to force the disclosure of documents or other physical evidence relating to the lawsuit.

dissolution A term used instead of divorce in some states.

district court In federal court and in some states, the name of the main trial court.

divorce The legal termination of a marriage.

doing business as (DBA) A situation in which a person or company operates a business under a name different from the person's or business's legal or registered name.

domain name A combination of letters and numbers that identifies a specific website on the Internet, followed by an identifier such as .com or .org.

down payment A lump sum cash payment made by a buyer when purchasing a major piece of property, such as a car or house.

durable power of attorney A power of attorney that remains in effect if the maker becomes incapacitated.

durable power of attorney for finances A legal document that gives someone authority to manage the maker's financial affairs if he or she becomes incapacitated.

durable power of attorney for health care A legal document that names someone to make medical decisions if the person who makes the document is unable to express his or her wishes for care.

E

emergency protective order Any court-issued order meant to protect a person from harm or harassment. This type of order is a stopgap measure, usually lasting only for a weekend or holiday.

escrow A document (such as a grant deed to real property) or sum of money that, by agreement of parties to a transaction, is held by a neutral third party until certain conditions are met. Once the conditions are met, the third party releases the funds or document from escrow.

estate Generally, all the assets a person owns at death.

estate taxes State or federal taxes imposed on property at a person's death. Some states also impose "inheritance taxes" on the people who inherit the property.

eviction Removal of a tenant from rental property by a law enforcement officer. Eviction cannot occur until the landlord has gone to court and obtained a court order, directing the tenant to move out.

evidence The many types of information presented to a judge or jury to convince them of the truth or falsity of the key facts in a case. Evidence may include testimony of witnesses, documents, photographs, items of damaged property, government records, videos, or laboratory reports.

executor The person named in a will to handle the debts and assets of someone who has died. Also called personal representative.

exempt property The items of property a debtor is allowed to keep if a creditor is trying to collect on a judgment or if the debtor files for Chapter 7 bankruptcy.

express warranty A guarantee made by a seller about the quality of goods or services provided. An express warranty is explicitly stated, either orally or in writing.

extended warranty contract Warranty coverage on an item that takes effect after the warranty coverage provided by the manufacturer or seller expires.

F

federal court A branch of the United States government with power derived directly from the U.S. Constitution. Federal courts decide cases involving the U.S. Constitution, federal law, and some disputes where the parties are from different states.

felony A serious crime, usually punishable by a prison term of more than one year or, in some cases, by death.

fictitious business name The name under which a business operates or by which it is commonly known. *See also* "doing business as."

fixed rate mortgage A mortgage loan with an interest rate that remains constant throughout the life of the loan.

for sale by owner (FSBO) A type of house sale in which the owner acts without the services of a listing real estate broker.

forbearance Voluntarily refraining from doing something, such as asserting a legal right. For example, a creditor may forbear on its right to collect a debt by temporarily postponing or reducing the borrower's payments.

foreclosure The forced sale of real estate to pay off a home loan or home equity loan on which the owner of the property has defaulted.

G

garnishment A process that takes property from a person to satisfy a debt. For example, a creditor may garnish a debtor's wages to collect a lawsuit judgment.

general partnership A business that is owned and managed by two or more people (called partners or general partners) who are personally liable for all business debts.

gift tax Federal tax assessed on any gift from one person to another that exceeds a certain amount ($14,000 in 2016 and indexed for inflation) in one year. Because everyone gets a gift/estate tax exemption of more than $5 million, very few people even owe gift tax.

grace period Following a borrower's or tenant's failure to make a timely payment on a loan or rent, a period of time during which the lender or landlord will refrain from taking legal action (calling a default on the loan or beginning eviction proceedings).

grant deed A deed containing an implied promise that the person transferring the property actually owns the title and that it is not encumbered in any way, except as described in the deed.

guarantor A person who makes a legally binding promise to either pay another person's debt or perform another person's duty if that person defaults or fails to perform.

guardian An adult who has been given the legal right by a court to control and care for someone known as a "ward." The ward may be either a minor child or an incapacitated adult. The guardian may make personal decisions on behalf of the ward (a "personal guardian"), manage the ward's property (a "property guardian" or "guardian of the estate"), or both.

guardian of the estate *See* "guardian."

guardianship A legal relationship created by a court between a guardian and a ward—either a minor child or an incapacitated adult. The guardian has a legal right and duty to care for the ward.

H

health care agent A person named in a health care directive or durable power of attorney for health care to make medical decisions for the person who signed the document, called the principal. A health care agent may also be known as a proxy, surrogate, or patient advocate.

health care directive A document in which you write out your wishes for end-of-life health care, in case you are unable to speak for yourself. *See also* "durable power of attorney for health care" and "living will."

holographic will A will that is completely handwritten and signed by the person making it. Holographic wills are valid in about half the states.

home warranty A service contract that covers major housing systems, such as plumbing or electrical wiring, for a set period of time from the date a house is sold. The warranty pays for repairs to the covered system and is renewable.

homeowners' association An organization of owners who jointly manage the common areas of a subdivision or condominium complex. The homeowners' association is also responsible for enforcing any covenants, conditions, and restrictions (CC&Rs) that apply to the property, including collecting dues.

hung jury A jury unable to come to a final decision, resulting in a mistrial.

I

implied warranty A guarantee about the quality of goods or services purchased. An implied warranty is not written down or explicitly spoken but is provided to consumers by law.

implied warranty of fitness An implied warranty that applies when someone buys an item for a specific purpose. If the buyer notifies the seller of his or her specific needs, this warranty guarantees that the item will meet those needs.

implied warranty of habitability A legal doctrine that requires landlords to offer and maintain livable premises for their tenants.

implied warranty of merchantability An implied warranty that a new item will work for its specified purpose.

independent contractor A self-employed person, as defined by the IRS (or another state or federal agency). Unlike employees, independent contractors retain control over how they do their work. The person or company paying the independent contractor controls only the outcome—the final product or service.

individual retirement account (IRA) An account to which a person may contribute up to a specified amount of earned income each year. The most common types of IRAs are traditional IRAs and Roth IRAs. With a traditional IRA, contributions and interest earned are not taxed until the participant withdraws funds at retirement. With Roth IRAs, contributions are taxed, but most distributions (investment returns and withdrawals at retirement) are not.

infraction A minor violation of the law that is punishable only by a fine—for example, a traffic ticket.

infringement (of copyright, patent, or trademark) The violation of a patent, copyright, or trademark owner's rights. Usually, this occurs when someone uses or benefits from a patented or copyrighted work, or a trademark or servicemark, without the owner's permission.

inheritance taxes Taxes levied by a few states on people who inherit property (compare "estate taxes").

interest A charge for the privilege of borrowing money or getting credit. An interest rate represents the annual percentage that is added to the balance of a loan or credit line. This means that if a loan has an interest rate of 8%, the creditor adds 8% to the balance each year.

interrogatories Written questions that one party to a lawsuit asks an opposing party. Interrogatories are designed to discover key facts about an opponent's case and are a common part of pretrial case investigation (discovery).

intestate succession The method by which property is distributed when a person dies without a valid will. Assets are distributed to the closest surviving relatives.

irrevocable trust A trust that cannot be revoked, amended, or changed.

J

joint custody An arrangement by which parents who do not live together share the upbringing of a child. Joint custody can be joint legal custody (in which both parents have a say in decisions affecting the child), joint physical custody (in which the child spends a significant amount of time with both parents), or both.

joint tenancy A way for two or more people to share ownership of real estate or other property. When property is held in joint tenancy and one owner dies, the other owners automatically receive the deceased owner's share.

judgment A final court ruling resolving the key questions in a lawsuit and determining the rights and obligations of the opposing parties.

judgment-proof A term used to describe a person from whom nothing can be collected because the person has little income and no property, or is protected from collection of the judgment by law—for example, a law preventing the collection of exempt property.

jury A group of people selected to apply the law, as stated by a judge, to the facts of a case and render a decision, called the verdict.

jury nullification A decision made by a jury to acquit a defendant who has violated a law that the jury believes is unjust or wrong, or should not be applied to the case.

L

landlord The owner of any real estate, such as a house, apartment building, or land, that is leased or rented to another person, called the tenant. Sometimes "landlord" is used to refer to a property manager.

lease An oral or written agreement between two people concerning the use by one of the property of the other. A person can lease either real estate (such as an apartment or business property) or personal property (such as a car or a boat).

legal custody The right and obligation to make decisions about a child's upbringing, including schooling and medical care. Compare "physical custody."

legislature The branch of government that has the responsibility and power to make laws. A state legislature makes state laws, and the federal legislature (the U.S. Congress) makes federal laws.

lemon A car that gives you serious trouble soon after you buy it.

liability (1) Legal responsibility for an act or failure to act. (2) Something for which a person is liable. For example, a debt is often called a liability.

liability insurance A contract that provides compensation to third parties who are injured or whose property is damaged due to the fault of the insurance policyholder.

license (of invention, copyright, or trademark) A contract giving written permission to use an invention, creative work, or trademark.

lien The right of a secured creditor to take a specific item of property if the borrower doesn't pay a debt.

life estate The right to live in or use, but not own, a specific piece of property until death.

life insurance A contract under which an insurance company agrees to pay money to a designated beneficiary upon the death of the policyholder. In exchange, the policyholder pays a regularly scheduled fee, known as the insurance premiums.

limited liability Restrictions on the amount a business owner can lose if the business is subject to debts, claims, or other liabilities. One of the primary advantages of forming a corporation or limited liability company (LLC) is that the business owners generally stand to lose only the amount of money invested in the business—creditors can't come after an owner's personal assets.

limited liability company (LLC) A business ownership structure that offers limited personal liability for business obligations and a choice of how the business will be taxed: either as a separate entity or as a partnership-like structure in which profits are taxed on the owners' personal income tax returns.

limited liability partnership (LLP) A type of partnership for professionals recognized in most states that protects partners from personal liability for negligent acts committed by other partners or by employees not under their direct control.

limited partnership A business structure that allows some partners (called limited partners) to enjoy limited personal liability for partnership debts while other partners (called general partners) have unlimited personal liability. Limited partners are usually passive investors; they are not allowed to make day-to-day business decisions.

living trust A trust created during the trustmaker's life to avoid probate after death. Property transferred into the trust during life passes directly to the trust beneficiaries after death, without probate.

living will A legal document that allows you to set out written wishes for health care. The document takes effect only if you are unable to make decisions for yourself.

loan broker A person who specializes in matching home buyers with appropriate mortgage lenders.

loan consolidation Combining a number of loans into a single new loan.

loss damage waiver (LDW) Rental car insurance that makes the rental car company responsible for damage to or theft of a rental car. Also called a "collision damage waiver."

M

malpractice (by an attorney) The delivery of substandard services by a lawyer. Generally, malpractice occurs when a lawyer fails to provide the quality of service that should reasonably be expected in the circumstances, with the result that the lawyer's client is harmed.

marital property Most of the property accumulated by spouses during a marriage, called "community property" in some states.

marriage certificate A document that provides proof of a marriage, typically issued to newlyweds a few weeks after they file for the certificate in a county office.

marriage license A document that authorizes a couple to get married, usually available from a city or county office in the state where the marriage will take place.

mediation A dispute-resolution method designed to help people settle disputes without going to court. In mediation, a neutral third party (the mediator) meets with the opposing sides to help them find a mutually satisfactory solution.

Medicaid A federal–state program that provides health insurance for financially needy people. The program is administered by each state.

Medicare A federal program that provides health insurance to elderly and disabled people.

meeting of creditors A hearing held by the bankruptcy trustee about a month after a debtor files for bankruptcy.

***Miranda* warning** A warning that the police must give to an in-custody suspect before conducting an interrogation; otherwise, the suspect's answers may not be used as evidence in a trial.

misdemeanor A crime, less serious than a felony, punishable in most states by no more than one year in jail.

mortgage A loan in which the borrower puts up the title to real estate as security (collateral) for the loan. If the borrower doesn't pay back the debt on time, the lender can foreclose on the real estate and have it sold to pay off the loan.

N

no-fault divorce Any divorce in which the spouse who wants to split up does not have to accuse the other of wrongdoing, but can simply state that the couple no longer gets along.

no-fault insurance Car insurance laws that require the insurance company of each person involved in an accident to pay for the medical bills and lost wages of its insured, up to a certain amount, regardless of who was at fault.

nolo contendere A plea entered by the defendant in response to being charged with a crime. A defendant who pleads nolo contendere neither admits nor denies committing the crime but is convicted and agrees to a punishment.

nondischargeable debts Debts that cannot be erased by filing for bankruptcy.

nondisclosure agreement A legally binding contract in which a person or business promises not to disclose specific information to others without proper authorization.

nonexempt property The property that a debtor risks losing to creditors after filing for Chapter 7 bankruptcy or when a creditor sues the debtor and wins a judgment.

nonprofit corporation A corporation formed to carry out a charitable, educational, religious, literary, or scientific purpose. Nonprofits receive certain benefits—for example, federal and state tax exemptions—that are not available to regular corporations.

notarization The act of certification by a notary public that establishes the authenticity of a signature on a legal document.

notary public A licensed public officer who administers oaths, certifies signatures on documents, and performs other specified functions.

nuisance Something that interferes with the use of property by being irritating, offensive, obstructive, or dangerous. Nuisances include a wide range of conditions, from a chemical plant's noxious odors to a neighbor's dog barking.

O

open adoption An adoption in which there is some degree of contact between the birth parents and the adoptive parents and sometimes with the child as well.

order A decision issued by a court. It can be a simple command—for example, ordering a recalcitrant witness to answer a proper question during a trial—or it can be a complicated and reasoned decision made after a hearing, directing that a party either do or refrain from doing some act.

ordinance A law passed by a county or city government.

own recognizance (O.R.) A way for a criminal defendant to get out of jail, without paying bail, by promising to appear in court when required to be there. Defendants charged with minor offenses who have strong ties to the community, such as a steady job, local family, and no history of failing to appear in court, are good candidates for O.R. release.

P

parenting agreement A detailed written agreement between a divorcing or separating couple that describes how they will deal with custody, visitation, holiday schedules, vacation, education, religion, and other issues related to their child.

partnership When used without a qualifier such as "limited" or "limited liability," this term usually refers to a legal structure called a general partnership: a business that is owned and managed by two or more people who are personally liable for all business debts.

party A person, corporation, or other legal entity that files a lawsuit (a plaintiff or petitioner) or defends against one (a defendant or respondent).

patent A legal monopoly, granted by the U.S. Patent and Trademark Office (PTO), on the right to use, manufacture, and sell a new and nonobvious invention.

pay-on-death (POD) designation A way to avoid probate for bank accounts, government bonds, individual retirement accounts, and in many states, securities or a car. A pay-on-death designation is created when the property owner names someone on the ownership document—such as the registration card for a bank account—to inherit the property at the owner's death.

pension A retirement fund for employees paid for or contributed to by an employer and/or the employee as part of a package of compensation for the employees' work.

personal property All property other than land and buildings attached to land. Cars, bank accounts, wages, securities, a small business, furniture, insurance policies, jewelry, patents, pets, and season baseball tickets are all examples of personal property.

petition A formal written request made to a court, asking for an order or ruling on a particular matter.

petitioner A person who initiates a lawsuit. The term is a synonym for plaintiff. It is used almost universally in some states and used in others only for certain types of lawsuits, most commonly divorce and other family law cases.

physical custody The right and obligation of a parent to provide a home for his or her child. Compare "legal custody."

plaintiff The person, corporation, or other legal entity that initiates a lawsuit. In certain states and for some types of lawsuits, the term "petitioner" is used instead of "plaintiff."

plant patent A patent issued for new strains of asexually reproducing plants.

plea The defendant's formal answer to criminal charges. Typically, defendants enter one of the following pleas: guilty, not guilty, or nolo contendere.

plea bargain A negotiation between the defense and prosecution that settles a criminal case. The defendant typically pleads guilty to a lesser crime (or fewer charges) than originally charged. In exchange, the defendant gets a potential —in some courts—guaranteed sentence that is shorter than what the defendant could face if convicted at trial.

pocket part The paper supplement found in the front or back of a book of laws—such as state statues—that contains annual changes to the law that are not included in the hardcover version of the book.

POLST forms A type of health care directive created by a patient with his or her doctor that informs emergency care providers what kinds of treatments the patient wants (and doesn't want) in a medical emergency. POLST forms cover many types of medical interventions, such as intubation, antibiotic use, and feeding tubes. They are available in most states, though they sometimes go by other names —including MOLST, POST, and COLST.

pot trust A trust for children—typically established in a will or living trust—in which the trustee decides how much to spend on each child, using trust funds to meet each child's specific needs.

power of attorney A document that gives another person (called the "attorney-in-fact" or "agent") legal authority to act on behalf of the person who makes the document, called the principal.

premarital agreement An agreement made by a couple before marriage that controls certain aspects of their relationship, usually the management and ownership of property, and sometimes whether alimony will be paid if the couple later divorces. Also known as a prenuptial agreement or "prenup."

preponderance of the evidence Evidence sufficient to convince a jury that one party's version of events is "more likely than not." In many civil lawsuits, the plaintiff must prove each element of his or her claim by a preponderance of the evidence in order to prevail.

private mortgage insurance (PMI) Insurance that reimburses a mortgage lender if the buyer defaults on the loan and the foreclosure sale price is less than the amount owed the lender (the mortgage plus the costs of the sale).

pro per A term derived from the Latin in propria persona, meaning "for one's self," used in some states to describe a person who handles his or her own case without a lawyer. In other states, the term "pro se" is used.

pro se *See* "pro per."

probable cause The standard by which judges evaluate arrests without warrants, many warrantless searches and seizures, and requests for arrest warrants and search warrants. There's probable cause if the facts support an objective belief that the person to be arrested has committed a crime—or that the place or item to be searched bears evidence of a crime.

probate The court process following a person's death that includes proving the authenticity of the will, appointing someone to handle the deceased person's affairs, identifying and inventorying the deceased person's property, paying debts and taxes, identifying heirs, and distributing the deceased person's property.

property guardian *See* "guardian."

prosecutor A lawyer who works for the local, state, or federal government to bring and litigate criminal cases.

provisional patent application (PPA) An interim patent application that has the legal effect of providing the inventor with an early filing date for an invention. The PPA does not take the place of a regular patent application, but it does confer patent pending status on the underlying invention for one year from the filing date.

public defender A government lawyer appointed to represent defendants who are charged with violations of criminal law and unable to pay for their defense.

Q

QTIP trust A trust for wealthy couples designed to reduce or postpone estate taxes.

quitclaim deed A deed that transfers whatever ownership interest the transferor has in a particular piece of real estate. The deed does not make any guarantees about what is being transferred.

R

real estate agent A foot soldier of the real estate business who shows houses and does most of the other nitty-gritty tasks associated with selling real estate in exchange for a commission on the sale.

real estate broker A real estate professional one step up from a real estate agent. A broker has more training and can supervise agents.

real property Another term for real estate. It includes land and things permanently attached to the land, such as trees, buildings, and stationary mobile homes.

recording The process of filing a copy of a deed or other document concerning real estate with the land records office in the county where the land is located. Recording creates a public record of ownership for all real estate in the state.

regulation A rule issued by a state or federal administrative agency for the purpose of implementing and enforcing a statute.

rent control Laws that limit the amount of rent landlords may charge—and state when and by how much rent can be raised. Most rent control laws also require a landlord to provide a good reason, or a "just cause," such as repeatedly late rent payments, for evicting a tenant.

rental agreement A contract, either oral or written, between a landlord and tenant that sets forth the terms of a tenancy.

renters' insurance Insurance that covers those who rent residential property against losses to their belongings that occur as a result of fire or theft. The liability portion of renters' insurance covers loss or damage to someone else's property, or injury to someone, caused by the renter's careless acts.

repossession A creditor's taking of property that has been pledged as collateral for a loan. A common example is when a lender repossesses a car when the buyer defaults on loan payments.

request for admissions A procedure in which one party to a lawsuit asks the opposing party to admit that certain facts are true. This occurs in the pretrial case-investigation phase of a lawsuit, known as "discovery."

request to produce (documents or things) A procedure in which one party to a lawsuit asks an opposing party to turn over certain documents or physical objects. Like a "request for admissions," this procedure is part of the pretrial case-investigation phase of a lawsuit, called "discovery."

respondent A term used instead of "defendant" in some states—especially for divorce and other family law cases—to identify the party who is being sued.

restraining order A court order directing a person not to do something, such as make contact with another specified person, enter the family home, or remove a child from the state.

Roth IRA *See* "individual retirement account."

ruling Any decision a judge makes during the course of a lawsuit.

S

S corporation A corporation organized under Subchapter S of the Internal Revenue Code. Shareholders enjoy limited liability status but are taxed on their individual tax returns in the same way as sole proprietors or owners of a partnership.

search warrant An order signed by a judge that allows the police to search an item or a place.

secret warranty program A program under which a car manufacturer will make repairs for free on vehicles with persistent problems, even after the warranty has expired, in order to avoid a recall and the accompanying bad press.

secured debt A debt for which a creditor has a lien on an item of property (often called collateral) to guarantee payment. The creditor can initiate a foreclosure or repossession to take the collateral to satisfy the debt if the borrower defaults.

security deposit A payment required by a landlord to ensure that a tenant pays rent on time and keeps (and leaves) the rental unit in good condition.

sentence Punishment in a criminal case. A sentence can range from a fine and community service to life imprisonment or death.

separate property In community property states, property owned and controlled entirely by one spouse.

service contract Another term for "extended warranty contract."

service mark A word, phrase, logo, symbol, color, sound, or smell used by a business to identify a service and distinguish it from those of its competitors.

settlement An agreement resolving a dispute between the parties in a lawsuit without a trial.

severance pay Funds that some employers offer to workers who are laid off, often based on length of service.

sexual harassment Unwelcome sexual advances or other offensive sex-based comments or behavior that must be endured as a condition of employment or that is severe or pervasive enough to create a hostile work environment.

shared custody *See* "joint custody."

shareholder An owner of a corporation whose ownership interest is represented by shares of stock in the corporation. Also called a "stockholder."

short sale (of a house) The sale of a house in which the proceeds fall short of what the owner still owes on the mortgage. Many lenders will agree to accept the proceeds of a short sale and may even forgive the rest of what is owed on the mortgage if the owner cannot make the mortgage payments.

sick leave Time off work for an employee's own illness, or in some cases, the illness of a family member.

small claims court A state court that resolves disputes involving relatively small amounts of money. Adversaries usually appear without lawyers—in fact, some states forbid lawyers in small claims court.

Social Security The general term that describes a number of related programs administered by the federal government, including retirement, disability, and dependents and survivors benefits. These programs provide workers and their families with benefits when their normal flow of income shrinks because of the retirement, disability, or death of the person who earned that income.

sole custody An arrangement in which only one parent has physical and legal custody of a child and the other parent often has visitation rights.

sole proprietorship A business owned and managed by one person (or a married couple in community property states). Business profits are reported and taxed on the owner's personal tax return, and the owner is personally liable for all business debts.

state court A court that decides cases involving state law or the state constitution. State courts have jurisdiction to consider disputes involving individual defendants who reside in that state or have minimum contacts with the state, such as using its highways, owning real property in the state, or doing business in the state.

statute A written law passed by Congress or a state legislature and signed into law by the president or a state governor.

statute of limitations The legally prescribed time limit for filing a lawsuit or bringing criminal charges.

subpoena A court order that requires a witness to appear in court. Subpoenas may be issued at the request of a party to a lawsuit.

subpoena duces tecum A type of subpoena, usually issued at the request of a party to a lawsuit, by which a court orders a witness to produce certain documents at a deposition or trial.

Supreme Court The United States Supreme Court is this country's highest court, which has the final power to decide cases involving the interpretation of the U.S. Constitution, certain legal areas set forth in the Constitution (called federal questions), and federal laws. It can also make final decisions in certain lawsuits between parties from different states. Most states also have a supreme court, which is the final arbiter of the state's constitution and state laws. In several states, the highest court uses a different name.

surviving spouse A widow or widower.

survivors benefits An amount of money available to the surviving spouse and minor or disabled children of a deceased worker who qualified for Social Security retirement or disability benefits.

T

temporary restraining order (TRO) An order that tells one person to stop harassing or harming another, issued after the aggrieved party appears before a judge. Usually, another hearing is held within a few days, in which both sides appear. It may result in a preliminary injunction if the judge believes the restraint should remain in place.

tenant Anyone, including a corporation, who rents real property, with or without a house or structure, from the owner (called the landlord). A tenant may also be called the "lessee."

trade dress The distinctive packaging or design of a product that promotes the product and distinguishes it from other products in the marketplace.

trade name The official or assumed name that a business uses when dealing with consumers.

trade secret In most states, a formula, pattern, physical device, idea, process, compilation of information, or other information that provides a business with a competitive advantage, and that is treated in a way that can reasonably be expected to prevent the public or competitors from learning about it.

trademark A word, phrase, logo, symbol, color, sound, or smell used by a business to identify a product and distinguish it from those of its competitors. Compare "trade dress," "service mark," "certification mark," and "collective mark."

transfer-on-death (TOD) deeds Deeds that pass property to named beneficiaries without probate when the property owner dies. Until the owner's death, a transfer-on-death deed has no effect, and the owner can revoke a TOD deed at any time. Transfer-on-death deeds (also called beneficiary deeds) are not available in all states.

treatise An extensive book or series of books written about a particular legal topic.

trial court The first court to hear a lawsuit.

trust A legal arrangement under which a person called a trustee manages property for the benefit of another.

trust deed The most common method of financing real estate purchases in California (most other states use mortgages). The trust deed transfers title to the property to a trustee—often a title company—which holds it as security for a loan. When the loan is paid off, the title is transferred to the borrower.

trustee The person who manages assets held in a trust. A trustee's job is to safeguard the trust assets and to invest and distribute trust income or principal as directed in the document that set up the trust.

U

unemployment insurance (UI) A program run jointly by federal and state governments that provides money benefits for a specified time after an employee has been laid off or fired from a job for reasons other than misconduct. In some instances, an employee who quits a job for a good reason (for example, because of sexual harassment at work) can also collect unemployment insurance benefits.

uninsured motorist coverage A type of car insurance that provides compensation for any injuries resulting from an accident with an uninsured motorist or a hit-and-run driver.

unlawful detainer An eviction lawsuit.

utility patent A patent issued for inventions that perform useful functions. Most patents issued by the U.S. Patent and Trademark Office (PTO) are utility patents.

V

visitation rights The right to see a child regularly, typically awarded by a court to the parent who does not have physical custody of the child.

W

warranty A guarantee by a seller to stand by its product or services by making repairs or offering replacements if something goes wrong. *See also* "express warranty" and "implied warranty."

warranty deed A seldom-used type of deed that contains express assurances about the legal validity of the title being transferred.

will A document in which a person specifies who is to inherit assets at death, names an executor to oversee the distribution of that property, and names a guardian for young children.

witness A person who observes an event (like a crime) or who testifies under oath at a deposition or trial, providing firsthand or expert evidence. In addition, the term also refers to someone who watches another person sign a document and then adds his name to confirm that the signature is genuine; this is called "attesting."

workers' compensation A state program that provides replacement income and medical expenses to employees who are injured on the job or become ill as a result of work.

Z

zoning The laws dividing cities into different areas according to use, from single-family residences to industrial plants. Zoning ordinances control the size, location, and use of buildings within these different areas.

APPENDIX

Legal Research

Legal research is how you learn about the law. It is not a skill reserved exclusively for lawyers; you can find the answers to your legal questions if you are armed with a little bit of patience and a good road map.

Which legal research method you should use depends on what you need to find out. Usually, people want to research the law in order to:

- understand a particular area of the law
- find and read a statute, regulation, ordinance, court decision, or piece of pending legislation (usually called a bill)
- find the answer to a specific legal question, or
- find a legal form.

This appendix explains how to use legal research to accomplish each of these tasks.

Learning About a Particular Area of the Law

Many people need to understand some area of the law before making an important decision. For example, you might want to know:

- Are there any legal rules I have to follow when selling a business?
- What's the difference between a living trust and a living will?
- Once I divorce, am I entitled to a share of my former spouse's pension?

Questions like these can be answered without regard to your specific circumstances; they involve a general understanding of the law. To find this type of information about a legal topic, you should turn to legal background materials.

Legal background materials are books, articles, and encyclopedia entries in which experts summarize and explain the basic principles of a legal subject area, such as bankruptcy, landlord–tenant law, or criminal law. These materials come in many forms; you can find them in law libraries and public libraries, and many are also available on the Internet.

How to Find a Law Library

Most counties have law libraries in the government buildings or courthouses at the county seat. These libraries are open to the public. County libraries are a good place to go if you're looking for legal encyclopedias, treatises, state laws, and court cases.

Law schools also maintain libraries for their students and staff. Although public access to some law school libraries is restricted, many are open to the general public—especially if the law school is part of a university that receives state funding.

Finally, don't limit yourself to law libraries. Most major public libraries in urban areas contain both local and state laws, self-help law books, and directories of organizations. Public libraries are also good sources of city, county, and state information.

Here are a number of legal background resources that you may find useful:

- **Nolo and other self-help law books.** Self-help law books, such as those published by Nolo, are written in plain English for a nonlawyer audience. They are an excellent starting point for cracking any legal area that is new to you. Law libraries, public libraries, and bookstores (including Nolo's online bookstore at www.nolo.com) often carry self-help law books. Nolo publishes titles on employment, small business issues, divorce, estate planning, and much more.
- **Organizations and advocacy groups.** Many nonprofit and professional organizations or advocacy groups—such as tenants' rights groups, the AARP (formerly the American Association of Retired Persons), and local business groups—publish articles or booklets on particular legal topics. Think about which groups might have the information you need, and then look for them in the yellow pages or on the Internet. Most public libraries have reference books that list organizations and associations by topic—these books are an easy way to find leads.
- **Legal encyclopedias.** You can often find a good introduction to your topic in a legal encyclopedia. The legal encyclopedias most commonly found in law libraries are *American Jurisprudence* and *Corpus Juris.* Many states have legal encyclopedias that are state-specific—for example, *Texas Jurisprudence.*
- **The Nutshell series.** Another good introduction to legal topics is the Nutshell series, as in *Torts in a Nutshell* and *Intellectual Property,* published by West Group. These books are available in most law libraries and some bookstores.
- **Treatises.** If you have the time and patience to delve deeply into a subject, you can find comprehensive books—generally known as treatises—on virtually every legal topic. For example, if you want to know about some aspect of trademark law, you could use *McCarthy on Trademarks and Unfair Competition*, a multivolume treatise on all aspects of trademark law.
- ***West's Legal Desk Reference.*** This book, by Statsky, Hussey, Diamond, and Nakamura, lists background materials both by state and by legal topic. In addition, *West's Legal Desk Reference* provides keywords and phrases that will help you use the other resources you may need during your research.
- **Nolo.com and other Internet resources.** Nolo's website, at www.nolo.com, explains many common legal issues

in plain English, includes extensive links to legal resources at www.nolo.com/legal-research, and provides 50-state law on many topics, such as landlord–tenant law. The other major legal websites (listed below) also provide helpful information and links to specific areas of the law. Finally, federal, state, and local government agency sites provide basic legal information for consumers, such as state marriage license requirements or publications on workplace rights. For example, if you visit the federal judiciary's website at www.uscourts.gov, you can download "Bankruptcy Basics," a pamphlet providing a good overview of bankruptcy. To find government agencies online, see "Finding Court and Government Agency Websites," below.

The Best Free Legal Websites

In addition to our own website at www.nolo.com, Nolo's favorite legal websites are:

- **The Legal Information Institute at Cornell Law School** www.law.cornell.edu
- **Justia** www.justia.com
- **The Library of Congress Guide to Law Online** www.loc.gov/law/help/guide.php

Finding a Specific Law

There are many reasons why you might need to find a specific statute, regulation, ordinance, or court decision. For example, you might hear about new state laws governing overtime wages and want to read the laws to see if they apply to your work situation. Or perhaps the city building department has referred you to a particular city ordinance that covers zoning laws in your neighborhood. Whatever the reason, finding a specific law is relatively straightforward. The steps depend on what type of law you seek.

City or County Laws

You can usually get copies of city or county laws (often called "ordinances") from the office of the city or county clerk. The main branch of your public library is also likely to have a collected set of these laws. Once you get there, ask the reference librarian for help.

Other good resources for finding local ordinances are www.statelocalgov.net and www.municode.com.

State or Federal Statutes and Regulations

Rules established by state and federal governments are called statutes and regulations. Federal statutes are passed by the United States Congress, while state statutes are passed by state legislatures. Regulations are issued by state or federal administrative agencies (such as the U.S.

Department of Transportation or the California Department of Public Health) to explain, implement, and enforce statutes.

You can find statutes and regulations in the library or on the Internet, such as at statelocalgov.net. You can also use legal background materials to point the way to the statute or regulation you should read.

Finding Statutes and Regulations at the Library

State and federal statutes and regulations can be found at a law library or the main branch of a public library. Depending on the state, statutes are compiled in books called codes, revised statutes, annotated statutes, or compiled laws. For example, the federal statutes are contained in a series called *United States Code,* and the Vermont statutes are found in a series called *Vermont Statutes Annotated.* (The term "annotated" means that the statutes are accompanied by information about their history and court decisions that have interpreted them.) Once you've located the books you need, search for the specific statute by its citation or by looking up keywords in the index.

After you find a law in the statute books, it's important to look at the update pamphlet in the front or back of the book (called the "pocket part") to make sure your statute hasn't been amended or deleted. Pocket parts are published only once per year, so brand-new statutes often have not yet made it to the pocket part. Law libraries subscribe to services and periodicals that update these books on a more frequent basis than the pocket parts. Ask the law librarian to help you find the most recent version of the statute.

Most federal regulations are published in the *Code of Federal Regulations (C.F.R.),* a well-indexed set of books organized by subject. If you don't have a citation for the regulation you want, check the index. To make sure the regulation is current, look at the monthly pamphlet that accompanies the books, called *C.F.R.-L.S.A. (List of C.F.R. Sections Affected).*

State regulations may be harder to find. If you know which agency publishes the regulation you want, you can usually call and get a copy (or check online). Many states also keep a portion of their regulations in a series of books called the "administrative code"; check the table of contents. If the regulation is not in an administrative code, look for loose-leaf manuals published by the individual agency. If you find a regulation in the administrative code or loose-leaf manual, you should still call the agency to make sure the regulation hasn't recently changed.

Finding Statutes and Regulations Online

What to do depends on the type of law you're looking for:

Federal laws. The easiest way to find federal laws online is to use Justia: https://law.justia.com/codes/us. From this site, you can search the U.S. Code by title, section, or keyword. You can also access federal laws at the Library of Congress Guide to Law Online, at www.loc.gov/law/help/guide.php. The website www.usa.gov is an excellent way to find information on federal laws.

You can also use the Google search engine. When using Google, provide the literal name or number of the law, in quotation marks. If the law has a lot of words, it usually works to just use the distinctive elements of the phrase. For example, when looking for the Bankruptcy Abuse Prevention and Reform Act of 2005, the phrase "bankruptcy abuse" would be sufficient for the statute's name. Similarly, if the law has a nickname, you can use that phrase. If you can think of key words that identify the law, provide those as well. For instance, if a new law creates an additional procedure for collecting child support, you could likely find it by typing in the terms: "child support" and "collection." If you know the year that the law was passed, add that as well (so that you don't get an out of date law by the same name).

Federal regulations. To find federal regulations online, the Justia website is a good place to start: https://law.justia.com/cfr.

State laws. To find state laws online, use the Cornell Law School website: www.law.cornell.edu/states/listing. Here, you will see a state-by-state index. You can also find state laws organized by topic at www.law.cornell.edu/wex/state_statutes. And usa.gov has links to many state government websites, such as consumer protection agencies, where you can find useful information on state laws and regulations.

State regulations. You can locate many state regulations by using Justia: https://justia.com.

Using Background Materials to Find Statutes and Regulations

When looking for a particular statute or regulation (state or federal), you may want to consult background materials, which often include relevant laws. For example, *Collier on Bankruptcy,* the leading bankruptcy treatise, contains a complete set of the federal bankruptcy laws. Even if the background resource does not include the text of the statutes or regulations, it will provide citations to the relevant laws and the books in which they are found.

Finding the Latest Legislation

If you are looking for a brand-new statute, you may have to search online for recently enacted legislation, because there is often a delay between the date a statute is passed and the date it shows up in the overall compilation of laws. Almost every state provides links to its legislature, where you can find pending and recently enacted legislation. These sites contain not only the most current version of a bill but also its history. For help locating your state's website, see below. To find out about pending federal legislation or to read the latest version of a bill, go to the Library of Congress website at www.congress.gov.

How to Read a Citation for a Statute or Regulation

A citation is an abbreviated reference that tells you where to find a legal resource. Citations for statutes usually include the name of the set of books where the statute appears, the volume or title number, and the section where you can find the statute. For example:

- 42 U.S.C. § 2000e is the citation of Title VII of the Civil Rights Act, which protects workers from discrimination. You can find the text of the law in Title 42 of the United States Code, starting at Section 2000e.
- Ariz. Rev. Stat. Ann. § 33-1321 is the citation to Arizona's law on tenant security deposits. You can find the text of the law in Title 33 of the Arizona Revised Statutes Annotated, Section 1321.

Citations for regulations usually include the name of the code where the regulations can be found, and the volume and section number. For example:

- You can find the regulations interpreting the Fair Credit Reporting Act at 16 C.F.R. § 600.1—volume 16 of the Code of Federal Regulations, Section 600.1.
- You can find California's regulations on pregnancy discrimination at 2 C.C.R. § 7291.2—Title 2 of the California Code of Regulations, Section 7291.2.

State Case Law

State case law consists of the rules established by courts in court decisions (also called "opinions"). Court decisions do one of two things. First, courts interpret statutes, regulations, and ordinances so that we know how they apply to real-life situations. Second, courts make rules that are not found in statutes, regulations, or ordinances. These rules are called the "common law."

Finding State Cases in the Library

State cases are found in a series of books called reporters. For example, California cases are contained in the *California Reporter.* You can also find state cases in books known as "regional reporters." These volumes contain cases from several states in a geographical region. For example, the *Atlantic Reporter* contains cases from several eastern states, including Delaware and Maryland.

Finding Cases Using a Citation

A citation indicates the name of the reporter, the volume number, and the page where the case appears. For example, 21 Cal. App.3d 446 tells you that the case is in California Appellate Reports, 3rd Series, Volume 21, on page 446.

Finding Cases Using the Name

If you don't have a citation but you know the name of one or both of the parties in the case—for instance, in the case named

Jones v. Smith, Jones and Smith are the names of the parties—you can use a "case digest" to find the citation. There are digests for individual states as well as federal and general digests. Look for the parties' names in the digest's Table of Cases. If you don't know the name of the case or the citation, then it will be very difficult to find the case in the law library.

Finding State Cases on the Web

If the case is recent (within the last ten years), there's a good chance it's available free on the Internet. A good place to start is Justia at www.law.justia.com. Also, most state court websites now publish recent cases.

If the case is older, you can still find it on the Internet, but you may have to pay a private company for access to its database. (Your local law library may also have online legal resources available for searching.) VersusLaw, at www.versuslaw.com, maintains an excellent library of older state court cases. You can do unlimited research on VersusLaw for $18.95 per month. You can also get state cases online through Lexis and Westlaw, commercial online legal research services. (For more information, see "Using Westlaw and Lexis to Do Legal Research on the Web," below.)

Federal Case Law

Federal case law consists of the rules established by federal courts. Like state cases, you can find federal case law both in the library and on the Web.

Finding Court and Government Agency Websites

Many courts and government agencies provide statutes and case law, plus other useful items like forms, answers to frequently asked questions, and downloadable pamphlets on various legal topics. The best resource for finding your state's website and other government websites is www.usa.gov. Other useful sites for finding state and local government laws are www.statelocalgov.net and www.municode.com.

Nolo's website provides links to courts across the country and access to small claims court information for most states. You can also find local, state, and federal court websites on the National Center for State Courts' website at www.ncsc.org. The federal judiciary's website at www.uscourts.gov lists federal court websites.

Finding Federal Cases in the Library

Cases decided by the U.S. Supreme Court are published in three different series of reporters. All three contain the same cases. The names of these series are:

- United States Reports
- Supreme Court Reporter, and
- Supreme Court Reports: Lawyers' Edition.

Well-stocked law libraries also have cases from other federal courts, including the Federal Circuit Courts of Appeal (federal appellate courts), U.S. District Courts (federal trial courts), and specialized courts such as bankruptcy or tax court.

To find a case in the Supreme Court reporters or any of the volumes containing other federal cases, follow the guidelines for finding state cases by citation or case name, above.

Using Lexis and Westlaw to Do Legal Research on the Web

Lexis and Westlaw are the chief electronic legal databases that contain the full text of many of the legal resources found in law libraries, including almost all reported cases from state and federal courts, all federal statutes, the statutes of most states, federal and state regulations, law review articles, commonly used treatises, and practice manuals.

Although Westlaw and Lexis databases are available over the Internet, subscriptions are pricey. For details, visit Westlaw at www.westlaw.com or Lexis at www.lexis.com.

Finding Federal and State Court Cases on the Web

Where to look depends on the type of case you want to find:

U.S. Supreme Court. Start at the Cornell Law School website: www.law.cornell.edu/supremecourt/text/home. It provides a thorough index of U.S. Supreme Court decisions.

If you want to search for a U.S. Supreme Court case using Google, type "Supreme Court" in quotation marks and then add any combination of the following elements:

- one or both names of the parties to the case (you can include the "v." abbreviation—for example, if you enter "Planned Parenthood v. Casey," you will retrieve a copy of the 1992 Supreme Court Case)
- one or more terms that describe the subject matter of the case (for example, if you enter "Betamax" and "Supreme Court," you will get the 1984 Supreme Court case, *Sony v. Universal*), or
- the year of the case.

Federal courts. Start at the Cornell Law School website: www.law.cornell.edu/federal. It provides a thorough index of federal court opinions.

If you want to search for a federal case using Google, type any combination of the elements described for U.S. Supreme Court cases, just above. You may also want to include the name of the court that decided the case, if you know it—for example, "Ninth Circuit Court of Appeals."

Note that cases decided before 1995—that is, before the Internet was used to catalog court cases—are usually only available in private databases that require a paid subscription.

State courts. Start with the Cornell Law School website: www.law.cornell.edu/opinions.html#state. It provides a thorough index of state court decisions.

If you want to search for a state court case using Google, type any combination of the elements described for U.S. Supreme Court cases, above. You may also want to include the name of the court that decided the case, if you know it—for example, "Vermont Supreme Court."

As with federal court cases, state cases decided before 1995 are usually available only through private databases that charge for a subscription.

Finding Answers to Specific Legal Questions

It's one thing to track down information on a recent case or statute or to read up on general information about a legal topic. It's quite another to confidently answer a question about how the law might apply to your own situation, such as:

- I live in North Carolina, and I've been charged with second offense drunk driving. My passenger was injured as a result of the accident. What penalties do I face?
- My brother is the executor of our parents' estate, and I don't like how he's handling things. What can I do?
- Can I run a home school in my state (North Dakota) if I've been convicted of a felony?

These are the types of questions that people have traditionally asked lawyers. To answer such questions, you may need to look at all of the legal resources we have mentioned thus far. You must also make sure that the law you find is current. If you want to undertake this type of legal research on your own, we recommend that you use a comprehensive legal research guide that walks you through the process step by step. (See the list of resources at the end of this appendix.) Here, we can provide just a brief overview of what you'll need to do.

When seeking the answer to a specific legal question, your ultimate goal is to predict, as near as possible, how a judge would rule if presented with the issues and facts of your case. The closer your facts are to the facts in previous cases or the more directly a statute applies to your situation, the more likely you'll be able to predict what a judge would decide. Sometimes, your question is so basic that the answer is easy to find. But often, a statute won't address each facet of your situation, and the facts of other cases won't match up 100%. Because of this, legal research cannot always provide a definitive answer, although it can often give you a good idea of what the answer will be. (That's why lawyers often hem and haw when asked a legal question.)

Basic or Common Legal Questions

If your legal question is basic and general, such as "What does it mean to file for Chapter 7 bankruptcy?" or "What kinds of expenses are child-support payments supposed to cover?" then you should begin your research by consulting one or more of the background resources discussed above. The answers to these types of questions are usually based on general legal information rather than on the nuances of your particular circumstances.

If your question is common and straightforward (such as "What is the filing fee for a Chapter 7 bankruptcy?" or "Can the state garnish my wages if I fall behind on child-support payments?") then it should be quite easy to find an answer, because these kinds of questions rely on factual information that many people need to know. Finding this kind of information doesn't involve any special legal-research methods. Think of the government branches or agencies that are likely to have the answers. For example, the U.S. Bankruptcy Court for your area probably has filing fees posted on its website, or you can call the court clerk. And every state has an agency that handles child-support payments. Look on your state's home page to find the agency website or a public information number. You can find phone numbers for city, county, state, and U.S. government agencies in the Government Pages section at the front of your local telephone book and on the government websites (find yours at www.usa.gov).

In some cases, the quickest way to find an answer is by contacting an organization or advocacy group that specializes in the subject of your question. Do you want to know the current estate tax rate? An organization that advocates for seniors, such as the AARP, may know the answer. If you're looking for information on evictions, a local tenants' rights group should be able to help. You can find almost any organization or advocacy group on the Internet. Most yellow pages directories also include listings of community resources.

Complex Legal Questions

If you can't get an answer to your legal question from a background resource—usually because your question involves unique facts related to your situation—you'll need to do more detailed research. Build on the information you found in the background materials.

To proceed further, first search for statutes, regulations, or ordinances that address your question. If you find relevant statutes, look for cases that have interpreted them. To do this at a law library, you can:

- look at the summaries of cases that follow the statute in an annotated code book
- use *Shepard's Citations* (a book that provides a complete list of cases that mention a particular statute, regulation, or constitutional provision), and
- search for cases in "case digests" (books that list cases by subject).

If you can't find a relevant statute or other legislative enactment, you need to look for case law only. To do this at a law library, you can:

- read any relevant cases mentioned in the background materials

- search in case digests by subject area or keywords
- if you find a relevant case, read the cases that it mentions, and
- if you find a relevant case, use *Shepard's Citations* to find more cases on point. (*Shepard's* provides a complete list of cases that mention your case.)

Making Sure the Law Is Up to Date

Because the law changes rapidly, you must make sure that the principles stated in your cases and statutes are still valid. A case may no longer be helpful to you if a more recent case has questioned its reasoning, ruled a different way, or expressly stated that your case is no longer good law. Likewise, you should check to make sure your statute has not been changed or eliminated.

Updating Your Research in the Library

If you are using the law library, there are a few things you should do to make sure your research is up to date.

- **Background resources.** If you use background materials, be sure to check the pocket part; it contains changes and new developments in the law.
- **Statutes.** Books containing statutes and regulations also contain pocket parts. Be sure to check these as well. Also check law library periodicals that contain more recent statutory updates.
- **Cases.** You can check the validity of every case you find by using *Shepard's Citations for Cases*. *Shepard's* will list every case that mentions your case, and tell you the reasons why it was mentioned. For example, it might show that a later case overruled your case, which means your case is no longer valid. Using *Shepard's* isn't easy—ask the law librarian for help.

Updating Your Research on the Web

On the Internet, the updating process is easier, but it might cost some money.

- **Statutes.** If you're checking a state statute, visit your state's website for current legislative developments. If you need federal information, track Congress's legislative developments at www.congress.gov. You can also get the most recent version of a statute (for a fee) through Westlaw or Lexis.
- **Cases.** You can check the validity of cases by using www.westlaw.com or *Shepard's* at www.lexis.com, but these services are only available to subscribers.

Finding Legal Forms

If you must take care of a legal matter, chances are good that you'll need to use a form of some sort—that is, a preformatted document that contains standard ("boilerplate") language addressing your specific situation. Leases, wills, trusts, and sales agreements are just a few examples of the thousands of legal forms that are used in the course of our daily personal and business affairs.

What Form Do You Need?

Figuring out what form you need is usually simple—someone will tell you. For example, suppose you are handling your own divorce, and when you try to file the papers, the clerk says you are missing a "disclosure" form. If the court can't give it to you, you'll have to find it on your own. Or, suppose you are trying to sell your car, and the buyer wants a bill of sale. Again, you'll have to track one down.

If you haven't been told what form you need, but you want to take care of a matter that you assume requires legal forms, start by trying to find a resource that explains the transaction. For example, if you want to sublet an apartment, you might look for a book about leases and rental agreements. This type of resource often provides the necessary forms and explains how to fill them out.

Keep in mind that some forms used by courts and government agencies are "mandatory." This means that you have to use their form, not a similar form that you or someone else has designed, even if your version contains the same information. If you need a form for a court or government agency, it's wise to ask the clerk whether the court has a mandatory form. Or you can check the court or agency's website—it may have forms you can download.

Finding the Form You Need

Fortunately, forms are readily available from many sources. Here are the best ways to get them.

- **Nolo and other self-help legal materials.** Self-help legal materials, including those published by Nolo, are a good place to find legal forms. Because self-help law materials are written for nonlawyers, the forms are usually accompanied by detailed instructions in plain English. You can find self-help legal materials in bookstores, law libraries, and on the Internet.
- **Law libraries.** Most law libraries have a large collection of books that contain forms for almost every legal transaction imaginable. They usually contain step-by-step instructions for completing the forms and highlight areas where the boilerplate language might not be appropriate.
- **Government forms on the Web.** Start by searching the government website www.usa.gov. Google is also an easy way to locate state or federal forms. Try typing any combination of the following elements into the search box:
  - the state that issued the form or, if it's a local form, the court where you will use it
  - the title of the form or a few unique terms that would likely be in the title—for example, "Petition Administer Estate" for a "Notice of Petition to Administer Estate"

    - the subject matter of the form in the absence of a specific name—for example "Summons Eviction," or
    - the term "form."
- **Stationery stores.** Many large stationery stores sell legal forms. However, these forms usually don't come with legal instructions, so you may need some help filling them in.
- **Commercial legal forms on the Web.** You can find almost any legal form you need somewhere on the Internet. Nolo.com, for example, has an extensive collection of forms in books and software, plus standalone products, such as Nolo's online will, online LLC, and California Residential Lease. There are sites that specialize in specific subjects, such as divorce or real estate, and there are mega sites like Findforms.com, where you can locate free or commercial legal forms. Many of our favorite legal research sites also have links to legal forms (see "The Best Legal Websites," above).

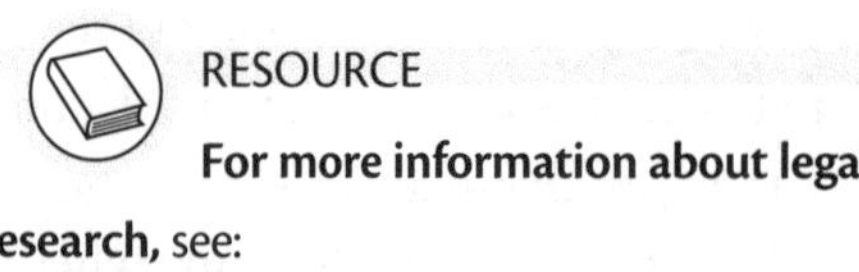

RESOURCE

For more information about legal research, see:

- *Legal Research: How to Find & Understand the Law,* by Stephen Elias and the Editors of Nolo (Nolo). An easy-to-read book that provides step-by-step instructions on how to find legal information, both in the law library and online. Includes examples, exercises (with answers), and sample legal memos.
- *Gilbert Law Summaries on Legal Research, Writing & Analysis,* by Peter Honigsberg (West Academic Publishing). A no-nonsense guide to commonly used law library resources.

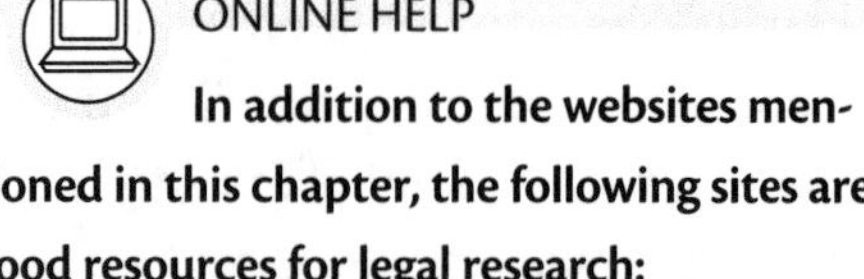

ONLINE HELP

In addition to the websites mentioned in this chapter, the following sites are good resources for legal research:

- **www.virtualchase.justia.com** The Virtual Chase offers guides to researching various legal topics, as well as general research tips and legal resources.
- **www.nolo.com/legal-research** At Nolo's Laws and Legal Research section, you can choose "Federal Law Resources" or "State Law Resources." The Federal link provides access to federal law. The State link takes you to individual state pages, which include links to that state's statutes. The FAQs in the Laws and Legal Research section provide basic advice on doing legal research, such as how to read a law and how to find Supreme Court cases. Nolo.com also includes thousands of free articles that cover the specifics of state and federal law (see the Legal Articles section).

Index

B

C

D

E

F

G

H

I

J

K

L

M

N

O

P

Q

R

S

T

U

V

W

Y

Z